# Rethinking
# Pull-Out Services
# in Early Intervention

*Nancy Lieberman*

This book is printed on recycled paper. ♺

# Rethinking Pull-Out Services in Early Intervention

## A Professional Resource

*edited by*

R.A. McWilliam, Ph.D.
*Frank Porter Graham Child Development Center*
*University of North Carolina, Chapel Hill*

·P·A·U·L·H·
BROOKES
PUBLISHING Cº

Baltimore · London · Toronto · Sydney

**Paul H. Brookes Publishing Co.**
Post Office Box 10624
Baltimore, Maryland 21285-0624

Typeset by AeroType, Inc., Amherst, New Hampshire.
Manufactured in the United States of America by
The Maple Press Company, York, Pennsylvania.

The case studies in this book are completely fictional. Any similarity to actual individuals or circumstances is coincidental, and no implications should be inferred.

**Library of Congress Cataloging-in-Publication Data**

Rethinking pull-out services in early intervention : a professional
  resource / edited by R.A. McWilliam
      p.  cm.
  Includes bibliographical references and index.
  ISBN 1-55766-242-8
  1. Handicapped children—Services for—United States.  2. Special
education—United States.  I. McWilliam, R.A.
HV888.5.R69  1996
362.4′048′083—dc20                                                        96-21471
                                                                              CIP

British Cataloguing in Publication data are available from the British Library.

# Contents

# Contributors

**Mary Beth Bruder, Ph.D.**
Professor of Pediatrics
Child and Family Studies
UConn Health Center, MC 6222
Farm Hollow, Suite A-200
University of Connecticut School of
   Medicine
309 Farmington Avenue
Farmington, CT 06032

**Angela Capone, Ph.D.**
Director of Early Childhood Programs
University Affiliated Program of Vermont
University of Vermont
499C Waterman Building
Burlington, VT 05405-0160

**Winnie Dunn, Ph.D., OTR, FAOTA**
Professor and Chair
Department of Occupational Therapy
   Education
School of Allied Health
University of Kansas Medical Center
3033 Robinson
3901 Rainbow Boulevard
Kansas City, KS 66160-7602

**Michael F. Giangreco, Ph.D.**
Research Assistant Professor
University Affiliated Program of
   Vermont
University of Vermont
499C Waterman Building
Burlington, VT 05405-0160

**Eva M. Horn, Ph.D.**
Assistant Professor
Department of Special Education
Box 328
Peabody College of Vanderbilt
   University
Nashville, TN 37203

**Karla Hull, Ed.D.**
Research Assistant Professor
University Affiliated Program of
   Vermont
University of Vermont
499C Waterman Building
Burlington, VT 05405-0160

**P.J. McWilliam, Ph.D.**
Research Investigator
Frank Porter Graham Child
   Development Center
CB#8185
University of North Carolina
105 Smith Level Road
Chapel Hill, NC 27599-8180

**R.A. McWilliam, Ph.D.**
Research Investigator
Frank Porter Graham Child
   Development Center
CB#8180
University of North Carolina
105 Smith Level Road
Chapel Hill, NC 27599-8180

**Beverly Rainforth, Ph.D., PT**
Associate Professor of Special Education
School of Education and Human
   Development
P.O. Box 6000
State University of New York at
   Binghamton
Binghamton, NY 13902-6000

**Pamela Roberts, M.A., PT**
Associate Professor of Allied Health
   Professions
School of Allied Health Professions
University of Connecticut
358 Mansfield Road
Storrs, CT 06269-2101

**Jane Ross-Allen, M.Ed.**
Lecturer
University Affiliated Program of
    Vermont
University of Vermont
499C Waterman Building
Burlington, VT 05405-0160

**Michelle S. Shannon, M.A.**
Faculty Research Associate
Department of Speech and Hearing
    Science
Box 871908
Arizona State University
Tempe, AZ 85287-1908

**Steven F. Warren, Ph.D.**
Professor of Special Education and
    Psychology
Department of Special Education
Box 328
Peabody College of Vanderbilt
    University
Nashville, TN 37203

**M. Jeanne Wilcox, Ph.D.**
Professor
Department of Speech and Hearing
    Science
Box 871908
Arizona State University
Tempe, AZ 85287-1908

**Pamela J. Winton, Ph.D.**
Research Investigator
Frank Porter Graham Child
    Development Center
CB#8185
University of North Carolina
105 Smith Level Road
Chapel Hill, NC 27599-8180

**Mark Wolery, Ph.D.**
Senior Research Scientist
Child and Family Studies Program
Allegheny-Singer Research Institute
320 East North Avenue
Pittsburgh, PA 15212

# Foreword

Several years ago Robin McWilliam and I began a series of informal discussions about the way in which services are provided for young children with disabilities. In these discussions, we reflected on the dual goals that constitute the basic thrust of early intervention: 1) to provide highly effective special services in order to maximize development and prevent the secondary consequences of disability, and 2) to promote children's success in normal and inclusive settings. It appeared to us that these two goals sometimes seem at odds with each other in the minds of both parents and professionals. For some, to be "specialized" means that the interactions between adults and children need to be provided in a fundamentally different way, and often in a different context from other types of interactions and experiences. From an operational perspective, "special" services seem to be defined as those in which a special education teacher or therapist pulls the child out of a regular classroom or preschool context and works individually with the child on special education or therapeutic goals. Although we knew that this type of instruction or therapy can be highly effective, we also knew that, for many children, the learning that occurs in this context does not transfer to other settings.

In a subsequent paper (Bailey & McWilliam, 1990), we argued that a primary goal of early intervention ought to be normalizing the life experiences of children with disabilities and their families. Although many people identify normalization with mainstreaming or inclusion, we argued that normalization is a much broader construct. Included in this concept was the notion that teaching and therapeutic strategies ought to be evaluated on the basis of three criteria: efficacy, efficiency, and normalcy. A good intervention ought to work, ought to work quickly, and ought to be conducted in settings and using techniques that are as normal as possible.

We realized, however, that incorporating the goal of normalization is not easy, owing to an array of factors. Robin then took the lead on writing a successful grant proposal in which he began to explore these issues in a more systematic fashion. That project, completed in 1995, reinforces how complex these issues are. He found that the decision to provide a particular set of services in a particular way to an individual child is based on a host of factors, including the attitudes, beliefs, and disciplinary training of professionals, the attitudes and beliefs of parents, characteristics of the child, the nature of the goal to be attained, and characteristics of the early intervention program, including the policy and administrative context in which the program is operated as well as the program's prior history with various service delivery models. No one model was found to be universally more effective for all children, and no systematic aptitude by treatment interaction was found.

*Rethinking Pull-Out Services* is a synthesis of the findings from this project, a review of the relevant early intervention literature, and the diverse experiences of the authors of the various chapters. Readers will be impressed with the nature and scope of the issues addressed in the book. They will also find themselves agreeing and disagreeing with the authors at different points in the text. McWilliam clearly articulates a preference for a model of service delivery that integrates teaching and therapeutic activities in the context of ongoing classroom activities and routines. Some readers will readily endorse this idea, whereas others will have serious concerns. These reactions reflect the natural tendency of educational and therapeutic fields to explore and question practices regarding children and families. The meaning of *appropriate services* in the context of young children with disabilities is a contested concept that is currently under considerable discussion in the early intervention arena.

Ultimately, we must recognize that no one model is likely to be best for all children and families. What we need are models for individualizing services that recognize that decisions regarding intervention activities must draw on data regarding effectiveness, efficiency, and normalcy in the context of the values espoused by parents and professionals. One example of how to individualize services is use of the continuum of six service delivery models described in Chapters 4, 7, and 13. This book makes a substantial contribution to that discussion by demonstrating the complex nature of the issue and by articulating the arguments in a more substantive fashion than has been done before. The text does not provide a definitive answer to the question of best practice, but I believe that such a goal is unrealistic. I am sure the reader will agree that this text lives up to its title by forcing the reader to rethink the way the services typically are provided, thus advancing our discussions and providing the foundation for a more informed approach to research and practice.

## REFERENCE

Bailey, D.B., & McWilliam, R.A. (1990). Normalizing early intervention. *Topics in Early Childhood Special Education, 10*(2), 33–47.

*Donald B. Bailey, Jr., Ph.D.*
*Frank Porter Graham Child Development Center*
*University of North Carolina at Chapel Hill*

# Acknowledgments

I am indebted to many professionals and students who contributed to the research on integrated therapy at the Frank Porter Graham Child Development Center: Karen Applequist, Don Bailey, Ashraf Chaudhary, Lisa Clifton, Ron Craig, Kathy Davis, Kathy Grabowski, Katie Harville, Krista Hicks, Miki Kersgard, Wayde Johnson, Lynette Keyes, Craig Pohlman, Barry Prizant, Joanne Roberts, Anita Scarborough, Darlene Sekerak, Kim Sloper, Amelia Spencer, Edgar Tyson, and Maureen Vandermaas.

Don Bailey's support for and participation in this project began before he became Director of the Frank Porter Graham Child Development Center and continued after he took his place on Mount Olympus. His encouragement has been most valuable.

Our research program, entitled Integrated Versus Isolated Treatment in Early Intervention, was funded by a field-initiated grant from the U.S. Department of Education (H023C00056). The opinions expressed in this book do not necessarily reflect the opinions of the Department of Education. One small project reported here, in which focus groups were conducted, was funded (with Part H Funds) through the North Carolina Interagency Coordinating Council for Children Birth to Five with Disabilities and Their Families.

The contributing authors of this book were magnificent in producing chapters of top quality under bothersome conditions (i.e., my nagging). The price I paid for having contributors of high caliber was that their lives proceeded apace during the writing of the book: One author had twins, another was awarded an early childhood research institute, and yet another published his own book.

One author deserves special mention because her contributions extended beyond the writing of her own chapter and beyond her office. This contributor had good ideas, honest appraisals, and views about how the editor spent his time. Many thanks go to the author of Chapter 12.

At the University of North Carolina at Chapel Hill, in addition to faculty colleagues already listed, Rune Simeonsson, Ron Wiegerink, and David Yoder were most helpful.

The book is much enhanced by the professionalism and friendliness of the staff at Paul H. Brookes Publishing Co., particularly Theresa Donnelly, Paul Klemt, and Sarah Cheney (who has now gone back to graduate school).

Finally, those who taught us the most and might be the last to know how much they have contributed are the children in our studies, their families, and the professionals working with them. Putting together this book has reminded me that much of early intervention research is a transactional endeavor. If we have done any good in studying practices that professionals employ with children, it is the least we could do in return for what they have taught us.

*To Kirsten*

I

# Issues in
# Providing Services in
# Early Intervention

# Chapter 1

# Service Delivery Issues in Center-Based Early Intervention

## R.A. McWilliam

Specialized services consist of occupational therapy, physical therapy, special education, and speech-language pathology. This book focuses on such services—those provided by professionals other than the teacher. Although the book concentrates on children with disabilities, it is true that 1) many children are in classrooms with typically developing children and 2) some children in early intervention programs do not have disabilities, but are at risk for developmental delays. A final introductory definition is that of *center-based programs;* this book is primarily about services in programs that children attend for a number of hours a day. These may be child care centers, part-time preschools, or full-time child care. We do not emphasize home- or clinic-based services, but some of the principles addressed here apply also to them. Major issues in service delivery are discussed first, followed by comments on research and theory, problems, and, finally, a rationale for a new approach.

## MAJOR ISSUES

Major issues in service delivery are collaboration, professional identity, functionality and intervention targets, and evaluation of effectiveness. Although these are not new issues, since the late 1980s new twists have arisen as practices have become refined (e.g., DEC Task Force on Recommended Practices, 1993; Odom, McLean, Johnson, & LaMontagne, 1995) and legislation has been put in place (e.g., PLs 99-457 and 102-119). Each issue is discussed in terms of problems and why the issue is important.

## Collaboration

Idol, Paolucci-Whitcomb, and Nevin describe collaborative consultation as an "interactive process which enable[s] people with diverse expertise to generate creative solutions to mutually defined problems" (1986, p. 1; see Chapter 2 as well). Yet, despite the benefits of collaboration, many professionals fear the collaborative process in practice. They fear that collaboration will limit their independence, create more work, be a threat to their professional identity, or challenge their basic views. Some of these fears are discussed in the following paragraphs.

*Desire to Work Independently*    The first problem with collaboration is that it violates many professionals' desire to work independently. In the traditional multidisciplinary model, each specialist conducts his or her own assessment, makes discipline-specific recommendations, writes discipline-specific individualized family service plan (IFSP) outcomes or individualized education program (IEP) goals, and provides discipline-specific services. In this traditional model, the only adults the therapist or educator really must think about are the parents, if the parents are lucky. Collaboration, on the other hand, means that specialists have to integrate what they do with other professionals and perhaps with paraprofessionals such as classroom assistants. The independence that characterized much of an early interventionist's work in the mid-1980s is now expected to give way to interdependence.

*More Work*    One of the appeals of independence is that less work is involved. Practitioners have long been able to set their own schedule and tell teachers when they would come to the classroom for the child. The only scheduling challenge might have been avoiding times that other therapists needed to work with the child. Collaboration, however, means making time to spend with the teacher, the family, and other therapists. Apart from the extra work this involves, practitioners have found that some Medicaid policies preclude charging for meeting time. Worse, practitioners say that Medicaid policies preclude any model but one-on-one services outside the classroom. Thus, although collaboration can result in shared responsibility for interventions (i.e., less work for any single therapist), getting there involves more work.

*Threats to Professional Identity*    The next section of this chapter discusses professional identity in detail. Suffice it to say here that a strong adherence to profession- or discipline-specific behaviors can sabotage the purposes of collaboration. If specialists cannot perform independently, they cannot maintain the illusion that they alone are responsible for treatment in the area of their specialty.

*Challenge to the Medical Model*    Collaboration in the medical model means letting each person handle certain problems (multidisciplinary); in the early intervention model, it means 1) each person handles some of the same problems and 2) one person handles most of the problems, with help provided by specialists as needed (transdisciplinary). Occupational therapy, physical therapy, and speech-language pathology have their roots in the medical model (see Chapter 11), which is quite different from the *educational* and *family-centered* models. Another, perhaps more pervasive, influence of the medical model is that habilitative therapy is like medical therapy: It should be administered on a regular schedule, the "patient" should passively accept the dosage and the treatment, and the problem will get better.

Given the problems cited previously, why should collaboration be considered in early intervention? There are three reasons:

1. All the professionals on a team need to be working on the same priorities.
2. They can learn from each other.
3. It promotes communication.

***Knowing the Family's Priorities***   In family-centered early intervention, everyone on the team should know what the family's priorities are for intervention. In multidisciplinary or medical-model treatment, each therapist needs to know only what the family wants with respect to that therapist's domain. However, this segmentation can lead to a therapist's failing to see the big picture. For example, a consulting special educator may be working on a child's on-task behavior by setting up many opportunities during the day for the child to complete tasks independently. The child is given a special place in the classroom and is encouraged to go there and play with puzzles and other materials that encourage task completion. What the special educator does not know, however, is that the speech-language pathologist is working on promoting the child's interactions with peers. The family's top priority is interactions with peers, but the special educator was not aware of this. The family talked to him or her only about staying on-task. In this example, the special educator is not only failing to attend to the family's first priority, because it was unknown, but also is inadvertently working against it. One of the principal advantages of collaboration, therefore, is ensuring that everyone is working on the same agenda—the family's.

***Learning from Each Other***   Collaboration provides an opportunity for on-the-job, functional in-service training. This is especially, but not exclusively, true for teachers, who with each child can learn about a strategy for addressing a particular developmental need. From a good therapist, a teacher can learn about the theory behind the intervention. Therapists can learn from teachers about learning styles, child engagement, and social competence. In actuality, many caregivers, especially in child care programs, do not have expertise to match that of therapists. But therapists can always learn from caregivers about individual children because caregivers spend much more time with the children. Therapists point out that, when they see children in distraction-free environments (e.g., pull-out situations), they can discover some capabilities of the children that may not be apparent in the classroom. Therefore, both skill- and child-related information can be shared through collaboration.

**Communicating to Build Teamwork** The importance of communication among service providers is repeatedly emphasized (see Chapter 6). Collaboration requires and promotes communication. Research has shown that, for children receiving in-class therapy, teachers and therapists consult with each other four times more than they do for children receiving out-of-class therapy (McWilliam & Bailey, 1992). In theory, the more practitioners communicate with each other, the better they function as a team.

The problems of collaboration involve attitude and values as well as systemic barriers such as Medicaid policies. The advantages of collaboration are also related to attitude and values; service providers who respect families' priorities, who see themselves as lifelong learners, and who believe in fostering teamwork are likely to embrace an approach that promotes collaboration.

## Professional Identity

The potential threat to professional identity is one of the problems associated with collaboration. It appears to be one of the major issues in integrated service delivery in early intervention. Possible problem areas include cultural discrepancy, role acceptance, role release, arrogance, and values paradoxes.

**Acculturation by Training Programs and Professional Organizations** Training programs, especially in the therapy disciplines, seem to do a good job acculturating students to their profession. The sense of professional identity is further enhanced by their professional organizations. Speech-language pathologists and psychologists, for example, are virtually required to be members of the American Speech-Hearing-Language Association and the American Psychological Association, respectively. An important component of the professional identity is having a specialized role. When therapists are confronted with the modern approach of transdisciplinary service delivery and collaboration, in which role release and role acceptance are required, that identity is threatened. They can no longer keep certain roles (i.e., interventions) to themselves, and they must adopt other, less specialized roles (i.e., classroom roles).

Acculturation means developing and fostering a particular culture; this happens in university training programs and professional organizations. Occupational therapy, physical therapy, and speech-language pathology are not simply disciplines, they are cultures. As in any culture, certain behaviors and attitudes are expected and are prevalent. It is a culture because the patterns of behavior and thought are discrete. Figure 1 shows four theoretical levels of culture that are evident in early intervention. The macroculture is the entire professional field, involving all disciplines (e.g., audiology, nursing, psychology, social work, vision specialists). (This theory is concerned with professional

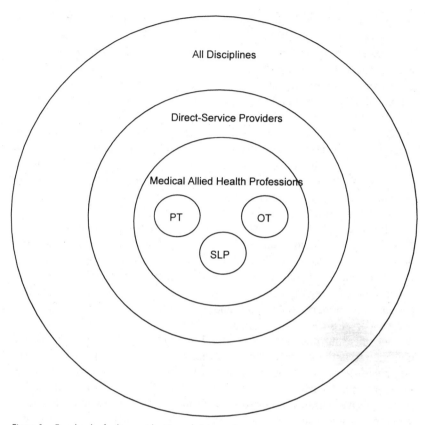

Figure 1. Four levels of culture evident in early intervention.

cultures and therefore excludes the very relevant legislative and family influences.) Within the macroculture, regular direct service providers (e.g.,
teachers, therapists) constitute the mesoculture. Within the mesoculture, the
medical allied health professions constitute a culture, with each of the therapies
constituting a subculture. According to this theory, the subcultures have the
strongest cultural identity.

Acculturation is not a bad thing. Educators, who have a less well-defined
culture, might envy the confederation, the status, and the professional identity
inherent in the specialized therapies. The advantages of cultural awareness
have been articulated for ethnic and racial cultures. The pitfalls of cultural
centrism as applied to ethnicity and race are the same when applied to early
intervention. One cannot maintain culture-specific behaviors if one wants to
work or play alongside people from other cultures. One has to adopt some of
their ways while not abandoning one's own. At the very least, one has to
understand others' ways and not force one's own on others. The theory of

therapies as cultures therefore points to both the strengths of professional identity as well as its frailty.

***Reluctance to Accept Roles from Other Disciplines*** With a strong sense of professional identity can come a disinclination to take on tasks from other disciplines. Integrated services require the therapists to concern themselves with areas of development outside their training, to work in unfamiliar settings (e.g., classrooms), and occasionally to perform tasks usually performed by group caregivers, such as changing diapers, restoring order, or wiping tables. Integrated services leave little room for the "*I don't do windows*" approach—an approach of which teachers may also be guilty. Teachers who do not want to incorporate range-of-motion activities, learn sign language, or work on independent spoon-feeding create barriers to effective service delivery.

***Reluctance to Let Others Take on Roles from One's Own Discipline*** The other side of the coin is a disinclination to allow other professionals to do what has traditionally been part of the expert arsenal. Deciding what other people can do is a complex task for specialists; they have to consider licensing regulations, the competence of the other person, liability, the potential for harm to the child, and so forth. For administrators, families, and even practitioners themselves, the problem is deciding whether the reasons for not releasing roles are legitimate. Therapists who have a philosophical objection to letting teachers "practice without a license" may find all sorts of legitimate-sounding reasons for insisting that they alone should carry out the interventions. A curious paradox is that, in home-based programs, therapists routinely give families things to do with their children, yet in center-based programs, teachers are often not proxy therapists. Clearly, families have very different opportunities from teachers to undertake therapeutic interventions; however, it can be said that teachers' opportunities are equally, albeit differently, available.

***Philosophical or Intellectual Arrogance*** Strong identification with a professional culture does not inevitably result in arrogance, but when combined with a condescending personality, arrogance can emerge. The difference in status between specialized therapists and generalist teachers can inhibit collaboration, if specialists reveal haughtiness about their status. Philosophical arrogance can emerge when a teacher's and a therapist's values are at odds, and intellectual arrogance can emerge when their degree of familiarity with technical jargon is different. A culturally sensitive approach helps prevent arrogance and also helps professionals respect each other's values and try to accommodate them.

***Cultural Beliefs and Values*** Different values and beliefs can inhibit teamwork. It is not simply that people from different disciplines have different knowledge: They often have very different views of the world, of families, of disability, of (re)habilitation, and of children. World views can range from believing that empirical evidence (research) should dictate what we do to believing that intuition (clinical judgment) should be our guide (Bogdan & Taylor, 1975). Views of families can range from parents as interferences to parents as partners (Dunst, 1985). Views of intervention can range from rehabilitation models to prevention models (Simeonsson, 1991). Views of children can range from children as unfinished adults to views based on developmental competence models (Goldberg, 1977). Hence, professionals from different disciplines (cultures) can have quite dissimilar ideas about how services should be delivered.

A cultural explanation has been proposed as an interpretation of problems with professionals maintaining too strong a connection with their disciplines. Despite the problems, some reasons for retaining cultural (i.e., discipline-specific) awareness exists. The confidence and contributions generated by identification with one's discipline can work for the benefit of children, families, and fellow professionals.

*Confidence* Having a healthy sense of one's own professional traditions, perspectives, and knowledge can give one enough confidence to respect the traditions, perspectives, and knowledge of other professionals.

*Valuable Contributions* It is likely that early childhood teachers who are aware of the rich background of their own discipline are more valuable contributors to teams than are those who are intimidated by the expertise of specialists.

*Ethics of Contention* There is nothing wrong with different perspectives, as long as we do not wage our ideological battles, whether actively or passively, using families as the fighting field. Unlike economics, literature, or even educational research, where mighty paradigm wars have been waged, early intervention at the point of service delivery is personal for families. It is likely that the personal characteristics of parents determine the extent to which they can handle professionals' different perspectives. But even the most educated, intellectually capable families are probably going to be more confused than enlightened by different perspectives. Families should be made informed consumers, so that they can take action when faced with controversies in treatment. For example, if some members of a team advocate craniosacral therapy as a treatment for cerebral palsy and others believe it to be at best ineffective and at worst harmful, the professionals have an ethical obligation to summarize the pros and cons and to help the family make a decision. They could suggest 1) seeing whether the child makes progress without the therapy or 2) trying the therapy for a specified time. Although contention might be illuminating for professionals, they need to evaluate the ethics of presenting a dispute to individual families before doing so.

Professional identity thus embodies the richness and the potential insularity of cultures, and it has a real impact on integrated service delivery.

### Functionality and Intervention Targets

What to work on and how to work on it reflect different approaches of disciplines. Consequently, one of the major issues in service delivery is the functionality of intervention targets and strategies (see Chapter 5 for more detail on functionality). This section discusses necessity, overspecificity, the number of goals, and family priorities.

*Necessity*   What is important to a specialist, from a relatively narrow, discipline-bound perspective, may not be important to ultimate child development, current adaptation, family routines, or family values. For example, working on protective reactions to the front, in which infants are taught to extend their arms forward to break their fall, is not an uncommon goal. The intervention often involves placing the baby prone over a large therapy ball and rotating the ball so that the infant's head goes toward the floor to elicit the desired protective extension. Unfortunately, 1) protective reactions are often found to be a need during a test of infant reactions; 2) there is no immediate need for the reaction, because often the infant cannot yet walk; 3) babies often cry (while tightening up, making extension even less likely) during this intervention; and 4) failure to use protective extension in infancy has not been found to predict failure to use it in later childhood. This is only one example of many interventions that have a nonfunctional target and intervention strategy. In a study of 100 randomly selected IFSPs from one state, the majority of intervention goals were of dubious functionality, and they were scored as such without the researchers even knowing the child (McWilliam et al., 1995). The necessity of discipline-specific intervention targets and strategies should be evaluated by answering the following questions:

1.  What difference will this skill make in the long run?
2.  What difference will it make in the short run (i.e., will it improve the current demands of daily functioning)?
3.  How well does it fit in with activities of daily living?
4.  How important does the family think it is?

*Overspecificity*   Development can be broken down into very small parts, primarily for assessing progress in developmentally delayed children and for understanding how development occurs. These very small parts may not be critical for eventual functioning. Although the necessity of a goal hinges on the connection with eventual functioning, overspecificity is related to isolation of a skill from its natural use. For example, using a three-chuck jaw grip (holding something with the thumb, index, and middle fingers) is useful (almost necessary) for finger-feeding. Taken out of the feeding context, the behavior has relatively limited application. Working on this skill in a traditional therapy session, using tiny paper pellets, then becomes illogical. It is better to focus on finger-feeding as the goal, rather than on mastery of a three-chuck jaw grip.

***Number of Goals*** The size of the outcomes or goals and objectives sections of many children's IFSPs and IEPs is much too large. There are simply too many things to work on. It has been recommended (McWilliam, 1992) that intervention plans be limited to 8–10 goals at any one time. Oversized IFSPs and IEPs are sometimes the result of multidisciplinary or interdisciplinary (as opposed to transdisciplinary) intervention planning.

***Family Priorities*** For most families, the priorities are still talking, walking, and acting normally, even while they acknowledge their children's limitations. Specialists can be helpful in identifying and addressing component skills that interfere with or enhance these priorities. Segregated services lamentably foster a focus on the trees to such an extent that the forest is unseen.

If a therapist or teacher understands what the child really needs, the intervention is likely to be more applicable to everyday routines. These interventions, however, must be limited in number to ensure that they are adequately implemented. These concepts are elaborated upon next.

***Understanding the Reason for Interventions*** When an objective is truly important for moving on, developmentally (e.g., head control), the goal (in this case, engagement) should be the focus. This allows everyone (parents and staff) to understand the value (functionality) of the objective and encourages them to look for alternative pathways to the eventual goal, which is vital for children whose usual pathways might be severely limited as a result of their disability. Without focusing on the goal, therapists and teachers might turn the intervention into a nonfunctional exercise. For example, if achieving head control is the objective, professionals can adapt seating, prompt the child to hold up his or her head, and provide physical therapy to elicit neck extension. If they do not give the child something to look at, though, their efforts are almost for naught. They need to remember that the reason for helping the child achieve head control is so he or she can be engaged.

***Keeping a Manageable Number of Goals*** This is especially important in center-based programs with many children. It is also recommended to help families, who have competing demands (e.g., jobs, housework, recreation) and limited time. If the number of goals is to be limited, one would hope that the goals are immediately useful.

***Maintaining Caregivers' Motivation*** If the people working with the child do not understand and accept the reason for working on a specific skill, they are less motivated to continue doing so. This is especially important for classroom teachers and families, who have many competing priorities (i.e., things that are just as important as working on the specialist's recommended interventions). Functional goals, almost by definition, are meaningful, so caregivers are likely to remain motivated to address them.

The relationship of functionality and intervention targets to service delivery is further addressed in Chapters 5 and 6. Functionality is neither the exclusive province of integrated services nor necessarily an *ipse qua non,* but intervention in context is more likely to foster or reinforce functionality than is intervention out of context.

## Evaluation of Effectiveness

A major issue in service delivery is the extent to which decisions are based on an evaluation of effectiveness. In a survey of about 800 early childhood special educators, occupational therapists, physical therapists, and speech-language pathologists working in early intervention, respondents were asked to rate the extent to which they would choose in-class versus out-of-class services under various conditions (McWilliam & Bailey, 1994). Some of those conditions were characteristics such as the child's age, severity of the disability, and distractibility. In the regression analyses, when child characteristics were considered by themselves, they predicted 49% of the variance. However, when child characteristics were entered last in the regression model after the respondent's discipline, specific techniques and goals of intervention, family preferences, therapist characteristics, and caseload characteristics, child characteristics accounted for only 10% of the variance. Results showed that discipline, techniques and goals, and family preference were stronger predictors than were child characteristics. Thus, the axiom that therapists base their decisions primarily on the needs of the child must be questioned.

Problems with evaluating the effectiveness of service delivery include 1) different views of evaluation, 2) reactions to unpopular research, 3) non–data-based service delivery, and 4) attribution theory.

***Different Views of Evaluation*** Different views of how to decide whether something works can make evaluation an elusive foundation for service delivery. Some practitioners need to see hard data, whereas others are satisfied with anecdotes of success; some believe that an approach works only if they have tried it themselves, so they try anything once. These discrepancies in evaluation philosophy apply both to approaches in the field and to effectiveness with a particular child. How to decide whether something works has become an issue with regard to broad approaches such as inclusion as well as narrowly defined techniques such as facilitated communication, patterning, Irlen lenses, holding therapy, myofascial release, craniosacral therapy, and so forth. Integration of services has not generated much discussion, although related topics such as collaboration and consultation have (e.g., File & Kontos, 1992), in the context of inclusion.

In early intervention, some approaches are backed by theory, anecdotes, and poorly conducted research. We have seen neurodevelopmental therapy, sensory integration, and motor planning have their ups and downs, and plenty of therapists still swear by them. Motor planning is fashionable in the mid-1990s, and some therapists are wholesale proponents of sensory integration. It is beyond the scope of this book to review research on specific treatments, but it is widely known that defensible research on many of these treatments is sorely lacking. Interestingly, research on the effectiveness of neurodevelopmental therapy has been conducted by early intervention researchers who are not therapists (e.g., Horn, Warren, & Jones, 1995).

Not only do anecdotes provide the underpinning of some techniques, values also play a part. This has been true especially in the acceptance of *developmentally appropriate practice* (Bredekamp, 1987) in early childhood and increasingly in early childhood special education. Other techniques, such as teaching through applied behavior analysis (Wolery, Bailey, & Sugai, 1988), have been by backed by minutiae-filled research. Behavioral approaches have not escaped controversy in early childhood special education (see Carta, Schwartz, Atwater, & McConnell, 1991, for a defense, and Mahoney, Robinson, & Powell, 1992, for an attack). Thus, both values and single-subject studies contribute to practitioners' concepts of what works.

**Reactions to Unpopular Research** Some studies with broad implications are attacked on methodological grounds. In a study by Palmer et al. (1988), physical therapy was administered to half of the participants for 12 months, and physical therapy for 6 months preceded by 6 months of the Learningames (Sparling & Lewis, 1979) early childhood curriculum was administered to the other half. The latter group was found to do better on motor quotient scores and on walking. Critics attacked the definition of the intervention and the outcome measure, and it is unclear whether, in light of these criticisms, any room was left for the possibility that physical therapy might not be as effective as supposed for children with cerebral palsy or that developmentally appropriate early childhood activities might have benefits.

Another controversial study was the meta-analysis of early intervention studies that purported to show that family involvement was not as effective as presumed (Casto & Mastropieri, 1986). Although the methodology of this study was also widely criticized (e.g., Dunst & Snyder, 1986; Strain & Smith, 1986), the response was in some ways quite different. Researchers reviewed extant studies carefully and conducted further investigations of family-centered practices (e.g., Dunst, Johanson, Trivette, & Hamby, 1991). More important for practice, however, early interventionists refined their approaches to working with families, acknowledging that the concept of parental involvement was paternalistic and narrow. Thus, unpopular research can either prevent further questioning or stimulate change.

**Non–Data-Based Service Delivery** With the exception of applied behavior analysts, failure to take a data-based approach has seriously hampered professionals' progress in individual interventions. Most interventions are conducted without even quasi-experimental evaluation. All the therapists we worked with in the course of our research (see Chapter 4) said they used clinical judgment to make decisions about how to serve children. We found, however, that therapists hardly varied in their approach between children; furthermore, there was little variability across disciplines within each program (McWilliam & Scarborough, 1994). If, over the years, practitioners had measured the effects of different models of service delivery with individual children, we would know much more than we do about what works with whom and why.

*Attribution Theory* Families sometimes attribute child success to therapy or education and sometimes to their own efforts. The latter attribution increases their sense of empowerment and, considering the amount of time many families put into helping their children, is likely to be valid. Considering the amount of time a therapist spends working directly with the child (e.g., 20 minutes a week), attribution of success to therapy is probably optimistic. The more therapy involves consultation, however, the more likely it can claim credit, for then the effects of therapy are enhanced by having others (e.g., teachers, parents) spend more time implementing the interventions. Because families obviously do not evaluate early intervention using quasi-experimental methodology, they are not isolating the critical independent variable, which might be the consultation rather than the hands-on work. When hands-on work is used for the purpose of collaboration (e.g., demonstrating a technique), it is likely to be a more important predictor of child progress. Families' attributions of the benefits of therapy and of service delivery models (e.g., individual hands-on) have undoubtedly reinforced the traditional status quo.

The importance of evaluation is obvious, but less evident reasons are 1) isolating the independent variable, 2) being honest about effectiveness, 3) elevating the quality of research, and 4) raising the quality of intervention.

*Isolating the Independent Variable* Data-based or well-conducted qualitative evaluation is necessary to determine the critical variables in our interventions. For example, in consultative services (defined as intermittent services provided by a specialist), we should attempt to discover the relative benefits of training or encouraging others to attend to interventions and carrying out direct interventions ourselves. When a speech-language pathologist visits a classroom, spends some time observing, takes two or three children out for therapy, and then spends a few minutes making suggestions to the teacher, and the children show progress in areas addressed by the therapist, how much does each of his or her activities (e.g., observation, therapy, consultation) contribute to that progress? Isolating the critical variables is valuable for guiding practitioners about which activities to emphasize and which to de-emphasize.

*Being Honest About Effectiveness* Research is needed to give practitioners the ability to be truthful about whether certain practices are proved or valued. The distinction between proof and values is not disingenuous: Both have their place, although practitioners may face a considerable challenge in recommending a values-based approach rather than a research-based one. Practitioners probably need to frame values-based recommendations in terms of theory, as has been done already with, for example, sensory integration and developmentally appropriate practice. Perhaps greater acceptance of the role of values in recommending interventions is also needed. In studies where no significant findings can be found to support one approach over another, values might well be the deciding factor on the recommended approach.

*Elevating the Quality of Research* A demand for data-based decision making in service delivery would foster the much-needed increase in high-quality research. Both more and better studies in service delivery models are needed. Examples of poor-quality research abound. For example, one study (DeGangi, Wietlisbach, Goodin, & Scheiner, 1993) purported to find that structured sensorimotor therapy was more effective than child-centered activity in the treatment of gross motor skills in preschool children with sensorimotor problems, and child-centered activity was more effective for treating fine motor problems. Yet this study 1) failed to measure treatment integrity, 2) did not report inter-rater agreement for observational measures, and 3) did not conduct analyses comparing the two treatments. Studies such as this serve no useful purpose and potentially set back practice.

*Raising the Quality of Intervention* Specialized therapies are characterized as 1) expensive, 2) atheoretically prescribed (i.e., on the basis of diagnosis more than on functioning need), and 3) less integrated than practitioners desire (McWilliam & Bailey, 1994). A research base in the literature and a commitment to conduct single-subject effectiveness analyses would go a long way toward improving service delivery. These expensive services could be allocated and decisions about how to provide the services could be made on the basis of empirical evidence.

Collaboration, professional identity, evaluation, and functionality have been discussed as major issues in classroom-based early intervention. The following section summarizes related research (see Chapter 4 for a discussion of studies specifically on integrated therapy).

## RESEARCH

Research related to service delivery includes studies of consultation and interdisciplinary collaboration. Unfortunately, the early intervention efficacy literature does not address issues of service delivery models beyond home-versus center-based locations. Analyses of cost, effectiveness, and efficiency are needed for different models of delivering specialized therapies in center-based programs.

Within special education for school-age children, some studies of integrated services (usually meaning integration between special and general education teachers) have been conducted. Students in Grades 2, 4, and 5 have been found to prefer pull-out if they are in the fourth or fifth grade (Jenkins & Heinen, 1989). The top two reasons for selecting pull-out were "get more/

better help there" and "embarrassing to have specialist come in," and the top two reasons for selecting in-class were "more convenient to stay" and "like to be with my class." For these school-age children, it was more embarrassing to have a specialist come in than for them to leave the classroom. They overwhelmingly preferred to receive help from classroom teachers versus specialists, although students receiving pull-out were more amenable to receiving help from specialists. From teachers' viewpoints, no particular type of student benefits from pull-out programs (Meyers, Gelzheiser, Yelich, & Gallagher, 1990). In this study, only 9% of the teachers ($N$ = 57) thought distracted students benefited from pull-out, whereas 19% thought these students did not benefit. Just over half of these teachers had no experience with alternatives to pull-out programs.

Some professional practices have been hypothesized to interfere with the integrated delivery of related services. Giangreco, Edelman, and Dennis (1991) found that the following six practices occurred frequently (i.e., above 5.5 on a 10-point Likert-type scale from *never happens* to *always happens*): summary reports that represent priorities from individual disciplines (8.17), discipline-specific recommendations for service delivery (8.01), IEP sections reflecting priorities of separate disciplines (8.28), service delivery recommendations for their own disciplines (7.84), recommendations preceding classroom placement decisions (6.59) and preceding determination of IEP goals (6.70), and placement decisions based on the need for related services (5.72). People who do not understand the concept of integrated services might be surprised that these practices are considered interferences, but this study should help to operationalize that concept.

### Consultation Research

What consultation practices have been shown to be effective in efficacy studies (i.e., comparing with no consultation) and in comparison studies (i.e., comparing with consultation practices)? Research on consultation effectiveness is found more in psychology than in special education journals; behavioral consultation has been studied more than mental health models; and student and teacher behavior has been the outcome in consultation studies more than student achievement (Fuchs, Fuchs, Dulan, Roberts, & Fernstrom, 1992).

In a study of the effectiveness of nondirective consultation, this approach was found to increase both instructional behaviors in targeted routines and student IEP-targeted behaviors (Hundert & Hopkins, 1992). Reviews of the research literature have documented 1) the importance of people skills and problem-solving skills of the consultant, 2) consultees' preference for the collaborative model over the expert (medical) model, and 3) the effectiveness of consultation (File & Kontos, 1992). In their review of educational consultation, Heron and Kimball (1988) found that model preferences may be different across educational roles (e.g., school psychologists preferring mental health consultation, but teachers preferring collaborative consultation) and that the collaborative model enhances success.

Problem-solving consultation about an individual child has been criticized as too restrictive to give teachers generalized information that will lead them to be more competent in the future (Witt & Martens, 1988). These authors argue that consultation should be focused more on helping teachers identify resources and developing self-sustaining competencies.

## Interdisciplinary Collaboration

What were the critical elements of collaboration (i.e., the independent variables)? Professionals from different disciplines and parents have been found to make decisions about related services (eligibility, frequency of service, and so forth) based on different criteria (Giangreco, 1990). Background data from this study showed that "all respondent groups indicated that related services still are provided primarily in direct modes and in physically isolated environments" (p. 27). In a study of interdisciplinary team members' attitudes toward speech-language services in public schools, educators had generally positive attitudes toward services, but some confusion about team member roles was evident (Tomes & Sanger, 1986). The most powerful predictor of positive attitudes was the extent to which educators felt they had input into developing treatment programs. In their interdisciplinary review of consultation research, West and Idol (1987) found that input variables, process variables, and situational variables could be identified as influencing various outcome variables. Input variables consist of consultee characteristics, consultant characteristics, and the nature of the problem presented. Process variables consist of the consultation model used, the consultation techniques or style used, the consultation stage, and whether an individual or group is receiving the consultation. Situational variables consist of time, location, organizational factors, and the learning environment. Outcome variables consist of teacher behavior and attitudes, student behavior and attitudes, and organizational or systemic change.

Barriers to effective consultation, in this case by special educators, were reviewed by Johnson, Pugach, and Hammitte (1988). They found that the literature pointed to pragmatic barriers of definition (i.e., defining the role of a consultant) and insufficient time as well as overwhelming caseloads. Conceptual barriers consisted of doubts about the credibility of special educators, possible mismatches between the thinking of general and special educators, hierarchical relationships that put consultants on a higher rung than classroom teachers, and different knowledge bases of consultants and consultees.

These studies show that, although not unequivocal, research on the related issues of consultation, interdisciplinary collaboration, and intervention foci suggests that an integrated approach to service delivery has merit. The following section describes some of the barriers to this approach. Because difficulties have been described previously, it might appear that this is a pessimistic introduction to the topic; rather, it sets the stage for the rest of the book. Problems with the way specialized services are delivered are, after all, what have prompted the innovations and research.

## PROBLEMS IN SERVICE DELIVERY

### Lack of Research

Empirical evidence has been unable to guide service delivery models because too little research exists and some of it is flawed, as discussed earlier in this chapter. (See Chapter 4 for an overview of comparative studies.)

### Superstitions, Beliefs, and Myths

Specific treatments predict the extent to which integrated therapy is likely to be chosen (McWilliam & Bailey, 1994). Although McWilliam and Bailey did not collect data on the more esoteric treatments, it seems conceivable that they are more apt to be provided outside the context of classroom routines. If the treatment requires specialized training or equipment, therapists will probably be inclined to provide therapy in a context where they have control and privacy. What are some of these esoteric treatments? They include facilitated communication (i.e., where the therapist's hand supports the child's hand in selecting communication-board items), auditory training (i.e., in which tones are provided to calm or stimulate brain activity), and craniosacral therapy (i.e., in which the therapist regulates the flow of cerebral spinal fluid through manipulation). Esoteric treatments tend to be controversial because they violate some people's values, they promise seemingly impossible cures, or the supporting research is flawed or lacking.

Sensory integration has a particularly interesting role in the lore of therapy. It is a theory and a set of practices that many, if not most, occupational therapists have adopted with devotion as a valid treatment. Yet educators and to some extent speech-language pathologists and physical therapists have been baffled by it. The theoretical links between such practices as brushing the skin or bouncing and such outcomes as concentration (as a result of more integration of the sensory pathways) have resulted in perplexing programming. For example, in a 2-year study of goals and therapy models, McWilliam and Scarborough (1994) came across brushing stimulation as a treatment for toileting, engagement, following directions, and appropriate use of hands (i.e., keeping hands out of the mouth). What is an accepted treatment in one discipline may be a superstition to another. This again points to a challenge in transdisciplinary approaches to early intervention.

Parents' beliefs in certain practices pose an especially difficult problem for integrated therapy. If we are trying to be family-centered, responding to families' concerns and priorities, and they want a model in which we have no confidence, we are caught in a bind. The recommended step is to make sure the family is fully informed (i.e., let them know of any reservations), but this can fail in two ways. First, they may not agree with us. Second, our doubts may only confuse the family and have detrimental effects. Families of children with hearing impairments have attested to this in the case of selecting total communication, Signed Exact English, American Sign Language, cued speech, or oral communication.

Another belief that may have an effect on the extent to which integrated therapy is used is that "more is better" (McWilliam et al., 1995). If "more" is interpreted to mean more direct therapy, more one-on-one, and more time in therapy generally, the relatively diffuse model of integrated therapy is unlikely to satisfy consumers and practitioners who believe there is a linear relationship between frequency or duration and effectiveness. In a study of the effects of developmental (occupational and physical) therapy on 3- to 15-year-old children with motor impairments, the frequency of therapy (once or thrice weekly) did not significantly affect improvement in gross motor skills (Jenkins et al., 1982). Families' beliefs that more is better pose a challenge to policy makers, program administrators, and practitioners.

Beliefs in specific treatments, such as sensory integrative techniques, of both professionals and families have little to do with research, but they are powerful forces in service delivery patterns in early intervention.

## The Politics of Early Intervention

The following problems are political in the sense that they are what Ambrose Bierce, in *The Devil's Dictionary,* called "a strife of interests masquerading as a contest of principles" (1941, p. 258). My sources for the observations in this section would not want to be identified, and I would not want to be the one to identify them. Strifes of interest have not escaped any of the disciplines. Although specific disciplines are identified here with each contest of principles, this is largely for illustrative purposes. Most of these problems also affect disciplines other than those in the example.

Some professions have sensed a loss of autonomy, especially since PL 99-457 (Education of the Handicapped Act Amendments of 1986) came into effect. Among some pediatric members of the American Physical Therapy Association, for example, there was a feeling that early intervention with infants and toddlers was their business, until legislation was passed under the U.S. Department of Education. Educators, however, perceive the law to be written with equal opportunity for all disciplines to be involved; unlike the terminology of PL 94-142 (Education for All Handicapped Children Act of 1975), for example, therapies are not called *related services,* and children can receive therapy regardless of any educational need. The way early intervention services are organized, starting at the federal level, therefore appears to be interpreted differently by the different disciplines.

In occupational therapy, some therapists worried that their clinic-based practices, especially for treatment of sensory integration, would become less accessible with legislation mandating that infants and toddlers should be served in settings most like those they would attend if they did not have disabilities. With respect to integrated services, this disquiet is played out in children being pulled out of their preschool or child care classrooms for therapy or even being transported by their parents to clinic-based therapy in the middle of the day.

Some speech-language pathologists have been concerned that private practice would suffer as public agencies gained resources for providing services. It appears as though private practitioners have still managed to provide services under contract to infant or toddler and preschool programs, but, from the perspective of private providers, every speech-language pathologist hired by a public program could represent the loss of a number of potential clients.

In at least one state, psychologists and speech-language pathologists fought the inclusion of assessment in training competencies for early childhood special educators. They argued that teachers could *screen* but not *test* children. This was not mere semantic quibbling; it represented anxiety that a critical function of psychologists (and speech-language pathologists in areas of communication) would be usurped. Ultimately, the ability of teachers to conduct assessment for intervention planning and monitoring progress was listed as a training competency.

Some special educators worry that inclusion is ineffective for some children and that the principles of the early childhood discipline are supplanting those of early childhood special education. Self-conscious efforts are being made at the national and state levels to bring together professionals from these two disciplines, but not without grumbling from some special educators about the dilution of their profession and the threats to individualization with inclusion.

For their part, some early childhood professionals are concerned that they will have to give up their constructivist principles with children with disabilities, under pressure from early intervention professionals. This is directly related to service delivery because the early intervention professionals who have the most contact with early childhood professionals are the special educators and therapists working with them and their children with special needs. For early childhood professionals, inclusion has meant not only learning to serve children with disabilities and their families but also learning to work with other professionals who also think they know what is best for the child.

The politics of early intervention are not always explicit in the literature, but it would be naive to ignore them, especially when proposing alternatives such as integrated service delivery.

## Lack of Clarity About the Purpose of Early Intervention

Finally, lack of clarity about the goal of early intervention causes problems in effecting service delivery. The following questions show the range of philosophies and concomitant strategies for the goal of intervention.

*Is it to treat the child or the condition for remediation or even cure?* Think about the claims of craniosacral therapy to cure cerebral palsy (Upledger & Vredevoogd, 1983) and of sensory integration to remedy learning disabilities (Ayres, 1978). With claims like these, families and professionals are likely to think that specific therapies need to be implemented exactly as prescribed by the specialist, which runs counter to integration of specialized services with general classroom routines.

*Is it to teach the child skills he or she has failed on developmental tests or to help the child catch up?* Similar to the remedial notion of early intervention, the catch-up philosophy promotes a deficit orientation to service delivery. In recommending goals, professionals are likely to emphasize children's weaknesses, with scant attention being paid to their strengths.

*Is it to provide support to the family, only part of which is to provide direct services to the child?* Early childhood special educators have embraced the family support philosophy (described by Dunst, 1985; Dunst, Trivette, & Deal, 1988), which is supported by research (Dunst, Trivette, Hamby, & Pollock, 1990). But the training of therapists still concentrates on direct services to children. This might be appropriate, considering that child-related skills are still needed and families value them (McWilliam et al., 1995), but the chasm between the two philosophies (direct services to children versus family support) exacerbates resistance to integrated service delivery.

*Is it to give children typical experiences to help them learn from typically developing peers and to learn through play?* This philosophy is consistent with inclusion (Buysse & Bailey, 1993), normalization (Bailey & McWilliam, 1991), and developmentally appropriate practice (Bredekamp, 1987). Again, acceptance of this approach as a purpose for early intervention is not universal; professionals more oriented to curative philosophies argue that this might be a goal of early childhood, but that children with disabilities need direct therapy to help them benefit from typical experiences, learn from peers, and learn through play.

*Is it to teach children those skills they need to succeed in everyday environments, modifying settings as necessary?* The problem with this approach, for some professionals, is that the need for certain foundational skills might not be apparent in everyday environments. For example, a child might sit with very bad posture but still survive in the classroom. Another child might use gestures instead of language and still be able to express him- or herself adequately. It could therefore be argued that the demands of the current environment are not a sufficient basis for service delivery and that the demands of subsequent environments justify working on skills that are not immediately necessary.

Different concepts of the purpose of early intervention, therefore, lead to different approaches to service delivery. Two well-known definitions of the mission of this field are those by Dunst (1985) and by Bailey and Wolery (1992). Dunst proposed that early intervention should be conducted using a social systems model, in which social support to families through a proactive approach, empowerment, and partnerships is a key ingredient. Bailey and Wolery's list of goals for early intervention is composed of the following:

1. To support families in achieving their own goals
2. To promote child engagement, independence, and mastery
3. To promote development in key domains
4. To build and support children's social competence
5. To promote the generalized use of skills
6. To provide and prepare for normalized life experiences
7. To prevent the emergence of future problems or disabilities

Theory and goals of early intervention show that this is a multifaceted, complex enterprise. In center-based service delivery, some goals can be used to justify practices opposing other practices that can be justified through other goals. For example, an occupational therapist might give a child a "chewy" (i.e., a cylindrical piece of rubber tubing) to wear around his or her neck to chew or suck on; this is designed to help the child calm, organize, and focus him- or herself (Scheerer, 1992). The occupational therapist would argue that the chewy addresses Bailey and Wolery's second and, possibly, seventh early intervention goals. However, the child's teacher might argue that chewing on rubber tubing worn around the neck violates the sixth and, possibly, fourth goals. Both professionals would have theoretical and philosophical bases for their arguments. This example demonstrates the challenge that conflicting philosophies pose for integrating services.

## CONCLUSIONS

Redefined goals of early intervention support a new approach to service delivery. Three arguments can be used to suggest that integrated services should be a component of this new approach.

First, the lack of data to support continuing traditional practices along with the problems identified earlier in this chapter call for a change. Although the data are not compelling in terms of benefits to children, they do suggest that children at least do no worse with an integrated approach. In the face of no clear advantage to children, values can be appropriately used to make a service delivery decision. If collaboration and normalization are valued, it would be reasonable to adopt an integrated services approach.

Second, the benefits of collaboration inherent in integrated therapy are that professionals can learn from one another, the child can receive frequent and context-appropriate intervention, and intervention can be linked across developmental domains. The success of a collaborative approach to consultation between special education and general education teachers has been documented in the literature. Research is needed to examine the effects of collaboration between specialists and teachers.

Third, integrated therapy can compensate, but not make up, for the shortage of allied health personnel (Yoder, Coleman, & Gallagher, 1990). Integrated therapy done well (see Chapter 7) requires just as much, if not more, therapist time as traditional pull-out therapy. Nevertheless, until there are enough therapists, is it better for intermittent therapy to be spent with one child at a time, away from the regular environment and regular caregivers (i.e., segregated), or in the regular environment (perhaps with more than one client child), collaborating with regular caregivers (i.e., integrated)?

This chapter presented an overview of major issues, research, and theory about service delivery, problems with current practices and alternatives, and a rationale for a new approach. The remainder of this book provides more information on issues related to the effectiveness of integrated therapy, discusses integrated therapy from the perspectives of different disciplines, and looks to future directions in service delivery.

## REFERENCES

Ayres, A.J. (1978). Learning disabilities and the vestibular system. *Journal of Learning Disabilities, 11,* 30–41.

Bailey, D.B., & McWilliam, R.A. (1991). Normalizing early intervention. *Topics in Early Childhood Special Education, 10*(2), 33–47.

Bailey, D.B., & Wolery, M. (1992). *Teaching infants and preschoolers with disabilities.* Columbus, OH: Charles E. Merrill.

Bierce, A. (1941). *The devil's dictionary.* Cleveland, OH: World Publishing Co.

Bogdan, R., & Taylor, S.J. (1975). *Introduction to qualitative research methods: A phenomenological approach to the social sciences.* New York: John Wiley & Sons.

Bredekamp, S. (1987). *Developmentally appropriate practice in early childhood programs serving children from birth through age 8: Expanded edition.* Washington, DC: National Association for the Education of Young Children.

Buysse, V., & Bailey, D.B., Jr. (1993). Behavioral and developmental outcomes in young children with disabilities in integrated and segregated settings: A review of comparative studies. *Journal of Special Education, 26,* 434–461.

Carta, J.J., Schwartz, I.S., Atwater, J.B., & McConnell, S.R. (1991). Developmentally appropriate practice: Appraising its usefulness for young children with disabilities. *Topics in Early Childhood Special Education, 11*(1), 1–20.

Casto, G., & Mastropieri, M.A. (1986). The efficacy of early intervention programs: A meta-analysis. *Exceptional Children, 52,* 417–424.

DEC Task Force on Recommended Practices. (1993). *DEC recommended practices: Indicators of quality in programs for infants and young children with special needs and their families.* Pittsburgh, PA: Division for Early Childhood.

DeGangi, G.A., Wietlisbach, S., Goodin, M., & Scheiner, N. (1993). A comparison of structured sensorimotor therapy and child-centered activity in the treatment of preschool children with sensorimotor problems. *American Journal of Occupational Therapy, 47,* 777–786.

Dunst, C.J. (1985). Rethinking early intervention. *Analysis and Intervention in Developmental Disabilities, 5,* 165–201.

Dunst, C.J., Johanson, C., Trivette, C.M., & Hamby, D.W. (1991). Family-oriented early intervention policies and practices: Family-centered or not? *Exceptional Children, 58,* 115–126.

Dunst, C.J., & Snyder, S.W. (1986). A critique of the Utah State University early intervention meta-analysis research. *Exceptional Children, 53,* 269–276.

Dunst, C.J., Trivette, C.M., & Deal, A.G. (1988). *Enabling and empowering families: Principles and guidelines for practice.* Cambridge, MA: Brookline Books.

Dunst, C.J., Trivette, C.M., Hamby, D.M., & Pollock, B. (1990). Family systems correlates of the behavior of young children with handicaps. *Journal of Early Intervention, 14,* 204–218.

Education for All Handicapped Children Act of 1975, PL 94–142. (August 23, 1977). Title 20, U.S.C. §§ 1401 *et seq.: U.S. Statutes at Large, 89,* 773–796.

Education of the Handicapped Act Amendments of 1986, PL 99–457. (October 8, 1986). Title 20, U.S.C. §§ 1400 *et seq.: U.S. Statutes at Large, 100,* 1145–1177.

File, N., & Kontos, S. (1992). Indirect service delivery through consultation: Review and implications for early intervention. *Journal of Early Intervention, 16,* 221–233.

Fuchs, D., Fuchs, L.S., Dulan, J., Roberts, H., & Fernstrom, P. (1992). Where is the research on consultation effectiveness? *Journal of Educational and Psychological Consultation, 3,* 151–174.

Giangreco, M.F. (1990). Making related service decisions for students with severe disabilities: Roles, criteria, and authority. *Journal of The Association for Persons with Severe Handicaps, 15,* 22–31.

Giangreco, M.F., Edelman, S., & Dennis, R. (1991). Common professional practices that interfere with the integrated delivery of related services. *Remedial and Special Education, 12*(2), 16–24.

Goldberg, S. (1977). Social competence in infancy: A model of parent-infant interaction. *Merrill Palmer Quarterly, 23,* 163–177.

Heron, T.E., & Kimball, W.H. (1988). Gaining perspective with the educational consultation research base: Ecological considerations and further recommendations. *Remedial and Special Education, 9*(6), 21–47.

Horn, E., Warren, S.F., & Jones, H. (1995). An experimental analysis of neurobehavioral motor intervention. *Developmental Medicine & Child Neurology, 37,* 566–583.

Hundert, J., & Hopkins, B. (1992). Training supervisors in a collaborative team approach to promote peer interaction of children with disabilities in integrated preschools. *Journal of Applied Behavior Analysis, 25,* 385–400.

Idol, L., Paolucci-Whitcomb, P., & Nevin, A. (1986). *Collaborative consultation.* Rockville, MD: Aspen Publishers, Inc.

Individuals with Disabilities Education Amendments of 1991, PL 102-119. (October 7, 1991). Title 20, U.S.C. §§ 1400 *et seq.: U.S. Statutes at Large, 105,* 587–608.

Jenkins, J.R., & Heinen, A. (1989). Students' preferences for service delivery: Pull-out, in-class, or integrated models. *Exceptional Children, 55,* 516–523.

Jenkins, J.R., Sells, C.J., Brady, D., Down, J., Moore, B., Carman, P., & Holm, R. (1982). Effects of developmental therapy on motor impaired children. *Physical & Occupational Therapy in Pediatrics, 2*(4), 19–28.

Johnson, L.J., Pugach, M.C., & Hammitte, D.J. (1988). Barriers to effective special education consultation. *Remedial and Special Education, 9,* 41–47.

Mahoney, G., Robinson, C., & Powell, A. (1992). Focusing on parent-child interaction: The bridge to developmentally appropriate practices. *Topics in Early Childhood Special Education, 12*(1), 105–120.

McWilliam, R.A. (1992). *Family-centered intervention planning: A routines-based approach.* Tucson, AZ: Communication Skill Builders.

McWilliam, R.A., & Bailey, D.B. (1992, December). *From integrated to pull-out services: Practices and perceptions of four disciplines.* Paper presented at the DEC Early Childhood Conference on Children with Special Needs, Washington, DC.

McWilliam, R.A., & Bailey, D.B., Jr. (1994). Predictors of service-delivery models in center-based early intervention. *Exceptional Children, 61,* 56–71.

McWilliam, R.A., Lang, L., Vandiviere, P., Angell, R., Collins, L., & Underdown, G. (1995). Satisfaction and struggles: Family perceptions of early intervention services. *Journal of Early Intervention, 19,* 43–60.

McWilliam, R.A., & Scarborough, A. (1994, September 23). *Does therapy carry over to the classroom? How to make early intervention more effective.* Paper presented at the North Carolina Association for the Education of Young Children/Division for Early Childhood Annual Study Conference, Greensboro, NC.

McWilliam, R.A., Tocci, L., & Harbin, G.L. (1995). *Services are child-centered and families like them that way—but why?* Chapel Hill, NC: Frank Porter Graham Child Development Center, University of North Carolina.

Meyers, J., Gelzheiser, L., Yelich, G., & Gallagher, M. (1990). Classroom, remedial, and resource teachers' views of pullout programs. *The Elementary School Journal, 90,* 533–545.

Odom, S.L., McLean, M.E., Johnson, L.J., & LaMontagne, M.J. (1995). Recommended practices in early childhood special education: Validation and current use. *Journal of Early Intervention, 19,* 1–17.

Palmer, F.B., Shapiro, B.K., Wachtel, R.C., Allen, M.A., Hiller, J.E., Harryman, S.E., Mosher, B.S., Meinert, C.L., & Capute, A.J. (1988). The effects of physical therapy on cerebral palsy: A controlled trial in infants with spastic diplegia. *The New England Journal of Medicine, 318,* 803–808.

Scheerer, C.R. (1992). Perspectives on an oral motor activity: The use of rubber tubing as a "chewy." *The American Journal of Occupational Therapy, 46,* 344–352.

Simeonsson, R.J. (1991). Primary, secondary, and tertiary prevention in early intervention. *Journal of Early Intervention, 15,* 124–134.

Sparling, J., & Lewis, I. (1979). *Learningames for the first three years.* New York: Walker & Co.

Strain, P.S., & Smith, B.J. (1986). A counter-interpretation of early intervention effects: A response to Casto and Mastropieri. *Exceptional Children, 53,* 260–265.

Tomes, L., & Sanger, D.D. (1986). Attitudes of interdisciplinary team members toward speech-language services in public schools. *Language, Speech, and Hearing Services in Schools, 17,* 230–240.

Upledger, J.E., & Vredevoogd, J.D. (1983). *Craniosacral therapy.* Chicago: Eastland Press.

West, J.F., & Idol, L. (1987). School consultation: Part I. An interdisciplinary perspective on theory, models, and research. *Journal of Learning Disabilities, 20,* 388–408.

Witt, J.C., & Martens, B.K. (1988). Problems with problem-solving consultation: A reanalysis of assumptions, methods, and goals. *School Psychology Review, 17,* 211–226.

Wolery, M., Bailey, D.B., & Sugai, G.M. (1988). *Effective teaching: Principles and procedures of applied behavior analysis.* Newton, MA: Allyn & Bacon.

Yoder, D.E., Coleman, P.P., & Gallagher, J.J. (1990). *Personnel needs: Allied health personnel meeting the demands of Part H, P.L. 99-457.* Unpublished manuscript, Carolina Institute for Child and Family Policy, University of North Carolina, Chapel Hill.

# Chapter 2

# Interdisciplinary Collaboration in Service Delivery

Mary Beth Bruder

Early intervention service delivery historically has included children and families who demonstrate a diversity of strengths and needs. These needs usually encompass a broad range of developmental, ecological, and health-related issues, resulting in an array of services delivered by a number of professionals from different disciplines. Although comprehensive in scope, this service methodology can result in confusion—children and families being served by a multitude of professionals with differing philosophies of intervention and differing treatment outcomes (Bruder, 1994). The major reason for this lack of coordination is the emphasis within personnel preparation programs (Bailey, Palsha, & Huntington, 1990) and state personnel standards boards (Bruder, Klosowski, & Daguio, 1991) to train and license professionals within a single disciplinary or developmental area without regard to the inherent overlap of a child's needs across areas. For example, a physical therapist is trained and licensed to provide interventions that affect motor development; a speech-language pathologist is trained and licensed to provide interventions that affect communication. However, children and families receiving early intervention services under the federal Individuals with Disabilities Education Act (IDEA) (PL 101-476) are entitled to receive special education and related services from a variety of professional disciplines, as listed in Table 1.

Although thorough, the model of multiple professionals working with one child to provide discipline-specific interventions can be overwhelming and cumbersome to all involved (Bruder & Bologna, 1993). There are also a number of questionable assumptions associated with the use of this model. First, this model assumes that a professional from a specific discipline is the most appropriate person to provide intervention within a developmental area.

Table 1. Disciplines in early intervention

Audiologist
Early childhood special educator
Nutritionist
Nurse
Occupational therapist
Physician
Psychologist
Physical therapist
Social worker
Speech-language pathologist
Vision specialist

This may not always be true. For example, some areas of intervention represent overlap between discipline-specific expertise (e.g., oral-motor interventions, social-cognitive interventions). In addition, a professional's expertise may be more representative of his or her training and experience as opposed to the traditional service boundaries of his or her discipline. In many parts of the country, the lack of availability of professionals from certain disciplines also is a concern. It has been well documented that there are critical personnel shortages within the disciplines of physical, occupational, and speech-language therapy (Hebbeler, 1994).

Another problematic assumption with this model is the belief that the child will progress in only the developmental area in which the discipline-specific intervention occurs. Although this may seem logical for children who show delay in one area of development (e.g., speech and language), most children who have disabilities and receive early intervention services demonstrate delays across many areas of development. It then becomes very difficult to design service delivery plans for these children, because the necessity and intensity of discipline-specific interventions becomes somewhat arbitrary and the effectiveness of one disciplinary intervention cannot be evaluated in isolation from other interventions. For children with severe delays across developmental areas, service delivery plans can represent an assortment of people, professional disciplines, and interventions, all delivered with varying degrees of frequency and intensity (Bruder & Bologna, 1993).

The third problematic assumption is the notion that both the child and family will be able to assimilate information and interventions from multiple professionals across multiple developmental areas. Many of the professionals who design and deliver the interventions may not have incorporated information from other disciplines and developmental areas into their own plans. This lack of integration often results in an overwhelming list of discipline-specific interventions that must be integrated into a child's daily routine by the family. This absence of coordination raises serious questions about the model's effectiveness.

## THE NEED FOR TEAM-BASED SERVICE DELIVERY

To avoid the inadequacy of this service methodology, many in the early intervention field have recommended that professionals from discipline-specific developmental areas combine their expertise and collaborate to meet the child's and family's needs (Bruder & Bologna, 1993). Collaborations can occur between two individuals as well as between groups of individuals. To formalize the collaborative process, it has been suggested that the involved individuals adopt a team model under which to operate (McCollum & Hughes, 1988). Creating a team, however, involves more than merely designating a group of individuals a *team* (Katzenbach & Smith, 1993; Lumsden & Lumsden, 1992); it requires their commitment to a process. A *team* has been defined as a group of people whose purpose and function stem from a common philosophy and shared goals (Maddux, 1988). Table 2 differentiates a group of individuals from a team.

## RESEARCH AND THEORY ON TEAMS

A rich body of literature about teams emanates from many disciplines, including business (Dyer, 1977; Harshman & Phillips, 1994; Kinlaw, 1991; Martin, 1993; Rees, 1991; Spiegel & Torres, 1994) and human services (Bailey, 1984; Dettmer, Thurston, & Dyck, 1993; Holm & McCartin, 1978; Maeroff, 1993). One of the most comprehensive studies of teams was conducted by Larson and LaFasto (1989). Their study examined the characteristic features or attributes of effectively functioning teams. They used qualitative methodology that included in-depth interviews with members of 27 teams representing business, science, medicine, sports, technology, higher education, government, the military, communities, nonprofit entities, and others (e.g., disaster relief, the presidential commission on the space shuttle Challenger accident). These teams represented a theoretically rich sample that was studied during a 3-year period. The distinguishing features of effectively functioning teams emerged with consistency, as described in the following sections.

### Characteristics of Effective Teams

The study by Larson and LaFasto (1989) identified numerous qualities of effective teams. Their findings have been supported by other such studies (Belbin, 1981; Harvey & Drolet, 1994; Katzenbach & Smith, 1993). These characteristics described effectiveness across all types of teams as listed in Table 3.

*A Clear, Elevating Goal* The Larson and LaFasto (1989) findings show that an effective team has a clear understanding of its goal as well as a belief that the goal is worthwhile and that its achievement will make a difference. In contrast, ineffective teams recognize that the absence of a purpose or goal contributed to their lack of productivity. The researchers found that the lack of

Table 2. Groups versus teams

| Groups | Teams |
|---|---|
| Members think they are grouped together for administrative purposes only. Individuals work independently, sometimes at cross-purposes with others. | Members recognize their interdependence and understand both personal and team goals are best accomplished with mutual support. Time is not wasted struggling over "turf" or attempting personal gain at the expense of others. |
| Members tend to focus on themselves because they are not sufficiently involved in planning the unit's objectives. They approach their job simply as a hired hand. | Members feel a sense of ownership for their jobs and unit because they are committed to goals they helped establish. |
| Members are told what to do rather than being asked what the best approach would be. Suggestions are not encouraged. | Members contribute to the organization's success by applying their unique talent and knowledge to team objectives. |
| Members distrust the motives of colleagues because they do not understand the role of other members. Expressions of opinion or disagreement are considered divisive and nonsupportive. | Members work in a climate of trust and are encouraged to openly express ideas, opinions, disagreements and feelings. Questions are welcome. |
| Members are so cautious about what they say that real understanding is not possible. Game playing may occur, and communications traps may be set to catch the unwary. | Members practice open and honest communication. They make an effort to understand each other's point of view. |
| Members may receive good training but are limited in applying it to the job by the supervisor or other group members. | Members are encouraged to develop skills and apply what they learn on the job. They receive the support of the team. |
| Members find themselves in conflict situations that they do not know how to resolve. Their supervisor may put off intervention until serious damage is done. | Members recognize conflict is a normal aspect of human interaction, but they view such situations as an opportunity for new ideas and creativity. They work to resolve conflict quickly and constructively. |
| Members may or may not participate in decisions affecting the team. Conformity often appears more important than positive results. | Members participate in decisions affecting the team but understand that their leader must make a final ruling whenever the team cannot decide or an emergency exists. A positive result, not conformity, is the goal. |

From Maddux, R.B. (1988). *Team building: An exercise in leadership*. Menlo Park, CA: Crisp Publications, Inc., 1200 Hamilton Court, Menlo Park, California 94025, 800-442-7477; reprinted by permission.

Table 3. Characteristics of effective teams

A clear, elevating goal
A results-driven structure
Competent team members
Unified commitment
A collaborative climate
Standards of excellence
External support and recognition
Principled leadership

From Larson, C.E., & LaFasto, F.M.J. (1989). *Team Work: What must go right/what can go wrong.* Beverly Hills, CA: Sage Publications; reprinted by permission.

a common goal can be attributed to a variety of factors such as the personal agendas of the team members or the contextual politics in which the team functions.

***Results-Driven Structure*** The structure of effective teams were found to revolve around the goal to be achieved. Three specific team structures were identified through the study, each with unique features. For example, the problem resolution team demonstrated a high level of trust among its members because it had to be able to focus on issues and solutions. A second team structure, the creative team, focused on discovering new possibilities and alternatives; autonomy was a critical feature of this structure, as was freedom from traditional boundaries of operation. The tactical team was the third structure identified; it was responsible for executing a well-defined plan, and a clear vision of the team's purpose, tasks, standards, and roles was essential. Across these team structures, Larson and LaFasto (1989) also defined four elements of effectiveness, which are listed in Table 4.

***Competent Team Members*** The researchers found that effective teams have team members who display two types of competencies. First, the members have technical competencies, including the knowledge, skills, and abilities needed to obtain the team's stated objective. Second, the members have collaborative competencies, including a strong desire to contribute and the ability to work together to address and resolve issues.

***Unified Commitment*** The researchers' findings show that effective teams demonstrate a dedication to the identification and purpose of the team and a willingness to do anything necessary to help the team succeed. These qualities seem to be facilitated by the team members' participation in all facets of group decision making.

***Collaborative Climate*** The study showed that effective teams demonstrate a collaborative climate in which team members feel they can work well together. Good climates are established on a foundation of trust, which includes elements of honesty, openness, consistency, and respect. Further analysis of Larson's and LaFasto's (1989) data reveals what trust means to people:

Table 4.  Necessary features of team structure

Clear roles and accountabilities
An effective communication system
Monitoring individual performance and providing feedback
Fact-based judgments

From Larson, C.E., & LaFasto, F.M.J. (1989). *Team Work: What must go right/what can go wrong.* Beverly Hills, CA: Sage Publications; reprinted by permission.

- Trust allows team members to stay focused on the problem, because problem solving relies on the open exchange of information.
- Trust promotes more efficient communication and coordination among members.
- Trust improves the quality of collaborative outcomes. Team members are not afraid to take risks, as evidenced by problems being brought up and addressed.
- Trust leads to team confidence because team members are able to compensate for each other when needed.

*Standards of Excellence*    The study found that effective teams work toward the attainment of a performance standard. Team members meet individual standards as well as team standards. Team standards are derived from both external (to the team) sources and internal sources (e.g., team leader). Larson and LaFasto (1989) found that it is important for individual team members to require one another to perform according to the established standards of excellence. Furthermore, it is important for a team to exert pressure on itself to establish and maintain performance standards that lead to improved outcomes.

*External Support and Recognition*    The researchers found that effective teams are given the resources to get the job done. The absence of such support is noticed more than its presence.

*Principled Leadership*    The study showed that this dimension of effectiveness seems to be the most critical. Effective leaders establish a vision, create change, and unleash talent. The team leader focuses attention on creating a supportive decision-making climate. Two characteristics of team leaders consistently identified through the study were a personal commitment to the team's goal and the ability to give team members the necessary autonomy to achieve results. In contrast, two characteristics identified as being indicative of poor team leadership are a leader's unwillingness to confront and resolve inadequate performance by team members and a leader's dilution of a team's effectiveness with too many priorities.

## TEAMS WITHIN EARLY INTERVENTION

Although the use of a team structure has been advocated for many years in working with children with disabilities (Allen, Holm, & Schiefelbusch, 1978;

Fewell, 1983; Holm & McCartin, 1978; Lyon & Lyon, 1980), comprehensive research on team functioning within early intervention service delivery structures is sparse. Most of the literature on the use of teams in early intervention has focused on the need to adopt such models of collaborative service delivery to ensure programmatic effectiveness (Allen et al., 1978; Bruder & Bologna, 1993; Bruder, Lippman, & Bologna, 1994; File & Kontos, 1992; Hanson & Widerstrom, 1993; McCollum & Hughes, 1988; McGonigel, Woodruff, & Roszmann-Millican, 1994).

Studies have been conducted, however, to examine various components of team functioning in working with children with disabilities. These components include individual levels of participation among members (Bailey, Helsel-DeWert, Thiele, & Ware, 1985; Gilliam & Coleman, 1981; Sands, Stafford, & McClelland, 1990); team meeting behaviors; the decision-making process (Bailey, Buysse, Simeonsson, Smith, & Keyes, 1995; Ysseldyke, Algozzine, & Mitchell, 1982); the development of cross-disciplinary service delivery plans (Campbell, McInerney, & Cooper, 1984); the use of collaborative consultation strategies (Hanline, 1990; Inge & Snell, 1985); and training of team members, at both the preservice level (Bailey, Simeonsson, Yoder, & Huntington, 1990; Courtnage & Smith-Davis, 1987) and the in-service level (Winton, McWilliam, Harrison, Owens, & Bailey, 1992).

Despite the limited database supporting the benefits of a team-based method of service delivery over other methods, teams of professionals are recommended as the preferred service delivery structure within early intervention (Bruder & Bologna, 1993; Garland & Linder, 1994; McGonigel, et al., 1994; McLean & Odom, 1993). Teams have been recognized for their value in assessment (Bagnato & Neisworth, 1991; Foley, 1990; Gibbs & Teti, 1990; Linder, 1993; McCune, Kalmanson, Fleck, Glazewski, & Sillari, 1990; Orlando, 1981), intervention planning (Linder, 1993; McGonigel & Garland, 1988; Noonan & McCormick, 1993), and service delivery (Fewell, 1983; Raver, 1991; Woodruff & McGonigel, 1988). However, much variation still exists in how early intervention teams actually function when services are being designed and delivered.

### Functions of Early Intervention Teams

Within early intervention, there are a number of phases in the service delivery process in which teams must function. The first phase is the assessment of the child and family. The unique needs of the child and family should dictate which assessment protocol is used. As such, the assessment team may have as many, or as few, members as needed by each situation. It is not uncommon for the number and type of team members to vary in relation to the assessment purpose. For example, a diagnostic assessment may require more in-depth involvement from numerous professionals from a variety of specialized disciplines. In contrast, a quarterly review of a child's progress may require only those professionals involved in day-to-day service provision.

Using Larson's and LaFasto's (1989) research, an effective assessment team would be described as having the structure of a problem resolution team. This structure requires a high level of trust among its members and a format for operating that focuses on issues rather than on predetermined positions or solutions (Larson & LaFasto, 1989, p. 49). This seems to aptly describe the uniqueness of each assessment protocol.

A second function of an early intervention team is intervention planning. This usually occurs within the context of planning the individualized education program (IEP) or individualized family service plan (IFSP). Again, the numbers of persons involved on the planning team can vary. At times, the family may want to limit the number of people involved in the planning to only those who will be providing services. At other times, additional professionals may be asked to consult to the planning process to ensure the comprehensiveness of service planning.

The second team structure identified by Larson and LaFasto (1989), the creative team, seems most applicable to the intervention planning function. A necessary feature of this team is autonomy from traditional systems thinking in order to facilitate the identification of flexible and unique outcomes and a clear set of performance standards. A service planning team must be able to respond to the individual needs of families and children across an array of dimensions, including culture, intervention techniques, natural environments, and functional outcomes (Bailey & McWilliam, 1990).

A third function of an early intervention team is service delivery to the child and family. This team's membership may vary over time in that as a child's and family's needs change, so should the early intervention services and the service providers. This team may have a core membership of those responsible for delivering services as well as consultant members who provide both direct (to the child) and indirect (to others involved with the child) services as needed.

Tactical teams, according to Larson and LaFasto (1989), have as their objective the execution of a well-defined plan, much as service delivery teams do. These teams must have an unambiguous role definition and a clear set of performance standards. As services are delivered to a child and family, the structure of a tactical team should ensure the effectiveness of both the individual team members and the team as a whole. Table 5 contains an overview of these team functions as they relate to Larson and LaFasto's structures.

## Types of Early Intervention Teams

Regardless of the function of the team, it must adopt a process by which to accomplish its goals. Within early intervention, the types of teams that have functioned have traditionally been identified as multidisciplinary, inter-

Table 5.  Team structure

| Broad objective | Dominant feature | Process emphasis | Early intervention function |
|---|---|---|---|
| Problem resolution | Trust | Focus on issue | Assessment |
| Creative | Autonomy | Explore possibilities and alternatives | Intervention planning |
| Tactical | Clarity | Be directive<br>Develop highly focused tasks<br>Clarify roles<br>Establish well-defined operational standards<br>Be accurate | Service delivery |

disciplinary, and transdisciplinary (McCollum & Hughes, 1988). These teams differ both in the role description of the members and in their functioning style. On a multidisciplinary team, the professionals typically represent their own disciplines and provide isolated assessment and intervention services. These include discipline-specific reports, goals, and interventions with the child or family. There is minimal integration and collaboration across disciplines, making it very difficult to develop coordinated, comprehensive programs for children and their families. This occurs because the team members focus only on their respective areas of expertise and roles with the child, and the family is viewed only as a recipient of services. This type of team is the most inefficient for children and families receiving services within center-based programs.

On the interdisciplinary team, each of the professionals carries out discipline-specific assessments and interventions; however, there is a formal commitment to sharing information throughout the process of assessment, planning, and intervention. Although each member views the child from his or her own discipline's perspective, the multiple perspectives are integrated into a holistic plan of intervention. This type of team lends itself to a center-based program that has access to multidisciplinary staff, assuming that the teacher acts as a service coordinator.

The transdisciplinary team approach further integrates the professionals and disciplines into a team. For this reason, it has been identified as ideal for the design and delivery of services for young children with disabilities receiving services within any type of setting (Garland & Linder, 1994; Hanson & Hanline, 1989; Linder, 1993; McGonigel & Garland, 1988; McGonigel et al., 1994). This type of team model is not new; it was developed in 1976 by the United Cerebral Palsy National Collaborative Infant Project (Hutchinson, 1978). Two fundamental beliefs of the transdisciplinary team model are that 1) children's development must be viewed as integrated and interactive and 2) children must be served within the context of the family (McGonigel et al., 1994).

The transdisciplinary team approach involves a greater degree of collaboration than other team models. Collaboration, in this instance, can be defined as a process of problem solving by team members (usually representing different disciplines), all of whom contribute their knowledge and skills equally (Vandercook & York, 1990). Collaboration requires a common philosophy and goal, which can be achieved only when joint activities focus on building relationships. Collaboration is inherent in a transdisciplinary team because team members are required to share responsibilities. The primary purpose of this type of team is to pool and integrate the expertise of its members so that more efficient and comprehensive service delivery may occur. As a result, there is a decrease in the number of professionals who interact with the child daily. Other characteristics of the transdisciplinary approach are joint team effort, joint staff development to ensure continuous skill development among members, and role release (Lyon & Lyon, 1980; McCollum & Hughes, 1988; Noonan & Kilgo, 1987; Woodruff & McGonigel, 1988).

Role release refers to the systematic crossing of traditional discipline boundaries by team members (Orelove & Sobsey, 1991). It involves a releasing of some functions traditionally associated with a specific discipline. For example, the physical therapist may provide training and support to the teacher to enable him or her to do much of the hands-on positioning and handling of a child with motor impairments. Likewise, the nurse may provide training to all team members to monitor a child's seizures. Effective implementation of the role release process requires team members to have a solid foundation in their own disciplines, combined with an understanding of the roles and competencies of the other disciplines represented on the team.

In the transdisciplinary approach, the child's program is primarily implemented by a single person or a few persons, with ongoing assistance provided by team members from the various disciplines (Orelove & Sobsey, 1991). In most center-based programs, teachers and program assistants take on the primary service delivery role. Related services support staff often serve as consultants to the teachers. Thus, the child's therapy and other needs are integrated into the daily routine of the classroom; however, therapists do not stop providing direct services to children (Orelove & Sobsey, 1991). For therapists to be effective, they need to maintain direct contact with the child with a disability.

## SERVICE DELIVERY MODELS AND THE USE OF TEAMS

McWilliam (1995) articulated a continuum of service delivery models used by therapists and teachers when providing services. These range from the individual pull-out (of the primary service site) model of service delivery to the integrated (into ongoing routines) model of service delivery. The transdisciplinary approach lends itself most readily to the more integrative models; however, the use of a more individual discipline-specific service model may be used on occasion by transdisciplinary teams. The critical factor for this model within a transdisciplinary team approach is the collaborative decision making of the team for the clinical necessity for less-integrative services and the continued use of collaborative consultation strategies by all team members.

## Collaborative Consultation

A number of models for collaborative consultation have been used to provide services for children with disabilities (Bruder, 1993; File & Kontos, 1992; Friend & Cook, 1992; Kontos, 1988; Wesley, 1994). Evidence suggests that both special and general educators prefer a collaborative model (Babcock & Pryzwansky, 1983; Buysse, Schulte, Pierce, & Terry, 1994; Pryzwansky & White, 1983; Wenger, 1979) rather than an expert model. The collaborative model, derived from Tharp and Werzel (1969), has been defined as

> an interactive process which enables people with diverse expertise to generate creative solutions to mutually defined problems. The major outcome of collaborative consultation is to provide comprehensive and effective programs for students with special needs within the most appropriate context, thereby enabling them to achieve maximum constructive interaction with their nonhandicapped peers. (Idol, Paolucci-Whitcomb, & Nevin, 1986, p. 1)

Collaborative consultation encompasses a number of interpersonal competencies that cross discipline boundaries. These include written and oral communication skills; personal characteristics, such as the ability to be caring, respectful, empathic, congruent, and open; and collaborative problem-solving skills (West & Cannon, 1988). The last attribute is critical to the development of a relationship of parity between both (or among all, if there are more than two) individuals involved in the consultation. However, the use of collaborative problem solving does not override the need for the consultant to use his or her specialized and discipline-specific skills to meet the consultee's need (Buysse et al., 1994).

## Team Process

Regardless of the function of the team, type of team, and service model, a functional process is necessary to ensure effectiveness (Gilliam & Coleman, 1981; Goldstein & Turnbull, 1982; Ysseldyke et al., 1982). In particular, five factors facilitating team process (Shonk, 1982) are described.

***Composition and Representation*** Although the number of people on a team varies according to the needs of the child, the parent always should be a member of the team. The regulations of Part H of IDEA (PL

101-476) require that a team for infants and toddlers with disabilities comprise two or more people representing different disciplines whose skills are necessary to enhance the child's development. Although adding more people to a team increases the expertise available for a child, a larger team can also negatively affect the collaborative process. For example, communication can become difficult, and coordination of team members for team meetings can become problematic. Rainforth, York, and Macdonald (1992) recommend the following guidelines when selecting team members:

> If two or more potential team members have overlapping information and skills related to the child's need, select only one of the team members to be involved.
> If one potential team member is able to address multiple challenges or needs of an individual child, select that team member.
> If two or more potential team members have similar competencies but one has more frequent or closer geographical access to the child's natural environment, select the individual who has closer and more frequent access.
> If none of the potential team members has adequate knowledge and skills to address a child's need, identify one team member who will obtain additional training and support either through student-specific technical assistance, or through various forms of continuing education and in-service training.
> If two professionals have similar but not overlapping knowledge and skill competencies, provide the opportunity for these two individuals to work together to train one another in complementary skills areas, with the ultimate goal being a divided caseload with each professional having more time to be involved with individual children. This is a capacity-building approach in that the capacity of one professional to meet more diverse learning needs is being developed. Ultimately, this can result in greater efficiency because the number of people involved with any one child can be streamlined without significant loss of expertise. (pp. 216, 218, 219)

**Goals** It has been suggested that all team members participate in establishing both the team goals and the steps to be used to accomplish each goal. In addition, team members should have expectations of what the final outcome of each goal should be and the criteria used for each outcome. Teams must establish goals for their structure and the methods used to accomplish goal outcomes.

**Roles** The members of the team are unique individuals with different skills, knowledge, and personalities. For a team to be effective, each individual must have a clear role and specific responsibilities. Ambiguity is a major cause of conflict; therefore, team members must continually clarify their current roles in relation to the task at hand. Preserving clarity sometimes can be challenging because there are many roles that overlap. At the beginning of each team interaction, each member's role should be restated and refined if necessary. Credibility is an important component of the roles of individual team members. In addition to the individual professional roles, responsibilities, and contributions of team members, there are other roles that members assume in facilitating a functional team process. Team members must provide support, including resource support, moral support, and technical support (York, Giangreco, Vandercook, & Macdonald, 1992), to other team members. This support must be ongoing to facilitate the team's effectiveness with children and families.

*Leadership* Leadership has been defined as "verbal and nonverbal communication behavior that influences a team's transactional and task processes in achieving members' and the team's needs and goals" (Lumsden & Lumsden, 1993, p. 260). Leadership is every team member's responsibility, because interdependence among members requires a shared commitment to maintaining a team process. Leadership is a set of behaviors that must be developed by each individual member to realize both individual and team success.

A designated team leader has specific expectations and responsibilities. The leader is expected to provide structure to the team process to ensure that outcomes are achieved. It has been suggested that the most appropriate leader is one who can lead others to lead themselves. A team leader is responsible for building and maintaining the team. The leader inspires the rest of the team to commit to reaching the team's identified goals and outcomes (Garland & Linder, 1994).

A number of personal qualities have been identified with effective leaders, including credibility, adaptability, communication, confidence, commitment, and concentration (Lumsden & Lumsden, 1993), as well as a lack of egocentricism and arrogance (Larson & LaFasto, 1989). Most important may be the ability of the leader to assess the maturity of the team members in relation to a specific task to be performed and lead accordingly. Hersey and Blanchard (1988) suggest that successful leaders adapt their communication according to the degree of maturity that members exhibit.

*Work Style* For a team to be functional, it must adopt a framework from which to achieve its goals. This framework revolves around the maintenance of a positive team climate, which is created by both the internal and external conditions experienced by a team. A positive climate is open, supportive, inclusive, challenging, and rewarding and encourages diverse ideas, change, and growth. It supports people's rights to express themselves, their feelings, and their opinions. A positive climate fosters a productive team. Figure 1 contains a checklist for assessing a team's climate.

The team must establish regular team meeting times during which much of the team's work is accomplished. Although informal collaboration around the needs of a family and child should occur frequently, a formal meeting ensures that the team process is maintained. Finding time for meetings should be a priority, and team members should adhere to a regular meeting schedule. The frequency with which teams meet varies according to the goals of the team. A meeting agenda should be used to structure meeting time and outcomes, and ground rules should be set to ensure meeting productivity. A regular meeting place should be established that is accessible and convenient and, if possible, should be free from distractions. Minutes and follow-up responsibilities should be recorded and distributed to all team members shortly after the meeting. Communication during the meeting should be open, and joint decision making should be prioritized.

A systematic process for problem solving should also be used to assist the team in making decisions during meetings (Johnson & Johnson, 1987). For example, Project BRIDGE (Prentice & Spencer, 1986) has developed a five-step decision-making model for teams to use in establishing service options for children and families. It has been recommended that each step in the problem-solving process be used as a checkpoint for teams to evaluate their ideas and practices against best practices for exemplary services in the field of early childhood special education. The following are the five steps of the model:

> *Problem formulation and information gathering.* The problem must be described in clear, observable terms. Resources should be identified, and the team should focus on the facts, rather than opinions.
> *Generating proposals for solutions.* As many alternatives as possible should be generated from all participants. Without being judgmental, the team must build positively on all suggestions.
> *Selecting alternatives and testing solutions.* The team must judge the available resources, and evaluate the alternatives for attaining the solution. The team should decide whether or not the solution makes good use of the resources, is cost effective, and fits the needs and goals of the child and family.
> *Action planning and implementation.* The team should assign specific responsibilities to individuals, determine timelines, and develop procedures for monitoring the plan. The plan should then be communicated to all relevant personnel.
> *Monitoring and evaluation.* The team should determine how to judge the success of their decision. The team should select a unit of evaluation, decide how often to evaluate, and modify the plan as needed. (p. 32)

## ISSUES IN TEAM-BASED SERVICE DELIVERY

### Problems in Delivering Team-Based Services

Although a team approach to early intervention seems to be an effective and accepted service methodology, it cannot be advocated without some caution. Teams are influenced by the organizational context in which they work (Harshman & Phillips, 1994; Sundstrom, DeMeuse, & Futrell, 1990), and there are many variables mediating team effectiveness within and across early intervention systems. Foremost is that many training programs for professionals (both graduate and undergraduate) neglect to prepare students to participate on collaborative teams (Bailey et al., 1990; Courtnage & Smith-Davis, 1987).

As honestly as you can, rate the climate in your group on each of the following statements, using the scale to the right.

| | Always | Usually | Sometimes | Rarely | Never |
|---|---|---|---|---|---|
| Members are able to say what they think. | ☐ | ☐ | ☐ | ☐ | ☐ |
| When there's a problem, members talk about it. | ☐ | ☐ | ☐ | ☐ | ☐ |
| Members do not blame one another for problems. | ☐ | ☐ | ☐ | ☐ | ☐ |
| People use words that are considerate of one another's feelings. | ☐ | ☐ | ☐ | ☐ | ☐ |
| There is a feeling that all members are equal in the group. | ☐ | ☐ | ☐ | ☐ | ☐ |
| Members support one another in other ideas and contributions. | ☐ | ☐ | ☐ | ☐ | ☐ |
| Members care about the team. | ☐ | ☐ | ☐ | ☐ | ☐ |
| Members care about one another. | ☐ | ☐ | ☐ | ☐ | ☐ |
| Members know that what they say will be treated in confidence. | ☐ | ☐ | ☐ | ☐ | ☐ |
| Members trust one another. | ☐ | ☐ | ☐ | ☐ | ☐ |
| If a member is upset, other members empathize. | ☐ | ☐ | ☐ | ☐ | ☐ |
| The team works on its transactional processes cooperatively. | ☐ | ☐ | ☐ | ☐ | ☐ |
| The team uses its transactional processes to make its task processes work effectively. | ☐ | ☐ | ☐ | ☐ | ☐ |
| Members are free to be assertive about what they think and feel. | ☐ | ☐ | ☐ | ☐ | ☐ |

Figure 1. Team climate checklist. (From Lumsden, G., & Lumsden, D. [1993]. *Communicating in groups and teams: Sharing leadership* [p. 212]. Belmont, CA: Wadsworth; reprinted by permission.)

41

Professionals usually receive training only in their area of expertise and, as such, see themselves primarily as representing their disciplines on a team, rather than as a collaborating component of a team (Sands et al., 1990). This has resulted in a work force poorly prepared to develop, implement, and evaluate a team-based service delivery model.

The absence of organizational support for a team approach is a second reason why teamwork is a problem. This lack of support can manifest itself in a variety of ways, including limited time set aside for team meetings and for collaborative consultation and an absence of funding to hire additional team members (Rainforth et al., 1992). These logistical barriers can be overwhelming, especially when the team is new or lacks strong team leadership.

## Rationale for the Use of Team-Based Service Delivery

Teams are a major factor in the delivery of effective early intervention services for a number of reasons. First, there is a growing number of infants, toddlers, and preschoolers with disabilities who receive early intervention. IDEA created a mandate for states to provide preschool services to eligible children and incentives to provide early intervention to infants and toddlers (Part H of IDEA). These services have resulted in an increased awareness of the developmental needs of young children and improved screening efforts for all young children.

In addition, more at-risk children are surviving due to advances in medical technology. For example, a greater percentage of low birth weight preterm infants are surviving than did 10 years ago. More than 90% of infants born weighing less than 1,500 grams currently survive (Pharoah & Alberman, 1990). Preterm infants as a group are recognized as having more neurological and developmental problems than healthy full-term infants do (Minde, 1993). There are also many more children growing up at risk for developmental delays because of environmental situations. The National Center for Children in Poverty (1990) has documented that more than 25% of all children under the age of 6 live in poverty. These increased populations have resulted in the provision of early intervention to children with a wide range of abilities and disabilities. It is not feasible to treat each child's developmental delay by area of development or discipline. Professionals need to pool their expertise to create holistic service models that best meet the needs of each child.

Second to the complexity of children's needs is the shortage of professionals available to provide services to these children. In 1991–1992, almost 7,000 more people were required to provide early intervention services, according to the 41 states and jurisdictions that reported data on the availability of professionals (Hebbeler, 1994). This figure is considered to be an underestimation because not all states reported their data and not all states were fully implementing Part H when these statistics were gathered. This shortage indicates that there are not enough individual professionals to address all developmental areas for every child in early intervention and early childhood.

There is also an important need to maximize resources across disciplines and agencies. The fiscal climate of the 1990s demands that service models maximize collaboration. Kagan (1991, 1993) suggests that collaborations represent the culmination of a process that comprises a hierarchy of components such as communication, cooperation, and coordination. A team-based model of service delivery requires collaborations that maximize the efficient use of resources.

### Recommendations for Expanding Team-Based Service Delivery

To implement a team approach, a number of recommendations should be in place. First is the need to recognize the necessity and benefits of a collaborative team. The formation and maintenance of teams that develop a joint philosophy and service goal must be a priority. The team-based philosophy should emphasize interdependence and a holistic view of the child and family, as opposed to a focus by individuals on a single developmental area. This philosophy of service must begin at the preservice level when professionals are becoming oriented to their field of study.

The second recommendation is associated with the first, in that we must provide opportunities for in-service training to both individuals and teams. The training should begin at the preservice preparation level (at both the undergraduate and graduate levels) as professionals begin to adopt behaviors appropriate to a collaborative model of service delivery. As professionals provide services through teams, training must be ongoing. Training also should be delivered through systematic applications of adult learning principles using validated methods such as case study and problem-solving applications. The training content should include communication and negotiation skills and more child-specific areas such as routine-based intervention and integrated therapy.

Service delivery models must be redesigned to support a team approach. Model redesign means that, administratively, support must be given to teams to form, develop, and maintain. This support must be logistical as well as philosophical because teams need resources and a structure to support their functions.

### REFERENCES

Allen, K., Holm, V., & Schiefelbusch, R. (1978). *Early intervention: A team approach*. Baltimore: University Park Press.

Babcock, N.L., & Pryzwansky, W.B. (1983). Models of consultation: Preferences of educational professionals at five stages of service. *Journal of School Psychology, 21,* 359–366.

Bagnato, S.J., & Neisworth, J.T. (1991). *Assessment for early intervention: Best practices for professionals*. New York: Guilford Press.

Bailey, D.B., Jr. (1984). A triaxial model of the interdisciplinary team and group process. *Exceptional Children, 51*(1), 17–25.

Bailey, D.B., Jr., Buysse, V., Simeonsson, R.J., Smith, T., & Keyes, L. (1995). Individual and team consensus ratings of child functioning. *Developmental Medicine and Child Neurology, 37,* 246–259.

Bailey, D.B., Jr., Helsel-DeWert, M., Thiele, J.E., & Ware, W. (1985). Measuring individual participation on the interdisciplinary team. *American Journal of Mental Deficiency, 88,* 247–254.

Bailey, D.B., Jr., & McWilliam, R.A. (1990). Normalizing early intervention. *Topics in Early Childhood Special Education, 10*(2), 33–47.

Bailey, D.B., Jr., Palsha, S.A., & Huntington, G.S. (1990). Preservice preparation of special education to serve infants with handicaps and their families: Current status and training needs. *Journal of Early Intervention, 14*(1), 43–54.

Bailey, D.B., Jr., Simeonsson, R.J., Yoder, D.E., & Huntington, G.S. (1990). Preparing professionals to serve infants and toddlers with handicaps and their families: An integrative analysis across eight disciplines. *Exceptional Children, 57*(1), 26–34.

Belbin, R.M. (1981). *Management teams: Why they succeed or fail.* New York: John Wiley & Sons.

Bruder, M.B. (1993). The provision of early intervention and early childhood special education within community early childhood programs: Characteristics of effective service delivery. *Topics in Early Childhood Special Education, 13*(1), 19–37.

Bruder, M.B. (1994). Working with members of other disciplines: Collaboration for success. In M. Wolery & J.S. Wilbers (Eds.), *Including children with special needs in early childhood programs* (pp. 45–70). Washington, DC: National Association for the Education of Young Children.

Bruder, M.B., & Bologna, T.M. (1993). Collaboration and service coordination for effective early intervention. In W. Brown, S.K. Thurman, & L. Pearl (Eds.), *Family-centered early intervention with infants and toddlers: Innovative cross-disciplinary approaches* (pp. 103–128). Baltimore: Paul H. Brookes Publishing Co.

Bruder, M.B., Klosowski, S., & Daguio, C. (1991). Personnel standards for ten professional disciplines servicing children under P.L. 99-457: Results from a national survey. *Journal of Early Intervention, 15*(1), 66–79.

Bruder, M.B., Lippman, C., & Bologna, T.M. (1994). Personnel preparation in early intervention: Building capacity for program expansion within institutions of higher education. *Journal of Early Intervention, 18*(1), 103–110.

Buysse, V., Schulte, A.C., Pierce, P.P., & Terry, D. (1994). Models and styles of consultation: Preferences of professionals in early intervention. *Journal of Early Intervention, 18*(3), 302–310.

Campbell, P.H., McInerney, W., & Cooper, M. (1984). Therapeutic programming for students with severe handicaps. *American Journal of Occupational Therapy, 38*(9), 594–602.

Courtnage, L., & Smith-Davis, J. (1987). Interdisciplinary team training: A national survey of special education teacher training programs. *Exceptional Children, 53*(5), 451–458.

Dettmer, P., Thurston, L.P., & Dyck, N. (1993). *Consultation, collaboration, and teamwork.* Needham, MA: Allyn & Bacon.

Dyer, W. (1977). *Team building: Issues and alternatives.* Reading, MA: Addison-Wesley.

Fewell, R.R. (1983). The team approach to infant education. In S. Garwood & R. Fewell (Eds.), *Educating handicapped infants: Issues in development and intervention* (pp. 299–322). Rockville, MD: Aspen Publishers.

File, N., & Kontos, S. (1992). Indirect service delivery through consultation: Review and implications for early intervention. *Journal of Early Intervention, 16*(3), 221–233.

Foley, G.M. (1990). Portrait of an arena evaluation: Assessment in the transdisciplinary approach. In E.D. Gibbs & D.M. Teti (Eds.), *Interdisciplinary assessment of infants: A guide for early intervention professionals* (pp. 271–286). Baltimore: Paul H. Brookes Publishing Co.

Friend, M., & Cook, L. (1992). *Interactions: Collaboration skills for school professionals.* New York: Longman.

Garland, C.W., & Linder, T.W. (1994). Administrative challenges in early intervention. In L.J. Johnson, R.J. Gallagher, M.J. LaMontagne, J.B. Jordan, P.L. Hutinger, J.J. Gallagher, & M.B. Karnes (Eds.), *Meeting early intervention challenges: Issues from birth to three* (pp. 133–166). Baltimore: Paul H. Brookes Publishing Co.

Gibbs, E.D., & Teti, D.M. (1990). Assessment of the infant with multiple handicaps. In E.D. Gibbs & D.M. Teti (Eds.), *Interdisciplinary assessment of infants: A guide for early intervention professionals* (pp. 177–188). Baltimore: Paul H. Brookes Publishing Co.

Gilliam, J.E., & Coleman, M.C. (1981). Who influences IEP committee decisions? *Exceptional Children, 47,* 642–644.

Goldstein, S., & Turnbull, A.P. (1982). Strategies to increase parent participation in IEP conferences. *Exceptional Children, 48,* 360–361.

Hanline, M.F. (1990). Project Profile: A consulting model for providing integration opportunities for preschool children with disabilities. *Journal of Early Intervention, 14*(4), 360–366.

Hanson, M.J., & Hanline, M.F. (1989). Integration options for the young child. In R. Gaylord-Ross (Ed.), *Integration strategies for students with handicaps* (pp. 177–194). Baltimore: Paul H. Brookes Publishing Co.

Hanson, M.J., & Widerstrom, A.H. (1993). Consultation and collaboration: Essentials of integration efforts for young children. In C. Peck, S. Odom, & D. Bricker (Eds.), *Integrating young children with disabilities into community programs: Ecological perspectives on research and implementation* (pp. 149–168). Baltimore: Paul H. Brookes Publishing Co.

Harshman, C.L., & Phillips, S.L. (1994). *Teaming up.* San Diego, CA: Pfeiffer & Co.

Harvey, T.R., & Drolet, B. (1994). *Building teams, building people.* Lancaster, PA: Technomic Publishing Co.

Hebbeler, K. (1994). *Shortages in professions working with young children with disabilities and their families* [Monograph]. Chapel Hill, NC: National Early Childhood Technical Assistance System (NEC*TAS).

Hersey, P., & Blanchard, K.H. (1988). *Management of organizational behavior: Utilizing human resources.* Englewood Cliffs, NJ: Prentice Hall.

Holm, V.A., & McCartin, R.E. (1978). Interdisciplinary child development team: Team issues and training in interdisciplinariness. In K.E. Allen, V.A. Holm, & R.J. Schiefelbusch (Eds.), *Early intervention—a team approach* (pp. 97–122). Baltimore: University Park Press.

Hutchinson, D. (1978). The transdisciplinary approach. In J. Curry & K. Peppe (Eds.), *Mental retardation: Nursing approaches to care* (pp. 65–74). St. Louis: C.V. Mosby Co.

Idol, L., Paolucci-Whitcomb, P., & Nevin, A. (1986). *Collaborative consultation.* Austin, TX: PRO-ED.

Individuals with Disabilities Education Act of 1990 (IDEA), PL 101-476. (October 30, 1990). Title 20, U.S.C. §§ 1400 *et seq.: U.S. Statutes at Large, 104,* 1103–1151.

Inge, K.J., & Snell, M.E. (1985). Teaching positioning and handling techniques to public school personnel through inservice training. *Journal of The Association for Persons with Severe Handicaps, 10*(2), 105–110.

Johnson, D.W., & Johnson, F.P. (1987). *Joining together: Group theory and group skills* (3rd ed.). Englewood Cliffs, NJ: Prentice Hall.

Kagan, S.L. (1991). *United we stand: Collaboration for child care and early intervention and education services.* New York: Teachers College Press.

Kagan, S.L. (1993). *Integrating services for children and families: Understanding the past to shape the future.* New Haven, CT: Yale University Press.

Katzenbach, J.R., & Smith, D.K. (1993). *The wisdom of teams.* New York: HarperCollins.

Kinlaw, D.C. (1991). *Developing superior work teams: Building quality and the competitive edge.* Lexington, MA: Lexington Books.

Kontos, S. (1988). Family day care as an integrated early intervention. *Topics in Early Childhood Special Education, 8*(2), 1–14.

Larson, C.E., & LaFasto, F.M.J. (1989). *Team Work: What must go right/what can go wrong.* Beverly Hills, CA: Sage Publications.

Linder, T.W. (1993). *Transdisciplinary play-based assessment: A functional approach to working with young children* (Rev. ed.). Baltimore: Paul H. Brookes Publishing Co.

Lumsden, G., & Lumsden, D. (1993). *Communicating in groups and teams.* Belmont, CA: Wadsworth.

Lyon, S., & Lyon, G. (1980). Team functioning and staff development: A role release approach to providing integrated educational services for severely handicapped students. *Journal of The Association for Persons with Severe Handicaps, 5*(3), 250–263.

Maddux, R.B. (1988). *Team building: An exercise in leadership.* Menlo Park, CA: Crisp Publications.

Maeroff, G.I. (1993). *Team building for school change: Equipping teachers for new roles.* New York: Teachers College Press.

Martin, D.E. (1993). *TeamThink.* New York: E.P. Dutton.

McCollum, J.A., & Hughes, M. (1988). Staffing patterns and team models in infancy programs. In J. Jordon, J. Gallagher, P. Hutinger, & M. Karnes (Eds.), *Early childhood special education: Birth to three* (pp. 129–146). Reston, VA: Council for Exceptional Children.

McCune, L., Kalmanson, B., Fleck, M.B., Glazewski, B., & Sillari, J. (1990). An interdisciplinary model of infant assessment. In S.J. Meisels & J.P. Shonkoff (Eds.), *Handbook of early childhood intervention* (pp. 219–277). New York: Cambridge University Press.

McGonigel, M.J., & Garland, C.W. (1988). The individualized family service plan and the early intervention team: Team and family issues and recommended practices. *Infants and Young Children, 1*(1), 10–21.

McGonigel, M.J., Woodruff, G., & Roszmann-Millican, M. (1994). The transdisciplinary team: A model for family-centered early intervention. In L.J. Johnson, R.J. Gallagher, M.J. LaMontagne, J.B. Jordan, P.L. Hutinger, J.J. Gallagher, & M.B. Karnes (Eds.), *Meeting early intervention challenges: Issues from birth to three* (pp. 95–131). Baltimore: Paul H. Brookes Publishing Co.

McLean, M.E., & Odom, S.L. (1993). Practices for young children with and without disabilities: A comparison of DEC and NAEYC identified practices. *Topics in Early Childhood Special Education, 13*(3), 274–292.

McWilliam, R.A. (1995). Integration of therapy and consultative special education: A continuum in early intervention. *Infants and Young Children, 7*(4), 29–38.

Minde, K. (1993). Prematurity and serious medical illness in infancy: Implications for development and intervention. In C.H. Zeanah (Ed.), *Handbook of infant mental health* (pp. 87–105). New York: Guilford Press.

National Center for Children in Poverty. (1990). *Five million children*. New York: Author.

Noonan, M.J., & Kilgo, J.L. (1987). Transition services for early age individuals with severe mental retardation. In R. Ianacone & R. Stodden (Eds.), *Transition issues and directions* (pp. 25–37). Reston, VA: Council for Exceptional Children.

Noonan, M.J., & McCormick, L. (1993). Intervention in natural environments. In M.J. Noonan & L. McCormick (Eds.), *Early intervention in natural environments: Methods and procedures* (pp. 237–265). Pacific Grove, CA: Brooks/Cole.

Orelove, F.P., & Sobsey, M. (1991). *Educating children with multiple disabilities: A transdisciplinary approach* (2nd ed.). Baltimore: Paul H. Brookes Publishing Co.

Orlando, C. (1981). Multidisciplinary team approaches in the assessment of handicapped preschool children. *Topics in Early Childhood Special Education, 1*(2), 23–30.

Pharoah, P.O.D., & Alberman, E.D. (1990). Annual statistical review. *Archives of Disease in Childhood, 65,* 147–151.

Prentice, R.R., & Spencer, P.E. (1986). *Project BRIDGE: Decision-making for early services: A team approach*. Elk Grove Village, IL: American Academy of Pediatrics.

Pryzwansky, W.B., & White, G. (1983). The influences of consultee characteristics on preferences for consultation approaches. *Professional Psychology: Research and Practice, 14*(4), 457–461.

Rainforth, B., York, J., & Macdonald, C. (1992). *Collaborative teams for students with severe disabilities: Integrating therapy and educational services*. Baltimore: Paul H. Brookes Publishing Co.

Raver, S.A. (1991). *Strategies for teaching at-risk and handicapped infants and toddlers*. New York: Macmillan.

Rees, F. (1991). *How to lead work teams: Facilitation skills*. San Diego, CA: Pfeiffer & Co.

Sands, R.G., Stafford, J., & McClelland, M. (1990). "I beg to differ": Conflict in the interdisciplinary team. *Social Work in Health Care, 14*(3), 55–72.

Shonk, J.H. (1982). *Working in teams: A practical manual for improving work groups*. New York: AMACOM.

Spiegel, J., & Torres, C. (1994). *Manager's official guide to team working*. San Diego, CA: Pfeiffer & Co.

Sundstrom, E., DeMeuse, K.P., & Futrell, D. (1990). Work teams: Applications and effectiveness. *American Psychologist, 45,* 120–133.

Tharp, R., & Wetzel, R. (1969). *Behavior modification in the natural environment*. New York: Academic Press.

Vandercook, T., & York, J. (1990). A team approach to program development and support. In W. Stainback & S. Stainback (Eds.), *Support networks for inclusive schooling: Interdependent, integrated education* (pp. 95–122). Baltimore: Paul H. Brookes Publishing Co.

Wenger, R.D. (1979). Teacher response to collaborative consultation. *Psychology in the Schools, 16,* 127–131.

Wesley, P.W. (1994). Providing on-site consultation to promote quality in integrated child care programs. *Journal of Early Intervention, 18*(4), 391–402.

West, J.F., & Cannon, G.S. (1988). Essential collaborative consultation competencies for regular and special educators. *Journal of Learning Disabilities, 21,* 56–63.

Winton, P.J., McWilliam, P.J., Harrison, T., Owens, A.M., & Bailey, D.B., Jr. (1992). Lessons learned from implementing a team-based model for change. *Infants and Young Children, 5*(1), 49–57.

Woodruff, G., & McGonigel, M.J. (1988). Early intervention team approaches: The transdisciplinary model. In J. Jordon, J. Gallagher, P. Hutinger, & M. Karnes (Eds.), *Early childhood special education: Birth to three* (pp. 163–182). Reston, VA: Council for Exceptional Children.

York, J., Giangreco, M.F., Vandercook, T., & Macdonald, C. (1992). Integrating support personnel in the inclusive classroom. In S. Stainback & W. Stainback (Eds.), *Curriculum considerations in inclusive classrooms: Facilitating learning for all students* (pp. 101–116). Baltimore: Paul H. Brookes Publishing Co.

Ysseldyke, J.E., Algozzine, B., & Mitchell, S. (1982). Special education team decision making: An analysis of current practice. *Personnel and Guidance Journal, 60,* 308–313.

# Chapter 3

# Family–Professional Partnerships and Integrated Services

## Pamela J. Winton

Integrated services can be viewed as part of the post–World War II evolution toward inclusive and normalizing approaches to human services delivery. Throughout the process of how the field defines acceptable and standard practice, parents have been central figures. They have served two important roles: 1) they have been the strongest and most powerful advocates for certain changes and directions, such as deinstitutionalization, normalization, and inclusion (Turnbull & Turnbull, 1990); and 2) they have been harsh and persuasive critics when the pendulum swings too far in the direction where change is leading (Boggs, 1978). Professionals have come to realize that the family is the enduring, long-lasting relationship for the child with disabilities. The service system needs to support children within the context of their families, and families are in the best position to know how that best can be accomplished. This is one reason why family perspectives on integrated services must be considered.

As stated in Chapter 1, the research on the efficacy of different service delivery models is scanty, methodologically flawed, and equivocal. There is little solid evidence for generating guidelines that can be applied to decision making about the level, types, context, and format for providing specialized services, which unfortunately has led to troubling results (Kaminer & Robinson, 1993). Some children receive a lot of direct therapy, perhaps even more than is helpful (Doernberg, 1978). Other children remain on waiting lists without any form of therapeutic intervention for long periods of time. Neither situation is an efficient or optimal use of resources. An individualized, family-centered approach provides an ecologically valid framework for providing specialized therapy. It is important to define what this approach means, what its potential advantages are, and what the strategies are for implementing this approach.

This chapter 1) describes the principles of a family-centered approach to early intervention as they are related to center-based programs, 2) presents issues and provides strategies related to taking a family-centered approach to deciding on and implementing center-based models for delivering specialized therapies, and 3) discusses strategies, including those promoting family–professional partnerships, related to moving toward more effective and collaborative service delivery models.

## FAMILY-CENTERED APPROACH TO CENTER-BASED EARLY INTERVENTION

The principles of a family-centered approach have been described extensively in the literature (Dunst, Trivette, & Deal, 1988; McGonigel, Kaufmann, & Johnson, 1991; Shelton, Jeppson, & Johnson, 1989). Central to these principles are the following notions:

- Families and professionals should operate as decision-making partners throughout the assessment and intervention process.
- Family priorities and interests should guide assessment and intervention decisions.
- Professionals should exhibit sensitivity to individual differences in family values, beliefs, and lifestyles.
- Throughout the intervention process there should be an emphasis on promoting and enhancing children and family interests and lifestyles.

An underlying belief is the importance of building relationships between the professionals and the families with whom they work. Mutual respect, trust, perspective sharing, and comfortable, predictable relationships are often described as the hallmarks to family-centeredness (Summers et al., 1990).

A question that is sometimes raised is how family-centered principles apply to center-based programs. There are fewer naturally occurring points of contact between families and professionals in many center-based programs. Professionals must therefore devise and consider strategies that maximize those opportunities and creatively build partnerships outside of face-to-face contacts. A second question is how a family-centered approach relates to decisions about models of service delivery. Is it really possible to provide families with choices of this nature when so many other variables (e.g., child characteristics, program characteristics, goals of therapy) influence the availability and appropriateness of different models? In this chapter, three points where contact does occur are considered in terms of building family–professional partnerships in center-based programs for the purposes of deciding on and implementing specialized therapies. They are the following:

- Assessment (determining the nature and extent of child need and family interests and priorities)
- Intervention planning (matching needs and priorities with strategies, activities, and models of service delivery and designing a shared plan for making and monitoring progress)
- Day-to-day activities and routines (implementing planned activities, monitoring and evaluating progress)

## FAMILY–PROFESSIONAL PARTNERSHIPS IN ASSESSMENTS

The following are three central tenets of the family-centered approach: 1) families' interests and priorities guide assessment and intervention, 2) families should be provided with information that will assist them in their decision-making role, and 3) assessment and intervention should be sensitive to and respectful of individual differences. This section describes the rationale and research basis for how these assumptions apply to the assessment process and the implications for family decisions about models of service delivery.

### Families' Interests

One of the global reasons that families contact early intervention programs is for help and information related to their children (McWilliam et al., 1995). Understanding more specifically what families hope to accomplish by making contact with a program should be an immediate goal for professionals, and this information should guide the assessment process. Some families may be seeking a diagnosis; they may want a specific label and explanation for why their child is different. Other families may want to know if their child is behind; they may not care as much about a specific label as about knowing if their concerns are valid. Others know their child is developing differently and want to know what they can do to help their child. Some families may want information on what types of child care environments are optimal for their child. These are just some examples of reasons why families may seek a professional's help and may become involved in assessment procedures. If families desire to do so, they should be part of an assessment process that leads toward answers to their questions.

The possibilities for family participation in assessment are numerous, ranging from being an observer with no active role to taking on the role of administering some test items themselves (Crais, 1993). The more families participate as partners in planning and conducting assessment procedures, the more prepared they are for making decisions about different approaches to intervention, including different models of service delivery. Building successful partnerships takes time. The more opportunities families have for getting to know the professionals who might be working with their children and for becoming familiar with the different interests and areas of expertise of these professionals, the more informed parents are when planning intervention activities and strategies.

Letting families know that their interests and concerns are of paramount importance from the first point of contact is an important strategy for increased participation in later stages of intervention. Partnerships do not usually start in the context of individualized family service plan (IFSP) meetings. Because this is the point of contact where parent participation has been mandated by the Education for All Handicapped Children Act of 1975 (PL 94-142) and by the Education of the Handicapped Act Amendments of 1986 (PL 99-457), IFSP/individualized education program (IEP) meetings have been the focus of efforts to involve parents in service delivery. Parents cannot be expected to enter the intervention process at the IFSP meeting, however, and automatically move into a partnership or leadership role.

### Families' Decision-Making Role

"You can give us a seat at the table, but you can't expect us to play a meaningful role without support, preparation, and information." This quotation from a parent illustrates an important point about family involvement. For families to make informed decisions about intervention and models of service delivery, parents need information about the treatment options. Focus group research conducted by McWilliam and colleagues (see Chapter 7) suggests that families prefer specialized services for their children delivered by one-on-one direct models of therapy. McWilliam speculates that this preference may not be based on accurate information about different models of service delivery. He reports that parents who participated in a child care program at the Frank Porter Graham Child Development Center and were offered and explained a continuum of service delivery models developed a preference for indirect models. McWilliam argues that families need exposure to properly implemented integrated therapy; without this exposure, their beliefs about the best model of service delivery may be based on assumptions that direct one-on-one therapy is better than indirect models for delivering therapeutic services. The assessment process should link treatment options with the concerns that families have about their children. If assessment procedures take place within the context of the natural environment, then a natural link between what the child is currently doing, areas in which the parents hope for progress, and strategies for accomplishing that progress can be made. The assessment process should provide families with information on each of their concerns; in this way, when intervention plans and models of service delivery are discussed, families can make informed decisions. For example, if a family's major interest is that their child develop language and communication skills because they see that as a key to their child being included in neighborhood and peer group activities, then integrating therapy into the context of the neighborhood and playgroup makes sense. It also makes sense that an assessment of the child's current skills should be made within the context of the neighborhood and peer group.

## Sensitive, Respectful, Goal-Oriented Assessment

Research by Gallimore and associates (Gallimore, Weisner, Bernheimer, Guthrie, & Nihira, 1993; Gallimore, Weisner, Kaufman, & Bernheimer, 1989) has provided numerous examples of the unique and individualized ways that families construct their lives to accommodate a child with a disability. They show that interventions that are not designed to support and enhance the naturally occurring adaptations that families have made are doomed to failure and have the potential for increasing stress in families' lives. What this means in terms of assessment is that strategies for gathering information about the ongoing routines and lifestyle choices of families should be used. For example, for families with two working parents, finding reasonably priced quality child care might be an interest; thus, assessment and intervention planning for this family might focus on this concern. Specifically, this might mean that toilet training becomes a priority for the child, if the child care or preschool environments have this requirement. It might also mean that families prefer a consultative model of service delivery whereby specialists consult with the family and the child care providers to implement certain aspects of the intervention plan, thus making people in the child's life, including siblings, child care providers, and baby sitters, important participants in the assessment process. If the child is attending a center-based program, the child's teachers and aides should participate in assessment and intervention planning, if at all possible. It might also mean that other aspects of the plan would require a period of one-on-one therapy.

## FAMILY INVOLVEMENT IN ASSESSMENT

Many professionals in the field of early intervention in the mid-1990s were trained to distrust what parents had to say about their children's abilities. In the not-too-distant past, training programs taught that parents overestimate their children's abilities and are unreliable reporters of assessment information. There are several possible explanations for why discrepancies between parent and professional reports of children's abilities were documented and emphasized in the past. Gradel, Thompson, and Sheehan (1981) made the point that parents have more opportunities to observe their children in naturalistic environments; they are more likely to see children performing at their best and to detect emerging skills. Therefore, parent estimates may be more accurate than professionals' estimates; professionals may be underestimating, rather than parents overestimating. The assessment tools used for young children have improved over time. Traditional tests often used a recall format to gather information from parents about children's skills (e.g., At what age did your child roll over?). Newer assessment tools rely more on parent reporting of current skill levels, a task that is much easier than recalling past events. Data gathered in the 1990s indicate that family–professional agreement is high when ecologically valid assessment measures are used (Snyder, McWilliam, & Lawson, 1995; Squires & Bricker, 1991).

## Strategies for Facilitating Family Involvement in Assessment

*Eliminate Models that Do Not Link Assessment with Intervention Planning and Implementation*   In some states and communities, child assessment has traditionally been the role of a small group of professionals whose sole job is conducting lengthy assessments of the child and writing long, professional reports about the assessment. Parents usually play a minor role in these assessments. They may be interviewed for family history information, or they may watch the procedures behind a one-way mirror. They are usually given the opportunity to hear a summary of the assessment and ask questions in a final interpretive conference and usually receive a written report some weeks later. Parents and teachers do not seem to find this approach to assessment helpful. What is often missing in these reports are practical strategies related to intervention. The reports are also notoriously hard to understand for the professionals and parents who are expected to develop and implement service plans. The reports usually focus on deficits, which sometimes results in the parents thinking that their child's condition is so bad that lots of specialized therapies are required. As one parent said, "After paying $300 for that assessment, I wish I could say that I learned one thing that helped me. I walked out of there still not knowing what I could do next to help my child."

*Plan the Assessment Process with Families*   An alternative approach is to provide families with a chance to shape the way the assessment is conducted. This involves families in give-and-take conversations about the possibilities and options. The first step is to discover family priorities and interests. Research suggests that families prefer to share this information through friendly conversations, rather than more formalized approaches (Summers et al., 1990). This does not necessarily mean that all families want an informal approach, but it does suggest that an informal approach should be one option that families are offered.

If parents are interested in information about their child, then an assessment may be in order. (This discussion ignores that assessments are also needed to determine eligibility and for that reason may need to be done even if parents are not particularly interested in undergoing a lengthy child assessment process.) Some parents may simply want help selecting a preschool or help with parenting; to serve them in this way, it may be necessary also to evaluate the child so that the family is eligible for services, but the evaluation should be explained to the family as simply a necessary step in the process. If an assessment is warranted, families often appreciate having input into the logistics of where, when, and who should attend. The short questionnaire developed by Project Dakota (see Figure 1) is one strategy for collecting this kind of information from parents.

The assessment should be designed around the questions that parents have about their child. For example, if a family wants to know where their child stands compared with other children his or her age, then a standardized approach to assessment may be warranted.

If a parent is worried about language development and wants to know how to promote more articulate speech, then another kind of assessment may be best. Families can be given options for playing active roles (administering test items), passive roles (watching others administer items), or evolving roles (parent starts administering items and professional takes over once the child warms up to the professional). This approach is more likely to provide information that parents can use and want to facilitate decision making about and monitoring of intervention strategies.

***Demonstrate and Reinforce Existing Intervention Strategies*** Using techniques in conducting assessments that also provide intervention information to participants can maximize this learning opportunity for all parties. For instance, a person trying to elicit a response from the child to a picture in a language test may use a prompt if the response is not forthcoming. If the child attempts to imitate the prompt, a professional might point out the child's ability to imitate as a strength and reinforce to others that this is a language-building strategy that might be used at home or in the classroom.

---

1. What questions or concerns do others have (e.g., baby sitter, clinic, preschool)?
2. Are there other places where we should observe your child?

   Place:
   Contact person:
   What to observe:

3. How does your child do around other children?
4. Where would you like the assessment to take place?
5. What time of day? (The best time is when your child is alert and when working parents can be present.)
6. Are there others who should be there in addition to parents and staff?
7. What are your child's favorite toys or activities that help your child become focused, motivated, and comfortable?
8. Which roles would you find comfortable during assessment?
   _____ a. Sit beside your child
   _____ b. Help with activities to explore your child's abilities
   _____ c. Offer comfort and support to your child
   _____ d. Exchange ideas with the facilitator
   _____ e. Carry out activities to explore your child's abilities
   _____ f. Prefer facilitator to handle and carry out activities with your child
   _____ g. Other

---

Figure 1.  Preassessment planning. (From Kjerland, K. [1986]. *Pre-assessment planning*. Eagan, MN: Project Dakota Outreach; reprinted by permission.)

***Use Specialized Assessment Approaches***   Some of the newer assessment models described in the literature, such as transdisciplinary play-based assessment (Linder, 1990) or arena assessments (Wolery & Dyk, 1984), provide families with opportunities to play an active role. These approaches use a natural play environment, familiar toys, and child-initiated play with adult facilitation as the means for collecting assessment information. Team members, including family members, observe the child playing in a comfortable and familiar environment. This provides all team members with the same basis for drawing conclusions about the child's strengths and needs. Intervention goals are generated immediately following the play situation.

Families often come to professionals for help and expertise related to concerns they have about their child. What families sometimes do not realize is that they have valuable information about their child that can greatly assist the professionals in answering their questions. If conducted in a family-centered fashion, the assessment process offers an opportunity for information sharing and building a common understanding of where and how to focus intervention efforts.

## FAMILY–PROFESSIONAL PARTNERSHIPS IN INTERVENTION PLANNING

One of the central tenets to a family-centered approach is that families are equal partners on the intervention team and that families have the final say about the intervention plans that are developed (McGonigel et al., 1991). This next section explores the status of that tenet and shares strategies related to realizing this goal.

### Families as Equal Partners

The importance of families feeling ownership for the goals set in early intervention planning meetings has been a theme in much of the early intervention literature (Bailey, 1987; Kaiser & Hemmeter, 1989; McGonigel et al., 1991). Despite this attention in the literature, there is little evidence that partnerships are built or manifest at team meetings. Intervention planning meetings in service delivery settings are notorious for being anxiety-producing and stressful for parents at worst and boring at best. Observational research on meetings to develop the IEP has demonstrated that parents play a passive role, with professionals doing most of the talking and presenting prepared plans for parents to sign (Goldstein, Strickland, Turnbull, & Curry, 1980). This research was conducted in 1980; unfortunately, anecdotal evidence suggests there have been few changes in the ways that IEP meetings are conducted.

The literature on the IFSP describes a process that should contrast with most IEP meetings. The planning meeting is described as being only one piece of a bigger planning process that involves families every step of the way

(McGonigel et al., 1991). The literature describes an active role for families in this process with those who are willing to serve as team leaders actually writing the IFSP using language and terms of their choosing. To what extent the reality of IFSP meetings matches this ideal has not been fully documented in the literature. Observational research is lacking. However, research based on professional perceptions of family-centered practices (Bailey, Buysse, Edmondson, & Smith, 1992) suggests that family participation in the intervention process is not occurring at the levels described in the literature. Clincial evidence supports that research. IFSP meetings, for the most part, continue to be somewhat formal events, dominated by professionals in terms of sheer numbers of participants and contributions (Able-Boone, 1993).

A number of factors can be identified that contribute to this status. The professionals in a program or agency who regularly come together for planning meetings usually all know each other. They develop a sense of "teamness," including team norms and expectations in terms of roles, leadership, and communication patterns. A team culture develops to which they all contribute and understand, even if only on a subconscious level. Parents are newcomers or occasional members of the team. It is possible that a parent could function as the leader of a preestablished team, but it would take a combination of personality, style, preparation, and acquiescence from the established team members for this to happen. This is unlikely unless a team makes a clear commitment to develop strategies for preparing and supporting families who express interest in assuming a leadership role.

Another reality related to intervention planning is that professionals are likely to have informal opportunities to discuss children. Families will not be privy to all of these conversations. Asking professionals never to discuss a child outside the presence of the family is an unreasonable request and one that is not in anyone's interests. It is another factor, however, that makes the premise of equal partnerships a difficult one to implement. A challenge for professionals is how to keep parents updated and informed about intervention goals and progress in the same ways that professionals are informing each other.

A third factor relates to the relationship between goals, strategies, and outcomes. The emphasis in the literature has been that family priorities should guide the intervention goals. Less has been said about the importance of continued family involvement in generating strategies to achieve the goals and about the family's role in monitoring progress. Once goals have been identified, professionals often take over the process. It is true that this is where professional expertise can be extremely helpful; it also is true, however, that families are capable of devising excellent strategies for achieving goals and of monitoring progress.

A fourth factor is the extent to which professionals truly believe that parents should have final decision-making authority about services. A study by

Giangreco (1990) on related service decisions and decision-making authority provided evidence that professionals do not accept this premise. In this study, the related-service specialists (i.e., occupational therapists, physical therapists, communication specialists) reported that they should retain final decision-making authority regarding related service provision. In contrast, special educators were divided in their opinion about who should have authority, and parents predominantly disagreed with professional retention of authority. Although the study focused on a school-age population, the findings have implications for early intervention.

## Strategies for Facilitating Family Involvement in Intervention Planning

*Spend Time in the Child's and Family's Natural Environment*  As mentioned earlier, one strategy is to involve families in the assessment process so that IEP and IFSP meetings are only part of an ongoing process. As part of the process, spending time in the home, on the playground, and in natural settings is important in intervention planning. Without the kind of information that can be gathered only through observation and time spent in natural settings, professionals are operating with limitations in their knowledge base.

Why is this so important? Sometimes families may not see the link between what they are naturally doing and official intervention strategies for accomplishing goals. For example, putting a favorite food like Cheerios on a highchair tray is an excellent way to encourage the development of the fine motor skill of using two fingers and a thumb to grasp. Letting parents and siblings know that the peek-a-boo game they are initiating is likely to promote a cognitive skill is another example of drawing family members into implementing strategies and monitoring outcomes. Recognizing what families are already doing that encourages movement toward a goal not only increases a family's sense of self-confidence but also reinforces an activity that has a great likelihood of being continued because it already exists in the natural environment of the child. Asking families to notice increased interest in certain games or greater success at picking up Cheerios can provide both professionals and families with meaningful outcome information. Using informal, imaginary scales can be a strategy for engaging families in monitoring progress. For instance, asking family members to rate a behavior or skill, or the absence of annoying behavior, on a scale of 1 to 10 each week is a way of noting changes. These same strategies can be effective with baby sitters, child care providers, and other people who interact with the child regularly. This kind of information sharing is best facilitated by specialists spending time in the child's home, neighborhood, and child care environment. It also means that specialists need to integrate their services with home and community routines, as well as classroom routines, whenever possible.

***Prepare Family Members for the Planning Meeting*** Even if parents have been involved in every step, planning meetings can be intimidating. Research by Brinckerhoff and Vincent (1987) demonstrated the efficacy of preparing parents for planning meetings. They conducted an experimental study in which one group of parents (experimental group) was asked to do the following before the IEP meeting: 1) complete a developmental assessment of their child's present performance, 2) complete a family profile, and 3) meet with a school–community liaison to discuss the upcoming meeting. Statistical analysis indicated that the experimental group of parents had significantly greater frequency of contributions, goals generated, and programming decisions made at the IEP meetings compared with a control group of parents. Preparation for each parent is different; this is not to suggest that every parent should be required to carry out the tasks reported in the Brinckerhoff and Vincent study; individualized preparation for planning meetings should be conducted, however. Important considerations in preparing parents for this meeting include the following:

- Determine the role they would like to play in the meeting.
- Determine who they would like to have in attendance and when are convenient times to hold the meeting.
- Describe generally the approaches to planning and ask parents what approach they prefer.

***Create a Welcoming and Friendly Environment*** Welcome the family. Show hospitality, especially if the setting is unfamiliar (e.g., location of the restroom, the drink machine, water fountain). Establish a relaxed atmosphere with informal and friendly conversation. The length and extent to which an informal settling-in period occurs depends on each family. Some families want to get to the business part of the meeting as soon as possible. For these families, a couple of minutes of informality is probably sufficient. Other families may feel very uncomfortable with the setting, the process, and the event. Some families may be used to a fairly lengthy informal relationship-building part of any formal transaction. These individual differences need to be taken into account by the team to try to accommodate each family within the time constraints. For some families, having professionals arrive one at a time so that individual, informal conversations are possible with those professionals who can stay longer may be a strategy for accommodating busy professionals and families who would like some informal time before the formal meeting begins.

***Use the Meeting to Brainstorm and Problem-Solve*** Collaboration is considered to be important in service delivery because no one discipline or person has all of the answers to the complexities of designing effective interventions. The planning meeting has the capacity to serve as a collaborative problem-solving session. Unfortunately, this does not always happen.

The traditions associated with planning meetings (IEP/IFSP) mitigate their usefulness as planning sessions. The time allotted is usually minimal (1 hour or less). As mentioned earlier, research by Giangreco (1990) indicated that professionals feel that they have the ultimate decision-making authority. If professionals view the final decision-making authority as theirs, they are more likely to view the planning meeting as simply a formality in which the decisions are presented for parental acquiescence. Research by McWillaim et al. presented in Chapter 7 indicates that most professionals do not consider giving families a choice about service delivery models. This suggests that discussing the merits of different models for providing therapies in a collaborative problem-solving fashion is not likely to take place in planning meetings.

Another mitigating factor is that when collaboration does take place, it often leads to differences of opinion and conflict. As a field, we are unprepared and ambivalent about how to deal with this inevitable phenomenon. Should professionals disagree in front of parents? Should parents be subjected to meetings in which there are no clear or easy answers or solutions? Should we present a united front to parents so they see us at our best and feel comforted by our expertise? Will disagreements and lack of consensus confuse parents and make their already difficult situation worse? These are some legitimate concerns that professionals have about using planning meetings as honest problem-solving sessions. Without skillful leadership and facilitation, planning meetings that include honest differences of opinion can be ineffective, upsetting, and unproductive. What follows are strategies to consider when designing meetings that will serve as effective problem-solving events.

- Identify a group facilitator who has facilitation skills so that both task and process issues are attended to effectively.
- Ensure that as many team members as possible have exposure to, knowledge of, and practice with communication skills. At the beginning of the meeting, generate ground rules to establish a respectful listening environment.
- Use a formalized brainstorming approach to ensure that all group members have an opportunity to contribute. This may be especially helpful when considering strategies for accomplishing goals. It is at this point that specialists are often turned to for their ideas, without other more generic strategies being considered. Observations in the home or classroom about naturally occurring activities that can be used to promote goals now can be brought into the discussion. Different models of service delivery can be explained, with the pros and cons of each described. If any differences of opinion can be aired in a somewhat structured and safe environment, it is less likely for the conflict to get out of hand. Providing parents with a list of questions about potential therapy (see Chapter 7) before the meeting is a strategy for conveying to them that it is acceptable to raise critical ques-

tions. Part of preparing families for the planning meeting might be a discussion about the differences of opinion that they might hear. Helping parents frame these differences as a positive outcome and letting them know they have the final say may be especially helpful in preparing them for the discussion. The importance of the professionals in the meeting being respectful of the opinions expressed by others cannot be overemphasized. Parents need to be able to make choices based on what they think will work best for them and their family. They should not feel that their choice will be seen as a personal rejection of one professional over another.

- Generate a collaborative monitoring plan. In a family-centered approach, families should have the final say about what approach to take and which strategies to try. This means that families might choose an approach that is not the choice of others. It is important to develop a monitoring plan to evaluate the family's choice; if it is not working, "Plan B" can be tried or the group can return to the drawing board. In this way, if things do not work as hoped, families and professionals have already paved the way for their collaborative efforts to continue. This lessens the fear that blame will be laid on anyone involved or "I told you so" messages will result from the lack of success.

***Use an Alternative Person-Centered Planning Process*** Person-centered planning has been described in the literature as an alternative to traditional IEP, individualized habilitation plan (IHP), and IFSP meetings (Stineman, Morningstar, Bishop, & Turnbull, 1993; Turnbull, Turnbull, & Blue-Banning, 1994). This approach has been used more frequently with school-age children (Forest & Pierpoint, 1992) and young adults (Stineman et al., 1993) than with infants and toddlers; however, the basic concepts apply across the life span. The following components of this approach distinguish it from more traditional approaches (Turnbull et al., 1994): 1) meetings are held in an informal setting; 2) visions and relationships rather than formal assessments guide the planning process; 3) proportion of participants from community and family are equal to or greater than professional participants; 4) emphasis on creative problem solving rather than formal, structured process; and 5) planning occurs on a regular basis (monthly) as opposed to once or twice a year. Families who have participated in this process are quite positive. There is no empirical research related to the efficacy of a person-centered approach, but as interest grows in this new approach, research should soon occur.

## INVOLVING FAMILIES IN DAY-TO-DAY ACTIVITIES

A frequent lament of professionals who work in center-based programs is how difficult it is to have ongoing communication with parents. This is especially unfortunate because research with families whose young children (3–5 years) with developmental delays were attending center-based programs indicated that informal and frequent conversations with their children's teachers were their most preferred form of parent involvement in the program (Winton & Turnbull, 1981). It is especially difficult to engage parents in this way when children are transported by bus or when programs serve as full-time child care for working parents who have few opportunities for extended visits to the center. When programs are implementing an interdisciplinary approach to early intervention that involves all team members (i.e., therapists, teachers, families) in implementation and monitoring of specialized therapies, the challenges are compounded. The teacher may have opportunities at drop-off and pickup times for updates, but the therapists are unlikely to be part of these informal exchanges. Research has indicated that therapists and teachers who take an integrated approach to therapy consult with each other four times more often than do teachers and therapists who do not use an integrated approach (McWilliam & Bailey, 1992). Although this level of collaboration is helpful in their relationship building, what about the parents? How do these uneven opportunities for sharing information affect collaborative relationships? What are some strategies for addressing these collaborative challenges of day-to-day information sharing?

### Strategies for Facilitating Family Participation in Ongoing Implementation and Collaboration

*Use Notebook for Information Exchange*  Short messages about therapy goals and related activities can be exchanged between home and the center using the notebook approach, in which the child brings a notebook from home to the center each day. It provides therapists and parents who may not meet often an opportunity to exchange information. A related strategy might be to share the Specialist's Documentation Form, which is used by therapists for recording what goals are addressed each day, the length of the session, and the model of therapy used (see Chapter 7). At the Frank Porter Graham Child Development Center, a copy of this form is sent home to parents each week to show what goals are being worked on and how they are being addressed. This strategy reinforces for therapists the importance of keeping families informed at a detailed level.

*Use Pictures to Share Information*  Sharing written information is an effective strategy for some parents, but not for all. Some parents may not read, or relate well to, written information. An alternative approach is using a Polaroid camera to capture an activity or to show an accomplishment. The picture can be taped into the notebook with a note. Reading members of the partnership (e.g., relatives, neighbors, other professionals who use the notebook) have more complete information, whereas nonreaders receive some information about what is happening. The picture also may serve as a catalyst for discussions about goals, activities, and progress.

*Use Videotape to Share Information*    Another approach to sharing an image is the use of a video camera. A teacher may use a video clip of a child as a means of asking for help from a specialist or a family member in understanding or treating a certain behavior that occurs irregularly. Video clips can also be a way to share information between home and school about special events or accomplishments.

*Attach Brief Notes to Child*    One teacher developed an effective and easy method for home–school communication in a center where children were transported by bus. She adhered sticky labels to the backpacks of students as they went to the bus at the end of the day. The labels had short sentences that were meant to engage the interest of the parents in asking their children about certain activities, such as "Ask me about the Piggy Song" or "Ask me what I did at snack" or "Ask about my new friend." Parents started using the same method in return. Therapists can also take part in this approach, if they have specific events or activities that they want the parent to know about through their child.

*Communicate Availability of Specialists to Families*    Often specialists are working on a consultative basis. They spend only a short time in the center and rarely are available at drop-off and pickup times. Sometimes the only time parents see them is at IEP or IFSP meetings. One therapist decided to write parents a friendly note that indicated times and places she could be called or seen if they simply wanted to talk or share information.

## Summary

A family-centered approach has the potential for helping families appreciate the importance and value of fun, play, leisure, and recreation in the lives of their child and their family. Too often families feel robbed of these pleasures because of their fear and concern that the more therapy they can provide for their child, the better off the child will be in the long run. A family-centered approach allows for a holistic approach to intervention that includes other considerations in addition to the need for therapies.

A family-centered approach also can engage family members, child care providers, baby sitters, and other important persons in the intervention process. These are the individuals who are likely to spend the most time with young children and whose participation is critical if intervention is to succeed. Creating a partnership with families is not just important; it is the only way to succeed. This quotation from a parent illustrates our dependence on parents:

> If I don't have the cooperation of a professional I am disappointed, but I know that I can move on and find another professional with whom to work. If a professional does not have my cooperation, they are stuck. They cannot move on and find different parents for my child.

## MOVING TOWARD COLLABORATIVE
## INTERPROFESSIONAL AND FAMILY–PROFESSIONAL
## RELATIONSHIPS IN CENTER-BASED PROGRAMS

The models of service delivery being espoused in the 1990s—integrated, family-centered, interdisciplinary—each represent a significant reconceptualization of how the early intervention service delivery system works (Shonkoff & Meisels, 1990). A question of major importance is how the programs, agencies, and individuals who are part of this system will make the necessary changes in practices, policies, and structures to move in these directions. Another question relates to the relationship between the different elements that make up the new directions in early intervention. Are these complementary or competing directions? In answering this question, it is important to point out that the major issues and strategies described for promoting a family-centered approach can also be applied to the interdisciplinary collaboration necessary to successfully implement integrated therapies. They include the following:

- The importance of building trusting relationships based on mutual respect and the honest belief that each person has something valuable to contribute to planning and implementing intervention
- The importance of communication skills in conveying information, respect, and appreciation of each person's perspective
- The time required to engage in planning, observation, relationship building, and meetings is "worth it," and the intervention will be better as a result
- The need to address administrative barriers, such as reimbursement policies. The approaches described in this chapter require time for planning and communicating with colleagues and families. Administrative policies must support time being allocated in these ways.
- The need to be sensitive to individual differences. Not everyone feels comfortable working in groups and being exposed to conflict; there are people who do not care to develop these skills. Accommodating these individual differences with respect to collaborative relationships across disciplines, sites, and people is an ongoing challenge that requires attention.

Issues and strategies related to assisting center-based programs in moving toward a family-centered approach in which families are provided with options for different service delivery models for providing therapies are described in the following sections.

### Individual Skill Levels

Models of service delivery are only as good as the professionals who implement them. One of the challenges in providing a family-centered approach and offering families options of different service delivery models is that effectiveness depends on the communication and collaboration skills of the individuals involved. Unfortunately, research indicates that most professionals in early intervention have not been provided with information and skill-building opportunities in these content areas in their preservice training programs (Bailey, Simeonsson, Yoder, & Huntington, 1990). This suggests that, for most professionals, these skills need to be acquired on the job or through in-service training opportunities.

## Systems-Level Issues

Throughout this chapter, the role of programmatic structures and policies in supporting a family-centered approach is emphasized. Creating more time for both informal and formal meetings, greater flexibility in assessment procedures, and more opportunities for home visits and observations are strategies that all require support from administrative levels. Research by Bailey and colleagues (Bailey, Buysse, Edmondson, & Smith, 1992) provides evidence that early intervention practitioners view systems variables as being more influential than their own knowledge and skills in their ability to implement a family-centered approach. In considering how programs can make changes, systems-level factors must be considered and addressed.

## A Team-Based Model of Change

A promising approach for assisting programs and individuals in making changes has been developed at the Frank Porter Graham Child Development Center (Bailey, McWilliam, & Winton, 1992; Bailey, McWilliam, Winton, & Simeonsson, 1992; Winton, McWilliam, Harrison, Owens, & Bailey, 1992). It proposes a team-based model of change as a strategy for building family-centered practices in early intervention. It is based on the following propositions related to the change process (Winton, 1990):

- It is difficult for individuals to develop new roles or behaviors unless social organizations are trained together so that the individuals within the organizations develop a shared knowledge and values base.
- Professionals often try to rationalize how their services are already compatible with the desired changes before they make any effort to change. They must recognize the gap between what they are currently doing and what is being recommended before they can move in the desired directions.
- Change is a gradual process that is best facilitated by ongoing staff development activities.
- The ultimate challenge for change agents (trainers) is how to empower trainees to become independent and competent problem solvers, capable of assessing and monitoring their own training needs.

The team-based model is implemented through a series of structured workshops that include the following key components:

- *Team participation* The key players in early intervention programs (i.e., administrators, teachers, therapists, families) are provided with the responsibility for decision making. This encourages programs to develop family-centered practices that fit the unique characteristics of the community and the children and families being served.
- *Guided decision-making activities related to individual and agency priorities* One of the primary purposes of the workshops is to help programs and individuals identify the gaps between current and ideal practice. Based on this knowledge, the key players are encouraged to prioritize specific practices and policies that they want to change. The FOCAS (Bailey, 1990) and BRASS TACKS I & II (McWilliam & Winton, 1990) tools were developed to assist programs in this self-assessment and priority-setting process.
- *Creating and monitoring a plan for change* A critical component of change occurring is for specific objectives, time lines, and responsibilities to be identified and monitored. This activity is an integral part of the workshop format; follow-up workshops are held to evaluate progress and identify new goals and objectives.
- *Family participation* The importance of including families in the process of making programmatic changes was demonstrated by a research study (Bailey, Buysse, Smith-Bonahue, & Elam, 1992) conducted as part of the model development. In this study, two sets of workshops were held: one that was attended only by the professionals in the agency and one that included both professionals and parents. Professionals attending the workshop that included parents identified more areas of practice in which change was desired compared with the professionals who did not participate with parents. In addition, the professionals who attended with parents felt very strongly that parent participation was a critical component to the success of the workshop.

For programs that desire to use a team-based approach to move toward a more integrated model of specialized services delivery, McWilliam and Bailey (1994) have created a tool for this purpose. Like the FOCAS and the BRASS TACKS I & II, it is designed to assist teams in identifying and prioritizing specific changes that will move them toward providing more options for service delivery models. Another resource related to team-based models of change is the Skills Inventory for Teams (SIFT), developed by Garland and associates at Child Development Resources (Garland, Frank, Buck, & Seklemian, 1992). It was developed for early interventionists to help them evaluate their ability to work effectively as a team and to identify strategies for making changes that foster greater collaboration and team effectiveness.

The long-term impact of the team-based model of change and the use of the instruments previously described is unknown. Longitudinal research charting changes identified and made through this process has not been conducted. This approach, however, offers promise as a strategy for building family–professional partnerships related to creating programmatic and policy changes that support a family-centered approach.

## CONCLUSIONS

A parent (Fialka, 1995) has compared the family–professional relationship to a dance: Each partner comes to the dance with a different piece of music and a different dancing style. She continued the analogy by stating that sometimes the dance turns into a square dance because of all the different partners who must somehow dance together. This analogy seems particularly relevant to this discussion of a family-centered approach and integrated therapies. There are many dancers, and the dancing seems to depend on some planned structures, and some shared music, but also on some flexibility in terms of how each player dances the steps. It is hoped that this chapter has provided some information about structures that may be useful and some ways that flexibility can be promoted.

## REFERENCES

Able-Boone, H.A. (1993). Family participation in the IFSP process: Family or professional driven? *Infant Toddler Intervention, 3*(1), 63–72.

Bailey, D.B., Jr. (1987). Collaborative goal-setting with families: Resolving differences in values and priorities for services. *Topics in Early Childhood Special Education, 7*(2), 59–71.

Bailey, D.B., Jr. (1990). *Family Orientation of Community and Agency Services (FOCAS)*. Chapel Hill, NC: Frank Porter Graham Child Development Center.

Bailey, D.B., Jr., Buysse, V.M., Edmondson, R., & Smith, T.M. (1992). Creating family-centered services in early intervention: Perceptions of professionals in four states. *Exceptional Children, 58*, 298–309.

Bailey, D.B., Jr., Buysse, V.M., Smith-Bonahue, T.M., & Elam, J. (1992). The effects and perceptions of family involvement in program decisions about family-centered practices. *Evaluation and Program Planning, 15*, 23–32.

Bailey, D.B., Jr., McWilliam, P.J., & Winton, P.J. (1992). Building family-centered practices in early intervention: A team-based model for change. *Infants and Young Children, 5*(1), 73–82.

Bailey, D.B., Jr., McWilliam, P.J., Winton, P.J., & Simeonsson, R.J. (1992). *Implementing family-centered services in early intervention: A team-based model for change.* Cambridge, MA: Brookline Books.

Bailey, D.B., Jr., Simeonsson, R.J., Yoder, D.E., & Huntington, G.S. (1990). Preparing professionals to serve infants and toddlers with handicaps and their families: An integrative analysis across eight disciplines. *Exceptional Children, 57*(1), 26–35.

Boggs, E.M. (1978). Deinstitutionalization jet lag. In A. Turnbull & R. Turnbull (Eds.), *Parents speak out* (pp. 39–54). Columbus, OH: Charles E. Merrill.

Brinckerhoff, J.L., & Vincent, L.J. (1987). Increasing parental decision-making at the individualized educational program meeting. *Journal of the Division of Early Childhood, 11*, 46–58.

Crais, E.R. (1993). Families and professionals as collaborators in assessment. *Topics in Language Disorders, 14*(1), 29–40.

Doernberg, N.L. (1978). Some negative effects on family integrations of health and educational services for young handicapped children. *Rehabilitation Literature, 39,* 107–110.

Dunst, C.J., Trivette, C.M., & Deal, A. (1988). *Enabling and empowering families: Principles and guidelines for practice.* Cambridge, MA: Brookline Books.

Education for All Handicapped Children Act of 1975, PL 94-142. (August 23, 1977). Title 20, U.S.C. §§ 1400 *et seq.: U.S. Statutes at Large, 89,* 773–796.

Education of the Handicapped Act Amendments of 1986, PL 99-457. (October 8, 1986). Title 20, U.S.C. §§ 1400 *et seq.: U.S. Statutes at Large, 100,* 1145–1177.

Fialka, J. (1995, May). *The dance of partnership or why do my feet hurt?* Keynote presentation at the Midwestern Consortium for Faculty Development Institute, Minneapolis, MN.

Forest, M., & Pierpoint, J.C. (1992, October). Putting kids on the MAP. *Educational Leadership,* 26–31.

Gallimore, R., Weisner, T., Bernheimer, L., Guthrie, D., & Nihira, K. (1993). Family responses to young children with developmental delays: Accommodation activity in ecological and cultural context. *American Journal of Mental Retardation, 98*(2), 185–206.

Gallimore, R., Weisner, T.S., Kaufman, S.Z., & Bernheimer, L.P. (1989). The social construction of ecocultural niches: Family accommodation of developmentally delayed children. *American Journal of Mental Retardation, 94,* 216–230.

Garland, C.W., Frank, A., Buck, D., & Seklemian, P. (1992). *Skills inventory for teams (SIFT).* Lightfoot, VA: Child Development Resources.

Giangreco, M.F. (1990). Making related service decisions for students with severe disabilities: Roles, criteria, and authority. *Journal of The Association for Persons with Severe Handicaps, 15*(1), 22–31.

Goldstein, S., Strickland, B., Turnbull, A., & Curry, L. (1980). An observational analysis of the IEP conference. *Exceptional Children, 46*(4), 278–280.

Gradel, K., Thompson, M., & Sheehen, R. (1981). Parental and professional agreement in early childhood assessment. *Topics in Early Childhood Special Education, 1,* 31–39.

Kaiser, A.P., & Hemmeter, M.L. (1989). Value based approaches to family intervention. *Topics in Early Childhood Special Education, 8,* 72–86.

Kaminer, R.K., & Robinson, C. (1993). Perspective: Developmental therapies in early intervention. *Infants and Young Children, 5*(4), v–viii.

Kjerland, K. (1986). *Pre-assessment planning.* Eagan, MN: Project Dakota Outreach.

Linder, T.W. (1990). *Transdisciplinary play-based assessment: A functional approach to working with young children.* Baltimore: Paul H. Brookes Publishing Co.

McGonigel, M.J., Kaufmann, R., & Johnson, B. (1991). *Guidelines and recommended practices for the individualized family service plan* (2nd ed.). Bethesda, MD: Association for the Care of Children's Health.

McWilliam, P.J., & Winton, P.J. (1990). *BRASS TACKS I & II.* Chapel Hill, NC: Frank Porter Graham Child Development Center.

McWilliam, R.A., & Bailey, D.B., Jr. (1992, December). *From integrated to pull-out services: Practices and perceptions of our disciplines.* Paper presented at the DEC Early Childhood Conference on Children with Special Needs, Washington, DC.

McWilliam, R.A., & Bailey, D.B., Jr. (1994). Predictors of service delivery models in center-based early intervention. *Exceptional Children, 61,* 56–71.

McWilliam, R.A., Lang, L., Vandiviere, P., Angell, R., Collins, L., & Underdown, G. (1995). Satisfaction and struggles: Family perceptions of early intervention services. *Journal of Early Intervention, 19*(1), 43–60.

Shelton, T.S., Jeppson, E.S., & Johnson, B.H. (1989). *Family-centered care for children with special health care needs* (2nd ed.). Bethesda, MD: Association for the Care of Children's Health.

Shonkoff, J., & Meisels, S. (1990). Early childhood intervention: The evolution of a concept. In S.J. Meisels & J.P. Shonkoff (Eds.), *Handbook of early intervention* (pp. 3–31). Cambridge, MA: Cambridge University Press.

Snyder, P.A., McWilliam, R.A., & Lawson, S. (1995, April 22). *Dependability and factorial validity of the Children's Engagement Questionnaire: A broad-based child status measure for early intervention*. Paper presented to the American Educational Research Association Conference, San Francisco, CA.

Squires, J., & Bricker, D. (1991). Impact of completing infant developmental questionnaires on at-risk mothers. *Journal of Early Intervention, 15,* 162–172.

Stineman, R., Morningstar, M., Bishop, B., & Turnbull, H. (1993). The role of families in transition planning for young adults with disabilities: Toward a method of person-centered planning. *Journal of Vocational Rehabilitation, 3*(2), 52–61.

Summers, J., Dell'Oliver, C., Turnbull, A., Benson, H., Santelli, E., Campbell, M., & Siegel-Causey, E. (1990). Examining the individualized family service plan process: What are family and practitioner preferences? *Topics in Early Childhood Special Education, 10*(1), 78–99.

Turnbull, A.P., & Turnbull, H.R. (1990). *Families, professionals, and exceptionality: A special partnership* (2nd ed.). Columbus, OH: Charles E. Merrill.

Turnbull, A.P., Turnbull, H.R., & Blue-Banning, M. (1994). Enhancing inclusion of infants and toddlers with disabilities and their families: A theoretical and programmatic analysis. *Infants and Young Children, 7*(2), 1–14.

Winton, P.J. (1990). A systemic approach for planning inservice training related to Public Law 99-457. *Infants and Young Children, 3*(1), 51–60.

Winton, P.J., McWilliam, P.J., Harrison, T., Owens, A.M., & Bailey, D.B., Jr. (1992). Lessons learned from implementing a team-based model of change. *Infants and Young Children, 5*(1), 49–57.

Winton, P.J., & Turnbull, A.P. (1981). Parent involvement as viewed by parents of preschool handicapped children. *Topics in Early Childhood Special Education, 1*(3), 11–19.

Wolery, M., & Dyk, L. (1984). Arena assessment: Description and preliminary social validity data. *Journal of The Association for Persons with Severe Handicaps, 9*(3), 231–235.

# Chapter 4

# A Program of Research on Integrated Versus Isolated Treatment in Early Intervention

R.A. McWilliam

This chapter reviews published and unpublished research on topics directly or closely related to integrated versus pull-out service delivery models. The chapter begins with descriptions of the few studies around the country. The majority of the chapter describes studies conducted at the Frank Porter Graham Child Development Center at the University of North Carolina at Chapel Hill. Challenges in conducting comparative research are apparent, as are the challenges of presenting complex findings in sound bites. We conclude that, although integrated therapy has only marginally better effects than segregated services on children's acquisition, generalization, and goal-related progress, 1) it has positive effects on collaboration and 2) true effects of either model can probably be amassed only over time.

**EXISTING RESEARCH**

The effectiveness of integrated services has been specifically addressed in relatively few studies. For the present purposes, *integrated services* are defined as 1) specialized instruction or therapy occurring in the classroom, 2) occurring with other children usually present, and 3) occurring in the context of ongoing routines and activities. Using a reversal, single-subject design, Giangreco (1986) compared isolated therapy and integrated therapy for instruction in the use of a microswitch. The subject was a 13-year-old girl with multiple disabilities. More trials were correct with integrated therapy, as confirmed by depressed performance during return to the baseline condition of isolated therapy.

71

Cole, Harris, Eland, and Mills (1989) compared in-class and out-of-class direct services for physical and occupational therapy. Both individual and small-group therapy were provided to 61 preschoolers with disabilities; services differed only in location. No significant differences were found on standardized scales of motor development, but classroom staff preferred the in-class model.

In a language study, 20 children ages 20–47 months were randomly assigned to either an indirect therapy condition or an individual pull-out condition (Wilcox, Kouri, & Caswell, 1991). Children in both groups received an interactive modeling procedure. It was found that their use of target words was the same in both conditions, but the classroom (indirect therapy) group better generalized to home settings. The researchers also found that cognitive ability predicted 46% of the variance in generalized word use for the classroom treatment group, which suggests support for others' findings of aptitude-by-treatment effects (Cole, Dale, & Mills, 1991; Yoder, Kaiser, & Alpert, 1991).

Direct service (one-on-one outside the classroom) and collaborative consultation (equal time discussing the child's needs, observing related behaviors, and making a plan for the next time) were compared through random assignment of 14 preschoolers and kindergartners receiving occupational therapy (Dunn, 1990). Children in both conditions achieved a similar percentage of individualized education program (IEP) goals, but teachers in the consultation condition reported much larger occupational therapy contributions to IEP goals and had more positive comments on an attitude scale.

In a comparison of individual and group consultation treatment methods for preschool children with developmental delays, participants in both groups demonstrated significant increases in both fine and gross motor skills (Davies & Gavin, 1994). No differences between the groups were found, and gains were seen in homes by parents as well as in clinical settings by therapists.

The studies described above provide a small but encouraging foundation for further research. Investigations are needed 1) to discover the perceptions of stakeholders, 2) to explore using single-subject methods with preschoolers, 3) to operationalize in-class and out-of-class models, 4) to study generalization in greater detail, and 5) to examine naturalistic practices and their long-term effects.

## STUDIES

Each of the studies conducted in our program of research on integrated versus isolated treatment in early intervention is briefly described.

### Perspectives of Benefits

*Purpose*  We designed a study to determine whether families' perspectives about in-class and out-of-class services would change over time (McWilliam, Bailey, & Vandermaas, 1991). We hypothesized that families would initially prefer what they were used to (predominantly pull-out), but that those who had experience with in-class treatment for the full year of data collection would change their preference.

***Method*** Sixteen families were interviewed and completed rating scales twice: once before the service delivery model was randomly assigned and once at the end of the year. All children were enrolled in the same program, and all received special education and speech-language, occupational, and physical therapy. Families were asked whether, if they had the choice (which they did not), they would rather have their child receive in-class or out-of-class specialized therapies and instruction.

***Results*** Table 1 shows that half the parents preferred in-class services and half preferred out-of-class services, excluding two families who had no preference. When they were randomly assigned, about half of each group received what they preferred. After 1 year of services, the question was repeated to families. Of the two parents who initially had no preference and who were each assigned to either in-class or out-of-class, both also had no preference at the end of the year. The three parents who initially preferred in-class and who received in-class still preferred in-class at the end of the year. Of the four who initially preferred in-class but received out-of-class, two still preferred in-class, one changed his or her mind, and one had no preference by the end of the year. Of the three parents who initially preferred out-of-class and were assigned to out-of-class, all still preferred out-of-class at the end of the year. Of the four who initially preferred out-of-class but who were assigned to in-class, three still preferred out-of-class and one had changed his or her mind by the end of the year.

***Discussion*** Families' preferences at the end of the year for the most part were the same as those at the beginning of the year, showing that our hypothesis was not proved. After the initial year, we decided that if we were going to ask families about their preferences, it would be more family centered to give them what they wanted. This has been the policy in the center ever since.

Table 1.  Parent preferences after 1 year's experience with either in-class or out-of-class specialized services

| | Child's random assignment | |
|---|---|---|
| Parent preference at beginning of year | In-class | Out-of-class |
| No preference (0) | 0 | 0 |
| In-class ( + ) | + + + | + + 0 – |
| Out-of-class ( – ) | – – – + | – – – |

From McWilliam, R.A., Bailey, D.B., & Vandermaas, M. (1991, November). *Research issues in comparing in-class and out-of-class special services for young children with disabilities.* Paper presented at the International Early Childhood Conference on Children with Special Needs (sponsored by the Division for Early Childhood, CEC), St. Louis, MO.

But that is not the end of the story. In 1991, 25% of the families chose out-of-class services; but by 1993, 90% did. This suggests that 1 year might be insufficient time for families to allow experiences to shape their preferences. The implications for service delivery are that, if families are given choices about service delivery models, one should wait for 2 years to determine whether experience with in-class therapy has an impact on its acceptability.

Why would families' preferences change in 2 years? When families were given choices, they could choose which model they wanted for each type of therapy, and they were given the opportunity to change their minds about any therapy at the quarterly individualized family service plan (IFSP) reviews. It is possible that, with families' trying in-class services a little at first, they perceived its benefits and gradually increased the amount of in-class. Another possibility is that those families who had chosen out-of-class heard from those who had chosen in-class and were converted. The robustness of parents' initial preferences was surprising, but our subsequent nonempirical observations point to the need for further research on treatment acceptability as it pertains to parents' experiences with different models.

## National Survey

***Purpose*** The purpose of this study was to determine what practitioners perceive as their typical and ideal practices and what influences their choice of service delivery models (McWilliam & Bailey, 1994).

***Method*** A survey was completed by 775 early intervention practitioners (65% of the expected appropriate respondents) from the fields of occupational therapy ($n$ = 141), physical therapy ($n$ = 311), early childhood special education ($n$ = 201), and speech-language pathology ($n$ = 122). The survey consisted of three parts: The first had six ratings of integrated practice, on which respondents rated their typical and ideal practices; the second part had a rating scale, from *always out-of-class* to *always in-class,* on which respondents rated services under various conditions; and the third had room for listing advantages and disadvantages as well as demographic questions.

***Results*** The predictors consisting of 1) discipline, 2) caseload characteristics, 3) respondent's age and experience, 4) family preference for service delivery models, and 5) child characteristics accounted for 51% of the variance in typical practices and 70% in ideal practices. Hierarchical regression was used, with variables entered in the order just listed. Discipline was by far the strongest predictor in this model, with family preference being a strong predictor ($R^2$ = .27) of ideal practice. Disciplines differed on five of the six areas of integrated practice (i.e., location, presence of other children, context, goals, role). See Table 2 for means and Chapter 6 for a discussion of these areas. Only typical child initiations did not differ among disciplines; all other typical practices and all ideal practices (including initiations) did differ.

Respondents identified consultation as the major advantage of the in-class model (McWilliam & Applequist, 1993), which had been defined in the survey as consisting of collaboration with the classroom teacher. They identified intensity of instruction as the major advantage of the out-of-class model. Table 3 shows the advantages and disadvantages of each model, as identified by 20% or more of the respondents. Opportunities for generalization were identified as an advantage of the in-class model by a relatively small percentage of respondents compared to those identifying consultation. It was seen as the primary disadvantage of the out-of-class model, however, albeit by a relatively small percentage. Table 4 consists of representative statements about each model.

*Discussion* The four disciplines in center-based early intervention have quite different perspectives about integrated practices. Special educators typically use and consider ideal the most integrated services, followed by occupational therapists. Physical therapists and speech-language pathologists did not differ from each other, and they were the least likely to use integrated services. Nevertheless, on average, practitioners reported favoring relatively integrated practices, with a range of 5.57 (physical therapists) to 7.35 (special educators), on a scale from 1 (least integrated) to 9 (most integrated). Differences between typical and ideal practices were significant, showing that practitioners could benefit from training and systems change to encourage integrated therapy (McWilliam, 1992).

Distractibility was an issue for practitioners as they considered the advantages and disadvantages of the in-class and out-of-class models. We were able to code responses about distractibility as setting or child related. This suggests that part of the distractibility issue is related to how distracting the in-class model might be for practitioners, not for children. Together, the closed-ended and the open-ended sections of the questionnaire provided much-needed information on the state of practitioners' perspectives about integrated therapy.

## In-Class Versus Out-of-Class Instruction

*Purpose* Calling integrated therapy an in-class model, as we did during the national survey, revealed our hypothesis that the location itself was important in integrated services. We therefore established a study to isolate location as an independent variable. The primary question was about the extent to which location affects the acquisition and generalization of skills taught by a specialist.

*Method* Four children with developmental disabilities were chosen to participate in this study (McWilliam & Grabowski, 1993) because they had demonstrated delays in cognitive functioning. Intervention occurred in two settings: the general classroom (in-class) and a small therapy room (out-of-class). Materials consisted of a shape sequence box ("shape sorter" toy), cylinder blocks, and a shape match board. These were chosen because they

Table 2(a). Means and standard deviations for self-ratings of typical practices

| Practice | Typical practice | | | | F | Univariate comparisons[d] |
|---|---|---|---|---|---|---|
| | OT (n=141) | PT (n=311) | SE (n=201) | SL (n=122) | | |
| Location (1 = always out of classroom, 9 = always in classroom | 5.21 (2.17) | 4.37 (2.11) | 7.25 (1.62) | 4.80 (2.60) | 80.29[c] | SE vs. OT<br>SE vs. SL<br>SE vs. PT<br>OT vs. PT |
| Presence of other children (1 = never, 9 = always | 6.02 (2.02) | 5.31 (2.07) | 7.01 (2.02) | 5.45 (2.34) | 29.08[c] | SE vs. OT<br>SE vs. SL<br>SE vs. PT<br>OT vs. PT |
| Context (1 = always separate from classroom routines, 9 = always within classroom routines) | 5.11 (2.09) | 4.35 (2.03) | 7.22 (1.58) | 4.86 (2.42) | 86.99[c] | SE vs. OT<br>SE vs. SL<br>SE vs. PT<br>OT vs. PT |

| | | | | | F | |
|---|---|---|---|---|---|---|
| Initiations (1 = always adult-initiated, 9 = always child-initiated) | 4.92 (1.72) | 4.93 (1.54) | 5.03 (1.59) | 4.75 (1.74) | 0.78 | SE vs. PT |
| Goals (1 = prerequisites only, 9 = immediately useful only) | 6.08 (1.70) | 6.16 (1.65) | 6.97 (1.42) | 6.59 (1.57) | 13.37[c] | SE vs. PT<br>SE vs. OT<br>SL vs. OT |
| Role (1 = direct service only, 9 = consultant only) | 4.42 (1.46) | 4.16 (1.49) | 4.57[a] (1.92) | 3.79 (1.20) | 5.07[b] | SE vs. SL<br>OT vs. SL |
| Overall mean | 5.29 (1.20) | 4.88 (1.15) | 6.60 (1.06) | 5.08 (1.50) | 88.94[c] | SE vs. OT<br>SE vs. PT<br>SE vs. SL<br>OT vs. PT |

From McWilliam, R.A., & Bailey, D.B., Jr. (1994). Predictors of service-delivery models in center-based early intervention. *Exceptional Children, 61*, 65–66; reprinted by permission.

[a]Only 56 special educators answered this question.
[b]$p < .01$.
[c]$p < .001$.
[d]$p < .05$.
OT, occupational therapy; PT, physical therapy; SE, special education; SL, speech-language.

Table 2(b). Means and standard deviations for self-ratings of ideal practices

| Practice | OT (n = 141) | PT (n = 311) | Ideal practice SE (n = 201) | SL (n = 122) | F | Univariate comparisons[c] |
|---|---|---|---|---|---|---|
| Location | 5.89 (1.76) | 5.30 (1.83) | 7.34 (1.33) | 5.43 (2.02) | 60.73[b] | SE vs. OT<br>SE vs. SL<br>SE vs. PT<br>OT vs. PT |
| Presence of other children | 5.71 (1.96) | 5.09 (1.97) | 7.41 (1.38) | 5.34 (2.03) | 67.89[b] | SE vs. OT<br>SE vs. SL<br>SE vs. PT<br>OT vs. PT |
| Context | 6.14 (1.79) | 5.61 (2.01) | 7.78 (1.36) | 5.98 (2.07) | 59.21[b] | SE vs. OT<br>SE vs. SL<br>SE vs. PT<br>OT vs. PT |
| Initiations | 5.88 (1.66) | 5.83 (1.53) | 6.65 (1.39) | 5.75 (1.69) | 14.03[b] | SE vs. OT<br>SE vs. PT<br>SE vs. SL |

| | | | | | | |
|---|---|---|---|---|---|---|
| Goals | 6.79 (1.88) | 6.78 (1.68) | 7.90 (1.90) | 7.31 (1.59) | 23.09[b] | SE vs. PT<br>SE vs. OT<br>SE vs. SL<br>SL vs. OT<br>SL vs. PT |
| Role | 5.05 (1.35) | 4.82 (1.16) | 5.98[a] (1.54) | 4.65 (1.15) | 16.14[b] | SE vs. OT<br>SE vs. PT<br>SE vs. SL |
| Overall mean | 5.91 (1.20) | 5.57 (1.19) | 7.35 (0.98) | 5.78 (1.34) | 104.71[b] | SE vs. OT<br>SE vs. SL<br>SE vs. PT<br>OT vs. PT |

From McWilliam, R.A., & Bailey, D.B., Jr. (1994). Predictors of service-delivery models in center-based early intervention. *Exceptional Children, 61,* 65–66; reprinted by permission.

[a]Only 54 special educators answered this question.

[b]$p < .001$.

[c]$p < .05$.

OT, occupational therapy; PT, physical therapy; SE, special education; SL, speech-language.

Table 2(c). Means and standard deviations for self-ratings: Difference scores

| | Difference scores | | | | | |
| Practice | OT (n = 141) | PT (n = 311) | SE (n = 201) | SL (n = 122) | F | Univariate comparisons[c] |
| --- | --- | --- | --- | --- | --- | --- |
| Location | 0.68 (1.57) | 0.93 (1.80) | 0.07 (1.62) | 0.63 (1.90) | 10.12[b] | SE vs. OT<br>SE vs. PT<br>SE vs. SL |
| Presence of other children | −0.31 (1.79) | −0.23 (1.96) | 0.36 (1.79) | −0.09 (1.75) | 5.01[a] | SE vs. PT<br>SE vs. OT |
| Context | 1.01 (1.58) | 1.26 (2.00) | .56 (1.46) | 1.12 (1.95) | 6.48[c] | SE vs. SL<br>SE vs. PT |
| Initiations | 0.94 (1.16) | 0.89 (1.29) | 1.60 (1.34) | 0.97 (1.30) | 13.99[c] | SE vs. OT<br>SE vs. PT<br>SE vs. SL |
| Goals | 0.72 (1.25) | 0.63 (1.35) | 0.94 (1.17) | 0.73 (1.11) | 2.50 | SE vs. PT |
| Role | 0.63 (1.23) | 0.66 (1.45) | 1.31 (1.65) | 0.85 (1.17) | 4.03[b] | SE vs. OT<br>SE vs. PT |
| Overall mean | 0.62 (1.20) | 0.69 (1.19) | 0.75 (0.98) | 0.69 (1.34) | .50 | |

From McWilliam, R.A., & Bailey, D.B., Jr. (1994). Predictors of service-delivery models in center-based early intervention. *Exceptional Children, 61,* 65–66; reprinted by permission.

[a]$p < .01$.
[b]$p < .001$.
[c]$p < .05$.

OT, occupational therapy; PT, physical therapy; SE, special education; SL, speech-language.

Table 3. Perceived advantages and disadvantages of each model across disciplines

| In-class model | | Out-of-class model | |
|---|---|---|---|
| Advantages | Disadvantages | Advantages | Disadvantages |
| Consultation (42%) | Setting distractions (55%) | Intensity of instruction (44%) | Poor generalization |
| Normalized activities (34%) | Child's distractibility (30%) | Minimized distractions (38%) | Less consultation (22%) |
| Teacher follow-through (21%) | Lack of equipment (24%) | Good for distractible children (25%) | Teacher follow-through (22%) |
| Normal setting (23%) | | Equipment/space (23%) | |
| Space (21%) | | | |
| Peer models (26%) | | | |
| Access to peers (20%) | | | |
| Generalization (20%) | | | |

From McWilliam, R.A., & Applequist, K. (1993, February). *National survey of four disciplines.* Paper presented at the annual conference of the North Carolina Federation of the Council for Exceptional Children, Greensboro, NC.

*Note:* Percentages in parentheses indicate the percentage of all comments.

1) had multiple components (a necessity for measuring progress), 2) required problem-solving and cognitive skills, and 3) were unfamiliar to the children before the study. An alternating treatments design was used because of its applicability to comparison studies (Wolery, Bailey, & Sugai, 1988); the interventionist also took qualitative field notes. Materials and settings were counterbalanced across children to control for possible effects on the outcome. Intervention consisted of a demonstration of the completed task, a prompt to begin, a test of unassisted performance, and forward-chaining instruction using pointing, and, when necessary, hand-over-hand assistance. Generalization probes were conducted by having the classroom teacher present the task to the child with a controlling prompt; she gave praise for correctly placed pieces, but no instruction. The independent variable was location, with in-class instruction defined as occurring in the general classroom, with a minimum of two other children present, and with general teachers in the classroom. Out-of-class instruction was defined as occurring in the therapy room, with no other children or general teachers present. Quantitative data sources were the number of pieces placed correctly and independently, and qualitative sources were the narrative reports of each session. Reliability was computed for 33 (19%) sessions; interobserver agreement on occurrence was 88%, on nonoccurrence was 92%, and κ was .77. Procedural reliability (i.e., treatment integrity) was calculated as the percentage of steps on procedural checklists

Table 4. Representative statements about each model

| In-class model | | Out-of-class model | |
| --- | --- | --- | --- |
| Advantages | Disadvantages | Advantages | Disadvantages |
| Work closely with teacher, aides, and other professionals to improve carryover and teach techniques that can be used throughout activities | Crowded and distractible conditions | Greater ability to focus on a specific activity | Carryover of functional skills may not be seen outside the therapy environment |
| Can incorporate therapy into educationally relevant activities | Child may be distracted and have difficulty attending to the instruction | Increased attentiveness with decreased distraction | We become "phantom therapists"; classroom staff do not get understanding of what we do or what our role is in educational setting |

completed. Procedural reliability on instructional steps ranged from 12% (on the step "invite child to play") to 82% (on the step "child correct followed by adult next item"). Independent variable procedural reliability (in- versus out-of-class) was 100%.

*Results* As seen in Figure 1, no difference in acquisition was found between tasks taught in class and those taught out of class. Cylinder toys were easier to master than the shape sorter for three of the four children. In assessing task reversal effects, we found that the nature of the task had more of an effect than location did. Generalization was not affected by where the task had been taught. Transfer was easier for the cylinder task than for the shape sorter, perhaps masking location effects.

Narrative field notes revealed three major themes. First, a constraint of the procedures was the children having to repeat similar steps within a session and the same task day after day; they became bored and uncooperative. Second, classroom peers were involved at different levels during in-class sessions and generalization probes, so the variability of peer presence was not systematically controlled. Third, general teachers seemed to have a significant impact on the success of in-class instruction (i.e., it was easier to teach in some teachers' classrooms than in others') and nonexperimental intervention (i.e., securing children's cooperation outside the prescribed procedures).

*Discussion* Because there was no difference between in-class and out-of-class instruction on acquisition or generalization, we concluded that

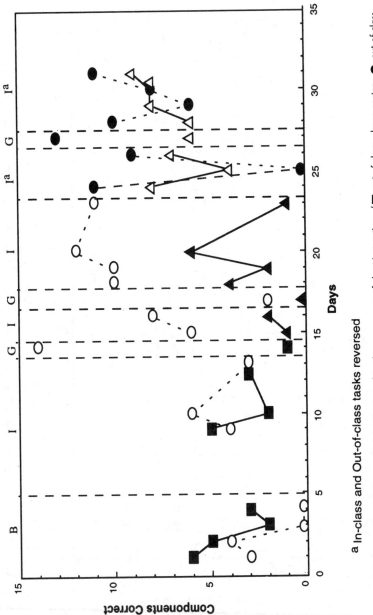

## a In-class and Out-of-class tasks reversed

Figure 1(a). Bonnie's acquisition and generalization of in-class versus out-of-class instruction. (■ out-of-class, shape sorter; ● out-of-class, cylinders; ○ in-class, cylinders; ▲ out-of-class, puzzle; △ in-class, puzzle.)

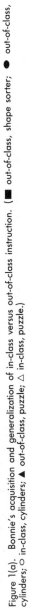

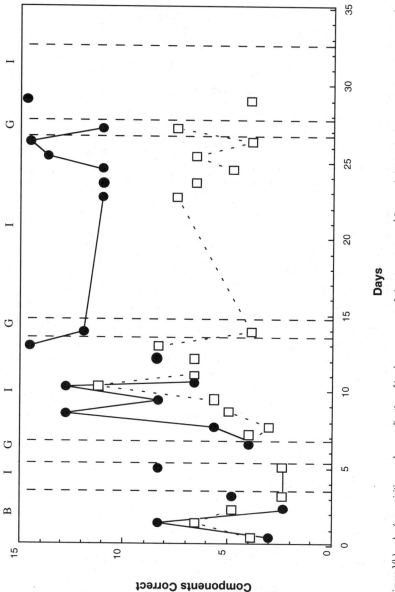

Figure 1(b). Jan's acquisition and generalization of in-class versus out-of-class instruction. ( ● out-of-class, cylinders; ■ in-class, shape sorter.)

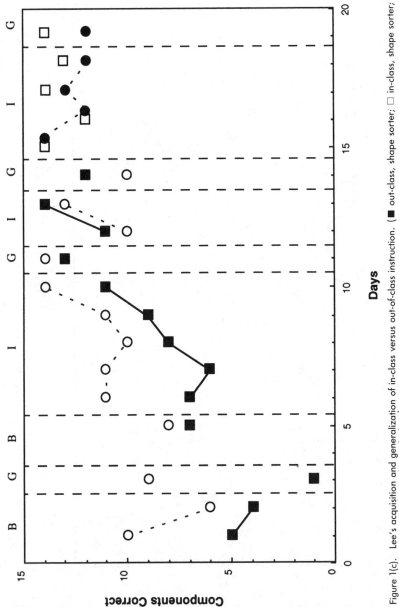

Figure 1(c). Lee's acquisition and generalization of in-class versus out-of-class instruction. (■ out-class, shape sorter; □ in-class, shape sorter; ● out-of-class, cylinders; ○ in-class, cylinders.)

85

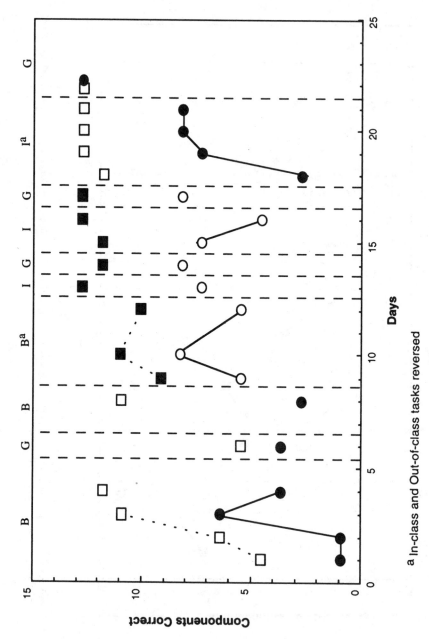

<sup>a</sup> In-class and Out-of-class tasks reversed

Figure 1(d). Ted's acquisition and generalization of in-class versus out-of-class instruction. (● out-of-class, cylinders; ○ in-class, cylinders; ■ out-of-class, shape sorter; □ in-class, shape sorter.)

86

interventionists can either stay with the more familiar model or move to a more consultative and transdisciplinary model. Experiences conducting this study suggested that, to make either in-class or out-of-class instruction successful, the teacher needs to vary the tasks, use responsive teaching, and pay attention to reinforcers. To make in-class instruction successful, the specialist needs to integrate instruction with ongoing routines, to form a partnership with the teacher, to combine group activities with naturally occurring private time with the child, and to monitor peer involvement.

### Integrated Versus Pull-Out Social Skills Intervention

***Purpose*** This study was conducted to provide some data-based information on the relative efficacy of two approaches a clinician might consider: integrated therapy and pull-out therapy (McWilliam & Spencer, 1993). We used a mixed-method research design to meet the four objectives of the study: 1) to compare the generalization effects of integrated therapy and pull-out therapy, 2) to compare the teachers' use of strategies the clinicians had recommended following integrated or pull-out therapy, 3) to capture the intentions and impressions of student clinicians and classroom teachers, and 4) to discover the effects on these professionals of using integrated therapy.

***Method*** Three children already receiving speech-language pathology services participated in this study consisting of a single-subject design in combination with qualitative methods. The children were observed in their classrooms, which were different for each child. In each of these classes there was one additional child with disabilities. Pull-out therapy sessions occurred in a therapy room furnished like a classroom. An adapted alternating treatments design (Wolery et al., 1988) was used, comparing integrated therapy with pull-out therapy. With the supervising speech-language pathologist in the child care center, we selected target behaviors consistent with each subject's IFSP. The children received speech-language therapy twice a week. For each child, 60-minute data collection sessions were conducted 2 days a week during general classroom activities (i.e., not during therapy times). The therapy sessions were conducted by two graduate students in speech-language pathology. Defining adult behaviors (i.e., operational definitions) for integrated therapy are contained in the Integrated Therapy Checklist (Figure 2) and the Teacher Participation Checklist (Figure 3).

The critical factors in *integrated therapy* were 1) that therapy had to occur in the classroom, 2) that the clinician and teacher collaborated during therapy time, and 3) that therapy occurred in the context of whatever classroom routine was occurring. *Pull-out therapy* was operationally defined as intervention by a specialist occurring outside the classroom and apart from other children; one other child could be involved for goals specifying interactions with peers. The most important criterion was to limit consultation with the teacher. Measures of treatment integrity showed that the two types of therapy were undertaken as

---

INTEGRATED THERAPY CHECKLIST

---

Target Child: _____     Date: _____

Did the specialist                                          ✓ Yes    X No     NA

1.   Communicate with you throughout the session (e.g., ask or tell you before he or she did anything with the child)?                                        _____

2.   Fit into the ongoing classroom routine or arrange with you beforehand to do otherwise?             _____

3.   Ask you or make recommendations about how you interact with the child (i.e., things you can do with the child)?                                                    _____

4.   Ask you how you feel about the suggestions she's made (e.g., "Are you OK with this idea?")?        _____

5.   Ask you or make recommendations about the classroom routines?                                      _____

6.   Involve or encourage you to involve the other children in carrying out the interventions?          _____

7.   Use discretion in talking about the child in front of the child or other people?                   _____

8.*  Assess the child's performance (by asking you, observing the child, or "testing" the child herself)?  _____

9.*  Assess how well the interventions are working (by asking or observing you)?                          _____

10.* Experiment or have you experiment with different interventions?                                     _____

11.* Make recommendations?                             _____

12.  Make at least one positive statement about what you are doing?                                      _____

*Optional integrated therapy functions

Figure 2.  Integrated therapy checklist developed by the Special Services Research Project at Frank Porter Graham Child Development Center, University of North Carolina at Chapel Hill.

described. For the qualitative component, we interviewed both clinicians and the three teachers, using a focused interview approach. Interrater agreement on the observations was 86%–99% ($\kappa = .38–.74$).

**Results**   Visual analysis is used to interpret the data. Figures 4–6 show that, in the generalization settings, more integrated therapy behaviors were displayed than were pull-out behaviors (i.e., more target behaviors were displayed for the integrated goals than for the pull-out goals). We were, however, looking for diverging or converging trends, which would indicate the relative efficacy of one intervention compared to the other. Diverging trends would consist of increasing differences between the two conditions, over time, and converging trends would consist of decreasing differences. Such trends were not apparent.

TEACHER PARTICIPATION CHECKLIST

Teacher's Name: _____     Child's Name: _____

Date: _____     Your Name: _____

Did the specialist                                          ✓ Yes    X No      NA

1.  Welcome you to the classroom (speak to you soon
    after you entered)?                                          _____

2.  Involve you in the activity in which the child is
    engaged?                                                     _____

3.  Provide information to ask questions?                        _____

4.  Try out or demonstrate interventions during the
    session?                                                     _____

5.  Thank you at the end of the session?                         _____

Figure 3.   Teacher participation checklist developed by the Special Services Research Project at Frank Porter Graham Child Development Center, University of North Carolina at Chapel Hill.

Figures 7–9 show that more teacher follow-through occurred for the integrated therapy goal of one of the children (Art), no difference between conditions in follow-through occurred with another child (Tanesha), and a pattern of initial benefits for the integrated therapy goal occurred for the third child (Timothy). Again, there was no evidence of the relative efficacy over time of one model compared to the other. Children's behavior frequencies generally paralleled teachers' use of strategies; this is most clearly seen in the two peaks in Tanesha's generalizations (Days 2 and 6–8) accompanied by the two peaks in her teacher's use of the strategies (Days 2 and 6) and in the initial peak in Timothy's integrated therapy goal generalization (Day 3) accompanied by the initial peak in his teacher's use of strategies for his integrated therapy goal (Days 3–4).

***Discussion***   Although the objective measures of child and teacher behavior indicated little difference over time between integrated and pull-out therapy, the teachers and clinicians perceived advantages of the integrated therapy model. The parallel patterns of teachers' follow-through and children's target behaviors at the beginning of the study suggest that teachers were willing to try a new idea and that children responded to teacher interventions.

Why did teachers find it hard to keep working on the goals? First, the single-subject data suggest that the improvement may have been too subtle to reinforce the teachers. Second, the qualitative data suggest that the positive social reinforcement from the clinicians and the shared burden of working on difficult behaviors may have indicated to the teachers that they were doing as well as could be expected. It might be argued that the teachers were not invested enough in the goals, because the goals were chosen by the specialists and researchers.

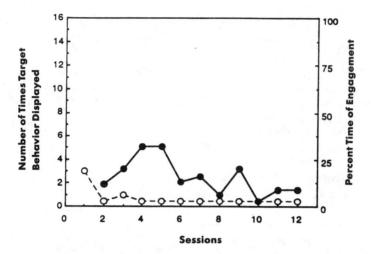

Figure 4.  Art's performance of target behaviors during nontherapy times. (● integrated [engagement]; ○ pull-out [imitation].)

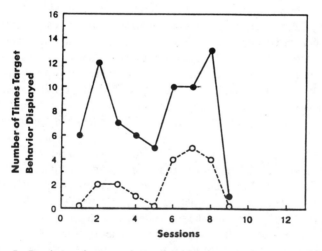

Figure 5.  Tanesha's performance of target behaviors during nontherapy times. (● integrated [language]; ○ pull-out (cooperative].)

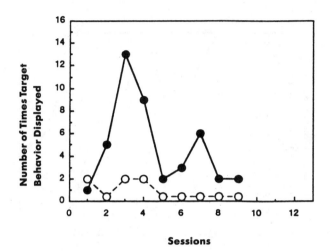

Figure 6. Timothy's performance of target behaviors during nontherapy times. (● integrated [cooperative play]; ○ pull-out [language].)

The interview data, however, do not support this notion; all three teachers expressed the importance of these goals for the children. Furthermore, the goals were taken from more general goals on the children's IFSPs, which the teachers were involved in formulating. Therefore, it is possible that a child's subtle progress and teachers' feelings about meeting expectations accounted for teachers' lack of persistence with the goals. Conclusions from this study were that 1) teachers seldom attend to the target goals during nontherapy time, 2) children do not display the target skills in nontherapy times, 3) teachers and therapists prefer integrated to pull-out services for the most part, and 4) therapists would like to use a combination of approaches.

## Communicative Interactions During Therapy

**Purpose**  Roberts, Prizant, and McWilliam (1995) compared the communicative interactions between children with disabilities and their speech-language pathologist during in-class and out-of-class therapy sessions.

**Method**  Fifteen children with disabilities who attended the Frank Porter Graham Family and Child Care Program participated in the study. Children ranged in age from 1 to 4 years of age, had mild or moderate cognitive and developmental delays, and represented a range of developmental disabilities. Children were matched in pairs by their age and developmental profile. One member of each pair was then randomly assigned to either in-class or out-of-class special services. Children received two 25-minute sessions of speech-language therapy in either in-class or out-of-class sessions. After children had received therapy for 3 months in either the in-class or out-of-class therapy

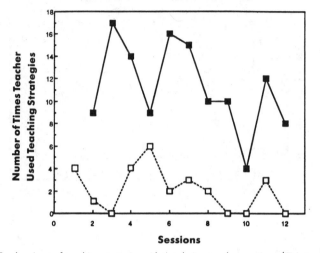

Figure 7. Teachers' use of teaching strategies with Art during nontherapy times. (■ integrated [engagement]; □ pull-out [imitation].)

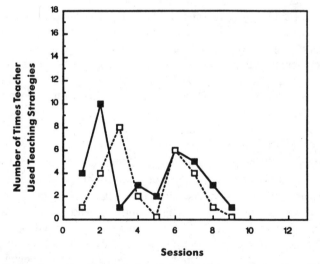

Figure 8. Teachers' use of teaching strategies with Tanesha during nontherapy times. (■ integrated [language]; □ pull-out [cooperative play].)

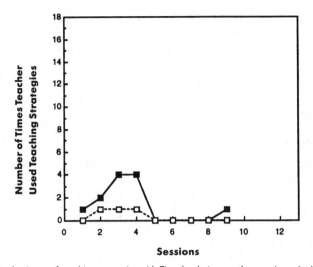

Figure 9. Teacher's use of teaching strategies with Timothy during nontherapy times. (■ integrated [cooperative play]; □ pull-out [language].)

model, videotapes were made of the therapy sessions. Two consecutive speech-language therapy sessions were taped for each child. Ten minutes from each tape for a total of 20 minutes were transcribed following the conventions in the computer program Systematic Analysis of Language Transcripts (SALT). Videotapes were reviewed for turn type, the function of communication, and the effect of communication.

**Results** Both the clinicians and children differed in the number of turns and types of turns they used during in-class and out-of-class sessions. The children and clinicians took more turns during the out-of-class therapy sessions compared with in-class sessions. Clinicians responded more often during out-of-class sessions and initiated more during in-class sessions. In contrast, children responded more often during in-class sessions and initiated more during out-of-class sessions. Differences also occurred in the children's use of language for joint attention, using more comments and requests for information during out-of-class sessions than during in-class sessions.

**Discussion** This study showed that the rate of interaction between child and specialist is, not surprisingly, higher in a one-on-one situation. It does not tell us, however, about the child's rate of interaction with other people, such as peers and classroom teachers. Specialists work at maintaining a high interaction rate, as seen in their frequent responses and initiations. Children's relatively high response rates during in-class sessions may be a reflection of the increased stimulation in classrooms compared with therapy rooms. Their relatively high initiation rates during out-of-class sessions, however, suggest that classrooms provide fewer opportunities for initiations than do traditional therapy situations. A further advantage of out-of-class sessions is that children use more comments and requests for information, presumably in part as responses to specialists' initiations. Therefore, out-of-class sessions have the advantage of giving the specialist an opportunity to create a more intensively interactive environment than that afforded by the classroom. For interventions requiring this level of intensity, out-of-class sessions are advantageous.

### Therapy Generalization Study

*Purpose* The Therapy Generalization Study (McWilliam & Scarborough, 1994) was undertaken to determine the extent to which 1) children transfer skills addressed in therapy to nontherapy situations and 2) teachers implement recommended facilitative techniques in the classroom.

*Method* Twenty-two children in five programs were observed during occupational therapy ($n = 9$), physical therapy ($n = 16$), and speech-language pathology ($n = 18$). Six sessions of each type of therapy were conducted in the classroom, and all other sessions were conducted out of the classroom. The therapist's style was rated during the session; a mean rating of the therapist's sensitivity, responsiveness, and elaborativeness constituted one score (for style), and the rating of the therapist's encouragement constituted the other. Children were then videotaped in the classroom, usually within 1 day of the therapy session; eight 10-minute observations were made throughout the day. Each child's generalization (i.e., classroom) sessions were coded for the frequency with which the child displayed the target behaviors and the frequency with which the teacher displayed facilitative techniques directly related to the child's target behaviors. The mean of each child's eight classroom observations following each type of therapy was used as the unit of analysis. This resulted in 32 observations nested within each child; because children had different amounts of therapies (6 received one type of therapy, 10 received two therapies, and 6 received all three types of therapy), Statistical Application Systems (SAS) mixed-models procedures for unbalanced data sets were used in analyses. The nested design was considered appropriate, despite theoretical lack of independence among the units of analysis, because multiple observations within subjects were found to be independent ($p < .0001$).

*Results* Mean frequencies of child generalization by type of therapy and location are shown in Table 5. The mixed-model procedure, with therapist's style, therapist's encouragement, teacher frequency of implementing facilitation strategies, type of therapy, location, and Type of Therapy × Location in the model, represent 45% of the variance in child generalization frequencies. This $R^2$ maximizes the explained variance; however, the Herzberg formula for estimating the measure of association shows that the model explains 17% of the unbiased variance (as described by Snyder & Lawson, 1994). The therapist's encouragement had a large effect on generalization, $F(1,27) = $

Table 5.  Mean frequencies of child generalization[a] by type of therapy and location

| Location | Therapy type[b] | N | Mean | Standard deviation |
|---|---|---|---|---|
| In-class | OT | 6 | 21.73 | 9.52 |
| | PT | 6 | 14.12 | 12.59 |
| | SLP | 6 | 14.86 | 25.42 |
| Out-of-class | OT | 3 | 8.56 | 1.68 |
| | PT | 10 | 5.40 | 5.57 |
| | SLP | 12 | 7.23 | 6.05 |

[a]Average frequency of generalized behaviors over 80 minutes, computed by dividing the total frequency by the number of target behaviors across all eight 10-minute observations. This controlled for differing numbers of target behavior among children.
[b]OT = occupational therapy; PT = physical therapy; SLP = speech-language pathology.

$6.12, p = .02, d = .95$). (Cohen's $d$ index measures the difference between two means in terms of their common standard deviation units [Ottenbacher, 1992].) Teacher use of facilitation strategies had a medium effect, $F(1,27) = 2.35, p = .14, d = .59$, and type of therapy, $F(2,27) = 2.89, p = .07, f = .12$, and location, $F(1,27) = 1.38, p = .25, d = .45$, had small effects. (Cohen's $f$ index gauges the relationship between the standard deviation of multiple group means and the common within-group standard deviation [Ottenbacher, 1992].) Contrast statement results consisted of occupational therapy resulting in more generalization than the other two types of therapy following both in-class and out-of-class therapy; large effects were found for the occupational therapy versus speech-language pathology contrast following in-class therapy, $F(1,27) = 6.87, p = .01, d = 1.01$. Physical therapy resulted in more generalization than speech-language pathology following in-class therapy. The only in-class versus out-of-class result by discipline was a medium effect for physical therapy, $F(1,27) = 3.09, p = .09, d = .68$, in which in-class therapy resulted in higher generalization than did out-of-class therapy. The frequency of teachers' use of facilitation strategies had no effect on generalization.

*Discussion*  This study shows that the therapist's style, especially encouragement, is even more important than the type of therapy or location. Examination of parameter estimates showed that, for every increase of 1 point on the 5-point rating scale, child-generalized behaviors would increase by 5 over the course of the 80 minutes of observation. Of the three types of therapy, only the location of physical therapy appears to have an impact on generalization, with in-class therapy being more successful than out-of-class therapy. Occupational therapy generally produced more generalization than other therapy types, regardless of location. The failure of teacher facilitation to account for any of the variance in generalization can be interpreted as disturbing. One explanation for this finding might be that the frequency of teacher facilitation is so low (3.76 in 80 minutes following in-class therapy, 5.12

following out-of-class therapy) that any beneficial effects would not be discerned. Examination of the parameter estimates shows that it would take 10 teacher facilitations to result in 1 child generalization. Low teacher facilitation frequencies are explained, in part, by the fact that teachers might not have known what the expected facilitation strategies were. This study, therefore, has serious implications for the manner in which therapists provide therapy, the location in which physical therapy, especially, is provided, and the amount of teacher facilitation necessary to help children generalize skills addressed in therapy.

### Field-Based Study of Goal Attainment

*Purpose*   This study was undertaken to determine the effects of different models of service delivery on children's IFSP and IEP goals (McWilliam, Scarborough, & Chaudhary, 1995).

*Method*   Eighty children with disabilities from seven sites were followed for up to 2 years. For each therapy or consultative special education session, the specialist was instructed to complete the Specialists Documentation Form (see Figure 1 in Chapter 7), which recorded the therapy model used predominantly (i.e., more than 50% of the session time) in that session, the goals addressed, and the length of the session. Approximately every 8 weeks, parents, classroom teachers, and specialists completed the Therapy Goals Information Form (see Figure 2 in Chapter 7), which consisted of two rating scales for selected IFSP and IEP goals. The rating scales (1–5) measured the frequency and independence with which the child displayed each target goal. Children were tested with the Battelle Developmental Inventory (BDI) at the beginning of the study, at midpoint, and at the end of the study. Data analyses to date have consisted of analyses of variance with the six models of service delivery, five of the sites (two sites had too few data for analysis), and BDI-computed deviation quotients in the model. After removal of the two sites, 71 participants remained in the study for analysis.

*Results*   Preliminary results show that the six models, site, and BDI accounted for 36% of the variance in frequency ratings and 33% of the variance in independence ratings. Table 6 shows the mean percentage of sessions using the six models and mean ratings of goal attainment, by site. After using a Bonferroni correction (dividing $p = .05$ by the number of statistical tests), only one significant finding emerged: The more the consultation model was used, in combination with the effects of site, the less frequently the behaviors were rated to occur, $F(5,172) = 3.95$, $p = .004$. The Consultation Model 6 × Site interaction effect was explained by Site A (see Table 6), in which consultation was used an average of only 5% of the time ($SD = 3.66$) per child; the other sites used this model even more rarely. In an analysis of congruence among raters across all measures of frequency and independence, statistically significant differences were found for both raters and sites. Contrast results showed that teachers rated frequency and independence significantly lower than did families (high scores mean lower frequency and less independence); Site E's

Table 6. Mean percentage of sessions using the six models per child, mean ratings of goal attainment, and mean Battelle quotients, by site (with standard deviations)

| Model | Sites | | | | | |
| --- | --- | --- | --- | --- | --- | --- |
| | A (N = 19) | B (N = 10) | C (N = 13) | D (N = 22) | E (N = 7) | All sites (N = 71) |
| Individual pull-out | 7 (8) | 2 (3) | 69 (33) | 69 (21) | 33 (31) | 39 (47) |
| Small group pull-out | 1 (2) | 0 (1) | 2 (4) | 13 (18) | 1 (2) | 5 (11) |
| One-on-one classroom | 8 (13) | 13 (11) | 20 (33) | 12 (20) | 8 (7) | 12 (20) |
| Group activity | 12 (7) | 51 (27) | 0 (0) | 1 (1) | 34 (27) | 14 (22) |
| Individualized during routines | 68 (15) | 33 (27) | 5 (9) | 7 (8) | 21 (16) | 28 (30) |
| Consultation | 5 (5) | 0 (1) | 3 (6) | 0 (0) | 3 (7) | 2 (5) |
| Frequency[a] | 2.59 (0.39) | 2.74 (0.18) | 2.71 (0.26) | 2.62 (0.36) | 2.27 (0.39) | 2.61 (0.35) |
| Independence[b] | 2.75 (0.39) | 2.91 (0.24) | 2.95 (0.49) | 2.69 (0.35) | 2.41 (0.41) | 2.75 (0.40) |
| Battelle quotient[c] | 62.19 (21.16) | 59.21 (21.79) | 54.21 (17.64) | 56.57 (24.56) | 64.83 (25.16) | 58.86 (21.79) |

[a]Ratings from 1 = All of the time to 5 = Never.
[b]Ratings from 1 = With no help to 5 = Needs total assistance.
[c]Computed as developmental age-to-chronological age ratio × 100 to avoid lowest possible score of 65 given in scoring manual.

frequency ratings were significantly lower (i.e., lower frequency) than other sites'; Site E's independence ratings were lower than those of Sites A, B, and C; and Site D's independence ratings were lower than Site C's.

***Discussion***   No pattern linking models and goal attainment could be found. The one significant finding, associating consultation (in interaction with site) with frequency, has little clinical significance because consultation occurred in only 5% of the sessions and the frequency score was not relatively high for Site A. Higher teacher ratings (i.e., behaviors occurring less often and with less independence) than family ratings of goal attainment suggest that families have more opportunity to see the target skills displayed or teachers use stricter criteria in their ratings. Low ratings for children in Site E are probably an artifact of the setting regardless of service delivery model, because the service delivery models were fairly evenly distributed among individual pull-out, group activity, and individualized during routine. Finally, children's developmental levels, as measured by the overall Battelle quotient, does not appear to influence goal attainment. This suggests that goals were developmentally appropriate, with more modest goals for children with more severe disabilities and more ambitious goals for higher functioning children. In summary, this study, at least in the preliminary stages of data analysis, appears to support findings from other studies showing that models of service delivery have little effect on child gains and progress.

## Focus Groups

***Purpose***   A focus group study (McWilliam, Young, & Harville, 1995) was conducted to determine the impact of shortages of specialized therapists on services. Shortages among medical allied health practitioners have been documented by Yoder, Coleman, and Gallagher (1990).

***Method***   Focus group participants consisted of early intervention therapists (e.g., occupational and physical therapists, speech-language pathologists), early intervention nontherapist professionals (e.g., home visitors, educators), mothers of children with disabilities, and administrators of early intervention (birth–5) programs. They were selected purposively to represent different agencies, geographic regions of North Carolina, and demographic regions (urban, suburban, and rural) from lists of nominations by members of the Children and Families Committee of the North Carolina Interagency Coordinating Council. Each group of participants was involved in its own focus group to encourage open discussion. The discussion was prompted by open-ended questions as well as statements and situations to which respondents could react. Discussions were audio- and videotaped and then transcribed. Transcriptions were analyzed using standard qualitative methods for the treatment of word data. Themes were generated, cross-researcher triangulation was checked, and member checks were used for validity verification.

*Results*   Table 7 shows the major themes emerging from the four focus groups.

*Discussion*   Across focus groups, it was apparent that real or perceived policies influenced how specialized therapies were provided. For example, although some professionals believed that Medicaid policies do not allow reimbursement for consultation, others believed that they do. Across groups, it was apparent that too little therapist time exists for 1) the number of children whose families and programs want some or more therapy and 2) the number of roles that therapists are expected to play (e.g., direct therapist, consultant,

Table 7.   Major themes emerging from the four focus groups

| Members | Major themes |
|---|---|
| Therapists | 1. Administrative and reimbursement policy constraints |
| | 2. Eligibility formulas a problem |
| | 3. Paradigm shifting from working with children to working with adults |
| | 4. Spread too thinly; caseloads too high |
| | 5. Shortage of pediatrically trained therapists |
| | 6. Value of some highly specialized treatments controversial |
| Early intervention nontherapist professionals | 1. Like working as a team; do not like not working as a team |
| | 2. See value in two-way learning |
| | 3. Shortage of pediatrically trained therapists |
| | 4. Therapy decisions based on diagnosis, not on need |
| | 5. Influence of DEC and MD recommendations |
| | 6. Shortage: Cannot meet IFSP/IEP requirements |
| | 7. Assistants are vital |
| Families | 1. More is better—in early years only (shortage) |
| | 2. Split in direct versus indirect |
| | 3. See value of indirect but do not want to give up direct (time) |
| | 4. Influence of DEC and MD recommendations |
| Administrators | 1. Therapies a priority; more is better |
| | 2. Cost is a problem, especially at contract rates |
| | 3. Shortage: Caseloads too high ("We can't make a silk purse out of a sow's ear, which is what [we] special ed administrators do") |
| | 4. Shortage: Long gaps during recruitment |
| | 5. Money wasted on undergraduate SLP programs |
| | 6. Therapy decisions based on diagnosis, even though ecology understood to be important |
| | 7. Influence of DEC and MD recommendations |
| | 8. Home health policies a problem (e.g., must receive two therapies, sessions must be 1 hour long) |
| | 9. Assistants provide most of direct services |

DEC, Developmental Education Center; IEP, individualized education program; IFSP, individualized family services plan; MD, medical doctor; SLP, speech-language pathology.

team member, evaluator). Therapists and nontherapists recognized the need to work together, but also pointed to difficulties in role release and role acceptance. Across groups, decisions about who gets therapy and how much appears to be based on an atheoretical basis: diagnosis, division of time available by the number of caseloads, and local custom seem to dictate which children receive differential amounts of different therapies. Ecological factors such as the family's participation, family resources, or classroom quality are rarely considered. Professionals conducting assessments, doctors, and to some extent other parents are influential over how much therapy is provided; families are especially, but not exclusively, susceptible to the belief that more is better. Assistants, especially certified occupational therapy assistants and physical therapy assistants, are much more involved in direct services than anticipated. Finally, the cost of providing specialized therapies inhibited hiring therapists as staff members and securing enough therapy time to meet expectations. When they made calculations during the focus group, administrators were surprised to realize that they were paying early childhood special educators per hour about 25% of therapists' contract fees. It appears, therefore, that improvements are sorely needed in the way specialized therapies are provided and that these improvements must come from training programs, policy makers and enforcers, and practitioners themselves.

## CONCLUSIONS

Research on service delivery models shows, in general, that in-class and integrated approaches have a negligible to weakly positive effect on children's progress or generalization compared with out-of-class and segregated approaches. Positive effects have been reported, however, for practitioners' perceptions (e.g., Cole et al., 1989). Location alone does not seem to be the issue, as shown in the McWilliam and Grabowski (1993) study. Opportunities for collaboration among professionals, regardless of immediate effectiveness with children, seem to be important benefits of an integrated approach (McWilliam & Spencer, 1993). The long-term benefits of therapy provided through different models of service delivery have yet to be established. Further analysis of the field-based longitudinal study described earlier (McWilliam, Scarborough, & Chaudhary, 1995) may shed light on this issue, but clearly more research is needed.

In the absence of conclusive findings for one approach over another, we can be guided by related, recommended practices. Principles of normalization (Bailey & McWilliam, 1991), inclusion (Giangreco, Cloninger, & Iverson, 1993), developmentally appropriate practice (National Association for the Education of Young Children, 1991), individualization (Wolery, 1991), and collaboration (Bickel & Hattrup, 1995) all suggest that integrated services are preferable to segregated services. Although the research does not overwhelmingly support this suggestion, neither does it support segregated services. Until conclusive evidence is found to support pull-out therapy that involves minimal contact with classroom teachers, integrated therapy is more compatible with current philosophical trends in early intervention.

## REFERENCES

Bailey, D.B., & McWilliam, R.A. (1991). Normalizing early intervention. *Topics in Early Childhood Special Education, 10*(2), 33–47.

Bickel, W.E., & Hattrup, R.A. (1995). Teachers and researchers in collaboration: Reflections on the process. *American Educational Research Journal, 32*, 35–62.

Cole, K., Dale, P., & Mills, P. (1991). Individual differences in language delayed children's responses to direct and interactive preschool instruction. *Topics in Early Childhood Special Education, 11*, 99–124.

Cole, K.N., Harris, S.R., Eland, S.F., & Mills, P.E. (1989). Comparison of two service delivery models: In-class and out-of-class therapy approaches. *Pediatric Physical Therapy, 1*, 49–54.

Davies, P.L., & Gavin, W.J. (1994). Comparison of individual and group/consultation treatment methods for preschool children with developmental delays. *The American Journal of Occupational Therapy, 48*, 155–161.

Dunn, W. (1990). A comparison of service provision models in school-based occupational therapy services: A pilot study. *The Occupational Therapy Journal of Research, 10*, 300–320.

Giangreco, M.F. (1986). Effects of integrated therapy: A pilot study. *Journal of The Association for Persons with Severe Handicaps, 11*, 205–208.

Giangreco, M.F., Cloninger, C.J., & Iverson, V.S. (1993). *Choosing options and accommodations for children: A guide to planning inclusive education.* Baltimore: Paul H. Brookes Publishing Co.

McWilliam, R.A. (1992). Predictors of service delivery models in center-based early intervention. (Doctoral dissertation, University of North Carolina at Chapel Hill, 1992). *Dissertation Abstracts International, 53*(09A), 3171.

McWilliam, R.A., & Applequist, K. (1993, February). *National survey of four disciplines.* Paper presented at the annual conference of the North Carolina Federation of the Council for Exceptional Children, Greensboro, NC.

McWilliam, R.A., & Bailey, D.B., Jr. (1994). Predictors of service-delivery models in center-based early intervention. *Exceptional Children, 61*, 56–71.

McWilliam, R.A., Bailey, D.B., & Vandermaas, M. (1991, November). *Research issues in comparing in-class and out-of-class special services for young children with disabilities.* Paper presented at the International Early Childhood Conference on Children with Special Needs (sponsored by the Division for Early Childhood, CEC), St. Louis, MO.

McWilliam, R.A., & Grabowski, K. (1993, December). *A comparison of in-class and out-of-class instruction.* Paper presented at the International Early Childhood Conference on Children with Special Needs, San Diego, CA.

McWilliam, R.A., & Scarborough, A. (1994, September). *Does therapy carry over to the classroom? How to make early intervention more effective.* Paper presented at the North Carolina Association for the Education of Young Children/Division for Early Childhood Annual Study Conference, Greensboro, NC.

McWilliam, R.A., Scarborough, A., & Chaudhary, A. (1995). [Patterns of service delivery models and ratings of individualized progress] Unpublished raw data.

Frank Porter Graham Child Development Center, University of North Carolina at Chapel Hill.

McWilliam, R.A., & Spencer, A.G. (1993). *Integrated versus pull-out speech-language services in early intervention: A mixed-method study.* Manuscript submitted for publication.

McWilliam, R.A., Young, H.J., & Harville, K. (1995). *Therapists', other early interventionists', mothers', and administrators' perceptions of service delivery models.* Unpublished raw data. University of North Carolina, Chapel Hill.

National Association for the Education of Young Children. (1991). Guidelines for appropriate curriculum content and assessment in programs serving children ages 3 through 8. *Young Children,* March, 21–38.

Ottenbacher, K.J. (1992). Practical significance in early intervention research: From affect to empirical effect. *Journal of Early Intervention, 16,* 181–193.

Roberts, J.E., Prizant, B., & McWilliam, R.A. (1995). Out-of-class vs. in-class service delivery in language intervention: Effects on communicative interactions with young children. *American Journal of Speech-Language Pathology, 4*(2), 87–93.

Snyder, P., & Lawson, S. (1994). Evaluating results using corrected and uncorrected effect size estimates. *Journal of Experimental Education, 61,* 334–349.

Wilcox, M.J., Kouri, T.A., & Caswell, S.B. (1991). Early language intervention: A comparison of classroom and individual treatment. *American Journal of Speech-Language Pathology, 1,* 49–61.

Wolery, M. (1991). Instruction in early childhood special education: "Seeing through a glass darkly . . . knowing in part." *Exceptional Children, 58,* 127–135.

Wolery, M., Bailey, D.B., & Sugai, G.M. (1988). *Effective teaching: Principles and procedures of applied behavior analysis.* Needham, MA: Allyn & Bacon.

Yoder, D.E., Coleman, P.P., & Gallagher, J.J. (1990). *Personnel needs: Allied health personnel meeting the demands of Part H, P.L. 99–457.* Unpublished manuscript, Carolina Institute for Child and Family Policy, University of North Carolina, Chapel Hill.

Yoder, P.J., Kaiser, A.P., & Alpert, C.A. (1991). An exploratory study of the interaction between language teaching methods and child characteristics. *Journal of Speech and Hearing Research, 34,* 155–167.

# Chapter 5

# Through Their Eyes

*Creating Functional, Child-Sensitive*
*Individualized Education Programs*

Karla Hull, Angela Capone,
Michael F. Giangreco, and Jane Ross-Allen

The landscape of early childhood special education is changing dramatically as young children with disabilities increasingly receive services in community-based preschools and child care settings attended primarily by children without disabilities. This emerging early childhood special education landscape is characterized by an emphasis on family-selected goals and the integrated provision of educational and related services through play, discovery, and problem solving (Bricker & Cripe, 1992; Bruder, 1993). Deficit-driven models of special education focusing on what a child cannot do are being replaced with practices that build on more positive characteristics, such as the child's abilities and interests. Several program-quality indicators support the underlying characteristics of a play-centered approach by acknowledging the importance of providing environments that are responsive to children's initiations, thereby encouraging participation, self-directed behavior, and engagement with the environment (McWilliam & Strain, 1993).

As early interventionists move toward providing services within the context of inclusive, play-centered environments, it will be important to examine existing practices that may be incongruent with a play-centered philosophy. This chapter describes briefly the philosophical beliefs that shape the play-centered approach guiding many inclusive early childhood special

Partial support for the preparation of this chapter was provided by the U.S. Department of Education, Office of Special Education and Rehabilitative Services, under the funding category Innovations for Educating Children with Deaf-Blindness in General Education Settings, CFDA 84.025F (H025F10008), awarded to The University Affiliated Program of Vermont at the University of Vermont. The contents of this chapter do not reflect the ideas or positions of the U.S. Department of Education; therefore, no official endorsement should be inferred.

education programs and highlights critical attributes of this philosophy that should be reflected in our daily practice with young children and their families. As we examine current practices, we reflect on the contradictions that surface when traditional individualized education programs (IEPs) are evaluated for their congruence with a play-centered philosophy. An alternative model of IEP development is presented that includes a refinement of our understanding of functional goals and objectives, is consistent with a play-centered philosophy, and supports the richness provided by inclusive settings.

## PHILOSOPHICAL BELIEFS THAT
## SHAPE A PLAY-CENTERED APPROACH

A play-centered approach is based on the "conviction that play provides the integrative context essential to support the growth of the whole child" (Van Hoorn, Nourot, Scales, & Alward, 1993, p. 9). It is widely recognized that play is instrumental in the development of intellect, creativity, a sense of self, and the capacity to interact with others (Almy & Genishi, 1982; Bergen, 1988; Cohen & Rae, 1987; Hendrick, 1990; Smilansky, 1968; Van Hoorn et al., 1993). Thus, play is critical to optimal child development; therefore, it is essential that educators develop an in-depth understanding of the nature of children's play and identify the interests, developmental levels, and learning history of individual children in the environment.

Play, by definition, is child-initiated, providing children with a meaningful curriculum that gives them choices that are interesting and challenging (Forman & Hill, 1984; Van Hoorn et al., 1993). A play-centered approach is characterized by the belief that children learn through play and from each other (Bricker & Cripe, 1992; Forman & Hill, 1984; Piaget, 1969; Vygotsky, 1962). Discussion of a play-centered approach focuses on the deliberate ways in which the materials, activities, schedules, teachers' behaviors, and peer interactions are creatively managed to reflect knowledge of the individual children in the environment while recognizing that children are active learners who learn from each other when presented with opportunities to engage in meaningful learning encounters. Play-centered environments are flexible and responsive, providing adult guidance that is appropriate and relevant to children's individual needs. Many educators in inclusive early childhood special education programs have learned that play provides a context that is intrinsically motivating, creating opportunities for children at all levels of development to participate. By engaging with peers in the various play scenarios offered in the areas of an early childhood environment (e.g., sand and water, block, dramatic play, art, woodworking), children "clarify and master many fundamental aspects of development in all basic areas: physical, intellectual, social, and emotional" (Maxim, 1989, p. 222). Environments guided by a play-centered philosophy create a community of learning partners whose discoveries, ideas, and curiosities are enhanced by the actions and reactions of each member, creating new and exciting opportunities for children to learn within a dynamic context.

## Children Are Active Learners

Knowledge is acquired through interaction with materials, peers, and adults, through questioning, poking, probing, and reflecting. Early childhood environments that translate a play-centered philosophy into action celebrate children as active explorers who seek to make meaning of their world. These environments respect the passions, styles, and needs of each child and challenge adults to design environments that address all aspects of development (e.g., social–emotional, cognitive, physical) while facilitating interactions among children, materials, and adults in such a manner that children use the environment productively and see themselves as capable learners (Johnson, Johnson, McMillan, & Rogers, 1989). Within the context of this approach, a well-designed early childhood program is defined by the extent to which the environment, activities, and interactions are rooted in the adult's 1) understanding of child development; 2) knowledge of each child's interests, abilities, needs, and learning history; and 3) ability to carefully orchestrate an environment that motivates each child to develop. In short, it is an environment that requires tremendous reflection and spontaneity on the part of educators and presents numerous and varied opportunities for children to explore and take risks.

## Children Learn from Each Other

Considerable evidence has accrued suggesting that children learn effectively from other children (Katz, Evangelou, & Hartman, 1990; Roopnarine & Johnson, 1983; Urberg & Kaplan, 1986; Vygotsky, 1962). Vygotsky (1962) spoke about this in his discussions of the "zone of proximal development," a concept suggesting children learn new skills that are only slightly outside their current skill repertoire. Bricker and Cripe (1992) state that "less able or developmentally younger children profited more from child-driven approaches (e.g., milieu teaching, interactive approach) than from more adult-controlled approaches" (p. 55), supporting trends toward providing services for young children with disabilities in inclusive, play-centered, early childhood programs. This is not to suggest that, in play, learning involves random interactions, but rather that learning occurs within the context of a carefully orchestrated environment that enhances each child's motivation to achieve through manipulation, exploration, and feedback (Graham & Bryant, 1993).

## Interrelatedness of Developmental Domains

Play-centered environments provide a learning context consistent with our knowledge of the interrelatedness of developmental domains (Berkeley & Ludlow, 1989; Van Hoorn et al., 1993). Play provides an integrated approach that encourages children to use skills from a number of developmental domains simultaneously. For example, the child engaged in a dramatic play scene may use cognitive abilities to identify roles or props, fine motor skills to manipulate props or put on a costume, gross motor skills to climb the mountain, and communication skills to assume a role or direct the play. There is room within a dramatic play scheme to accommodate children with a diverse array of developmental competencies. Within this approach, adults must look at activities from a broad perspective to ensure that fine motor, gross motor, and other domain-specific activities are integrated into children's natural play. The goal is for children to self-select activities that foster growth in all developmental domains.

## Role of the Adult

Conceptualizing the role of adults as facilitators of learning challenges educators to devote time to exploring the ways adults can become involved in children's play, without dominating the play, and to enhancing their abilities to observe children's play to develop hypotheses about what children are learning or working on. The information gained from these observations is used to deliberately modify the environment so that activities, materials, and adult behaviors constantly and consistently provide opportunities for children to use existing competencies more often, in more settings, and with greater complexity, thus developing greater competence. The role of adults in a play-centered environment is flexible and responsive to the individual needs of children, ensuring that all children are able to participate in the environment in ways that respect their interests, current level of ability, and learning history. Importantly, daily observations and stated goals and objectives for individual children provide the underlying structure to guide a teacher's intentional modification of the learning environment.

## Learning Occurs Within the
## Context of Relevant, Meaningful Activities

Play-centered environments provide children with opportunities to select from an array of activities that are related to the real world of the child. In early childhood environments reflecting this belief, the general interests of young children and the individual interests of children in the program are considered when planning activities. Children seem to learn and remember best when the activities in which they are engaged are related to experiences they have or to materials with which they are familiar. Interest in an activity leads children to explore an object, materials, or an event to discover more about it. Children discover concepts and information through hands-on interactions with materials that have been chosen by the child and are used in the manner in which the child decides. The ultimate challenge here is that the adult's role is to set the context, the "lure," and then as unobtrusively as possible to support the child's exploration. The ultimate goal is to motivate children actively to discover concepts, enlarging their repertoire of learning (Dodge & Colker, 1992).

An observer in a well-defined, developmentally appropriate, play-centered environment may well feel like a spectator at a ballet. The stage is set with the props clearly visible and carefully selected, waiting for the children whose curiosities prompted their presence. The adults engage in what might be termed a dance throughout the day, each moving about the room, supporting yet not dominating children's play, responding to children's discoveries and issues, and supporting children's decisions and activities. As the day progresses, the activities create an explosion of discoveries and queries that set the stage for tomorrow's learning.

## FORGING A NEW RELATIONSHIP: THE MARRIAGE OF PLAY AND THE IEP

As early interventionists move toward the provision of services in inclusive settings, as well as incorporating a play-based philosophy into more traditional settings, they are challenged to reexamine the focus of IEP goals and objectives and refine prevailing beliefs about functional goals and objectives. As a result of this process, there is greater consistency between the content of the IEP and the context in which it is implemented. Ultimately, these discussions blur the lines between early intervention or early childhood special education and early childhood education practice and create a more unified and effective approach to the education of young children with disabilities.

The IEPs we develop are designed to serve as a map, guiding our practice and creating markers that determine the route we have taken and how far we have come. A 1994 analysis of traditional IEPs suggests that they do not "adequately communicate the individual needs of the students nor did they appear to serve as a useful resource to guide their general educational experience" (Giangreco, Dennis, Edelman, & Cloninger, 1994). These findings support Smith's (1990) research indicating that IEPs frequently are not useful documents. Specifically, Giangreco et al. (1994) identified five critical issues presented in Table 1.

The authors of this chapter live in Vermont, a rural state divided by a mountain range that becomes impassable during the long winter months, making the adage "you can't get there from here" a favorite saying of seventh-generation Vermonters. Similarly, many IEPs leave us wondering how we can integrate stated goals and objectives into the daily activities and experiences that a young child encounters. The current form of IEPs has changed very little over the years, even though IEPs were originally designed to guide services that primarily occurred in segregated settings. It is time to update our IEP map to guide our practice more effectively in inclusive, play-centered settings, so that we do not find ourselves looking at an IEP and feeling like we "can't get there from here."

Table 1. Illustration of IEP characteristics with alternative practices

| Problematic characteristics | Potential alternatives |
|---|---|
| 1. Sweeping statements: "José will improve communication skills." | 1. Individualized learning outcomes: "José will initiate the use of 15 new signs in interactions with peers in his preschool." |
| 2. Functional rhetoric without substance: "Gina will enlarge her circle of friends." | 2. Family-centered priorities based on valued life outcomes: "Gina will initiate and maintain social interactions with her peers throughout activities encountered at preschool." |
| 3. Making promises that are hard to keep: IEPs filed away, lengthy, and not incorporated into general education activities. | 3. Useful IEPs: Use of a one-page "program-at-a-glance" to summarize a child's individualized education program within the learning areas of a play-centered setting. |
| 4. Goals for staff rather than for children: "Mary Ann will have hearing aids checked daily by the audiologists" written as an IEP goal is actually a goal for the staff, not Mary Ann. | 4. Goals for children are distinguished from supports provided by staff: "A teacher assistant, taught by an audiologist, will check Mary Ann's hearing aids daily" is written in the IEP as a support rather than a goal. |
| 5. Discipline-referenced: "Darren will improve articulation of bilabial sounds in speech therapy." | 5. Discipline-free shared goals: "Darren will increase intelligibility of speech in one-to-one conversation with parents, siblings, peers, and teachers." |

Adapted with permission from Giangreco, M., Dennis, R., Edelman, S., & Cloninger, C. (1994). Dressing your IEPs for the general education climate: Analysis of IEP goals and objectives for students with multiple disabilities. *Remedial and Special Education, 15*, 288–296.

## Reexamining the Focus of IEP Goals and Objectives

Typically, IEP goals and objectives are identified based on a child's performance on standardized tests or other developmental or criterion-referenced checklists. Items on these measures that the child passes are used to identify the child's current level of performance, and items that the child fails are identified as areas of need and frequently become IEP goals and objectives. Although the resulting individualized plan is unique relative to a particular child's performance on a developmentally sequenced set of skills, the plan emphasizes limitations rather than maximizes capabilities and sets a course that is driven by a standard set of skills rather than one that reflects the child's individual preferences, dislikes, passions, coping strategies, and approaches to life. As play becomes the primary vehicle for learning, the IEP team is challenged to enhance its knowledge of the child by expanding the information gleaned from test situations with detailed descriptions of a child's behavior as observed in play. This new information creates a context for an IEP discussion that leads to the identification of goals and objectives that are consistent with the activities encountered in a play-centered environment, reflect parent's priorities, and facilitate the development of a more complex and varied play repertoire.

## Creating a New Definition of Functional Goals and Objectives

The field of early intervention has promoted the development of functional goals and objectives as professionals have become increasingly sensitive to the fact that children learn best when they engage in activities that are meaningful. Functional goals and objectives are described as those that are useful and meaningful within a child's life circumstances and promote generalization across materials and settings (Bricker & Cripe, 1992; Notari & Drinkwater, 1991). This movement has encouraged early interventionists to abandon the practice of writing goals and objectives that address isolated skills, focusing instead on objectives that are considered functional. Because functional goals and objectives are central to the creation of relevant IEPs that support development within the context of a child's life, it is essential that educators refine their understanding of functionality as it applies to the development of IEP goals and objectives.

Art, for example, provides a context for reflecting on more traditional perspectives related to the identification of functional goals and objectives and allows us to reconceptualize functionality within the context of play. Because it is widely accepted that children enjoy interacting with art materials and using their imagination to create with paper, glue, and color, arts and crafts activities are common elements of early childhood environments. Art projects provide opportunities to practice such skills as copying a model, following a direction, cutting on lines, or tracing. In turn, art products become tangible evidence of fine motor, cognitive, and linguistic competence and the acquisition of new skills. Are goals and objectives that are linked to arts and crafts projects functional? Many would answer yes, arguing that art activities are useful and meaningful within the context of preschool, child care, and early childhood special education programs; however, they may not be useful and meaningful for a particular child.

Although some projects may appear to provide a more functional context for practicing isolated skills such as grasp and release, the activity is not necessarily meaningful for a child who has not chosen either the activity or to use the materials in the prescribed way. Because most projects are designed to facilitate the acquisition of new skills or the refinement of an emerging skill, adult-directed projects frequently frustrate children by concentrating on their limitations rather than on maximizing their capabilities. Finally, although some activities may appear to provide a context for implementing functional goals and objectives, these activities may impose an external structure to the learning environment that may inhibit imagination, experimentation, creativity, individuality, self-esteem, initiation, self-control, and organization, the very skills that most early childhood environments are designed to encourage.

Forman and Hill (1984) urge us to remember that "learning encounters must always be defined from the child's point of view" (p. 5). As we develop IEP goals and objectives that are consistent with a play-centered curriculum, we must approach the discussion of functionality from an in-depth understanding of the child to ensure that all goals and objectives are 1) relevant to the child's ability, experience, current learning environment, and passions; and 2) consistent with the definition of play as a child-initiated activity.

## AN ALTERNATIVE MODEL FOR IEP DEVELOPMENT: CREATION OF A COMMON VISION

Creating a common vision has been cited as one of the single most important aspects of the IEP meeting. It is widely acknowledged that the effectiveness of an IEP team is greatly increased when the team shares a common vision regarding the relevant, functional outcomes for a child (York, Rainforth, & Giangreco, 1990). The process of developing an IEP for a young child must be guided by four critical factors: 1) knowledge of how the individual child functions in typical settings on a daily basis, 2) knowledge of the family's priorities, 3) a shared understanding of the characteristics of a play-based environment, and 4) a shared vision of how the team will work together. These four factors create the foundation for development of the IEP and serve to focus the discussion in ways that facilitate the creation of a common vision for the educational program.

### Knowledge of the Individual Child

The IEP, by definition, must include a discussion of the child's current level of performance, which is determined through an assessment that is guided by evaluation questions formulated from parents' concerns and other referral information. In the traditional model for developing an IEP, this discussion of a child's current level of performance is framed by an assessment process driven by a developmental milestone model that is characterized by categorizing information into discrete domains. Typically, these milestones reflect discrete skills that are exclusively domain-referenced and hierarchically arranged.

In the alternative IEP model, the discussion of current level of performance is framed by an assessment process guided by a parent interview. This interview assists in providing a picture of the child and acts as a vehicle for noting parental concerns. The discussion of current level of performance is driven by observations of how a child integrates his or her skills in all domains during play. Bredekamp and Rosegrant (1992) remind us that the learning process should be viewed as a cycle rather than a hierarchy; that is, "utilization is not necessarily a more highly valued goal than is awareness and exploration" (p. 35). Thus, observations of children's participation in dramatic play yield information about the way children currently use their cognitive, motor, communication, social and emotional, and self-help skills in the relevant, motivating context of play. Similar observations of children participating in the sand and water, art, dramatic play, and other critical component areas provide information about a child's material and activity preferences. This information presents the team with relevant integrated facts about how the child currently negotiates in the key learning areas of a play-centered environment. With this knowledge of a child's interests, preferences, and styles of interacting with a variety of materials, the team can begin to determine the kinds of learning outcomes that would be most likely to increase a child's repertoire immediately and effectively.

## Knowledge of Family's Priorities

The family's active role in the process of IEP development is critical in forging the common vision. Research and declarations of best practice are unified in their assertion that the family is the constant in a child's life, and that services should reflect families' cultures and priorities (Bailey, McWilliam, Winton, & Simeonsson, 1991; Bruder, 1993). A commitment to respecting the family as the primary decision maker implies constant attention to the ways our practices actively include families and support their ability to guide the direction of services that they choose to receive.

Building a relationship with a family begins with the initial referral contact and continues throughout the assessment process, forming a basis for gathering information about the family's priorities. By the time the IEP meeting is held, the professionals should have a clear picture of family priorities, and parents should have the clear message that their participation is critical to the successful development of an IEP for their child. There are several models to assist professionals in eliciting family priorities, but the basis for each of these models is the development of a respectful relationship guided by the belief that the family is the primary decision maker.

## A Shared Understanding of a Play-Centered Approach

The development of a relevant plan requires knowledge of the family's priorities and a shared understanding of the characteristics and goals of environments reflecting a play-centered approach to learning. Knowing the typical activities, experiences, and materials that are an integral part of a play-centered approach, the team can determine how a particular child may need to be supported to gain access to the richness that the environment offers in support of the child's pursuit of clearly identified learning outcomes. This knowledge of how young children increase the complexity of their play supports teams in making meaningful decisions for an individual child and reflects an understanding about the interrelatedness of learning in young children.

## A Shared Vision of How the Team Will Work Together

The process of creating a common vision implies the development of a particular relationship between members of the IEP team. In this relationship, team members use their specialized knowledge to create a relevant and discipline-free educational plan. *Discipline-free* refers to practices driven by consensus decision making and shared goals that "avoid the parochial practices of retaining separate goals and decision authority by each discipline" (Giangreco, Edelman, & Dennis, 1991, p. 17). Early childhood special educators who work with preschoolers with disabilities and their families must be prepared to "reach beyond the traditional boundaries of practice to integrate a range of services in order to meet multiple and complex needs" (Fenichel & Eggbeer, 1990, p. 6). Teams move closer to developing a common framework as they strive to "purposely identify and pursue a unified set of goals" (Giangreco, Cloninger, & Iverson, 1993, p. 9) as they begin to address critical issues such as 1) educational relevance; 2) gaps, overlaps, and contradictions in services; 3) the role of various related service providers; and 4) contradictions in services.

## Criteria for Selection of Annual Goals

As the IEP team strives to develop an educational program that increases a child's available repertoire for coping with daily living, it must ensure that the annual written goals are authentically individualized and prioritized. The annual goals serve to keep a team focused by providing direction for the development of more detailed short-term objectives and instructional plans. The annual goals should be observable, measurable, and reasonably achievable within 1 year.

***Authentically Individualized*** *Authentically individualized* is a term used by Johnson and Johnson (1992) to describe "the willingness to change the task to fit the specific situation, as well as the learner's needs and level of interest at the time" (p. 444). Authentically individualized annual goals are based on knowledge of a child's current level of performance, preferences, learning history, and educational needs, and they include activity-based outcomes for a child. Knowledge of the child's current levels of performance provides information on how a child moves, communicates, and thinks in each of the learning areas of a play-centered environment. This information lays the foundation for a team discussion of the learning outcomes that reflect the obvious next steps leading to an increase in the child's repertoires. The team can generate a list to determine which activities best reflect a child's interests while providing an integrated context for development and learning. Annual goals, which include the context as well as the expectations for a child's behavior, serve to remind the IEP team about the relevant activities in which the targeted behaviors are authentically used.

*Prioritized* The effectiveness and efficiency of an IEP is highly related to the ability of the team to identify and prioritize the areas of a child's repertoire that will be addressed in the IEP. Annual goals can be prioritized by considering family priorities, immediate relevance, and the long-term benefit to the child. It is essential that teams agree on a reasonable number of goals that will be the focus of the educational program. Creating IEPs with a large number of discipline-specific goals and objectives increases the probability that implementation of the IEP will be less efficient and may result in parts of the IEP being addressed by single team members in isolation and without important input from other members. The team checklist presented in Figure 1 is designed to assist teams in developing or refining an IEP process that results in authentically individualized goals and objectives.

1.0 The team has gathered information about the child from
    ☐ 1.1 Significant people in the child's life (e.g., parents, caregivers, siblings)
    ☐ 1.2 Observations conducted in natural settings (home, child care, play groups)
    ☐ 1.3 Appropriate standardized/curriculum-based measures/ checklists
2.0 The team has developed a knowledge of the child that includes
    ☐ 2.1 Knowledge of child's preferences (e.g., favorite materials, activities, peers)
    ☐ 2.2 Knowledge of child's learning history (e.g., pace, context variables, modality preferences)
    ☐ 2.3 A description of the ways the child integrates his or her skills in all domains during play and daily routines
3.0 The team has engaged in discussions focusing on
    ☐ 3.1 Identifying family priorities
    ☐ 3.2 Describing the activities, materials, and routines that are characteristic of a play-based environment
    ☐ 3.3 Identifying the child's educational needs
    ☐ 3.4 Determining the naturally occurring activities or routines that support the accomplishment of the child's identified educational needs
    ☐ 3.5 Describing the supports or accommodations that will ensure that the child has access to all aspects of a play-based environment (e.g., peers, materials, activities)
4.0 The team has developed goals and objectives that
    ☐ 4.1 Reflect its holistic knowledge of the child
    ☐ 4.2 Are linked to activities typically engaged in by young children
    ☐ 4.3 Support interaction with peers
    ☐ 4.4 Lead to the development of more complex play schemes
    ☐ 4.5 Are discipline-free
5.0 The team has prioritized goals and objectives based on
    ☐ 5.1 Family priorities
    ☐ 5.2 Immediate relevance
    ☐ 5.3 Long-term benefit

Figure 1. Team checklist for developing authentically individualized goals and objectives.

**Case Study** *Abby*

The story of Abby's IEP meeting provides an illustration of the alternative model of IEP development presented in this chapter. Abby is a 4-year-old child who has received home-based services from birth and began attending a segregated preschool program for young children with disabilities when she turned 3. As Abby's parents thought about her upcoming entry into kindergarten, they became committed to finding a community-based preschool program that would provide Abby with opportunities to develop friendships that could continue into kindergarten. As Abby's IEP team developed her plan for the upcoming year, three things were notably different. First, the team had grown to include the community-based preschool teacher as a member of the team. Second, Abby's parents had selected a preschool program that placed play at the center of the curriculum. Finally, as the team began to talk about Abby's current level of performance, the discussion centered on Abby's interests, play activities, and strengths, rather than focusing on test scores and developmental milestones. In short, when developing Abby's goals and objectives, the team reflected on Abby's current competencies relative to participating in a play-centered environment. The resulting goals and objectives were designed to build on those competencies, facilitate the development of more complex play behaviors, and facilitate more complex and varied interactions with peers.

**Current Level of Performance: Social**

Abby initiates interactions with adults through eye gaze, gestures, and vocalizations. Her initiations are typically related to requests for help or to show an adult something that is of interest to her; she does not seek adults as playmates. When approached by adults trying to enter into her play or to prompt her to engage in an activity, Abby frequently initiates a "come and chase me" game by leaving the area, moving quickly around the room, and laughing. Abby maintains the game for as long as the adult continues to play the role of pursuer, and delights in being caught if it results in a game of tickling. Abby typically does not engage in adult-selected activity if caught. If the adult does not follow, Abby moves on to observe another area of the room. Abby is observed to watch her peers intently from a distance (approximately 5

*(continued)*

*(continued)*

feet). She does smile in response to peer initiations; however, she allows only one particular child, Sarah, to either enter her play or sit next to her. To date, Abby's initiations toward peers have been limited to requests for help (primarily at snack time) and sharing (presenting an item for a peer to look at with no accompanying vocalizations). When exploring the environment, Abby watches from across the room, circles around the activity, then approaches when others have left. While exploring the activity, Abby consistently engages in functional and tactile play, although recently she has been observed to imitate the behaviors of the children she observes at the water table. While Abby is exploring the play materials she also remains vigilant about other activities occurring around the classroom (distracting her from the activity at hand). In other words, Abby appears to go through the motions while looking elsewhere. Currently, Abby appears to maintain focused eye contact with her chosen activity for approximately 20–30 seconds.

## Annual Goals

1. Abby imitates the play behaviors of peers in at least one additional area of the room.
2. Abby allows at least two new children to play beside her in at least two areas of the room.
3. Abby responds to peer requests and comments during play with vocalizations and gestures.

Abby's IEP document and IEP process clearly illustrate the concepts introduced in this chapter. First, in addition to facilitating the development of more complex behaviors, the goals are responsive to the strengths and interests that Abby has demonstrated in a play-based environment. Second, the goals are consistent with Abby's parents' priorities related to establishing play partnerships before entering kindergarten. Finally, the goals are consistent with the play-based philosophy of the program.

Although Abby's written IEP signifies an accomplishment, it also presents a challenge to her preschool teacher, who must now translate the IEP into action. Because the teacher is key to a play-centered aproach to learning (Van Hoorn, Nourot, Scales, & Alward, 1993), Abby's teacher must begin the process of combining her

*(continued)*

*(continued)*

knowledge of Abby with her knowledge of children and play and arranging the environment so that Abby will accomplish her goals and objectives through her play. Her approach can best be described as a continuous cycle of observation and action.

## Observation

It is highly likely that Abby's teacher will spend time over the next few days observing how Abby is currently using her environment. Although the current level of performance section on Abby's IEP is fairly detailed, Abby's teacher wants to be sure that it is current and related to the specific goals and objectives that the team has identified. To ensure that her observations are purposive, Abby's teacher will most likely develop a detailed set of questions, such as the following, to guide her observations:

- What attracts Abby's attention most?
- What action schemes is Abby imitating?
- What areas of the room or materials or activities support these schemes?
- What other children in the room are experimenting with the same concepts and actions?
- What activities does Abby's friend, Sarah, prefer?

It is important to note that although the observations are designed to ensure that the environment supports Abby's play, the teacher's observations do not focus solely on Abby. To make effective decisions, the teacher must gather information about the other children and the physical environment relative to the goals she has for Abby. As a result of her observations, Abby's teacher has discovered that Abby is using crayons in a circular motion, that Abby's friend, Sarah, prefers gooey substances like ooblick and finger paints, and that a number of other children are experimenting at the easel.

## Action

Feeling somewhat like a mad scientist, Abby's teacher begins rearranging her environment driven by her new knowledge and a series of questions. Her first decision is to expand the art area to include some sensory-based activities. By putting a shaving cream activity next to

*(continued)*

*(continued)*

the crayons and paper, she is hoping the gooey shaving cream encourages Abby's friend to play near Abby while Abby is using the crayons. If Abby notices her friend using the shaving cream, perhaps she will be tempted to explore the shaving cream (a new experience). But what if Abby does not join her friend in exploring the shaving cream? What will the plan be then? Having thought through a number of scenarios, the teacher decides that if she observes the two children in the area at the same time, she will quietly enter the area, sit so that Abby can see her (if she chooses), and imitate Abby's circular motion in the shaving cream. Perhaps the combination of her action (suggesting that Abby can do a preferred motion in a new place) with the fact that her friend is there will be just the lure Abby needs to try a new experience. Abby's teacher is also toying with expanding the art area to include the easels, paints, sensory materials, crayons, and glue—creating what might be called a messy area. But first she must observe again.

- What was the impact of adding another activity to the art area?
- Did Abby still use the crayons, or was there now too much activity there for her?

Each action creates a reaction that must be observed and interpreted. Each interpretation prompts an action. Children's play (and, more specifically, Abby's play) creates an explosion of discoveries and queries that must be observed and interpreted to set the stage for tomorrow's learning in a fashion that reflects the marriage of IEP goals and objectives and a play-centered approach to learning.

## CONCLUSIONS

The emphasis on family-selected goals and the integrated provision of educational and related services through play, discovery, and problem solving is permeating the consciousness of early interventionists involved in the continual reflection and refinement of their practices. Partnerships with families and early childhood educators have broadened and deepened our understanding of young children, creating a need to reframe some of our practices to reflect knowledge about the ways young children learn. Although some argue that young children with disabilities are distinctively different from their peers without disability labels, many early interventionists who provide services for young children with disabilities in inclusive play-centered settings support a philosophy affirming that children are children and focusing on children's competence, recognizing that the similarities among children far outweigh the differences. This is not to say that young children with disabilities do not have distinct and unique needs, but rather to emphasize that all children have distinct and unique needs and that play-centered environments are designed specifically to be responsive to the wide diversity that exists in inclusive settings.

## REFERENCES

Almy, M., & Genishi, C. (1982). *Ways of studying children* (Rev. ed.). New York: Teachers College Press.

Bailey, D.B., McWilliam, P.J., Winton, P.J., & Simeonsson, R.J. (1991). *Implementing family-centered practices in early intervention: A team-based model for change.* Chapel Hill, NC: Frank Porter Graham Child Development Center, University of North Carolina.

Bergen, D. (Ed.). (1988). *Play as a medium for learning and development: A handbook of theory and practice.* Portsmouth, NH: Heinemann.

Berkeley, T.R., & Ludlow, B.L. (1989). Toward a reconceptualization of the developmental model. *Topics in Early Childhood Special Education, 9*(3), 51–66.

Bredekamp, S., & Rosegrant, T. (1992). Reaching potentials through appropriate curriculum: Conceptual frameworks for applying guidelines. *Reaching potentials: Appropriate curriculum and assessment for young children.* Washington, DC: National Association for the Education of Young Children.

Bricker, D.D., & Cripe, J.W. (1992). *An activity-based approach to early intervention.* Baltimore: Paul H. Brookes Publishing Co.

Bruder, M.B. (1993). The provision of early intervention and early childhood special education within community early childhood programs: Characteristics of effective service delivery. *Topics in Early Childhood Special Education, 13*, 19–37.

Cohen, S., & Rae, G. (1987). *Growing up with children.* New York: Holt, Rinehart & Winston.

Dodge, D., & Colker, L. (1992). *The creative curriculum.* Washington, DC: Teaching Strategies Press.

Fenichel, E.S., & Eggbeer, L. (1990). *Preparing practitioners to work with infants, toddlers, and their families: Issues and recommendations for educators and trainers.* Washington, DC: National Center for Clinical Infants Programs.

Forman, G., & Hill, F. (1984). *Constructive play: Applying Piaget in the preschool.* Reading, MA: Addison-Wesley.

Giangreco, M.F. (1994). Effects of a consensus-building process on team decision-making: Preliminary data. *Physical Disabilities: Education and Related Services, 13*(1), 41–56.

Giangreco, M.F., Cloninger, C.J., & Iverson, V.S. (1993). *Choosing options and accommodations for children: A guide to planning inclusive education.* Baltimore: Paul H. Brookes Publishing Co.

Giangreco, M., Dennis, R., Edelman, S., & Cloninger, C. (1994). Dressing your IEPs for the general education climate: Analysis of IEP goals and objectives for students with multiple disabilities. *Remedial and Special Education, 15*, 288–296.

Giangreco, M., Edelman, S., & Dennis, R. (1991). Common professional practices that interfere with the integrated delivery of related services. *Remedial and Special Education, 12*(2), 16–24.

Graham, M.A., & Bryant, D.M. (1993). Developmentally appropriate environments for children with special needs. *Infants & Young Children, 5*(3), 31–42.

Hendrick, J. (1990). *Total learning: Developmental curriculum for the young child.* Columbus, OH: Charles E. Merrill.

Johnson, J.E., & Johnson, K.M. (1992). Clarifying the developmental perspective in response to Carta, Schwartz, Atwater, & McConnell. *Topics in Early Childhood Special Education, 12,* 439–457.

Johnson, P., Johnson, L., McMillan, R., & Rogers, C. (1989). *Early childhood special education program design and evaluation guide.* Columbus, OH: Ohio Department of Education.

Katz, L., Evangelou, D., & Hartman, J. (1990). *The case for mixed age grouping in early education.* Washington, DC: National Association for the Education of Young Children.

Maxim, G.W. (1989). *The very young.* Columbus, OH: Charles E. Merrill.

McWilliam, R.A., & Strain, P.S. (1993). Service delivery models. In Council for Exceptional Children, *Division of Early Childhood Recommended Practices: Indicators of quality in programs for infants and young children with special needs and their families.* Reston, VA: Council for Exceptional Children.

Notari, A.R., & Drinkwater, S.G. (1991). Best practices for writing child outcome: An evaluation of two methods. *Topics in Early Childhood Special Education, 11*(3), 92–106.

Piaget, J. (1969). *The language and thought of the child.* New York: World Publishing.

Roopnarine, J.P., & Johnson, J.E. (1983). Kindergarten play with preschool and school-aged children within a mixed-age classroom. *The Elementary School Journal, 86*(5), 579–586.

Smilansky, S. (1968). *The effects of sociodramatic play on disadvantaged preschool children.* New York: John Wiley & Sons.

Smith, S. (1990). Individualized education programs (IEPs) in special education: From intent to acquiescence. *Exceptional Children, 57,* 6–14.

Urberg, K., & Kaplan, M. (1986). Effects of classroom age composition on the play and social behaviors of preschool children. *Journal of Applied Developmental Psychology, 7*(4), 403–415.

Van Hoorn, J., Nourot, P., Scales, B., & Alward, K. (1993). *Play at the center of the curriculum.* Columbus, OH: Charles E. Merrill.

Vygotsky, L.S. (1962). *Thought and language.* Cambridge, MA: MIT Press.

York, J., Rainforth, B., & Giangreco, M.F. (1990). Transdisciplinary teamwork and integrated therapy: Clarifying some misconceptions. *Pediatric Physical Therapy, 2*(2), 73–79.

# Chapter 6

# Generalization Issues in Providing Integrated Services

## Steven F. Warren and Eva M. Horn

At the heart of the debate about appropriate service delivery models is the issue of the relative effectiveness of different approaches in promoting generalization of targeted skills. The amount, type, durability, and meaningfulness of generalization is a litmus test by which the efficacy of any service delivery model must, at least partially, be evaluated. It has been accepted as an article of faith by some (e.g., Dunn, 1991; Giangreco, Edelman, & Dennis, 1991) that when services such as physical therapy and speech-language therapy are fully integrated, their effects should generalize better than when such services are delivered primarily in a segregated therapy model. The data on which to base this assumption, however, are minimal and inconclusive.

A reason for the development of integrated service delivery systems is the assumption that this approach produces more robust, meaningful generalization and is more effective than segregated models. Indeed, each of the six principles that together define integrated therapy has evolved from concerns that its antithesis can inhibit generalization (Dunn, 1991; Rainforth, York, & Macdonald, 1992). These principles are as follows:

1. Therapy and instruction should occur in the child's classroom.
2. Other children should be present.
3. Therapy and instruction should be embedded in ongoing classroom routines and activities.
4. Therapy and instruction should follow the child's attentional lead.
5. Goals should be functional and immediately useful.
6. The primary role of the specialist is as a collaborator with the other members of the child's team.

McWilliam (1995) has pointed out that the extent to which services are segregated or integrated can vary along dimensions that reflect each of these six principles. These dimensions are 1) where services are provided, 2) who is present, 3) what intervention style is used, 4) what kinds of goals are addressed, 5) what types of activities are used, and 6) what role the specialist plays.

This chapter focuses on the issue of skill generalization and its facilitation. It begins with a case study of a child's inability to generalize. This story illustrates some of the complex issues that cannot be ignored if intervention efforts are ultimately to be successful. The chapter then discusses what generalization is, how it relates to learning and competence, and why both strong and weak generalization can be misleading. Two studies are discussed: One is a report of an early motor skills intervention, and the other is an attempt to facilitate early prelinguistic communication skills. Both achieved unusually strong generalization with partially integrated approaches. The chapter concludes with a set of recommendations on how to promote optimal generalization and how to ensure, via the application of a few simple guidelines, that intervention efforts are effective.

---

### Case Study  *Brian's Story*

At age 32 months, Brian is used to having lots of adults around. Doctors, specialists, and educators have moved in and out of Brian's daily routine since he was diagnosed as having quadriplegic spastic cerebral palsy and global developmental delays. He tries to respond to their many demands, learning to hold his head up for longer periods and more steadily, maintaining eye contact, looking at one object or picture rather than others, and even waving good-bye after a fashion. When Brian tries some demands of his own, however, showing that he is uncomfortable or bored or wet, only his mother usually understands.

Brian attends a community parents-day-out (PDO) program for toddlers 3 days a week. An early interventionist regularly works with the child care teachers on supporting his development. He also sees a physical therapist once a week in a hospital outpatient clinic, where he has learned to maintain an upright posture in supported sitting. He receives speech therapy services with a group of similar children twice a week at a university-based speech and language clinic. Here he works on early augmentative or alternative communication system use and has learned to use gaze for indicating preference. Finally, Brian sees an occupational therapist who works for a home health care agency and visits with him in the PDO during the nap time. (That is

*(continued)*

*(continued)*

the only time that worked into the therapist's very busy schedule.) The occupational therapist is working with him on biting and chewing and feels that he has made tremendous progress. In short, Brian receives many important intervention services and is making good, steady progress. Nevertheless, currently his mother comes each day that he attends the PDO to feed him his lunch. No one else can get him to eat. All of the skills described above should logically come together at mealtime. But Brian experiences extreme difficulty using these skills when they are naturally called for and sequencing or combining these skills for meaningful use. Brian's story is not unusual.

## WHAT IS GENERALIZATION?

Stokes and Baer (1977) defined *generalization* as the "occurrence of relevant behavior under different, nontraining conditions without the scheduling of the same events in those conditions as had been scheduled in the training conditions" (p. 350). They made the point that a "therapeutic behavior change, to be effective, often (not always) must occur over time, persons, and settings, and the effects of the change sometimes should spread to a variety of related behaviors" (p. 350). When generalization of a skill has occurred fully and appropriately, the individual can and will use that skill whenever and wherever he or she needs it and will not typically use it (overgeneralization) inappropriately. Thus, the end product of generalization is what we normally think of as competence with a skill.

It may be useful to think of generalization as a key part of the process of learning. For example, a young child might first acquire very limited use of the word "more." Initially, he or she might have trouble pronouncing this word, may fail to use it in a variety of situations in which it would be very functional, and, in the course of learning its effects and pragmatic privileges, might try it out in some situations in which it is nonfunctional or minimally functional (e.g., perhaps requesting more juice after his or her cup has just been filled). With experience, his or her knowledge of the phonology, meaning, and pragmatics of "more" would solidify, and he or she would use it (generalization) appropriately and rarely use it inappropriately. In other words, he or she would become fully competent with "more."

At any point in the learning process, we may attempt to measure generalization by applying various probes to indicate the child's working knowledge of the target skill. Based on such probes, researchers often estimate the extent to which an individual has generalized a target skill. Mistakes or errors in using a skill (either under- or overgeneralization) as observed anecdotally or via a probe are a clear sign of learning. Mistakes or errors that become stable patterns, however, are often an indication of a learning problem. We can apply this same logic to virtually any human skill that is learned. Indeed, generalization is a basic part of learning, regardless of whether learning is self-initiated, the result of natural contingencies, or the result of therapists' and/or teachers' diligent efforts (Billingsley, Burgess, Lynch, & Matlock, 1991; Haring, 1988; Horner & Billingsley, 1988). The measurement of generalization presents a wide range of conceptual and methodological problems (Warren, 1985). For example, just because a child fails to generalize a given skill under a certain set of probe conditions, this does not mean the child will not generalize that skill under other types of conditions, or even later under the same conditions. Measures of generalization are susceptible to error, as are most types of measurements and assessments. Furthermore, historically, the social sciences have a long history of either not measuring generalization at all (Warren, 1977) or measuring it under easy conditions that do not allow a good estimate of the extent to which the patient or client or student or child is actually competent with the skill (Gazdag & Warren, 1992). Finally, it may be difficult to measure the generalization of some types of skills or knowledge (no matter how precise and valid our measures), because they are acquired so quickly that the learning process is virtually invisible. For example, around age 4, many typically developing children appear to learn new words from a single exposure, a process called fast mapping (Miller & Gildea, 1987). One day they do not know a given word, and the next day they do.

Our primary concerns in this chapter are how to interpret generalization failures and successes and how to promote meaningful generalization. We are specifically concerned about the extent to which generalization is related to the components of integrated service delivery. We have evidence that each of these components *can* effect generalization (e.g., Hart, 1985; Stokes & Baer, 1977; Stremel-Campbell & Campbell, 1985). But we also have clear evidence that an intervention approach can omit some of these components, and yet robust generalization and learning still occur. In fact, a child's ability to generalize across a variety of stimulus differences (i.e., across settings, interaction styles) is strong evidence that he or she truly has acquired a skill and is competent with it.

## THE NATURE OF GENERALIZATION RESEARCH

Ideally, we would now turn to the published research on generalization as a result of different types of interventions (i.e., communication, motor) and get a clear indication of the effects of different therapy models (e.g., segregated versus integrated) or the effects of different components of these models (e.g., pull-out versus in-class therapy) as established by a substantial number of well-executed experimental studies. Unfortunately, this is not easily accomplished, owing to certain limitations with the present databases. To highlight these limitations, we briefly consider the nature of generalization research in the domains of motor and communication intervention. These limitations are relevant to the recommendations offered at the end of this chapter.

## Communication and Language

The extraordinary importance of measuring and analyzing generalization resulting from communication and language intervention efforts was noted early (Schiefelbusch & Lloyd, 1974). In the 1960s and 1970s, formal generalization analyses were omitted from the majority of behavioral research studies (Stokes & Baer, 1977; Warren, 1977). Since then, the trend has reversed itself. Generalization analyses are now included in the majority of published language intervention studies (Goldstein & Hockenberger, 1991). Although this trend is good news, generalization is a complex, multifaceted concept that can be measured on many levels. For example, at least four basic types of language generalization are possible (Warren, 1988). These are cross-modal (e.g., receptive to productive language, spoken to written words), stimulus-and-response class (e.g., word meanings and uses), recombinatory (e.g., syntactic and morphological expressions), and stimulus (e.g., across contexts, pragmatics). Similar complexity is inherent with motor development (Horn, 1991) and social skill development (Brown & Odom, 1994). Unfortunately, many reported measures of generalization appear to be superficial and even trivial. Such measures can give a misleading impression of the effects of an intervention.

Gazdag and Warren (1992) conducted an analysis of 23 studies of language intervention with children with mental retardation published between 1979 and 1989. To be included in this analysis, a study had to include an experimental analysis of stimulus generalization. This is the type of generalization necessary for pull-out therapy to be effective. It is the most frequently reported type of generalization in the literature (Horner, Dunlap, & Koegel, 1988; Stokes & Baer, 1977). In the Gazdag and Warren (1992) analysis, stimulus generalization referred to the use of the targeted verbal responses across five dimensions: persons, settings, materials, peers, and interaction styles. The 23 studies yielded a total of 64 separate tests of stimulus generalization. The number of stimulus generalization tests was calculated by determining the number of tests that varied from each other (within a study) in terms of the five dimensions assessed (i.e., persons, settings, materials, peers, interaction styles).

Of the 64 tests analyzed, 44% reported a strong generalization effect (i.e., occurrence of the target form on 67% or more of the possible occurrences) and 41% reported moderate generalization (i.e., occurrence of the target form between 33% and 66% of the possible occurrences). In sum, 85% of the tests revealed strong to moderate stimulus generalization—a very encouraging result.

The data reported by Gazdag and Warren (1992) are obviously susceptible to a publication bias; that is, positive results tend to be published, but failures do not. However, a more significant factor may have been that 52% of the reported generalization tests differed from the training context on only a single stimulus dimension (e.g., the person doing the test), whereas an additional 36% differed in only two dimensions. That is, 88% of the tests differed from the intervention on only one or two of the possible five stimulus dimensions. It has been demonstrated experimentally (Halle, 1989; Halle & Holt, 1991) that changing only one or two stimulus dimensions does not serve as a robust test of generalization and may indicate very little about the actual generality of the skill in question.

The primary point of the Gazdag and Warren (1992) analysis is that many reported stimulus generalization successes constitute relatively superficial analyses. In studies that reported strong to moderate generalization, it is not known (without a careful reading of the specific studies) whether this is a trivial result or a true indicator of the general efficacy of the intervention used. This observation corresponds with other analyses of subsets of the communication intervention literature (e.g., Kaiser, Yoder, & Keetz, 1992; Tannock & Girolametto, 1992), which, although reporting positive effects, also noted that the majority of studies reviewed assessed generalization in very limited ways, making it difficult to estimate overall intervention effects.

## Motor Skills

The importance of measuring generalization resulting from intervention designed to enhance motor skills has also been widely acknowledged since the late 1980s (Harris, 1988). The experimental intervention literature for this domain is plagued with serious problems, however. In a critical review of 28 studies of various motor intervention approaches applied to children under age 10 with cerebral palsy, Horn (1991) reported a wide range of major conceptual and methodological problems. These included an absence of well-defined and well-implemented intervention techniques, narrowly conceived treatment targets and outcome measures, poor subject description, flawed experimental designs, and a virtual absence of comprehensive measurements of generalization. In most studies, generalization was neither programmed to occur nor measured as it might have occurred. Furthermore, an analysis of the data that were available was inconclusive regarding the relative efficacy of any of the approaches investigated (i.e., neurodevelopmental therapy, sensory integration, behavioral programming).

Given the small number of studies published on any one approach to motor skill intervention, and the substantial conceptual and methodological limitations identified by Horn (1991) and others (e.g., Harris, 1988; Ottenbacher & Peterson, 1985), we might conclude that it is simply premature to concern ourselves with whether motor interventions are more effective when delivered via segregated or integrated approaches. However, several well-conceptualized motor intervention studies suggesting that at least some dimensions of an integrated approach can substantially enhance the effectiveness of motor intervention have been conducted (e.g., Horn, Warren, & Jones, 1995). Also, physical therapists, a prime agent of motor interventions, tend to use the most isolated approaches of all therapy types (McWilliam & Sekerak, 1995). Given that the effectiveness of traditional physical therapy services to children with cerebral palsy has been seriously questioned in several studies (e.g., Palmer et al., 1988; Piper et al., 1986; Rothberg, Goodman, Jacklin, & Cooper, 1991), the need for this therapy to move toward integrated services, assuming that they are more effective in promoting generalization, should not be understated.

## INDICATIONS FROM DATA

To our knowledge, no full-scale comparisons have been made of segregated versus integrated services in which all six defining principles have been systematically varied. There is a very limited database comparing the effects of pull-out versus in-class therapies that is relevant to this issue. There are also data on across-setting and across-adult generalization effects that are relevant to this same dimension. We briefly consider what these data indicate in the next sections.

### Comparative Studies

Several researchers have suggested that incorporating therapy into a child's daily routines where the skills are required may help ensure functional outcomes, continued use, and appropriate responding to natural cues in the environment (Bruder, 1993; Dunn, 1991; Rainforth et al., 1992; Snell & Brown, 1993; see also Chapter 5). Several intervention studies carried out directly in the environments in which children are expected to use the skills have demonstrated promising effects (e.g., Giangreco, 1986). Nevertheless, research on the relative effectiveness of integrated versus pull-out models has been inconclusive (McWilliam & Bailey, 1994); that is, no clear advantage for integrated models has been shown. Several of these comparative studies are briefly reviewed below.

Cole, Harris, Eland, and Mills (1989) found no significant differences on standardized measures of motor development between preschoolers receiving in-class and pull-out direct services for physical therapy and occupational therapy. The services delivered to the subjects differed only in terms of location and group size (individual or small group). Wilcox, Kouri, and Caswell (1991) investigated the relative effects of in-class versus pull-out use of an interactive modeling procedure to promote lexical acquisition in 20 preschool children randomly assigned to the in-class or pull-out therapy. Results indicated that use of the target words as measured by treatment data was equal between the two groups, but that children in the in-class treatment group demonstrated a greater degree of productive use of the target words on a generalization measure taken in their homes. Roberts, Prizant, and McWilliam (1995) investigated the effects of in-class versus pull-out language intervention with 15 preschool children with disabilities. Their data were inconclusive regarding the relative efficacy of these service delivery modes. Finally, McWilliam and Spencer (1993) compared the effects of pull-out versus in-class therapy on the social skills of three children. Children's generalization of the target behaviors to nontherapy classroom times was measured. No consistent pattern of differences between pull-out and in-class therapy was shown in terms of the children's generalization.

Research comparing in-class versus pull-out therapy is so minimal at present that no conclusion about the relative effects of these service delivery variables should be made. Other research, however, does suggest that generalization from pull-out therapy to the classroom may be more difficult to achieve than generalization from in-class training, because children need to generalize skills across more stimulus dimensions. We turn now to a brief discussion of across-setting and across-adult generalization research associated with milieu language intervention.

## Across-Setting and Across-Adult Generalization

Generalization occurs more readily when the differences between the treatment and generalization contexts are relatively minimal. This has also been demonstrated by experimental learning research over the years (McReynolds & Spradlin, 1989). Furthermore, generalization across a number of stimulus dimensions suggests that a child is approaching a level of competence with a skill (Warren, 1988). Generalization of a treatment target by a child across settings and adults is the same type of generalization necessary for pull-out therapy to be effective.

Milieu language teaching has generated a substantial body of empirical research over the past 15 years. As an intervention approach, it can be used in a variety of contexts, including pull-out, in-class, and at home. Kaiser et al. (1992) conducted a detailed evaluation of the effects of milieu teaching. Nineteen of the studies they reviewed included data relevant to the issue of generalization across settings, adults, or both. Kaiser et al. summarized these data as follows:

> The results of assessments of generalization across settings and trainers appear to be related to the specific type of format used to evaluate child behavior. When only one aspect of the generalization setting (i.e., setting or trainer) varied from the original training setting, generalization was typically strong. When two (setting and trainer) or three (setting, trainer, and task format) aspects were changed, child generalization was more varied. The two most difficult tests of generalization (as reported in studies by Warren and Bambara, 1989, and Warren and Gazdag,

1990) had the most inconsistent results. These were generalization to truly naturalistic interactions with untrained teachers in nontraining settings and generalization
to probe formats in which alternative responses could be used to answer appropriately. (p. 28)

The across-settings and across-adult generalization effects reported with
milieu teaching are similar to the effects reported with other approaches and in
other domains (Brown & Odom, 1994; Horn, 1991; Horner et al., 1988;
Tannock & Girolametto, 1992). This research suggests that in-class instruction
may have an advantage over pull-out therapies in terms of generalization. This
advantage may be more artifactual than real, however. That is, if pull-out and
in-class therapies are compared on equally difficult tests of generalization (i.e.,
same number and difficulty of stimulus differences), do these differences
disappear? The very limited comparative research reviewed earlier hints at
this possibility. Perhaps making an issue of where or who does the training
sets up the proverbial straw man, diverting us from the more important
differences and dimensions of integrated versus segregated service delivery. To
bring this issue into focus, we now examine two intervention approaches
studied in a pull-out context, but incorporating many elements of integrated
therapy models. These studies have reported unusually strong generalization
across a number of dimensions.

## Neurobehavioral Motor Intervention

Neurobehavioral motor intervention is a hybrid combination of behavioral
teaching principles and neurodevelopmental handling and positioning principles. Historically, the effects of behavioral and neurodevelopmental approaches on the motor skill acquisition of children with cerebral palsy
and other impairments have been investigated separately. On their own,
neither approach has generated impressive results (Horn, 1991). These approaches are compatible in application, however, although perhaps not in
theory (Bobath, 1980). The approach with the strongest empirical base,
behavioral programming, provides a technology and set of guidelines on
how to teach, but does not specify what to teach (e.g., Filler & Kasari, 1981;
Horn & Warren, 1987; Lee, Mahler, & Westling, 1985). It was used to guide
the development of highly motivating, functional activities as a context
for training. The neurodevelopmental approach (Bobath, 1980) specifies the
underlying components of movement that must be acquired for normalized
motor functioning as well as techniques to facilitate their expression, but
not how to use the movement components to achieve a functional outcome
(Gordon, 1987).

Horn and colleagues investigated the effects of a neurobehavioral approach on the acquisition and generalization of specific movement components
by 11 infants and toddlers (ages 7–34 months at the start of the intervention)
with cerebral palsy (Horn, Jones, & Warren, 1995a, 1995b; Horn, Warren, &

Jones, 1995). For each of the 11 children, three components of movement and two exemplar skills for each movement component were selected and defined based on a comprehensive assessment. One exemplar skill of each movement component was trained, and the other untrained exemplar skills were probed for response generalization. Children received 30 minutes of training per day, 4 days per week. A comprehensive analysis of stimulus and response generalization was conducted. Only two of the six principles of integrated therapy were implemented (i.e., training embedded in routines, functional skills taught), not because these dimensions are incompatible with this approach, but because of the experimental nature of this initial analysis of the neurobehavioral approach.

At the beginning of the intervention, none of the children could do any of the target skills. By the final three intervention measures, the children executed the treated exemplar skills correctly on 89% of the opportunities. In follow-up probes in the intervention context, they executed the treated exemplars correctly on 96% of the opportunities. During baseline, the children executed the untreated exemplar skill on 2% of the occasions on average. Concurrently with the end of intervention on the treated skill, they executed the untreated skill correctly on 71% of the occasions, and on 73% of the occasions during the post-treatment follow-up. Stimulus generalization was measured to the classroom teacher (but not in the classroom setting). During baseline, all children failed to generalize the treated exemplar skill with their classroom teacher. By the end of treatment, they demonstrated generalization in an average of 75% of possible occasions with their classroom teacher and in an average of 87% of such occasions on post-treatment follow-ups. It is important to note that these basic results were replicated across 11 children, 33 treated exemplar skills, and 33 untreated exemplar skills. No treated or untreated exemplar skill failed to generalize.

The results of the Horn et al. analyses suggest that a neurobehavioral approach can be used to enhance the acquisition of specific movement components as they are exhibited in a treated exemplar skill and in a second untreated skill requiring the targeted movement component for execution. Furthermore, the children demonstrated stimulus generalization of the trained exemplar skill by performing it in probes with their classroom teachers. The results were replicated across 11 children and 33 movement components. The consistency and robustness of these results combined with the degree of generalization attained across all treated and untreated exemplar skills and children represent unusually strong effects relative to those reported in most early motor intervention studies (cf. Harris, 1988; Ottenbacher & Peterson, 1985; Palmer et al., 1988; Parrette & Hourcade, 1984).

What accounts for the unusually consistent and robust effects obtained in this research? Two features of the intervention provide plausible explanations. First, the combination of neurodevelopmental and behavioral approaches brings together a compatible set of techniques for facilitating functional movement through specific handling and positioning with techniques to stimulate and reinforce the frequent use of discrete motor skills. Second, by focusing the intervention on the underlying components of movement necessary to execute various skills, this approach avoids the common pitfall evident in many other published studies: a too narrow emphasis on specific milestone skills (e.g., head control) as either the focus of intervention or the outcome measure (e.g., Palmer et al., 1988). In the first case, this leads to an artificial splintering of skills with minimal carryover to other functional movements—for example, the training of head control in supported sitting, with no carryover of the head control skills in other positions or situations that require a more dynamic use of head control. Other studies focused their interventions on the facilitation of movement components, but then used milestone skill assessments (i.e., developmental skill assessments) as outcome measures (e.g., Sommerfeld, Fraser, Hensinger, & Beresford, 1981). The reported failure of these studies to demonstrate change in milestone skills may be related to the lack of integration during training. That is, movement components were trained in isolation without addressing their functional use as they are exhibited within specific milestone skills. In contrast, in Horn et al.'s (1995) research, the children appeared to have acquired the underlying movement components necessary for the development and execution of a variety of movement patterns, not just a narrow set of specific behaviors.

Despite its strengths, this research has a number of limitations. First, although the analysis of generalization was extensive relative to other studies in the literature, it was still limited for practical reasons. For example, it simply was not feasible to probe both the treated and untreated exemplars in the teacher generalization context. Second, there was no effort to measure the overall impact on the children's general motor development beyond the treated and untreated exemplar skills. Third, the implementation of the intervention was constrained by the requirements of the experimental design and should not be taken to represent a best practice example of implementation of the neurobehavioral approach. For example, with seven of the children, treated skills were trained serially, not concurrently. Classroom teachers did not directly participate in the intervention so that we could measure generalization with them. Parents were not directly involved in the intervention either. It should be noted, however, that the training was provided by educational personnel. Finally, direct intervention was provided for only 30 minutes, four times per week. If it had been integrated throughout the children's days. much more instructional time might have occurred.

In three 1995 studies (Horn et al., 1995a, 1995b; Horn, Warren, & Jones, 1995), impressive and robust generalization was demonstrated using an approach that contained elements of both segregated and integrated therapy. A neurobehavioral approach could be implemented in a more integrated context than it was here, perhaps with even stronger effects. But the fact that it generated such powerful effects with only two integrated principles suggests that the six principles of integrated therapy are not equal in their effects.

## Prelinguistic Milieu Teaching

Since 1970, a relatively large amount of research has focused on developing effective early language intervention approaches. Although a great deal of knowledge accumulated during this time on the nature of prelinguistic communication development (e.g., Bates, 1979), there was very little intervention research on this topic until the 1990s (Yoder & Warren, 1993). Warren, Yoder, Gazdag, Kim, and Jones (1993), Wilcox (1992), and Yoder, Warren, Kim, and Gazdag (1994) have all reported very positive effects of prelinguistic intervention with young children with developmental delays. Warren's and Yoder's research program uses a version of milieu language teaching (Warren et al., 1993; Yoder et al., 1994) modified to teach initial prelinguistic forms of requesting and commenting. Although various modifications necessary to adapt the basic milieu approach to the prelinguistic level were made, the distinguishing characteristics of this model were maintained. These included a focus on following the child's attentional lead, embedding instruction within ongoing routines and interaction, arranging the environment to elicit child responses, focusing on specific target behaviors (e.g., requesting), and using discrete prompts when deemed necessary (e.g., time delays, models).

Warren, Yoder, and their colleagues have published two analyses of the effects of prelinguistic intervention (Warren et al., 1993; Yoder et al., 1994). Warren et al. (1993) used prelinguistic milieu teaching to teach commenting and requesting to four young children with developmental delays and little or no intentional communication. Yoder et al. (1994) replicated the effects reported by Warren et al. (1993) and extended them to an analysis of generalization by the children to interactions with their mothers and their mothers' responses. Both studies examined generalization across stimulus materials, settings, teachers, and interaction styles. In both studies, the children received 20 minutes of intervention daily, 4 days per week. For experimental reasons, the intervention was delivered in a one-to-one pull-out context. Teachers and parents were purposefully kept naïve regarding the specific goals of the intervention or techniques used so that generalization with them could be assessed. Of the six principles of integrated practice specified by McWilliam (1995), three were employed. The intervention was child-directed and embedded in routines, and functional skills were taught. But no other children were present during training, the child was removed from the classroom for training, and there was no consultation with classroom personnel or teachers.

In the Warren et al. (1993) study, all four children demonstrated robust generalization from the trainer to the classroom teacher and across settings, materials, and adult interaction styles. Two of the children demonstrated similar effects with additional classroom teachers and in additional classroom contexts (e.g., snack time). Substantial increases in general communication abilities, as measured by the Communication and Symbolic Behavior Scales (Wetherby & Prizant, 1990), were also reported. Yoder et al. (1994) replicated the basic effects reported by Warren et al. (1993) and extended them by showing that the intervention effects generalized to the children's interactions with their mothers. Substantial increases in linguistic mapping (e.g., providing a label for an item the child has requested) by teachers and parents occurred concurrently with increases in the children's rates of requesting in both studies.

There are some intriguing reasons why interventions that teach children to communicate, that teach them how to comment and request prelinguistically and thus move from preintentional to intentional communication, may have unusually strong generalized effects. First, during their initial acquisition of intentional communication forms, children are actually acquiring basic communication functions (e.g., requesting, commenting, protesting, greeting), not simply new forms for expressing old functions (e.g., saying "more" as a request form or "no" as a protest), which is much of what later communication and language acquisition is concerned with. Acquiring these basic functions provides children with their first effective means of intentional communication— a powerful means of controlling any environment they are in.

Second, these functions are acquired against the backdrop of a very restricted repertoire of intentional behavior. This small repertoire makes it relatively easy for adults to recognize and respond differentially to new behaviors. In contrast, it is obviously difficult for even sensitive, attentive parents and teachers to recognize and respond contingently and positively to most new instances of behavior by a 3-year-old child who is learning an average of 10 new words per day and has a large, frequently used, complex repertoire of intentional behavior and sophisticated language. Warren, Yoder, and colleagues report data (Warren et al., 1993; Yoder et al., 1994) demonstrating that teachers and parents do respond differently to the display of prelinguistic requests by young children with mental retardation. For example, they more frequently supply a label contingent on whatever the child has requested (linguistic mapping) in addition to fulfilling the request. This transactional effect is potentially important because linguistic mapping is thought to be one of the primary devices used by adults to teach vocabulary to children (Nelson, 1989). This leads us to a compelling question: If we "turn on" prelinguistic communication via intervention, does this also "turn on" the environment in ways like linguistic mapping that enhance further communication and language development?

## DIMENSIONS OF INTEGRATED THERAPY

What are we to conclude from the neurobehavioral motor intervention and prelinguistic milieu intervention research? That the location of therapy is irrelevant, at least compared to other variables? That the presence of peers is more superficial than functional? That the use of a specialist as a consultant is a minor detail? These studies do not directly address these issues. They do suggest that the child's attentional engagement, the functionality of the skills taught, and embedding instruction into meaningful interaction may be relatively more important than the other three principles. We now discuss the six principles of integrated therapy in terms of their likely contribution to meaningful generalization.

## Therapy in the Child's Classroom

In-class instruction facilitates communication between specialists and teachers and minimizes the differences between therapy and the child's normal environments, thus promoting generalization. It should help to make therapy more normalized and relevant to the child and to others who interact with him or her. As we noted previously, in-class instruction may make generalization easier, but not necessarily stronger or more robust. All things considered, we favor in-class instruction. The data that support this as a critical dimension of instruction or therapy are weak at best, however.

## Presence of Other Children

Some types of instruction, notably social and communication skills, can be aided by the presence of other children. It may even be critical to have other children present for social skills instruction to have a reasonable chance of generalization (Brown & Odom, 1994). It may also be the only feasible way to conduct instruction in many classrooms because of child-to-teacher ratios and the lack of space to conduct pull-out therapy. Evidence suggesting that the presence of peers specifically promotes generalization is weak, however. We favor the presence of other children, assuming that it does not interfere with instruction. Except for social skills instruction, however, we do not consider it an important variable.

## Therapy and Instruction Should Be Embedded in Ongoing Classroom Routines and Activities

We think the critical requirement is that routines be highly engaging, not that they necessarily be based in the classroom. Routines are defined as repetitive, predictable, turn-taking games, rituals, or activities (Yoder & Warren, 1993). The predictability of routines is important because routines allow children to devote greater attentional resources to actually learning new skills. This is where the quality of moderate novelty within a routine influences learning. If all aspects of a routine are familiar, the child may become bored and unresponsive, as sometimes occurs in rote learning tasks. Yet, if an activity is too novel or not yet a routine, children may spend much of their attentional energy exploring the activity and trying to establish their role. In contrast, moderate novelty typically attracts the child's attention. It is created when a new element or twist is added to a familiar routine (Jones & Warren, 1991).

Established caregiving, play, and social routines provide contexts in which young children can be comfortable with their role. This familiarity directly aids in the learning of new skills (e.g., words, movements) that represent novel stimuli against the familiar backdrop of the predictable routine. Instruction is the art of constantly introducing new (i.e., moderately novel) knowledge and skills that are linked directly to the child's present knowledge base and embedded in ongoing, predictable routines (Bricker & Cripe, 1992).

Attentional engagement and embedded instruction are closely linked concepts (Warren, 1991). Conceptually and empirically, there is clear evidence that they are essential elements of effective instruction and lead to efficient learning and generalization.

## Therapy and Instruction Should Follow the Child's Attentional Lead

It is difficult to overstate the importance of attentional engagement to learning. When the rate and quality of attentional engagement are high, then learning is maximally efficient and teaching can work optimally. The adult's ability to follow the child's attentional lead, particularly with children who are developmentally young, can directly affect the quality of the child's attention.

The quality of a child's attention is substantially greater to objects or events of the child's choosing, rather than to objects or events of the adult's choosing (Bruner, Roy, & Ratner, 1980). Thus, the specialist's or teacher's ability to follow the child's attentional lead and focus on the child's topic of interest is superior to directly recruiting the child's attention. When the child engages an object, event, or person, he or she is identifying what, for the moment, is of prepotent interest to him or her. If the adult focuses on the same topic, joint attention is established. In this context of joint attention, direct instruction can proceed for as long as the child's attention is maintained (Hart, 1985; McCathren, Yoder, & Warren, 1995).

The role of attentional engagement and the procedure of following the child's attentional lead to ensure it are of fundamental importance to effective instruction and generalization. Poor attentional engagement is likely to drastically affect generalization. This aspect of integrated therapy may have little to do with where instruction is done, who is present, or who does it, but its importance to promoting generalization and learning can hardly be understated.

## Goals Should Be Functional and Immediately Useful

Functional, immediately useful goals aid generalization. Virtually every teacher and specialist favors teaching functional skills. But some functional goals may be more functional than others. We suspect that one of the reasons why the neurobehavioral motor intervention and the prelinguistic milieu intervention previously discussed achieved such strong generalization was that the targeted skills were both functional and foundational. Foundational skills are behaviors that theoretically prepare a child for more successful functioning, but do not necessarily lead to immediate utility (McWilliam, 1995). For example, teaching presumed cognitive prerequisites of intentional communication (e.g., means–ends relationships) would be a form of foundational instruction, but perhaps not functional instruction.

Horn and colleagues (Horn, Jones, & Warren, 1995a, 1995b; Horn, Warren, & Jones, 1995) focused on the underlying components of movement necessary to execute various skills but taught children to manifest these components in meaningful motor acts. Warren et al. (1993) and Yoder et al. (1994) taught basic functions that are both immediately useful and set the stage for the development of more advanced communication skills based on these foundational building blocks of intentional communication. In both the motor and communication studies, these new functions or foundations were not pitted against any competing forms or functions. For example, children had no alternative requesting strategy with a long history of effectiveness with which a new form of requesting had to compete, prove itself more effective, and ultimately replace or at least complement.

Goals that are both functional and foundational in nature will probably generalize relatively well, regardless of the context in which they are specifically acquired. In a sense, these goals are truly functional. But for other functional goals, the struggle to become established in a child's repertoire may be more difficult. For example, to begin using two-word request forms instead of one-word forms (e.g., "more") combined with a pointing gesture may depend on differential responding by adults in the child's environment, contingently reinforcing the more elaborate response instead of the simpler form. Perhaps, in these cases, where instruction occurs (i.e., in the classroom and/or at home) and who does it (i.e., those who interact most with the child) become much more crucial for generalization to occur efficiently and completely.

## The Specialist as Collaborator

If a specialist is too narrowly trained and thus is not skilled at creating a high degree of attentional engagement, at creating routines and embedding instruction in them, and at developing goals that are both foundational and functional, then his or her direct training efforts may not lead to robust generalization. Furthermore, if his or her caseload is too high (as it often is) and he or she cannot work with the child several times per week, then his or her efforts may simply be too diluted to have much impact. In addition, if ineffective efforts keep others from addressing the child's motor or communication needs in the classroom, then the specialist is a hindrance to the child's optimal development. If the specialist can work with the child frequently and meets the other conditions noted above, however, then his or her efforts may aid the child directly even as pull-out therapy. If not, then, from the perspective of learning and generalization, the specialist should work primarily as a consultant to the classroom teachers and parents.

## PROMOTING GENERALIZATION

Skills that are both functional and foundational may generalize strongly. But there are a very limited number of foundational skills (e.g., to request, to greet, to indicate, to reach and grasp). Thus, most learning (and instruction) involves displacing an established but less sophisticated form of a function with a new form. Inevitably, this creates a competition between the new and old forms. The old form may have a long history of valuable service to the child as a good enough solution to a particular problem (Thelen, 1995). To displace it, the new form must represent a more successful solution to the given problem (e.g., getting the cookie, getting mom's attention, getting a favorite program on the television, getting out of something that is no fun, propelling oneself across the floor, indicating which doll is wanted ).

Awareness that old and new forms of a function may compete in the natural environment provides a different perspective of the generalization process. Variability in a child's use of a new form suggests that response competition is occurring and that learning may still be unstable (Thelen, 1995). Stable, broadly generalized responding indicates that the new form has successfully displaced the old form. From this perspective, interventions must compete with the child's current solution to a given problem. How can we ensure that the new target skill will win this competition?

We believe that integrated therapy is an important part of the answer to this question because to ensure that a new form (but not a new function) is established in a child's repertoire, we need to determine the factors that may influence generalization. This implies that we attempt to take a broad systems approach to instruction (Warren, 1988, 1993), which is intended to ensure that new forms are taught and supported by as many elements of the instructional context as possible. The six principles of integrated therapy reflect a substantial portion of what we can control and program. Other aspects of instruction also may be critically important. We offer four general recommendations below.

### Increase Rate of Use

The more frequently a child initiates a newly learned skill or behavior, the more feedback he or she gets from the environment about the effects of that skill, its optimal form and uses, and the appropriate contexts for its use. To quote Lois Bloom (1995), "[I]t turns out that frequency matters" (p. xi). Rate of behavior or skill use can be directly influenced by ensuring that children have opportunities and encouragement to use a new skill or behavior, which can be provided by activity-based curriculum approaches (Bricker & Cripe, 1992) or by the embedded use of milieu teaching strategies during a child's day (e.g., Hart, 1985; Warren, 1991).

## Increase Follow-Through

McWilliam and Scarborough (1994) found that teachers facilitated skills trained in therapy (i.e., provided follow-through) less than 5% of the time and at a frequency of less than one event per 10 minutes in the day following the therapy session in question. Poor follow-through provides insufficient support for a new form to displace an old form in a child's repertoire. Effective follow-through should be one of the primary goals of frequent consultation between specialists, teachers, and parents. It is often the weak link preventing truly effective instruction. Fully integrated therapy provides a better context for effective follow-through, but does not guarantee it.

## Take a Developmental Perspective

Development is not a linear process. Different skills develop differently, and their differences have very important implications for intervention. The truth of these statements is self-evident, but do we apply these truths to our expectations of children and to our intervention approaches? For example, it takes a typical child several months to acquire his or her first 10 words productively (Fenson et al., 1994). If typical children take this long, what expectation should we have for children with developmental delays? Many syntactic skills also take months and years to acquire from the point at which the child first begins actively acquiring them. Meanwhile, the acquisition of various elements of phonology (i.e., sounds) takes years, as do many gross and fine motor skills. In contrast, there are points in development when typical 4-year-olds are "fast mapping" several new words a day into their lexicon (Rice, 1990). Knowledge of the development trajectories of a variety of skills and the typical variability associated with these trajectories can allow individualization of interventions to the characteristics of the skills being taught and to the characteristics of the individual learner. This may help us to continue with skills that naturally take a long time to learn as well as to reevaluate an approach that may not be working with a type of skill that perhaps should proceed more quickly (e.g., vocabulary learning with children who are developmentally advanced).

## Accurately Interpret Generalization Effects

As noted earlier, some of the literature documenting generalization effects can be misleading. Many studies report moderate to strong generalization, but these tests were relatively easy and involved only one or two stimulus differences. Our goal should be strong, robust generalization across a variety of contexts and conditions. Anything less should be viewed as insufficient. Again, we should also take into account the characteristics of the targeted skill. For example, social and pragmatic skills are notoriously affected by the context in which they are measured and thus can easily give the impression of meaningful change where there is only a fleeting, context-dependent change. In contrast, motor skills and syntactic rules tend to be less context-determined in general. To ensure that our interventions are effective, we should probe widely for stable, generalized use. Finally, we should be mindful that generalization is strictly an individual phenomenon that varies from skill to skill, child to child, and context to context. How much training will be necessary to achieve robust, stable effects cannot be determined a priori.

## CONCLUSIONS

Our choice of therapy models should be driven by empirical evidence of their relative effectiveness. We presently lack this evidence. Thorough, meaningful generalization analyses, however, can act as self-correcting mechanisms guiding us steadily toward increasingly effective intervention approaches. These analyses suggest that three principles compatible with either integrated or segregated therapy (e.g., following the child's attentional lead, embedding instruction in routines, teaching functional skills) can produce powerful generalization effects when applied to foundational skills. Fully integrated models may have their strongest effects, in relative terms, when intervention focuses on teaching new forms for old functions.

## REFERENCES

Bates, E. (1979). *The emergence of symbols.* New York: Academic Press.

Billingsley, F.F., Burgess, D., Lynch, V.W., & Matlock, B.L. (1991). Toward generalized outcomes: Considerations and guidelines for writing instructional objectives. *Education and Training in Mental Retardation, 4,* 351–360.

Bloom, L. (1995). Foreword. In B. Hart & T.R. Risley, *Meaningful differences in the everyday experience of young American children.* Baltimore: Paul H. Brookes Publishing Co.

Bobath, K. (1980). *A neurophysiological basis for the treatment of cerebral palsy.* London: William Heinemann Medical Books.

Bricker, D., & Cripe, J.W. (1992). *An activity-based approach to early intervention.* Baltimore: Paul H. Brookes Publishing Co.

Brown, W.H., & Odom, S.L. (1994). Strategies and tactics for promoting generalization and maintenance of young children's social behavior. *Research in Developmental Disabilities, 15*(2), 99–118.

Bruder, M.D. (1993). Working with members of other disciplines: Collaboration for success. In M. Wolery & J.S. Wilbers (Eds.), *Including children with special needs in early childhood programs* (pp. 45–70). Washington, DC: National Association for the Education of Young Children.

Bruner, J., Roy, C., & Ratner, N. (1980). The beginnings of request. In K.E. Nelson (Ed.), *Children's language* (Vol. 3, pp. 91–138). New York: Gardner Press.

Cole, K., Harris, S., Eland, S., & Mills, P. (1989). Comparison of two service delivery models: In-class and out-of-class therapy approaches. *Pediatric Physical Therapy, 1,* 49–54.

Dunn, W. (1991). Integrated related services. In L.H. Meyer, C.A. Peck, & L. Brown (Eds.), *Critical issues in the lives of people with severe disabilities* (pp. 353–377). Baltimore: Paul H. Brookes Publishing Co.

Fenson, L., Dale, P.S., Reznick, J.S., Bates, E., Thal, D.J., & Pethick, S.J. (1994). Variability in early communicative development. *Monographs of the Society for Research in Child Development, 59*(5, Serial No. 242).

Filler, J., & Kasari, C. (1981). Acquisition, maintenance, and generalization of parent taught skills with two severely handicapped infants. *Journal of The Association for Persons with Severe Handicaps, 6*(1), 30–38.

Gazdag, G., & Warren, S.F. (1992, March). *An analysis of stimulus generalization reported in language intervention studies.* Paper presented at the 24th Annual Gatlinburg Conference on Research and Theory on MR/DD, Gatlinburg, TN.

Giangreco, M. (1986). Effects of integrated therapy: A pilot study. *Journal of The Association for Persons with Severe Handicaps, 11,* 205–208.

Giangreco, M.F., Edelman, S., & Dennis, R. (1991). Common professional practices that interfere with integrated delivery of related services. *Remedial and Special Education, 12*(2), 16–24.

Goldstein, H., & Hockenberger, E.H. (1991). Significant progress in child language intervention: An 11-year retrospective. *Research in Developmental Disabilities, 12,* 401–425.

Gordon, J. (1987). Assumptions underlying physical therapy intervention: Theoretical and historical perspectives. In J.H. Carr, R.B. Shepherd, & J. Gordon (Eds.), *Movement science: Foundation for physical therapy in rehabilitation* (pp. 41–57). Rockville, MD: Aspen Publishers, Inc.

Halle, J.W. (1989). Identifying stimuli in the natural environment that control verbal responses. *Journal of Speech and Hearing Disorders, 54,* 500–504.

Halle, J.W., & Holt, B. (1991). Assessing stimulus control in natural settings: An analysis of stimuli that acquire control during training. *Journal of Applied Behavior Analysis, 24,* 579–589.

Haring, N.G. (1988). A technology for generalization. In N.G. Haring (Ed.), *Generalization for students with severe handicaps: Strategies and solutions* (pp. 5–11). Seattle: University of Washington Press.

Harris, S. (1988). Early intervention: Does developmental therapy make a difference? *Topics in Early Childhood Special Education, 7,* 20–32.

Hart, B. (1985). Naturalistic language training techniques. In S.F. Warren & A. Rogers-Warren (Eds.), *Teaching functional language* (pp. 63–88). Austin, TX: PRO-ED.

Hart, B., & Risley, T.R. (1995). *Meaningful differences in the everyday experience of young American children.* Baltimore: Paul H. Brookes Publishing Co.

Horn, E. (1991). Basic motor skills instruction for children with neuromotor delays: A critical review. *Journal of Special Education, 25,* 168–197.

Horn, E., Jones, H., & Warren, S.F. (1995a). *Concurrent skill intervention in motor development for young children with cerebral palsy: An experimental analysis.* Unpublished manuscript, Vanderbilt University, Nashville, TN.

Horn, E., Jones, H., & Warren, S.F. (1995b). *Systematic replication of neurobehavioral motor skills intervention with young children with cerebral palsy.* Unpublished manuscript, Vanderbilt University, Nashville, TN.

Horn, E., & Warren, S.F. (1987). Facilitating the acquisition of sensorimotor behavior with a microcomputer mediated teaching system: An experimental analysis. *Journal of The Association for Persons with Severe Handicaps, 12,* 205–215.

Horn, E., Warren, S.F., & Jones, H. (1995). An experimental analysis of neuro-behavioral motor intervention. *Developmental Medicine and Child Neurology, 37,* 566–583.

Horner, R.H., & Billingsley, F.F. (1988). The effect of competing behavior on the generalization and maintenance of adaptive behavior in applied settings. In R.H. Horner, G. Dunlap, & R.L. Koegel (Eds.), *Generalization and maintenance: Life-style changes in applied settings* (pp. 197–220). Baltimore: Paul H. Brookes Publishing Co.

Horner, R.H., Dunlap, G., & Koegel, R.L. (Eds.). (1988). *Generalization and maintenance: Life-style changes in applied settings.* Baltimore: Paul H. Brookes Publishing Co.

Jones, H.A., & Warren, S.F. (1991). Enhancing engagement in early language teaching. *Teaching Exceptional Children, 23,* 48–50.

Kaiser, A.P., Yoder, P., & Keetz, A. (1992). Evaluating milieu teaching. In S.F. Warren & J. Reichle (Eds.), *Causes and effects in communication and language intervention* (pp. 9–47). Baltimore: Paul H. Brookes Publishing Co.

Lee, J.M., Mahler, T.J., & Westling, D.L. (1985). Reducing occurrences of an ATNR. *American Journal of Mental Deficiency, 89*(6), 617–621.

McCathren, R.B., Yoder, P.J., & Warren, S.F. (1995). The role of directives in early language intervention. *Journal of Early Intervention, 19*(2), 91–101.

McReynolds, L.V., & Spradlin, J.E. (Eds.). (1989). *Generalization strategies in the treatment of communication disorders.* Philadelphia: B.C. Decker.

McWilliam, R.A. (1995). Integration of therapy and consultative special education: A continuum in early intervention. *Infants and Young Children, 7*(4), 29–38.

McWilliam, R.A., & Bailey, D.B. (1994). Predictors of service-delivery models in center-based early intervention. *Exceptional Children, 61,* 25–39.

McWilliam, R.A., & Scarborough, A. (1994, September). *Does therapy carry over to the classroom? How to make early intervention more effective.* Paper presented at the North Carolina Association for the Education of Young Children/Division for Early Childhood Annual Study Conference, Greensboro, NC.

McWilliam, R.A., & Sekerak, D. (1995). Integrated practices in center-based early intervention: Perceptions of physical therapists. *Pediatric Physical Therapy, 7,* 51–58.

McWilliam, R.A., & Spencer, A.G. (1993, December). *Integrated versus pull-out speech-language services in early intervention: A mixed-method study.* Poster presented at the International Early Childhood Conference on Children with Special Needs, San Diego, CA.

Miller, G.A., & Gildea, P.M. (1987). How children learn words. *Scientific American, 257,* 94–99.

Nelson, K.E. (1989). Strategies for first language teaching. In M.L. Rice & R.L. Schiefelbusch (Eds.), *The teachability of language* (pp. 263–310). Baltimore: Paul H. Brookes Publishing Co.

Ottenbacher, K., & Peterson, P. (1985). A meta-analysis of applied vestibular stimulation research. *Physical and Occupational Therapy in Pediatrics, 5,* 119–134.

Palmer, F.B., Shapiro, B.K., Wachtel, R.C., Allen, M.C., Hiller, J.E., Harryman, M.S., Mosher, B.S., Meinert, C.L., & Capute, A.J. (1988). The effects of physical therapy on cerebral palsy. *New England Journal of Medicine, 318,* 803–808.

Parrette, H.P., & Hourcade, J.J. (1984). How effective are physiotherapeutic programs with young mentally retarded children who have cerebral palsy? *Journal of Mental Deficiency Research, 28,* 167–175.

Piper, M.C., Junos, V., Willis, D., Mazer, B.L., Ramsay, M., & Wilver, K.M. (1986). Early physical therapy effects on the high-risk infant: A randomized controlled trial. *Pediatrics, 78,* 216–224.

Rainforth, B., York, J., & Macdonald, C. (1992). *Collaborative teams for students with severe disabilities: Integrating therapy and educational services.* Baltimore: Paul H. Brookes Publishing Co.

Rice, M.L. (1990). Preschooler's QUIL: Quick incidental learning of words. In G. Conti-Ramsden & C.E. Snow (Eds.), *Children's language* (Vol. 7). Hillsdale, NJ: Lawrence Erlbaum Associates.

Roberts, J.E., Prizant, B., & McWilliam, R.A. (1995). Out-of-class versus in-class service delivery in language intervention: Effects on communication interaction with young children. *American Journal of Speech-Language Pathology, 4,* 87–94.

Rothberg, A.D., Goodman, M., Jacklin, L.A., & Cooper, P.A. (1991). Six-year follow-up of early physiotherapy intervention in very low birth weight infants. *Pediatrics, 88,* 547–552.

Schiefelbusch, R.L., & Lloyd, L.L. (Eds.). (1974). *Language perspectives: Acquisition, retardation, and intervention.* Baltimore: University Park Press.

Snell, M.E., & Brown, F. (1993). Instructional planning and implementation. In M.E. Snell (Ed.), *Instruction of students with severe disabilities* (pp. 99–151). New York: Macmillan.

Sommerfeld, D., Fraser, B.A., Hensinger, R.N., & Beresford, C.V. (1981). Evaluation of physical therapy services for severely mentally impaired students with cerebral palsy. *Physical Therapy, 61,* 338–344.

Stokes, T., & Baer, D.M. (1977). An implicit technology of generalization. *Journal of Applied Behavior Analysis, 10,* 349–367.

Stremel-Campbell, K., & Campbell, C.R. (1985). Training techniques that may facilitate generalization. In S.F. Warren & A. Rogers-Warren (Eds.), *Teaching functional language* (pp. 251–288). Austin, TX: PRO-ED.

Tannock, R., & Girolametto, L. (1992). Reassessing parent-focused language intervention programs. In S.F. Warren & J. Reichle (Eds.), *Causes and effects in communication and language intervention* (pp. 49–79). Baltimore: Paul H. Brookes Publishing Co.

Thelen, E. (1995). Motor development: A new synthesis. *American Psychologist, 50,* 79–95.

Warren, S.F. (1977). A useful ecobehavior perspective for applied behavior analysis. In A.K. Rogers-Warren & S.F. Warren (Eds.), *Ecological perspectives in behavior analysis* (pp. 173–196). Baltimore: University Park Press.

Warren, S.F. (1985). Clinical strategies for the measurement of language generalization. In S.F. Warren & A.K. Rogers-Warren (Eds.), *Teaching functional language* (pp. 3–24). Austin, TX: PRO-ED.

Warren, S.F. (1988). A behavioral approach to language generalization. *Language, Speech, and Hearing Services in the Schools, 19,* 292–303.

Warren, S.F. (1991). Enhancing communication and language development with milieu teaching procedures. In E. Cipani (Ed.), *A guide for developing language competence in preschool children with severe and moderate handicaps* (pp. 68–93). Springfield, IL: Charles C Thomas.

Warren, S.F. (1993). Early communication and language intervention: Challenges for the 1990s and beyond. In A. Kaiser & D. Gray (Eds.), *Enhancing children's communication: Research foundations for intervention* (pp. 375–395). Baltimore: Paul H. Brookes Publishing Co.

Warren, S.F., & Bambara, L.M. (1989). An experimental analysis of milieu language intervention: Teaching the action-object form. *Journal of Speech and Hearing Disorders, 54,* 448–461.

Warren, S.F., & Gazdag, G.A. (1990). Facilitating early language development with milieu intervention procedures. *Journal of Early Intervention, 14,* 62–68.

Warren, S.F., Yoder, P.J., Gazdag, G.E., Kim, K., & Jones, H.A. (1993). Facilitating prelinguistic communication skills in young children with developmental delay. *Journal of Speech and Hearing Research, 36,* 83–97.

Wetherby, A., & Prizant, B. (1990). *Communication and symbolic behavior scales— research edition.* Chicago: Riverside.

Wilcox, M.J. (1992). Enhancing initial communication skills in young children with developmental disabilities through partner programming. *Seminars in Speech and Language, 13,* 194–212.

Wilcox, M.J., Kouri, T., & Caswell, S. (1991). Early language intervention: A comparison of classroom and individual treatment. *American Journal of Speech-Language Pathology, 1,* 49–62.

Yoder, P.J., & Warren, S.F. (1993). Can developmentally delayed children's language development be enhanced through prelinguistic intervention? In A. Kaiser & D. Gray (Eds.), *Enhancing children's communication: Research foundations for intervention* (pp. 35–61). Baltimore: Paul H. Brookes Publishing Co.

Yoder, P.J., Warren, S.F., Kim, K., & Gazdag, G.E. (1994). Facilitating prelinguistic communication skills in young children with developmental delay II: Systematic replication and extension. *Journal of Speech and Hearing Research, 37,* 841–851.

# II

# Application

# Chapter 7

# How to Provide
# Integrated Therapy

## R.A. McWilliam

This chapter is devoted to guidelines for the implementation of integrated therapy. Integrated therapy works best when administrators, specialists, teachers, and families endorse the concept. The chapter is divided into two sections: getting started and methods of implementation.

### GETTING STARTED

Moving from traditional methods of service delivery, which focus on direct, hands-on therapy, usually in a segregated setting (i.e., a therapy room), to integrated methods of service delivery, which focus on providing therapy in context and in collaboration with regular caregivers, can be a dramatic change. Shifting focus has been described as a difficult process in early intervention (Bailey, McWilliam, & Winton, 1992), despite the fairly rapid evolution of the field. How do practitioners, administrators, and families negotiate the change to integrated therapy? The following section describes my sources of information about implementing integrated therapy and advantages for all the stakeholders of an integrated approach.

### Sources of Information

Almost every study we have conducted on integrated versus isolated treatment (see Chapter 4) has contributed to the guidelines for implementation. First, the national survey (McWilliam & Bailey, 1994) revealed what predicted the use of an integrated approach and what practitioners considered to be the advantages and disadvantages of in-class and out-of-class services. Second, the interviews in the therapy generalization study (McWilliam & Scarborough, 1994) delineated in more detail the perceptions of specialists, teachers, and parents. Third, the focus groups (McWilliam & Young, 1995) provided the perceptions of these same groups in terms of ideal practices, barriers to ideal practices, and proposed solutions for overcoming the barriers. Fourth, the effectiveness study (McWilliam, Scarborough, & Chaudhary, 1995) demonstrated the value of the data collection tools. Together these studies have given us a wealth of information on which to base our recommendations.

Another important source has been my participation in and observation of the implementation of an integrated therapy approach in our own child care program at the Frank Porter Graham Child Development Center. In 1988, almost all specialized services were provided through a pull-out model. In 1991, we gave families the choice of in-class or out-of-class therapy for each type of therapy their child received. More families chose out-of-class therapy. By 1993, when we were continuing to give families choices (now expanded to six models), almost all families chose one of the integrated options. In the meantime, we have had to work with an unfortunately frequent turnover of consulting occupational and physical therapists, which means these therapists have been introduced to a sometimes quite unfamiliar approach to therapy. (We are not sure whether the rapid turnover was a result of having to use integrated therapy!) Teachers also have altered their expectations. The process of walking families, specialists, and teachers through a change of approach has contributed greatly to our understanding of the challenges and delights inherent in this process.

The following four sections describe the advantages of integrated therapy. People adopt innovations for different reasons and as a result of different influences. Some people are quick to try new things that might make their work more effective, whereas others stick with what they consider the tried and true. Some people are influenced by research, others by the effect on their working lives, and others by acquaintances who have undergone the change.

## Advantages for Administrators

***Team Cohesion*** When therapy is provided in the classroom, teachers and specialists consult with each other four times as much as they do when therapy is provided out of class (McWilliam, 1994). Integrated therapy sets the stage for staff to work together rather than autonomously. They must coordinate functions or at least come to agreement about roles and responsibilities while the therapist is in the classroom.

***Integrated Programming*** Traditional isolated therapy and special education promote a two-box system in inclusive settings. In the two-box system, typically developing children receive the general curriculum, and children with special needs receive a separate, specialized curriculum. By integrating therapy into the classroom curriculum, there can be a single curriculum with individual modifications.

***Space Saving*** Integrated therapy obviates the need for separate therapy rooms.

*Cautions* Each of the advantages for administrators comes with potential disadvantages. First, the interdependence inherent in integrated therapy can lead to staff disputes, whereas the independent, isolated model can avoid disputes through lack of contact. Second, an integrated curriculum works only if the teacher actually provides the individualization needed by the children with special needs. Research shows that, regardless of therapy model, teachers use specialized techniques very little of the time and very infrequently (McWilliam & Scarborough, 1994a). Integrating therapy into the curriculum involves far more than simply locating therapy in the classroom (McWilliam & Grabowski, 1993). Third, programs still need space for some out-of-class activities by therapists. Some assessments are most appropriately conducted in isolated settings, and some families choose out-of-class therapy. Programs that currently devote multiple rooms for therapy should be able to save space; those that have only one or two therapy rooms would be well advised to preserve them as therapy rooms. A fourth caution for administrators is that integrated therapy is not likely to be a method for saving costs. Although the time spent with children can be used more efficiently, the time needed to collaborate properly with other professionals and with families requires at least as much of the therapist's time. Finally, administrators might encounter difficulties with respect to reimbursement policies that restrict allowable activities. Some third-party payers and administrative units (e.g., local education agencies) pay only for direct hands-on therapy. Although it may seem as though the disadvantages outweigh the advantages, the advantages for specialists, teachers, and children and families should also be taken into consideration.

## Advantages for Specialists

*Opportunities to Work with the Child in the Context Where the Skills Are Needed* A functional approach to therapy involves helping children acquire the skills they need to succeed in current and future environments. By working in the classroom, with other children present, and in concert with classroom activities, therapists work on the acquisition, generalization, accuracy, and fluency of skills the child needs to be a fully engaged classroom participant. In contrast, working outside the classroom, or even within the classroom but isolated from the other children, requires the child to take a second step—to apply the skills where needed, in context. Integrated therapy is efficient in conducting intervention in a single step.

*Opportunities to Address Problems as They Arise* The reactive corollary of addressing skills as needed is addressing problems as they arise. When the child with cerebral palsy attempts to step over blocks to get into the block area, the physical therapist (PT) can teach the child how to step over objects right then and there. The child is motivated and the PT has everything needed, without creating an artificial situation.

*Opportunities to Work with the General Teaching Staff* Two opportunities to work with teachers are planning for the therapy sessions and collaborating once the therapist is in the room. Planning is important for determining what specialists and teachers will do when specialists are in the classroom; without planning, misunderstandings can arise. Minimally, specialists, teachers, or both might consider what specialists do in the classroom ineffective, unless they have talked about each other's roles and responsibilities. As for in-class collaboration, the PT can call the teacher's attention to how he or she is helping the child learn to step over blocks. In a different situation, where the teacher might have removed the blocks for the child (a natural thing to do), the therapist might tell the teacher then or later how that can be an opportunity to address an individualized family service plan (IFSP)/individualized education program (IEP) goal.

*Cautions* Contexts, immediate interventions, and collaboration can also pose difficulties. First, some contexts appear unsuitable for specialists, such as crowded classrooms, unruly children, or classrooms bereft of materials. This requires specialists to consult at the program or classroom level; specialists need to adopt this perhaps unfamiliar role, but when they realize that they will help the child between therapy sessions, one assumes they will readily take on the role of consultant. The second caution is that on-the-spot intervention can break the child's engagement, disrupt an activity, or make the child resist. Specialists need to intervene in such a manner that they preserve the flow of the child's engagement, and they must be prepared to let some opportunities go by. Some therapists feel a pressure to be doing something constantly; that, after all, is what happens in clinical therapy. An effective integrated therapist spends some time observing. When specialists realize that they are not solely responsible for teaching a skill to a child, and when they are realistic about the potential effectiveness of once-a-week bursts of therapy, they are free to observe the whole environment and the focal child's functioning in that environment. With observation, specialists can determine the best times to intervene or can advise the teaching staff on how to intervene naturally. Finally, specialists might find working with adults from other disciplines a challenge. In one of our focus groups, a therapist said plaintively, "We were never trained to work with people from other disciplines—or parents—in fact, with any adults" (McWilliam, Young, & Harville, 1995). Among the shifts in mindset required for effective integrated therapy is the realization that therapy in early intervention involves working with adults as much as, if not more than, with children. Specialists should therefore prepare themselves to become consultants in environments and child engagement.

## Advantages for Teachers

*Opportunities to Work with Specialists* Teachers often do not have opportunities to receive expert advice on working with children. In early intervention, specialists can help teachers be effective in teaching children with many different needs.

***Knowledge of Goals and Strategies*** Teachers' participation in intervention planning (i.e., IFSP or IEP development) ranges from not attending the meeting to leading the meeting. Some child care teachers are not involved in intervention planning, especially when the plan is developed before the child begins attending the child care center. Some teachers attend the meetings but have no meaningful role; these meetings tend to follow the traditional specialist-dominated format consisting of the presentation of assessment results and specialists' recommendations. Some teachers provide the classroom perspective, informing team members about barriers the child needs to overcome to participate fully in the classroom. Some teachers, particularly early childhood special education teachers in self-contained programs, lead the meetings. This range of teacher involvement is associated with teachers' knowledge and later recollection of goals for the child: The more involved the teachers are in intervention planning, the more likely they are to know what the goals are for the children with special needs. Even on teams with high teacher involvement, if specialists write goals for their own area of expertise, other team members are not as likely to be aware of these goals. With all this variability in methods for becoming knowledgeable about goals and strategies, many teachers can benefit from prompts, such as having the therapist work in the classroom. This benefit was most strikingly seen when teachers working with pull-out therapists were vague about goals and strategies, whereas teachers working with integrated therapists were more knowledgeable.

***Continuity by Having Children Stay in the Classroom*** As children get older and activities are more structured, at least in the sense of being more organized (e.g., special materials, special activities, following a theme), when children leave the classroom for therapy, the teacher is faced with the challenge of these children missing information and experiences the other children received. When the children who miss classroom activities have developmental disabilities, the compensation challenge is even greater for the teacher. Because scheduling therapy is such a nightmare (i.e., rigid or unpredictable schedules, short sessions) in most settings, teachers and therapists often find it difficult to coordinate schedules so that children with special needs miss only nonessential activities. When children can continue to participate in classroom activities (with a supportive therapist), however, the teacher is able to ensure some sense of continuity.

***Additional Adults in the Classroom*** Many classrooms are understaffed for the needs for individualization, so having a therapist in the room for part of the day can help with individual attention to children. Specialists can spend time either with one child, in what we would call the one-on-one-in-classroom or individualized-within-routines model, or with a group of children, in what we would call the group activity model. Whether the specialist is working with one child or more, that is one or more children the teacher does not have to worry about.

*Cautions* We found that personality emerged as a theme predicting success or failure in collaboration. Thus, although working with specialists is generally an advantage for teachers, either the teacher's or the specialist's personal characteristics can become a disadvantage. Teachers who, for example, are unsure of themselves might not appreciate a specialist giving input to classroom management. Similarly, specialists who like autonomy might not appreciate compromising. Remembering to attend to goals and strategies might be difficult for teachers who already feel overburdened; they might see the disadvantages of the added responsibility more clearly than the advantages of better serving the child and family. Some teachers like to have children leave the classroom for therapy because that eases overcrowding, decreases the number of children they must attend to, and sometimes removes the child with the most challenging behavior. Finally, in some settings, an extra adult in the classroom simply adds to the overcrowding. Advantages to teachers of integrated services must be weighed against the possible disadvantages.

## Advantages for Families and Children

*Specialists Can See Needs in Context* This advantage begins with functional assessment, as opposed to standardized or decontextualized assessment. When the therapist can evaluate children's functioning in the environments in which the children need to succeed, the chances are that interventions will be more functional. For example, an early childhood special educator who bases interventions on test results might work with the child on stacking blocks, looking for objects under a cloth, or putting together an 11-piece form board. But a teacher who sees the child in the classroom might work with the child on cleaning up stackable toys, looking for a favorite toy in a basketful of classroom materials, or completing a puzzle that the child sees other children completing. Similar examples of functional interventions, derived from assessing child functioning in context, apply in the areas of gross motor, fine motor, communication, and social skills.

*Integrated Programming Leads to Integrated Functioning* The multidisciplinary approach, which so often is associated with segregated services, is congruent with a domain concept of testing, but not with a holistic concept of child development. Tests are divided into domains or subscales on the basis of statistical analyses that show which items load on to factors. Simplistically put, these factors become the domains. Child development, however, proceeds in a cross-modal fashion: Development in one area can enhance and sometimes even impede development in another area. Many parents have noticed, for example, that language plateaus when major motor milestones are being accomplished. Once the child has become competent at the new motor milestone, however, language often resumes at a rapid rate. If this is how normal development interacts across different areas, then the importance of a coordinated approach to intervention for children with developmental delays or disabilities becomes clear. An integrated approach is the best way of increasing the likelihood of coordination among specialists and developmental areas.

***Continuity by Having Child Stay in the Classroom*** This advantage was mentioned earlier as an advantage for teachers, but it also applies to children. When children who might have difficulties with transitions or change have to shift environments for therapy, their capacity for organized behavior is unnecessarily challenged. The most common disadvantage of integrated services mentioned by specialists is distraction; pull-out therapy is less distracting. Yet a similar cognitive process that challenges a child to attend (i.e., the ability to concentrate on one thing at a time) is tested when the child is taken from the everyday environment to a different environment. After therapy, when children return to the classroom, they not only have to make a switch of environments again but also have to fit into the ongoing classroom routines. Furthermore, some children later find gaps in their knowledge because they missed something when they were out of the classroom. For example, infants might find that their favorite caregiver has disappeared without saying goodbye, toddlers might find that previously accessible toys have been removed, and preschoolers might find that the teacher is talking about a story read while therapy was in progress. Distractibility is certainly a problem for some children, but whether pull-out therapy helps that problem in the long run is still unknown.

***Normalization*** Although researchers have found that middle school and high school students with special needs do not like to be singled out by their exodus to special services, younger children do not mind and even enjoy the special attention. For parents, however, segregated services reinforce the message that their child is different from other children who get to stay in their classroom. Without overinterpreting families' reactions, it is possible that traditional models have spawned notions of lower expectations and differentness, whereas integrated models could reinforce concepts of higher expectations and sameness. Some interventionists believe their duty is to ensure that parents have realistic expectations; these interventionists would not have a problem with this effect on families. Other interventionists, however, recognize that hope and aspiration is a vital part of adjusting to a child's special needs and would not want to promote non-normative ideas.

***Realistic Expectations About the Value of Specialized Interventions*** We have been surprised at how early and strongly families want specialized services for their children. Our focus groups revealed that the value of one-on-one, direct, separate therapy begins with doctors' prescriptions, evaluators' recommendations, practitioners' (including generalist early interventionists') beliefs, and other parents' prompts. It appears that families come to see segregated therapy, including weekly clinic visits, rather like a treatment in which repeated doses eventually have a curative effect. They acknowledge that much goes on between visits and that, during therapy sessions, they expect to learn things to do with their children. But we have descriptions of service delivery models that contradict this logic. For example, in some communities, standard practice is for families to take their child for therapy once a week to a clinic—and the parent hands the child over to the therapist. These families receive cursory, if any, recommendations for home activities. Another example is pull-out services in classroom programs where therapists and teachers have little time to exchange information at the end of therapy sessions. These teachers often have no idea what goes on in therapy. When these two common service delivery models are used, it is not surprising that families (not to mention practitioners, administrators, extended family members, etc.) develop a belief that weekly direct therapy or instruction is effective. Integrated therapy, however, cultivates families' expectations that therapy should be connected to nontherapy times, people, and places.

*Cautions*   Our national survey showed that specialists recognize the need to use more integrated practices than they typically do, but families do not necessarily know this. What families see as common practice must be the best way to get help for their child, so they develop strong faith in whatever service delivery model their child is receiving or in models they have heard about from others (McWilliam, Young, & Harville, 1995). We have come across this phenomenon of families believing in a service delivery model that reflects typical but not recommended practice in another area—families believing that a child focus is preferable to a family focus (McWilliam, Tocci, & Harbin, 1995). Borrowing a term from marketing, we have called this the phenomenon of the "uninformed consumer" because the families' preference stems from no experience with an alternative.

Compounding this problem is that the national shortage of pediatric therapists has led some early intervention systems to adopt a consultative approach as a way of spreading out the resources. This solution is disingenuous because a consultative or integrated approach done well probably requires just as many hours as the traditional, segregated direct therapy model. Parents with children might correctly assume that the consultative model as applied by these systems is a diminution of service. Our experiences in research and service provision suggest that, when families see properly implemented integrated therapy, they come to see its advantages. Families' initial perceptions and preferences for segregated therapy might be a considerable challenge to implementing integrated therapy.

## METHODS OF IMPLEMENTATION

Administrators, teachers, specialists, and families can enhance the practice of integrated therapy. This section describes specific steps we have either seen or heard about in our research.

### Administrators

Administrators are concerned with finances and how personnel time is used; with the IFSP or IEP process; and with planning, implementing, and evaluating services. All of these functions are affected by methods of delivering specialized services.

#### Finances and Time

*Hire Therapists Rather than Contract for Services* Integrated therapy works best when therapists can be flexible with schedules, which is easier with staff therapists than with contracted therapists. Furthermore, the integrated approach is as much a philosophy as a set of practices, and administrators find it easier to have a unified program philosophy when key players are employees rather than vendors.

*Learn What Is Covered by Medicaid or Other Third-Party Insurance Providers for Direct and Indirect Services* Much confusion reigns about what is covered by insurance and Medicaid, and some therapists have seen reimbursement guidelines as barriers to providing integrated services. Administrators need to guide staff about these guidelines and to verify or disaffirm practitioners' notions about restrictions.

*Learn About Any Caps on Third-Party Reimbursement* Although caps on reimbursement are not solely an issue for integrated therapy, they are for service delivery in general. Therapists have reported pressure to provide the most intensive therapy possible when caps are in effect. Intensity is sometimes translated as providing the maximum one-on-one segregated therapy before the cap is reached. Administrators need to find out about caps and guide therapists regarding the best use of their limited time with a child, which may not necessarily be in providing traditional pull-out services.

*Guide Therapists and Teachers About Creative Uses of Direct Service Time* Therapists have reported following the letter of the law for what counts as direct service and what counts as indirect service. When the reimbursement rate is higher per minute (or per 15-minute block) for direct therapy, they tend to provide what they consider direct therapy. This leaves little room for such indirect therapy as consulting with teachers and families and attending intervention planning meetings. Administrators should help practitioners interpret *direct service* in the most flexible light, so that practitioners are reimbursed at the maximum rate while not neglecting their *indirect service* obligations.

*Establish Guidelines for Amount of Time Spent on Indirect Service, Planning, and Consultation*   The bias in favor of direct service, despite being based on false assumptions as outlined earlier, is so strong that administrators may find it beneficial to guide practitioners about the amount of time they are expected to perform indirect services. Guidelines should be established based on individual therapists rather than on individual children, because children need different types of services at different times. For the same reason, administrators' guidelines should be guidelines, not rules. By guiding practitioners in how their time should be spent, administrators are both notifying them of the importance of so-called indirect services and establishing a backup should they have to intervene with therapists not spending enough time in consultation.

*Ask Referral Sources, Doctors, and Evaluation Centers to Specify Only in What Areas Children Need Help*   A pervasive problem in early intervention is the feeling of referral sources, doctors, and evaluation personnel that they need to advocate for children's treatment; this is a problem when the advocacy takes the form of specific recommendations for therapy in the absence of information about the child's and family's everyday environments. The focus group of early intervention nontherapist professionals revealed that they made assumptions about therapy such as recommending therapy before the intervention plan was developed (on the assumption that certain disorders merit therapy) and assuming that a fairly standard intensity of therapy (usually once a week) was necessary across the board. When presented with different scenarios, however, the professionals realized that therapy should be assigned more judiciously. One scenario involved a child with spastic quadriplegia who was the only child, age 12 months, of a stay-at-home mother married to a father who was very active in the care of the child. These parents understood the PT's recommendations and religiously incorporated the exercises and movements into everyday routines. How much time with a therapist does this family need? Compare this scenario with one involving a child of the same age, also with spastic quadriplegia, but whose mother works in a chicken plant every day and has two other preschoolers. After picking up her children in the evenings, she has to prepare dinner, wash clothes, and get the children bathed. She is too busy either to work in any therapy or to foster any social time for herself. How much therapy time does this family need? Both children have the same degree of cerebral palsy and are the same age. The professionals recognized that the second child would need more time with a therapist than would the first, but they admitted that decisions are rarely made on ecological bases. One of the reasons is that children come to the program with predetermined prescriptions or recommendations for therapy, including the recommendations for the intensity of therapy. These decisions should be made at the program level once ecological needs have been assessed.

*Request Eligibility Be Determined by Need* In some systems, children qualify for therapy only if their performance in a given developmental area (e.g., language) is significantly different from their overall level of development. By these types of criteria, children with no expressive communication and with extremely low developmental quotients do not qualify for speech-language services. Similarly, a relatively high-functioning child with a few easily correctable errors in a developmental area may not qualify for specialized therapy. Clearly, the intent of legislation is for services to be based on need, which the discrepancy criterion cannot be said to represent. Systems with this type of criterion often have methods for waiving it, and administrators should vigorously pursue such waivers.

### The IFSP/IEP

*Use Routines-Based Assessment and Intervention Planning* To ensure that interventions, especially those associated with therapeutic or special education services, are functional, assessment and intervention planning should be based on everyday routines, such as described in McWilliam (1992). The traditional method of basing these functions on developmental domains reinforces discipline-specific intervention, which in turn reinforces segregated therapy. Administrators can require integrated intervention planning and assessment by having the staff work with families on a structured yet informal review of what the child needs to succeed in home and classroom routines.

*Develop Policies Regarding Family Choice of Preferred Models of Service Delivery* Therapists have reported that they, not families, make decisions about what service delivery models to use (McWilliam, Young, & Harville, 1995). Nationally, early intervention practitioners across disciplines have reported that, hypothetically, they would honor family preferences (McWilliam & Bailey, 1994). Those who tend to use integrated services, however, report that they would most often honor family preferences for in-class therapy, and those who tend to use segregated services report that they would most often honor preferences for out-of-class therapy. Because families who have exposure to integrated therapy tend to choose it when given the choice, administrators should develop policies making such a choice possible.

*Ensure that Families Learn About Indirect Service, Planning, and Consultation* Therapists are under pressure to provide maximum direct services because they feel families do not appreciate the need for time spent in other activities (McWilliam, Young, & Harville, 1995). When families see that their children are to receive two 30-minute sessions of physical therapy a week, for example, they are not too sympathetic if they find that children receive only one such session because the therapist is in meetings (even if the meetings are related to their children). Administrators should educate families about how indirect service, planning, and consultation can be as beneficial as direct service, if not more so.

*Ensure that Therapy Services Meet Specific Needs* This necessity has been mentioned earlier. During the IFSP or IEP process, administrators should monitor the basis on which therapy decisions are made.

*Specify Total Therapists' Time per Month per Child, Rather than per Week* In an earlier example, the pitfalls of specifying therapists' time per week for each child were highlighted: Families rightfully expect that amount of therapy. Specifying time per month for each child allows the therapist to use the time more flexibly, and therefore children who need more intensive therapy time can receive it. Administrators need to check local and state requirements about specifying intensity of services, but they should advocate for the monthly rather than weekly allocation.

*Seek Balance of Power Between Teacher and Therapists* Teachers feel less powerful than therapists in the IFSP or IEP process (McWilliam, Young, & Harville, 1995), which can cause problems when an integrated approach is to be used. Integrated programming requires that 1) therapists apply their expertise to fit nontherapy routines and 2) teachers incorporate specialized interventions within their classroom management. Both parties must therefore be able to negotiate what can be managed in the classroom and in therapy sessions. Administrators need to be aware of therapists, especially those with strong personalities (McWilliam, Young, & Harville, 1995), who dominate less assertive teachers. Sometimes the balance of power can be reversed; administrators should seek to level that balance.

### Planning

*Ensure that Each Classroom Has a Schedule and that Lesson Plans Are Developed* Therapists have difficulty planning integrated therapy if they do not know what is happening in classrooms when they enter. Administrators, who presumably need to ensure that lesson plans are in place, have an additional reason to be vigilant with this requirement.

*Discuss Roles and Responsibilities with Therapists and Teachers* Misunderstandings about teachers' and therapists' roles and responsibilities often happen simply because of a lack of communication (McWilliam & Scarborough, 1994). Both parties need to know 1) where therapists will spend their time, 2) whether therapists desire children other than the target child around, 3) the extent to which target children will be allowed to establish what they are engaged with, 4) when and how the therapist and teacher will discuss the child, and 5) what types of interventions (particularly highly specialized ones) the therapist intends to use. Administrators can help establish this communication.

*Ensure that Therapists and Teachers Can Identify Reason for Each Intervention* Administrators are often in a good position to ask, What is this child working on? and then, Why? These questions in tandem help to define the functionality of interventions. If a child is seen working on a lacing board, the administrator can ask the first question. Presumably, the answer would be, "Lacing." The answer to the second question, perhaps, would be, "So he can lace his shoes." At that point, the administrator can explore the necessity of the child lacing his or her own shoes. If the administrator is convinced that it is a functional and age-appropriate activity for the child, the question about why a lacing board rather than a shoe is being used might ensue.

*Monitor How Much and How Well Teachers Incorporate Therapy into Teaching* If intervention planning occurs in a functional manner, therapy would be virtually indistinguishable from teaching. In many programs, however, therapists have recommendations for teachers to use in the classroom. We found that teachers rarely apply the techniques therapists expect them to (McWilliam & Scarborough, 1994). Reasons for this lack of application vary, ranging from therapists' failure to work collaboratively with teachers to teachers' refusal to adopt additional responsibilities. Administrators should take responsibility for monitoring the extent to which individualized plans are carried out in the classroom.

*Encourage Reciprocal Consultation Between Therapists and Teachers* Breakdowns in communication have been noted earlier. For reasonable consultation to occur, professionals need time and sometimes structure. Using one of the in-class models of service delivery precipitates about four times as much unscheduled consultation as an out-of-class model (McWilliam, 1994). Structure might be needed, however, to ensure that time is devoted to discussing children and interventions; it might also be needed to ensure that consultation works both ways. Therapists need to convey particular information and techniques to teachers, and teachers need to convey everyday needs as well as strengths and constraints. Administrators must encourage time and structure for this exchange.

### Implementation

*Monitor Consultation at Beginning of, During, and After Therapists' Visits* Consultation is sometimes treated as an add-on to therapy — something that should be done to complement direct therapy. Administrators can help practitioners realize the importance of consultation before (i.e., planning how therapists will use their time), during (i.e., collaborating while therapists are in the classroom), and after (i.e., exchanging information resulting from therapists' time in the classroom). Many constraints, such as insufficient planning time and too much activity in the classroom, will arise. This only emphasizes the importance of the administrator helping to solve consultation problems.

*Assess Classroom Atmosphere for Incorporating Therapists* Some classrooms are difficult environments for therapists to work in. Here the issue is the classroom atmosphere, including the children's engagement, classroom organization, the flexibility and rigidity of classroom activities, and the teaching staff's openness to specialists. It might be hard for therapists, especially contract therapists perceived as outsiders, to address classroom challenges. Administrators need to assess the atmosphere and give direction, if necessary, to make it conducive to integrated therapy.

*Arrange for Joint In-Service Training by a Teacher and a Therapist*  Therapists rarely attend in-service training for classroom-based early interventionists and vice versa. Administrators would be well advised to secure on-site in-service training, where a trainer comes to the classroom and works with the staff while children are present. Critical to the success of integrated therapy, however, is that therapists participate in such training. If teachers receive only on-site training, therapists who did not participate may subvert the strategies introduced during training.

### Evaluation

*Monitor Which of Six Models Therapists Use*  Six models of service delivery have been described as a continuum from one-on-one segregated practice to consultation involving no hands-on work with the child (Mc-William, 1995). Table 1 shows the six models with descriptions of associated roles of other children, teachers, and therapists. The conceptualization of six models provides more options than simply in-class versus out-of-class or the three-level model used by some professional organizations (i.e., direct, monitoring, consultation).

A simple form, the Specialists Documentation Form (SDF), has been devised for tracking what goals are addressed during therapists' time and what models therapists used (see Figure 1). We have used this by printing current goals for each child and updating as needed. This reminds each specialist of all the goals, not just those on which he or she is concentrating. At the end of each session, the therapist checks which goals were addressed and which of the six models was used predominantly. Some therapists have found the form simplistic when they use more than one model in a session, so a more sophisticated method could be devised. We found that having therapists check only one model, the one used for the most time, rendered the task of completing the SDF less odious. Another part of the form is used to indicate the length of the session. Therapists who go to a classroom and share their time among children apportion that time as best they can so that the total session lengths for all the children do not exceed the amount of time the therapist is in the classroom. This method of accounting for time is useful for tracking the amount of time the therapist spends in the program, but it underestimates the total time with a therapist that an individual child receives. For example, if a therapist conducts a half-hour group activity and two of the children in the group are target children, then both children benefit from the full 30 minutes. Recording this amount of time on each child's SDF, however, would look as though the therapist spent 60 minutes in the program. It is an imperfect system, but the primary value of the SDF is a structure for monitoring the service delivery model the therapists employ.

Table 1. Continuum of six consultative models

| Model | Location | Therapy focus | Context | Peers | Teacher's role |
|---|---|---|---|---|---|
| Individual pull-out | Therapy room or other place apart from the regular class | Directly and exclusively on child functioning, usually on areas of greatest need | Can vary from drill to work to play-based intervention, determined by therapist | Not present | To provide information before therapy and receive information after therapy |
| Small-group pull-out | Therapy room or other place apart from the regular class | Directly on functioning by child(ren) with special needs; some attention to children without special needs, if present | Can vary from group to drill work to play-based intervention, determined by therapist | One to six peers present, all or some of whom may have special needs | To provide information before therapy and receive information after therapy, to schedule group session, to decide with therapist which peers will participate |
| One-on-one in classroom | Classroom,[a] often apart from other children | Directly and exclusively on child functioning, usually on areas of greatest need | Therapist- or child-initiated, unrelated to concurrent classroom activity | In classroom, but not involved in therapy | To conduct activities and play with other children, keep children from disrupting therapy; rarely, to watch therapy session, to provide information before therapy, and receive information after therapy |

*(continued)*

161

Table 1. (continued)

| Model | Location | Therapy focus | Context | Peers | Teacher's role |
|---|---|---|---|---|---|
| Group activity | Classroom; small or large group | On all children in group and on peer interactions, with emphasis on meeting special needs of one or more children | Therapist- or child-initiated; may be planned with teacher | All or some children in group have special needs | When small group, to conduct activities and play with other children; if possible, to watch or participate in therapist's group. When large group, to watch or participate in group activity. To participate in planning large- and possibly small-group activity. |
| Individual during routine | Classroom, wherever focal child is | Directly but not exclusively on the focal child | Ongoing classroom routines, which includes structured activities, self-help, free play, and outside. Mostly child-initiated. | Usually present | To plan and conduct activity (including free play) including focal child, to observe therapist's interactions with child, to provide information before therapy, to exchange information with therapist after routine |
| Consultation | In or out of classroom | Teacher, as related to the needs of the child; can vary from expert to collegial model | Therapist- or teacher-initiated concerns, priorities, recommendations | Present if occurring in class; not present if occurring out of class | To exchange information and expertise with therapist, to help plan future therapy sessions, to give and receive feedback, to foster partnership with therapist |

From McWilliam, R.A. (1995). Integration of therapy and consultative special education: A continuum in early intervention. *Infants and Young Children, 7*(4), 29–38; reprinted by permission.

*"Classroom" includes any regular play area, such as the playground.

# FPG

## Specialist's Documentation Form
*Special Services Research Project - YR 3   Frank Porter Graham Child Development Center*

Today's Date: ___ / ___ / ___

Specialist (initials) _____

Child (full name): _____   IFSP/Rev. Date: _____   Session Length (min.): _____   Special Service:   SE   SLP   PT   OT   Other (specify)

| Outcome # | Outcome | Outcome Addressed | Check the model used for most of the time in today's session: (Check one only)* | |
|---|---|---|---|---|
| | | Yes    No | **Individual Pull-Out** | |
| | | Yes    No | **Small Group Pull-Out** | |
| | | Yes    No | **1:1 in Classroom** | |
| | | Yes    No | **Group Activity** | |
| | | Yes    No | **Individual During Routine** | |
| | | Yes    No | **Consultation** | |
| | | Yes    No | *See Reverse Side for Descriptions | |
| | | Yes    No | | |
| | | Yes    No | | |
| | | Yes    No | | |

University of North Carolina at Chapel Hill, CB No. 8180, 105 Smith Level Road, Chapel Hill, NC 27599-8180

Child ID: _____

Figure 1.  Specialist's documentation form. IFSP, individualized family services plan; OT, occupational therapist; PT, physical therapist; SE, special educator; SLP, speech-language pathologist.

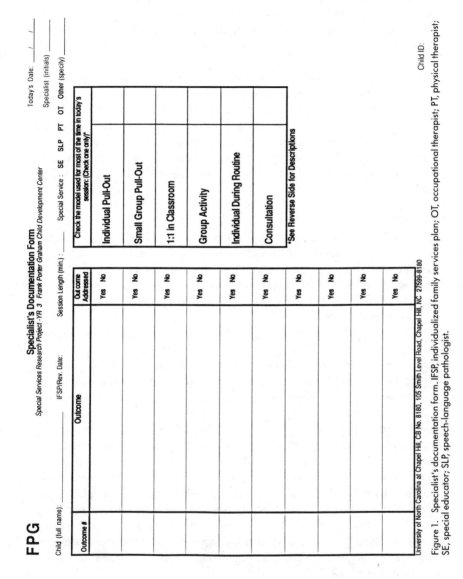

163

*Monitor How Often Teachers Provide Intervention on Highest-Priority Objectives*   Program evaluation when children with special needs are enrolled should include the extent to which individualization occurs. Because of the concern raised by our finding that teachers rarely apply specialized techniques (McWilliam & Scarborough, 1994), administrators should monitor the extent to which teachers address at least the top-priority goals.

*Have Teachers, Therapists, and Parents Rate Child Independence and Frequency on Each Objective Every 8 Weeks*   In research, we have used the Therapy Goals Information Form (TGIF) for these ratings, shown in Figure 2. The same goals listed on the SDF are listed on the TGIF. We found little difference between independence and frequency ratings, but it may be useful to retain both to make it easier for teachers, therapists, and parents to score children's abilities. Administrators would use the TGIF as a goal attainment measure.

## Teachers

This section provides steps for the classroom teacher to follow when implementing integrated therapy. Although not all classroom teachers, such as many early childhood teachers in inclusive programs, are directly responsible for developing the IFSP or IEP, early childhood special education teachers often are. The other areas in this section apply to all classroom teachers.

### The IFSP or IEP

*Report Child Functioning by Routine, Not by Domain*   During the assessment stage of developing the IFSP/IEP, the teacher should describe how the child performs during each type of classroom routine, as discussed by McWilliam (1992). In traditional programming, domains (i.e., cognitive, communication, gross motor, fine motor, social, self-help) and disciplines (i.e., special education, occupational therapy, physical therapy, speech-language pathology) have dominated the assessment and intervention planning process. This domination tended to decontextualize what a child could do and needed to do. A very useful role of the teacher is to ground the discussion in everyday functional activities. Thus, by talking about a child's functioning during arrival (e.g., taking off a coat, greeting others), free play (e.g., engagement with objects and peers), structured activities (e.g., following directions, sitting posture), outside play (e.g., movement quality, taking turns), meals (e.g., self-feeding, making requests), and other classroom routines, the teacher makes a critically important contribution to the IFSP or IEP development process.

*Consider Which of the Six Models Would Be Most Helpful for Each Specialized Service*   As child needs become identified, the teacher can think about which of the six service delivery models would be most effective for each type of support (i.e, early childhood special education, speech-

**TGIF**

*Therapy Goals Information Form - Year 4*

FAMILY

Child (full name): _____

Date This Form Was Completed: _____ / _____ / _____

Family Member: _____

For Period Ending: November

How well does the child do each of the following
(Check one box for frequency and one box for independence for each outcome)

| Outcome # | Outcome | 1 | 2 | 3 | 4 | 5 | 6 | |
|---|---|---|---|---|---|---|---|---|
| | | All of the time | Almost all of the time | About half the time | Almost Never | Never | Does not apply (Don't know) | FREQUENCY |
| | | With no help | With very little help | With some help | With lots of help | Needs total assistance | Does not apply (Don't know) | INDEPENDENCE |
| | | All of the time | Almost all of the time | About half the time | Almost Never | Never | Does not apply (Don't know) | FREQUENCY |
| | | With no help | With very little help | With some help | With lots of help | Needs total assistance | Does not apply (Don't know) | INDEPENDENCE |
| | | All of the time | Almost all of the time | About half the time | Almost Never | Never | Does not apply (Don't know) | FREQUENCY |
| | | With no help | With very little help | With some help | With lots of help | Needs total assistance | Does not apply (Don't know) | INDEPENDENCE |
| | | All of the time | Almost all of the time | About half the time | Almost Never | Never | Does not apply (Don't know) | FREQUENCY |
| | | With no help | With very little help | With some help | With lots of help | Needs total assistance | Does not apply (Don't know) | INDEPENDENCE |
| | | All of the time | Almost all of the time | About half the time | Almost Never | Never | Does not apply (Don't know) | FREQUENCY |
| | | With no help | With very little help | With some help | With lots of help | Needs total assistance | Does not apply (Don't know) | INDEPENDENCE |
| | | All of the time | Almost all of the time | About half the time | Almost Never | Never | Does not apply (Don't know) | FREQUENCY |
| | | With no help | With very little help | With some help | With lots of help | Needs total assistance | Does not apply (Don't know) | INDEPENDENCE |
| | | All of the time | Almost all of the time | About half the time | Almost Never | Never | Does not apply (Don't know) | FREQUENCY |
| | | With no help | With very little help | With some help | With lots of help | Needs total assistance | Does not apply (Don't know) | INDEPENDENCE |
| | | All of the time | Almost all of the time | About half the time | Almost Never | Never | Does not apply (Don't know) | FREQUENCY |
| | | With no help | With very little help | With some help | With lots of help | Needs total assistance | Does not apply (Don't know) | INDEPENDENCE |
| | | All of the time | Almost all of the time | About half the time | Almost Never | Never | Does not apply (Don't know) | FREQUENCY |
| | | With no help | With very little help | With some help | With lots of help | Needs total assistance | Does not apply (Don't know) | INDEPENDENCE |
| | | All of the time | Almost all of the time | About half the time | Almost Never | Never | Does not apply (Don't know) | FREQUENCY |
| | | With no help | With very little help | With some help | With lots of help | Needs total assistance | Does not apply (Don't know) | INDEPENDENCE |

Special Services Research Project, Frank Porter Graham Child Development Center, UNC-CH

Form: FAM-APR93

Child ID:

Figure 2. Therapy goals information form.

language pathology, occupational therapy, physical therapy) that may be needed for each goal. Table 1 shows some factors to consider for each model. Other considerations may be based on individual characteristics of specialists if the teacher knows who they will be. Some specialists disrupt classroom routines, whereas others enhance them, for example. In integrated therapy, teachers work collaboratively with specialists in making decisions about programming, and this step helps teachers contribute to a previously underemphasized decision point—how and where specialized services are to be provided.

*Request Part of Allocated Therapy Time for Planning* Teachers, like specialists, often find that not enough time is allotted for consultation with specialists. The IFSP/IEP development process is an appropriate time to negotiate with administrators, therapists, and families for such planning. The intensity of services is a required component of the document, so teachers can request, for example, that one-fourth of the child's therapy time be used for consultation. Teachers must be prepared to justify this request to 1) administrators who may consider this a waste of expensive therapy time, 2) specialists who may consider this unnecessary, and 3) families that may feel that this detracts from services to their child.

### Planning

*Give Schedule and Lesson Plans to Therapists* Integrated therapy forces changes on teachers as well as specialists. Teachers who have not had to prepare very much, because they alone were responsible for classroom activities, will find themselves having to be better prepared. For specialists to make the best use of their time in the classroom, teachers should provide them with the classroom schedule and weekly lesson plans.

*Discuss Roles and Responsibilities with Therapists* "Can we talk about this?" Comedienne Joan Rivers's famous line needs to be heard in early intervention classroom programs. Too often classroom programming and specialized programming are disconnected because teachers and specialists do not talk about how they will work with each other. Even when they do make time to talk to each other, the discussion is on child-functioning issues. What is missing, however, is a negotiation about their own behavior during therapy time. The teacher should be prepared to discuss where the therapist will work with the child, how to manage children other than the focal child(ren), what teaching or intervention style works best for the focal child(ren), how the teacher would like to ensure that consultation is built into therapy time, and what goals and techniques the specialist recommends. Talking about these issues is critical to the success of integrated therapy.

*Emphasize the Need for Functional Interventions* The teacher can provide the impetus for therapists to work on necessary skills using immediately relevant strategies. One of the most significant contributions of the field of education is to apply interventions in functional contexts. Specialists may approach a problem with ideas that were cultivated in clinic or laboratory settings; the teacher needs to work with specialists to figure out how these ideas translate to the real world of a classroom program. Both the specific goals of intervention and the techniques may need to be discussed. For example, if a physical therapist points out the need for the child to remain in a kneeling position for a given length of time, the teacher would be well advised to ask how this is functional for the child. If the teacher, the physical therapist, and the family agree that remaining in a kneeling position is necessary and immediately relevant (see Chapter 5), the teacher can then set up classroom activities to promote this behavior. If a speech-language pathologist says a child should have his or her gums massaged with an electronic rubber-tipped toothbrush before meals, the teacher might ask why this technique is needed. After hearing about the theory that oral stimulation promotes better chewing, the teacher and therapist are likely to have a discussion about 1) whether this technique is necessary or simply a good idea, 2) whether other ways of stimulating the mouth are available, and 3) whether the family considers this a technique that absolutely must be used.

*Ask Therapist to Incorporate Therapy into Your Teaching* When teachers are faced with the challenge of adding strategies suggested by therapists to their teaching, they can share the responsibility with therapists for fitting in the strategies. Teachers may ask therapists for ideas when they feel that they could be doing more for a child. Having both professionals consider how the strategies can be incorporated into classroom activities reminds therapists of the need to keep strategies functional for the classroom and promotes interdisciplinary collaboration.

*Plan for Reciprocal Consultation with Therapist* Too often, when therapists use the expert model of consultation (as discussed by Coleman, Buysse, Scalise-Smith, & Schulte, 1991), they and teachers assume that it is the therapist's responsibility to give feedback to the teacher about how therapeutic strategies are being incorporated into the classroom. In the collaborative model of consultation, both teachers and therapists can agree to give feedback to each other. Teachers would give feedback to therapists about how therapy time and suggestions for follow-through activities (i.e., when therapist is not present) are fitting into classroom routines. This mutual feedback promotes the concept of two professionals working in partnership, rather than one (the teacher) working under the direction of the other (the therapist).

### Implementation

*Build in Consultation Time at Beginning and End of Therapist's Visit* Traditional models of service delivery consisted of the therapist coming to the classroom, taking the child out for therapy for the prescribed amount of time, and returning the child to the classroom at the end of therapy. Then perhaps another child would be taken out. With in-class models of service delivery, some therapists go into the classroom and immediately begin working with children; when they have to leave, they may say good-bye to the child and exit. Teachers and therapists, although appreciating the lack of disruption, miss the opportunity to work together. The slipping-in-and-out model is child-centered, but not collaborative. Teachers can work with therapists to ensure that they have time to talk about issues at the beginning and end of the therapist's time with children in the classroom. This is a challenge for both professionals; therapists may perceive this as taking away from therapy time, and teachers may perceive it as disrupting classroom teaching. They will probably find that it is better to miss collaboration as the exception (e.g., when the therapist comes in during story time) than as the rule.

*Reduce Interference While Promoting Involvement of Other Children* Nonfocal children (i.e., those not receiving therapy) can be a blessing and a curse to therapists, so teachers need to take responsibility for crowd control when therapists are in the classroom. Interference may be a matter of perception; nonfocal children who try to get involved with a therapist's play with the focal child are seen as intrusive by some therapists and as an opportunity to promote social competence in the focal child by other therapists. The teacher, who in most cases knows the children best, needs to 1) find out how the therapist feels about having other children around; 2) be nearby, helping to manage the group; 3) limit the number of children who can be involved in the classroom zone where the therapist is working; or 4) encourage the therapist to fit his or her work into existing classroom routines, to promote children's regular engagement in activities rather than focusing on the therapist.

*Try to Observe and Hear the Therapist* Many classroom factors, such as the size of the group and the amount of help the teacher needs to keep the children engaged, can impinge on a teacher's availability during the therapist's time in the classroom. But to the extent possible, teachers (and therefore children) benefit the most if they are aware of what the therapist is doing with focal children. Assuming therapists are using therapeutic strategies in their play with children, teachers can observe these strategies for use during times when the therapist is not in the classroom. Observing and hearing the therapist also gives teachers an opportunity to give feedback (positive, we hope).

*Facilitate Activities that Promote the Child's Opportunities to Perform Skills Targeted for Attention by Therapist* A frustration for therapists trying in-class models of service delivery is that the children with whom they are working are not engaged in activities that give therapists an opportunity to address IFSP/IEP goals. For example, a consulting special education teacher working on a child's problem solving with objects might come into a classroom during circle time, which is followed by outside play. Teachers, knowing the special education teacher's focus for the child, can 1) incorporate toys into the circle time, 2) ask the specialist if another time of day would be possible, or 3) as a last resort, suggest using the one-on-one in-classroom model, where the specialist takes the child aside and works on something different from what the rest of the class is doing.

*Ask Therapists for Feedback* Itinerant or consulting therapists often have much experience with many different classrooms. Although they are not expected to have the experience of teachers when it comes to classroom operations, they may have constructive ideas. Classroom teachers do not often have the opportunity to receive feedback from someone who spends much time in the classroom, and therapists providing integrated therapy become familiar with how the classroom is managed. More important than classroom management, however, is the area of individualizing for children with special needs in which the in-class therapist can provide useful feedback. Therapists are most comfortable providing feedback in their areas of expertise. An occupational therapist, for example, might show the teacher how his or her teaching a child to play with small toys is enhancing or hindering the child's ability to be engaged with toys independently. (Note my hopeful thinking that the therapist would focus on the functionality of the intervention, independent engagement, rather than on a limited outcome such as fine pincer grasp.) Finally, by asking therapists for feedback, teachers set the tone for collaboration; they convey that they want to learn from their colleagues for the good of the children.

*Ask Therapist to Demonstrate* "Can you show me what you mean?" Demonstration from the specialist is particularly useful when the specialist has recommended a strategy that seems difficult to implement. For example, if a therapist suggests that the teacher hold a child with severe spastic quadriplegia in his or her lap during circle, the teacher might think this would be very difficult while trying to lead group finger-plays and songs. The physical therapist could demonstrate to the teacher, showing how to use his or her chest to keep the child flexed through the spine and how to use his or her forearms to keep the child's shoulders rounded. Asking therapists to demonstrate can have the added benefit of their experiencing the difficulties involved in implementing their suggestions while continuing classroom management.

*Evaluation* Although classroom teachers often do not systematically evaluate their classroom activities, it is a worthwhile endeavor. The following steps are designed to give classroom teachers practical methods for tracking the effectiveness of specialized interventions with their children.

*Monitor Which of the Six Models Therapists Use* All forms of therapy can be categorized as one of six models, as shown in Table 1. The benefit of monitoring which models are used for which children is that teachers can suggest different models if 1) therapy is not changing what the child can do, 2) the child is improving, or 3) the usual model is interfering with classroom operations. For example, the teacher might document that, in a 3-month period, the speech-language pathologist has taken a child out of the classroom by him- or herself 10 times, has taken a child out of the classroom with a couple of other children 10 times, and has worked with the child (apart from the other children) 4 times. If the child is making progress or communicating relatively well in the classroom, the teacher might suggest that the therapist spend more time in the classroom. In the absence of some form of monitoring, therapists and teachers can engage in a nonproductive exchange (e.g., "But I do come into the classroom," "Not very often," "I was in just last week," "What about the week before?") about the extent that different models are used.

*Monitor How Often Interventions on Highest-Priority Objectives Are Provided* One of the questions that has arisen from our research is the extent to which teachers do what therapists hope they are doing to carry over therapy to nontherapy times. Failure to follow through with interventions should not, however, be interpreted as failure by the teacher alone. If an intervention strategy is nonfunctional for the classroom or does not make sense to the teacher, it is unrealistic to expect the teacher to implement it frequently. Nonfunctional interventions, unfeasible recommendations, unclear expectations, competing demands, or teacher reluctance can all account for teachers not implementing strategies. If teachers kept data on how often they provided interventions, they could ask the therapist for alternative suggestions for those interventions that they are not implementing frequently. Because collecting data on the extent of individualization can be challenging, teachers may consider doing so only on the highest-priority objectives. (Note that this suggests that the team has used the recommended practice of placing objectives in the family's order of priority, as described by McWilliam [1992].)

*Rate Child Independence and Frequency on Each Objective Every 8 Weeks* In our research, we used the TGIF to rate parents', teachers', and therapists' perceptions of child progress on IFSP/IEP goals addressed by specialists. Figure 3 shows an example. Every child has an individual TGIF on which his or her current goals are listed. Goals must be observable and functional and cannot be general (nonfunctional) statements such as, "Jerome will improve communication." Sometimes objectives are more salient than goals; it depends on the specificity with which goals are written. Each goal or objective is rated on how often the child performs the behavior/skill/activity and the extent to which the child can perform it independently. Completing TGIFs gives teachers an opportunity to assess child progress at fairly frequent intervals. They can use their perceptions as recorded on these forms to recommend 1) that alternative interventions be tried, 2) that existing interventions be continued, or 3) that different goals be established.

*Report Data to Therapist, Family, and Administrator* Recommendations based on the TGIF would be made to therapists and families when teachers reported their perceptions of child progress. Families should appreciate the fairly frequent progress reports, and therapists should appreciate the reports of generalization (i.e., generalization from therapy sessions to nontherapy times). Administrators can use these data to help with their program evaluation, and teachers would be enhancing their professionalism by presenting outcome data for their children.

# SAN

TEACHER

## TGIF
### Therapy Goals Information Form

Child (full name): John Asan Example    Date This Form Was Completed: ___/___/___

Teacher: _____    For Period Ending: November

**How well does the child do each of the following**
(Check one box for frequency and one box for independence for each outcome)

| Outcome # | Outcome | 1 | 2 | 3 | 4 | 5 | 6 | |
|---|---|---|---|---|---|---|---|---|
| 1 | John will have conversations with peers and adults; exchanges of 3 turns each at least 4 times per day. | All of the time | Almost all of the time | About half the time | Almost Never | Never | Does not apply (Don't know) | FREQUENCY |
| | | With no help | With very little help | With some help | With lots of help | Needs total assistance | Does not apply (Don't know) | INDEPENDENCE |
| 2 | John will take off a long-sleeved pullover or button down shirt by himself, given verbal help only, for 5 days in a row. | All of the time | Almost all of the time | About half the time | Almost Never | Never | Does not apply (Don't know) | FREQUENCY |
| | | With no help | With very little help | With some help | With lots of help | Needs total assistance | Does not apply (Don't know) | INDEPENDENCE |
| 3 | John will eat neatly by keeping food on plate or in his mouth, with mouth closed, without prompts, daily for a week. | All of the time | Almost all of the time | About half the time | Almost Never | Never | Does not apply (Don't know) | FREQUENCY |
| | | With no help | With very little help | With some help | With lots of help | Needs total assistance | Does not apply (Don't know) | INDEPENDENCE |
| 4 | John will draw three simple pictures or shapes after a demonstration and with verbal prompts, on 3 occasions for each of 3 pictures. | All of the time | Almost all of the time | About half the time | Almost Never | Never | Does not apply (Don't know) | FREQUENCY |
| | | With no help | With very little help | With some help | With lots of help | Needs total assistance | Does not apply (Don't know) | INDEPENDENCE |
| 5 | John will attempt to solve problems involving relating to people and things (e.g., completing an art project) by using assorted strategies, for at least 50% of the problems he encounters. | All of the time | Almost all of the time | About half the time | Almost Never | Never | Does not apply (Don't know) | FREQUENCY |
| | | With no help | With very little help | With some help | With lots of help | Needs total assistance | Does not apply (Don't know) | INDEPENDENCE |
| 6 | John will step one foot per step when going downstairs, without using a handrail or hand support, but with verbal prompts, daily for a week. | All of the time | Almost all of the time | About half the time | Almost Never | Never | Does not apply (Don't know) | FREQUENCY |
| | | With no help | With very little help | With some help | With lots of help | Needs total assistance | Does not apply (Don't know) | INDEPENDENCE |
| 7 | John will use a modified tripod grip (3 fingers only) to use assorted tools (tongs, tweezers, clothespins, pencils) on 5 occasions for at least 2 different tools. | All of the time | Almost all of the time | About half the time | Almost Never | Never | Does not apply (Don't know) | FREQUENCY |
| | | With no help | With very little help | With some help | With lots of help | Needs total assistance | Does not apply (Don't know) | INDEPENDENCE |
| 8 | John will say K and G sounds in words, 60% of the opportunities during the week. | All of the time | Almost all of the time | About half the time | Almost Never | Never | Does not apply (Don't know) | FREQUENCY |
| | | With no help | With very little help | With some help | With lots of help | Needs total assistance | Does not apply (Don't know) | INDEPENDENCE |
| 9 | John will make smooth transitions between activities, people and places 75% of the time. | All of the time | Almost all of the time | About half the time | Almost Never | Never | Does not apply (Don't know) | FREQUENCY |
| | | With no help | With very little help | With some help | With lots of help | Needs total assistance | Does not apply (Don't know) | INDEPENDENCE |
| | | All of the time | Almost all of the time | About half the time | Almost Never | Never | Does not apply (Don't know) | FREQUENCY |
| | | With no help | With very little help | With some help | With lots of help | Needs total assistance | Does not apply (Don't know) | INDEPENDENCE |

Special Services Research Project, Frank Porter Graham Child Development Center, UNC-CH    Child ID: _____

Figure 3.    Sample completed therapy goals information form.

## Specialists

Specialists are usually involved in IFSP/IEP development, planning their time with children and other clients (i.e., families and other interventionists), implementing interventions, and (sometimes) evaluating the effectiveness of their work. The following steps have been shown to support an integrated approach to these functions.

### The IFSP/IEP

*Report Child Functioning by Routine*   During IFSP/IEP meetings, specialists may dominate the time while presenting assessment findings and making recommendations. As described in *Family-Centered Intervention Planning: A Routines-Based Approach* (McWilliam, 1992), this way of conducting meetings puts families in an unnecessarily passive role and emphasizes the professional–client chasm. It is better for specialists to report how the child functions in everyday routines. For example, specialists need to share the assessment of a child's communication with regular caregivers during those routines (i.e., parents or teachers). Assessment reports and interpretives should be saved for other times. Giving up the opportunity to demonstrate single-handed expertise is uncomfortable for some specialists, but the advantages of collaborating with others and keeping an eye on child functioning should compensate somewhat.

*Consider Which of the Six Models Would Be Most Helpful*   Alternatives for service delivery have not been emphasized in training programs for therapists and special educators or in the literature. (In speech-language journals, a number of articles have been written on service delivery, but our research showed that many speech-language pathologists still are more reluctant than other specialists to use integrated approaches.) We now know that therapy can be provided in six ways. Our field-based study (McWilliam, Scarborough, & Chaudhary, 1995) showed that specialists do not vary the models they use within children or across children; furthermore, specialists within any one program tend to use the same model. Because each model has its potential uses, it is worthwhile to consider all of them. From an integrated therapy approach, specialists should assume that the group activity, individual during routine, or consultation model will be tried first. In deciding which of these or which of the segregated models should be planned, specialists can consider 1) how the goals can be addressed in classroom routines, 2) how the specific techniques can be used in classroom routines, 3) what model the family would like used, 4) what classroom characteristics would enhance or impede the intervention, and 5) how effective each model would be for the child. It may seem unusual to consider child characteristics last, but our data showed that this factor predicts choice of models less than do the other factors.

*Plan Time for Consultation/Planning*   Parents in a focus group (McWilliam, Young, & Harville, 1995) on specialized services were asked what specialists had to do in addition to hands-on therapy with their children. They mentioned writing reports, consulting with parents and with teachers, and preparing equipment. Later in the meeting, the facilitator asked, "How many minutes out of, say, a total of 60 minutes of therapy—perhaps broken into two 30-minute sessions—would you want the therapist working directly with your child?" The answers from parents were 45, 50, and 60 minutes. They were unapologetically, good-naturedly abashed when they realized what they expected of therapists. Therefore, therapists should ensure that other team members, especially family members, realize what goes into allocated therapy time. Unlike prevailing political presumptions in the field of education that we should strip away all nondirect service functions (i.e., cut out all the bureaucracy and just let teachers teach), integrated therapy embraces the complexity of early intervention services and promotes people working together to ensure that regular caregivers can make everyday routines therapeutic.

*Give the Family the Choice of the Six Models* Many practitioners who completed the national survey questionnaires (McWilliam & Bailey, 1994) wrote, unprompted, that they had never considered giving families a choice about service delivery models. This was in response to the questions about what they would do if families had a preference. Furthermore, in my years of presenting about service delivery models and of visiting early intervention programs, when I have asked about giving families choices, only two or three teams out of hundreds have done so. It is true that many families initially say they do not care and that they will leave it up to the therapists, but therapists who explain the choices to families are providing them with valuable information, without parent-training them. In my experience, families whose therapists use one or more of the integrated models (e.g., group activity, individual during routine, consultation) speak positively about how those therapists provide therapy; that is, they say how good it is that therapy occurs where the child needs the skills, that the child does not have to be taken away from friends, and that the teacher and therapist are both involved. However, families whose therapists tend to use the segregated models (e.g., individual pull-out, small-group pull-out, one-on-one in classroom) speak positively about the fact that their child receives therapy. The difference is that for families with experience with integrated models, therapy is not a unidimensional service: They have more information about therapy.

### Planning

*Plan Classroom Visits During Optimal Times* Therapists can be frustrated when they go into classrooms and find that the children with whom they want to work are engaged in activities that do not provide much opportunity for the therapist to help. By planning visits during times of the day when children are more likely to be engaged in compatible activities, therapists will feel that their time is better spent. For example, if an occupational therapist working on perceptual-motor skills with a child can visit the classroom when tabletop activities are available (e.g., art, centers, even free play in some settings), the opportunities to assess the child's perceptual-motor functioning and to try out interventions are enhanced.

*Discuss Roles and Responsibilities with Teachers*  This guideline applies to teachers and therapists equally. If both parties know the issues, it doubles the chance that communication will occur. This guideline is discussed in the section about roles and responsibilities for teachers.

*Concentrate on Functional Skills More than Foundational Skills*  The clinical literature, especially in the fields with origins in the medical model (e.g., occupational therapy, physical therapy, speech-language pathology), emphasizes habilitation or rehabilitation to prepare the child for future needs. In physical therapy, therefore, children are taught to walk on a balance beam to help their balance in everyday functioning, which presumably does not usually entail walking on 4-inch boards. In speech-language pathology, children may be taught to blow a feather across a table to prepare them to use adequate breath control while speaking. In occupational therapy, children may be taught to tolerate brushing of the palms to prepare them to handle different textures. The more functional therapists can make the goals, the more therapy can be integrated into regular routines. Thus, the physical therapist would work with the child and teacher to teach the child to keep his or her balance on the playground, the speech-language pathologist would work with the child and teacher to teach the child to use his or her diaphragm to speak loudly enough, and the occupational therapist would work with the child and teacher to increase the familiarity of textures of highly desired objects.

*Help the Teacher Incorporate Therapy into General Teaching*  If therapists feel that particular interventions are needed, they can work with teachers to incorporate them into fun activities. The balance beam can become part of an obstacle course, the feather can become part of a game to fill a container without using hands, and the brushed palms can become part of . . . a tickling game? (All right, so some interventions are so foreign to everyday functioning that it is almost impossible to work them in!) Creative, flexible therapists can usually find alternative ways of addressing functional goals; very few problems have only one prescribed intervention. Therapists using integrated approaches often need to think about the alternatives and present those most compatible with the child's, the family's, and the teacher's regular routines.

*Use Individual During Routine Model, with Option of Using Group Activity or One-on-One in Classroom*  We found dividing therapy approaches into *in-class* and *out-of-class* to be simplistic; hence, our formulation of six models. After hours of observation and reams of self-report data, we have concluded that the individual during routine model is the most useful of the integrated approaches for the following reasons:

- Ongoing classroom activities are not disrupted.
- Children are engaged in activities they would be doing when the therapist was not around.
- Therapists can observe and assess functioning in normal routines.
- Milieu teaching (Kaiser, Hendrickson, & Alpert, 1991; Warren & Bambara, 1989; Warren & Gazdag, 1990), in which practitioners work within the context of children's engagement, can be used.
- Teachers can see how interventions can fit into regular routines.
- The child's peers can be incorporated into therapy.
- The child learns to cope with distractions.
- Therapists can work with more than one child at a time.

If this model does not work with a given child, perhaps for reasons that have nothing to do with the child (e.g., classroom characteristics), the therapist does not have to resort to a pull-out model right away. Other in-class models retain some of the benefits of individual during routine but give the therapist more control over the situation. The group activity model entails therapists' planning with teachers to have therapist-led activities, which means that intervention can occur 1) where the child usually spends his or her time, 2) with peers, and 3) with the teacher present. If this does not work, therapists can try the one-on-one in-classroom model, in which they work with the child in the classroom but apart from the regular routine and apart from other children. This is a segregated model, but the child stays in a familiar environment, the teacher may have an opportunity to observe what is going on, and the child learns to cope with distractions. Therapists therefore approach service delivery alternatives by starting with a highly integrated model and gradually using less integrated models if necessary. This method is quite different from either starting with a segregated model or changing to pull-out when in-class does not work.

*Plan for Reciprocal Consultation with Teacher*   When beginning to work with a teacher, the therapist can set the stage for collaboration by stating that he or she hopes the teacher will speak up when he or she sees things the therapist could be doing differently. The therapist can also say that he or she hopes to be able to give the teacher suggestions. Most teachers welcome both opportunities.

### Implementation

*Build in Consultation Time at Beginning and End of Classroom Visit*   If a therapist knows he or she will be in a classroom for 2 hours, because four children theoretically receive 30 minutes each, it is advisable to plan for the first few minutes and the last few minutes to be spent with the teacher. This may be difficult for teachers who are busy with classroom management responsibilities, but by planning for these times and letting teachers know this would be the most effective use of therapy time, therapists give the message that consultation is important.

*Join Child(ren) in Ongoing Activities, Using One-on-One In Classroom Only When Absolutely Necessary* When therapists go into the classroom (regardless of whether they have spent time consulting with the teacher), they can see what the focal child is doing and join the child in that activity. Sometimes therapists find the child is nonengaged, so their first task is to help get the child engaged in the routines (free play provides many different options). If the routines or the child's engagement are such that therapists cannot conceive of any way to work on needed skills, they have the last resort option of taking the child to a part of the classroom where they can work with the child apart from the ongoing routines.

*Watch Teacher to Give Feedback and Learn About Managing this Group* Therapists are often eager to work directly with children, in part because the *zeitgeist* of therapy is that anything else is less valuable. Therapists would be well advised, however, to observe the teacher to gather information for making constructive suggestions and for ideas for working with that particular group of children.

*Demonstrate Interventions for Classroom Staff* Demonstrating or modeling alone can be doomed to failure, to which many therapists will attest. Caregivers do not necessarily imitate the things they see others doing with children. For modeling to succeed, teachers need to see a purpose for changing what they do and to see commonalities between themselves and modelers; that is, people do not imitate the behaviors of people they see as fundamentally different from themselves. Therapists can offer to model a strategy they would like the teacher to carry out, but modeling and hoping for imitation has little chance of succeeding, as does insisting that teachers watch.

*Ask the Teacher for Feedback* Requesting teachers' opinions has three benefits. First, it conveys to teachers that specialists do not see themselves as superior. Second, it trains teachers to evaluate therapy. Third, it helps both the effectiveness of therapy time and collaboration. The teacher might, for example, suggest ways to limit the number of children participating in the therapist's activity. Teachers can also give the therapist ideas about successful methods of interaction with a given child.

### Evaluation

*Monitor Which of the Six Models Are Used* At the beginning of our field-based research, therapists told us the models they used most of the time. After asking them to report through the SDF (see Figure 1), however, we found that perceptions in the absence of documentation were different from the self-report data. Specifically, therapists who said they used in-class approaches at least half of the time actually used out-of-class approaches almost exclusively. Of course, they may originally have given what they thought was the socially desirable response to the question. The discrepancy did alert us that, to avoid therapists possibly deluding themselves, they may be well-advised to record how they provide each session of therapy. They can then use this information to make decisions about service delivery models at the next review with the family and other professionals.

*Monitor How Often Interventions on Each Objective Are Provided*   Some therapists try to address many goals, only to find they have to concentrate on one or two priorities at a time. For example, a physical therapist might have four goals to work on with an infant: independent sitting, protective reactions to the side, head control in prone, and relaxation in side-lying. (Note that these goals are not stated in context and therefore are not functional; we assume that the IFSP provides the context.) During therapy time, however, the therapist finds him- or herself working on the first two goals, which are related, most of the time. If the child progresses in sitting skills but not in head control or relaxation, one possible explanation is that the last two goals were not addressed very much during therapy times. That information is critical when deciding what changes to make; clearly, if head control and relaxation are important to families, the therapist will know to concentrate on those goals rather than suggesting a change in interventions or in the goals themselves. The SDF provides a structure for therapists to document quickly 1) how much time was spent with a child, 2) what was addressed, and 3) what model was used. The key to the SDF actually being used is to have copies with the child's current objectives already written on the form. If therapists have to write in the goals, they are unlikely to use it, because of the extra time needed to complete it.

*Rate Child Independence and Frequency on Each Objective Every 8 Weeks*   The TGIF, described earlier, can be completed by therapists as it is by teachers and families. Therapists' ratings are important because they see the children from a different perspective than teachers and families. All three perspectives are important and should be considered when reviewing child progress. The TGIF is a quick way to document progress, and many therapists may want to provide additional information.

*Report Data to Teacher, Family, and Administrator*   For the same reasons as previously given for teachers, specialists can use TGIF data to report child progress to other interested people.

## Families

Whereas the steps outlined previously have focused on what service providers can do, this section discusses families' potential roles in implementing integrated services. Families, like professionals, may be interested in issues of finances and time, the IFSP/IEP, implementation, and evaluation. These steps complement issues discussed in Chapter 3.

### *Finances and Time*

*Learn What Is Covered by Medicaid or Other Third-Party Insurance Providers for Direct and Indirect Services*   Therapists have identified third-party restrictions as a barrier to integrating therapy into regular routines. Families would be well advised to find out exactly what rules come with their insurance or Medicaid policies, because sometimes perceived restrictions are in fact hearsay. For example, if the policy states that therapy must be provided by a qualified professional and must consist of direct treatment, it does not necessarily mean that in-class therapy is precluded. Families may find that they are able to provide information to therapists about what is allowed. Furthermore, families can make the case to third-party payers that a flexible arrangement is in their child's best interests and is the best use of insurance or Medicaid funds.

*Learn About Any Caps on Third-Party Reimbursement* Before determining how much therapy a child should receive (i.e., before deciding on the intensity listed in the IFSP/IEP), families should find out about any caps imposed by third-party payers. That will help the family decide on the frequency of therapy sessions. For example, if an insurance company will pay for only 12 sessions, the family might elect to spread the sessions out over the year (i.e., monthly sessions) rather than having them all at the beginning of the year and then not having contact with the therapist for months.

*Learn How Therapy Is Effective* Families have traditionally been passive recipients of information and recommendations from therapists. If a therapist or a doctor says the child needs twice-weekly speech-language therapy, for example, the family should ask the following types of questions:

- Why does it have to be this often or this infrequently?
- What would happen if my child had more or less therapy?
- What exactly happens during therapy?
- What are the teacher's and the family's roles in supporting therapy?
- What is the therapist's role in supporting the teacher and the family?
- If the family and the teacher are to benefit directly from therapy (i.e., if the therapist will be suggesting interventions to carry out between therapy sessions), how will therapy be provided?
- If the child is to benefit directly from therapy (i.e., if the therapist will be teaching skills or conducting other interventions), what can the family expect to see as a result of therapy?
- If the therapist is providing direct intervention during therapy sessions, can the family and other caregivers (e.g., teachers) provide the same intervention between sessions?
- If the family and teachers are providing intervention, how often will therapy sessions occur and why?

These questions should give families some idea about the effectiveness of therapy. It is not so much a question of whether therapy is effective, but how therapy is effective. If the effectiveness of therapy hinges on the therapists providing expert consultation to families and other caregivers, families should ask therapists to spend their time in ways that maximize that process (i.e., talking to them as much as, if not more than, to the child). If it hinges on the therapists intervening directly with children, families should ask therapists to work on immediately relevant skills in relevant contexts.

### The IFSP/IEP

*Ask for Routines-Based Rather than Domain-Based Assessment and Intervention Planning; Report on Home Routines* Some programs give families the opportunity to be involved in making decisions about assessment and intervention planning, whereas others do not. Families can ask for assessments to be handled as they see fit, such as asking professionals to assess how their child functions in everyday routines. Whether professionals provide domain- or discipline-specific assessment, families can say that they want routines-based assessment and intervention planning. Families can also tell the other team members that they would like to report on how the child functions during home routines and for that information to be used in determining intervention goals.

*State Which of the Six Models of Service Delivery Are Desired for Each Therapy* Families have not characteristically been given opportunities to choose therapy models, but they can familiarize themselves with the six models that have been presented in this book and elsewhere (McWilliam, 1995). Therapists have reported that, generally, they are willing to follow families' preferences (McWilliam & Bailey, 1994), but that parents should know that therapists who favor in-class models are more likely to follow families' preferences for in-class and therapists who favor out-of-class models are more likely to follow preferences for out-of-class. Because one of the attributes of early intervention providers is that they respond to families' concerns (McWilliam et al., 1995), families should at least make their preferences known.

*Emphasize Functional Needs Rather than Those from a Test or Curriculum* Families can take two approaches in advocating for functional interventions. First, they can identify behaviors they would like to see their children doing to function successfully in everyday routines. Second, they can ask why recommended skills are important and how they are immediately relevant. If a special educator suggests matching objects by colors, for example, the family can ask why this is important. If the answer is that this is a skill that all children of this developmental level learn, the family can ask, "But how will that help my child right now?" If the special educator says it will help the child learn to put toys away, the family can say, "All right, let's change the goal to putting toys away."

*Ask Staff When Indirect Service, Planning, and Consultation Will Take Place* Four times as much consultation between specialists and teachers occurs when in-class therapy is provided than when out-of-class therapy is provided (McWilliam, 1994). Although this may be perceived as a drawback to in-class therapy, it can also be an advantage: It generates collaboration. Nevertheless, consultation takes time, and professionals are likely to have the notion that it is less valuable than direct hands-on work with the child.

Parents would therefore be well advised to ensure that both teachers and professionals plan to set aside time to talk to each other.

*Decide on Therapy Needed and Intensity After Deciding on the Child's Needs* Too often in early intervention, specialized services are identified before the child's and family's needs are. For example, if a child has cerebral palsy, it is assumed that he or she should receive early childhood special education, occupational therapy, physical therapy, and speech-language therapy. Furthermore, it is assumed that these services should be provided as often as possible. Assumptions about services needed and their intensity are often made on the basis of diagnosis and age. For example, children with Down syndrome might not receive intensive speech-language services until the age of 2 years. This whole concept is atheoretical and absurd for at least three reasons: 1) the knowledge and skills of specialists can be valuable at any time for any child and family, 2) services should be allocated only to support the attainment of specific activities, and 3) each child's environment (e.g., home, early intervention program, support network) has unique characteristics that influence his or her development. Taking these points in order, every family with or without a child with special needs can benefit from the advice of an early childhood specialist; the value of specialists is not unique to developmental disabilities, let alone to specific diagnoses.

The World Health Organization makes useful distinctions between impairments, disabilities, and handicaps: The impairment is the equivalent of the diagnosis, the disability is the resulting aberration from normal functioning, and the handicap is the interference with functioning. For example, the child with mental retardation (MR) or developmental delays (DD) can have the impairment of MR/DD. The disability may be that the child does not understand cues in the environment (i.e., does not respond well), and the handicap may be that the child does not eat independently, does not communicate, and does not move independently. Clearly, children with certain diagnoses or impairments are likely to benefit more than others from specialized services, but the allocation of resources should be made on the basis of the handicaps, not the impairment. How much an impairment results in a handicap is in part a function of what the child needs to be able to do to succeed in everyday routines and how the environment supports or impedes the child's abilities. Therefore, families should assess what their children need to be able to do before deciding on services and how often the services are provided.

An often overlooked component of planning for specialized services is the resources already available for the child. The child with cerebral palsy who lives in a home where a parent has much time to play, is happy spending time this way, and understands how to incorporate therapy into everyday routines is likely to need less of a therapist's time than the child who does not have these resources. An extremely important point is that parents who have these resources may need much support, but that is different from needing much child-oriented therapy. For children in classroom-based programs, the resources of the program similarly should influence the decision about needed therapies and intensity. The child in a program with 1) a small number of children in each classroom, 2) well-trained and sensitive staff, and 3) a curriculum or philosophy of developmentally and individually appropriate practices is likely to need less of therapists' time than a program that is overcrowded, staffed by less qualified personnel, and developmentally and individually inappropriate. Therefore, the family should decide on the child's needs first and then decide on what therapies and intensity of services are needed to support the regular caregivers in meeting those needs.

*Allow Therapists Maximum Flexibility Rather than Holding Them to a Certain Amount of Time per Week* Families may be torn between wanting therapists to spend time working directly with their child and wanting them to provide effective consultation. One way to allow therapists flexibility while ensuring that specialized services are provided is to ask for a certain amount of therapy time per month rather than per week. Another way is to request that therapy sessions alternate between a child focus and a caregiver focus. Families should be concerned about getting the allocated amount of therapist time, but they increase the likelihood of services being integrated if they allow therapists flexibility, particularly in the amount of time spent on direct hands-on treatment.

### Implementation

*Monitor How Much and How Well Teachers Incorporate Therapy into Teaching* Families can observe in the classroom and can ask for documentation about the extent to which teachers incorporate therapists' suggestions into classroom teaching. To observe, families should find out from therapists what types of techniques they have recommended for each goal. During observations, families can look for how often and for how long teachers use the strategies. It is important to recognize that teachers' failure to follow through with recommendations may not be their fault. The goals or strategies may be nonfunctional, therapists may not have communicated with teachers, and teachers may have too many competing demands to be effective individualizers. Families can advocate for the situation to be corrected; they can ask for the goals and strategies to be redefined; they can ask therapists and teachers to meet; and they can ask for a change in the learning environment (e.g., more resources for the classroom or a change in placement). If families use teachers' documentation as the method of monitoring follow-through,[1] they would be

---

[1]The concept of teachers' following through with strategies recommended by therapists suggests an expert model of consultation that I do not endorse in most situations. If therapists and teachers *collaborate,* as described in Chapter 2, teachers implement strategies that are mutually agreed upon (i.e., the agenda is as much theirs as the therapists'). Other ways of describing *follow-through* are *using facilitating strategies* or *individualizing,* but both the use of facilitating strategies and individualizing teaching can emanate from teachers themselves, so I am left with the awkward and imprecise term *following through.*

well advised to explain that they understand that infrequent or irregular follow-through is not necessarily the teacher's fault. This encourages teachers to report their follow-through activities honestly. Families can propose either a systematic method or an informal method for teachers' documentation. The systematic method can consist of a form on which the strategies are listed; teachers record the number of times each day they implemented each strategy. Some interventions, especially communication interventions, may occur frequently enough that it is unrealistic for teachers to keep track of the number of times they implemented them. In that case, they can use a simple rating scale with 0 = not at all, 1 = a few times, 2 = quite often, and 3 = a lot. The informal documentation can consist of a notebook in which the strategies are listed at the front as a reminder. Teachers record in narrative form what they do with the child each day. Whether using observation or documentation, families can assess the success of integrated therapy by how much the strategies are used during nontherapy times.

*Visit the Classroom Occasionally When the Therapist Is There* Visits occurring when the therapist is in the classroom can inform families about the therapist's service delivery model. Assuming that families have participated in deciding on the model(s) to be used, they can determine whether the plan is being carried out. This may be especially important if families discover that the teacher is not following through. If little communication or coordination occurs between teacher and therapist, the family might be able to pinpoint one of the problems. It should be noted, however, that some professionals mostly collaborate outside scheduled therapy times, so families should not jump to conclusions based solely on their observations during visits.

*Ask How Therapy Can Be Incorporated into Normal Home and Community Routines* In classroom programs, professionals sometimes forget that intervention occurs outside the program. If families want to carry intervention strategies over to the home or community, they should ask both therapists and teachers for ideas.

### Evaluation

*Ask for Documentation of Which of the Six Models Therapists Use at Each Session* Families can ask therapists to complete the SDF, previously described. As a parent, I find it hard to ask professionals to complete extra paperwork, but this form takes only a few seconds. If therapists seem resistant, families can ask teachers to complete it, because they should be able to tell which models are used. The recommendation for documentation at each session comes from the discrepancy we found between therapists' reported usual model of service delivery and the models they reported on the SDF; most therapists report using more integrated models than they actually do.

*Ask Teachers How Often They Provide Intervention on Highest-Priority Objectives* Receiving this report seems to be critical because of our finding that teachers implement strategies that specialists recommend about 5% of the time or only once or twice in a 10-minute observation. Teachers have reported that they do other activities with the children to support the goals, but this report is an indication that collaboration is not occurring. If teachers are providing interventions other than those that specialists have recommended, teachers and specialists should have agreed that those interventions should be considered facilitation strategies or follow-through. Sometimes what teachers consider an intervention specialists would not, because it is too weak. For example, a speech-language pathologist might recommend that teachers try to get children to elaborate on one-word utterances (to promote two-word utterances and the use of descriptors) by giving them descriptive choices (e.g., "You want the baby doll? Which one? Big baby or little baby?"). If the teacher says that he or she is working on two-word utterances by modeling (e.g., "You want the baby doll? Here's the big baby doll."), the speech-language pathologist might feel that this method is too indirect because it does not elicit the child's production of the target behavior. Families' monitoring of the teacher's follow-through can reveal such incongruities and help the professionals decide on what constitutes an intervention. Most importantly, families need documentation of follow-through because the teacher's role in intervention is at the heart of the philosophy of integrated services. If teachers are not individualizing, for whatever reason, the value of therapy is considerably diminished.

*Rate Child Independence and Frequency on Each Objective Every 8 Weeks* Families can use the TGIF, previously described, to monitor children's goal attainment.

## CONCLUSIONS

The guidelines presented in this chapter are designed to help administrators, therapists, teachers, and families prepare for integrated therapy and to outline implementation steps. Commonalities exist across the four groups in the advantages, cautions, and procedures of this approach, so some repetition is inevitable. Yet each group has a different perspective; thus, the repetition is not redundant.

Despite the listing of implementation steps, this chapter does not provide a recipe for integrating services. A "cookbook" approach is inappropriate in early intervention because of the concept of individualization and the recognition of ecological differences. The guidelines presented here, however, in combination with the discipline-specific chapters that follow, should provide a thorough foundation for individual programs, professionals, and families to design integrated service delivery.

## REFERENCES

Bailey, D.B., McWilliam, P.J., & Winton, P.J. (1992). Building family-centered practices in early intervention: A team-based model for change. *Infants and Young Children, 5*(1), 73–82.

Coleman, P.P., Buysse, V., Scalise-Smith, D.L., & Schulte, A.C. (1991). Consultation: Applications to early intervention. *Infants and Young Children, 4,* 41–46.

Kaiser, A.P., Hendrickson, J.M., & Alpert, C.L. (1991). Milieu language teaching: A second look. *Advances in Mental Retardation and Developmental Disabilities, 4,* 63–92.

McWilliam, R.A. (1992). *Family-centered intervention planning: A routines-based approach.* Tucson, AZ: Communication/Therapy Skill Builders.

McWilliam, R.A. (1994, October). *Integrated therapy/instruction: Synthesis of four years of research.* Paper presented at the International Early Childhood Conference on Children with Special Needs and Their Families, St. Louis, MO.

McWilliam, R.A. (1995). Integration of therapy and consultative special education: A continuum in early intervention. *Infants and Young Children, 7*(4), 29–38.

McWilliam, R.A., & Bailey, D.B. (1994). Predictors of service delivery models in center-based early intervention. *Exceptional Children, 61,* 56–71.

McWilliam, R.A., & Grabowski, K. (1993, December). *A comparison of in-class and out-of-class instruction.* Poster presented at the International Early Childhood Conference on Children with Special Needs and Their Families, San Diego, CA.

McWilliam, R.A., Harbin, G.L., Snyder, P., Mittal, M., Vandiviere, P., Porter, P., & Munn, D. (1995). *Self-rated family-centeredness of Part H services.* Chapel Hill: Frank Porter Graham Child Development Center, University of North Carolina.

McWilliam, R.A., & Scarborough, A. (1994, September). *Does therapy carry over to the classroom? How to make early intervention more effective.* Paper presented at the North Carolina Association for the Education of Young Children/Division for Early Childhood Annual Study Conference, Greensboro, NC.

McWilliam, R.A., Scarborough, A., & Chaudhary, A. (1995). *Effects of therapy and consultation models on young children's goal attainment.* Unpublished data, University of North Carolina, Chapel Hill.

McWilliam, R.A., Tocci, L., & Harbin, G.L. (1995). *Services are child-oriented—and families want them that way.* Chapel Hill: Early Childhood Research Institute on Service Utilization, Frank Porter Graham Child Development Center, University of North Carolina.

McWilliam, R.A., Young, H.J., & Harville, K. (1995). *Themes related to specialized services for infants, toddlers, and preschoolers with disabilities.* Manuscript in preparation.

Warren, S.F., & Bambara, L.M. (1989). An experimental analysis of milieu language intervention: Teaching the action-object form. *Journal of Speech and Hearing Disorders, 54,* 448–461.

Warren, S.F., & Gazdag, G. (1990). Facilitating early language development with milieu intervention procedures. *Journal of Early Intervention, 14,* 62–86.

# Chapter 8

# Early Childhood Special and General Education

## Mark Wolery

Issues related to integrating practice recommendations from two disciplines, early childhood special education and early childhood general education, are described in this chapter. Because two disciplines are discussed, the terms involved in the two disciplines are defined, and the historical factors that influence practice are identified. Subsequently, the practices of both disciplines are noted, and myths about those practices are presented. Barriers to integrating the practices are discussed, and recommendations for practice integration are proposed.

## DEFINITION OF TERMS

The two disciplines, early childhood general education and early childhood special education, share three words in their names, and they each have a unique term. One of the shared terms, *early childhood,* refers to young children, usually from birth to age 8. In some cases, the term refers to children from birth to age 5, but both the National Association for the Education of Young Children (NAEYC) and the Division for Early Childhood (DEC) of the Council for Exceptional Children address children through age 8. For this chapter, *early childhood* refers to infants, toddlers, and preschoolers (i.e., through age 5). The unique terms in the disciplines' names, *general* and *special,* also are easily defined. *General* refers to programs designed for typically developing children, and *special* refers to programs designed for children with exceptional needs, including those with identified disabilities and those who are gifted or talented. Both disciplines, however, are interested in children who are at risk for learning and developmental problems. Thus, although both disciplines have defined populations, they overlap considerably in terms of serving young children who are at risk. Also, the inclusion of young children with disabilities in programs for typically developing children blurs the distinction between the two fields.

The third shared term, *education,* is most problematic to define. Discussion of educating any group implies a curriculum and stimulates images of schools and pedagogy. But what is the curriculum for young children? What should they be taught? What methods of instruction should be used? What are the goals of teaching young children? How is that teaching evaluated? These questions have produced a substantial amount of discussion. For this chapter, *education* is defined as purposeful manipulations of environmental variables to increase the likelihood that particular outcomes will occur; deciding what those outcomes are also is an issue open to debate (cf. Johnson & Johnson, 1994). Furthermore, *education* as used in this chapter is restricted to programs that involve groups of young children (i.e., classrooms). One can argue appropriately that all interactions the child has with the social and physical environment in and out of classrooms should be designed to promote adaptive development (Wolery, 1996a) and that "education" is too restrictive. A more appropriate word is "intervention," which includes practices such as family support and home-based services. Many young children, however, spend considerable amounts of time in group care settings, and both disciplines have practice guidelines for such contexts. Thus, this chapter focuses on the issues and practice recommendations relevant for such contexts.

## HISTORICAL AND CONTEXTUAL ISSUES

The practices in education, particularly early education, are based on conceptualizations of how children develop and learn; in short, they are based on whether nature, nurture, or some combination of the two influences what children do and become. Most experts maintain that both forces are operating, and, with advancing age, environmental exchanges exert relatively greater influence (Bijou, 1993; Bornstein & Lamb, 1992; Gallagher & Ramey, 1987; Harel & Anastasiow, 1985). During the 1940s, a maturational perspective was dominant as reflected by the writings of Gesell and colleagues (e.g., Gesell et al., 1940). In the 1960s, evidence from developmental psychology (e.g., Hunt, 1961), the translation of Piaget's work into English (Piaget, 1951, 1952, 1954), the emergence of behavior analytic methods (Bijou & Baer, 1961, 1965; Harris, Wolf, & Baer, 1964), and activist political agendas (e.g., the war on poverty) caused the maturational perspective to diminish and constructivism and cultural transmission to gain prominence. The general early education community tended to adopt constructivist views based on the work of Piaget and more recently on the writings of Vygotsky (1978), and the special early education and intervention community tended to adopt a cultural transition view emphasizing behavioral (Strain et al., 1992) and ecological (e.g., Bronfenbrenner, 1977; Dunst, 1985) perspectives. Despite these tendencies, cultural transmission programs existed in general early education (cf. Evans, 1975) and constructivism influenced special early education (Bricker & Bricker, 1974; Dunst, 1981; Stephens, 1977). Despite the ascendancy of these views, the maturational view continues to influence both general (cf. Bredekamp, 1987) and special (Goodman, 1992) early education. For discussions of various perspectives, see Baltes, Reese, and Nesselroade (1977); Dunst (1981); and Horowitz (1987).

During the 1980s, public dissatisfaction with education became evident, and numerous reports called for reform and increased attention to academic success (Anderson, Heibert, Scott, & Wilkinson, 1985; Bennett, 1986). This produced an emphasis on academic performance in many early childhood programs and often resulted in inappropriate practices (Elkind, 1989). Some children were denied access to kindergarten because they were not ready, and others were retained (Shepard & Smith, 1988). In response to these trends, NAEYC convened working groups to describe appropriate practices (Johnson & Johnson, 1992). Their work produced a widely disseminated document describing developmentally appropriate practice guidelines (i.e., Bredekamp, 1987). This document focused on general early education and addressed children with disabilities in only a cursory manner, but it produced interest in both general and special early education. Discussions in the general early education community centered around the definition of the practices and their relevance to children from other than European-American origins and to children across the economic distribution (Bredekamp, 1991; Kessler, 1991; Kostelnik, 1992; Lubeck, 1991; Mallory & New, 1994; McGill-Franzen, 1992; Spodek, 1991; Walsh, 1991). In special early education, the discussion focused on the relevance of the guidelines for young children with disabilities (Atwater, Carta, Schwartz, & McConnell, 1994; Bredekamp, 1993; Carta, 1995; Carta, Atwater, Schwartz, & McConnell, 1993; Carta, Schwartz, Atwater, & McConnell, 1991; Cavallaro, Haney, & Cabello, 1993; Guralnick, 1993; Johnson & Johnson, 1992, 1993; Mahoney, Robinson, & Powell, 1992; Mallory & New, 1994; McLean & Odom, 1993; Norris, 1991; Novick, 1993; Wolery & Bredekamp, 1994; Wolery, Strain, & Bailey, 1992).

Interest in the practice guidelines occurred in the early special education community because of the firm commitment to including young children with disabilities in general early childhood programs. Such integration (e.g., mainstreaming, inclusion) emerged in the 1970s through the work of Bricker and Bricker (1973) and was later supported by research and program evaluation efforts (e.g., Allen, 1992; Bailey & McWilliam, 1990; Buysse & Bailey, 1993; Guralnick, 1978, 1981, 1990; Odom & McEvoy, 1988; Peck & Cooke, 1983; Peck, Odom, & Bricker, 1993; Safford, 1989; Strain, 1983). By 1989, a majority of general early childhood programs reported enrolling at least one child with a disability (Wolery, Holcombe, et al., 1993). If children with disabilities are served in programs for children without disabilities, then the practice of those programs will influence how services are provided. Also, early special education researchers have developed an impressive array of intervention strategies (Bailey & Wolery, 1992; Barnett & Carey, 1992; Bricker & Cripe, 1992; Kozloff, 1994; Odom, McConnell, & McEvoy, 1992; Odom & McLean, in press; Wolery & Wilbers, 1994). If the guidelines of developmentally appropriate practice are different from those of special education practice, then procedures are needed for integrating the two sets of practices.

Thus, historically different views of how children develop and learn influence which early education practices are considered acceptable. Although both general and special early education tend to be influenced by different theoretical positions, they also share some common conceptual foundations. Furthermore, values and research related to integrating young children with and without disabilities create the need to analyze the two sets of practices.

## DISCIPLINE-SPECIFIC PRACTICES

In this section, broad statements about practices specific to general and special early education are noted, as are outcomes that may be achieved through the use of the practices. After the practices are presented, myths about both practices are noted.

### General Early Childhood Education

Recommendations concerning general early childhood practices can be found in many sources (e.g., Spodek, 1993; Teale & Sulzby, 1986); however, the developmentally appropriate practice document (Bredekamp, 1987) is used extensively to guide practice. Developmental appropriateness contains two components: age-appropriateness and individual-appropriateness (Bredekamp, 1987). Age-appropriateness is based on the notion that relatively predictable sequences of development occur in young children and across various areas of development. Individual appropriateness acknowledges the variation that exists in development and allows practices to accommodate individual differences in interests, needs, and abilities. Recommendations in the document are made on the curriculum, adult–child interactions, relationships between program personnel and the home, and assessment practices. Emphasis is placed on all areas of development, children's interests and developmental levels, active interaction with people and materials through play, use of concrete materials relevant to children's lives, responsive guidance by the adult based on observations of the children, frequent child choice of materials and activities (i.e., child-initiated learning), and use of stimulating questions (Bredekamp, 1987). When interacting with children, adults individualize their responses to children, provide opportunities for children to communicate, promote task completion through nonintrusive means, encourage exploration, identify and respond to indications of stress, and promote the development of self-esteem and self-control (Bredekamp, 1987).

Assessment practices emphasize use of multiple sources of information (e.g., observations), attention to diversity issues, and communication with family members.

In the early 1990s, there were clarifications of the developmentally appropriate practice guidelines (Bredekamp & Rosegrant, 1992a), and NAEYC, in conjunction with the National Association of Early Childhood Specialists in State Departments of Education (NAECS/SDE), published a position statement about curriculum content and assessment practices (NAEYC & NAECS/SDE, 1991). The position statement is based on seven explicit assumptions, which are presented in Table 1. Also, the joint position statement contains several lists of specific recommendations. The curriculum recommendations are captured in the following statement:

> The NAEYC and NAECS/SDE guidelines call for meaning-centered, integrated, "mindful" curriculum, but such a curriculum is only achieved if the other perspectives that inform curriculum are activated—child development knowledge, discipline-based knowledge, and knowledge of the individual developmental/ learning continuum of each child. The curriculum guidelines therefore require that curriculum not only be meaning centered but that it be age appropriate (reflect knowledge of child development domains), be individually appropriate (based on children's needs, interests, and individual differences), and have intellectual integrity (reflect the knowledge base of the disciplines). (Rosegrant & Bredekamp, 1992, p. 70)

For assessment practices, guidelines are presented for planning instruction, identifying children with disabilities, and program evaluation and accountability (NAEYC & NAECS/SDE, 1991). Assessments for planning instruction emphasize considering the whole child, attending to diversity issues, collaborating with others, integrating the assessment and curriculum activities, using informal and authentic procedures, including ongoing observation, attending to children's strengths, and communicating regularly with family members.

Table 1. Assumptions from the position statement by NAEYC and NAECS/SDE

1. Children learn best when their physical needs are met and they feel psychologically secure.
2. Children construct knowledge.
3. Children learn through social interaction with adults and other children.
4. Children's learning reflects a recurring cycle that begins in awareness and moves to exploration, to inquiry, and, finally, to utilization.
5. Children learn through play.
6. Children's interests and "need to know" motivate learning.
7. Human development and learning are characterized by individual variation.

From National Association for the Education of Young Children and the National Association of Early Childhood Specialists in State Departments of Education. (1991). Guidelines for appropriate curriculum content and assessment in programs serving children ages 3 through 8. *Young Children, 46,* 21–38; reprinted by permission.

These practices are designed to promote a range of outcomes for children that vary substantially by child's age, child's abilities, and program emphasis. Bredekamp and Rosegrant (1992b) indicate that the guidelines of developmentally appropriate practices are not a curriculum, but a framework for use in making curricular decisions and carrying out curricular activities. Furthermore, they emphasize that the "curriculum is not child development" (p. 5). Rather, knowledge of child development, curriculum theory, and content disciplines (e.g., literacy, mathematics, arts) is integrated to design meaningful programs. In the NAEYC and NAECS/SDE (1991) position statement, sample goals were offered for illustrative purposes of the outcomes that may be achieved by use of the curriculum and assessment guidelines. These are listed in Table 2.

## Special Early Childhood Education

Until 1993, practices in early childhood special education had to be gleaned from various texts and periodicals. In 1991, DEC established the Task Force on Recommended Practices to develop practice recommendations. The resulting document (DEC Task Force on Recommended Practices, 1993) described

Table 2. Sample goals for general early education programs

Responsible adults want children to
- Develop a positive self-concept and attitude toward learning, self-control, and a sense of belonging
- Develop curiosity about the world, confidence as a learner, creativity and imagination, and personal initiative
- Develop relationships of mutual trust and respect with adults and peers, understand perspectives of other people, and negotiate and apply rules of group living
- Understand and respect social and cultural diversity
- Know about the community and social roles
- Use language to communicate effectively and to facilitate thinking and learning
- Become literate individuals who gain satisfaction, as well as information, from reading and writing
- Represent ideas and feelings through pretend play, drama, dance and movement, music, art, and construction
- Think critically, reason, and solve problems
- Construct understanding of relationships among objects, people, and events, such as classifying, ordering, number, space, and time
- Construct knowledge of the physical world, manipulate objects for desired effects, and understand cause-and-effect relationships
- Acquire knowledge of and appreciation for the fine arts, humanities, and sciences
- Become competent in management of their bodies and acquire basic physical skills, both gross motor and fine motor
- Gain knowledge about the care of their bodies and maintain a desirable level of health and fitness

From National Association for the Education of Young Children and the National Association of Early Childhood Specialists in the State Departments of Education (1991). Guidelines for appropriate curriculum content and assessment in programs serving children ages 3 through 8. *Young Children, 46,* 21–38; reprinted by permission.

recommended practices in several relevant areas. The acceptability of those practices was then established through a survey of parents and DEC members (Odom, McLean, Johnson, & LaMontagne, 1995). A book describing these practice recommendations also was developed (Odom & McLean, in press). The task force document contains more than 400 practice recommendations; thus, they cannot be listed here.

However, based on the task force report and other documents, some general principles of early childhood special education can be identified. First, the curricular activities should be individualized and based on a thorough assessment (Barnett & Carey, 1992; Bricker, 1986). Second, the assessment activities should involve multiple measurement strategies conducted over time under natural conditions using familiar adults and routines (McLean, Bailey, & Wolery, 1996; Neisworth, 1993). Third, family-centered practices that honor families as decision makers and use family support principles should be employed (Dunst, Trivette, & Deal, 1994). Fourth, planning, implementing, and evaluating children's early education experiences are inherently a team effort that involves members of relevant disciplines and family members (Bruder, 1994; McGonigel, Woodruff, & Roszmann-Millican, 1994). Fifth, services should be provided in normalized contexts using normalized procedures (Bailey & McWilliam, 1990; McWilliam & Strain, 1993; Peck et al., 1993). Sixth, intervention strategies should be used within the context of ongoing routines and activities (Bricker & Cripe, 1992; Wolery, 1994a). Seventh, ongoing monitoring and adjustment of intervention practices are necessary (Wolery, 1996b). Eighth, transitions between service programs should be planned, implemented, and evaluated on an individual basis (Atwater, Orth-Lopes, Elliott, Carta, & Schwartz, 1994; Rosenkoetter, Hains, & Fowler, 1994).

These practice principles are used to produce a range of outcomes. Bailey and Wolery (1992) identified some common outcomes that are generalizable across programs; these are shown in Table 3. However, as specified in the Individuals with Disabilities Education Act of 1990 (PL 101-476) and subsequent regulations, the goals for each child with disabilities are to be specified individually and formalized in an educational plan.

Early education for children with and without disabilities is a complex undertaking. It requires the adults in the program to make many decisions and modifications within each day and across days. It varies considerably depending on the children being served and the goals being promoted. It requires coordination with family members and with other professionals. It involves a large range of procedures from environmental arrangements to highly specialized instructional techniques (Barnett & Carey, 1992; Bredekamp & Rosegrant, 1992a). Capturing this complexity in a list of recommendations is difficult and open to substantial misinterpretation. Despite efforts to articulate the intent of the recommendations and the conditional statements that

Table 3.  General outcomes for young children with disabilities

1.  To support families in achieving their own goals
2.  To promote children's engagement, independence, and mastery
3.  To promote children's development in key domains
4.  To build and support children's social competence
5.  To promote children's generalized use of skills
6.  To provide and prepare children for normalized life experiences
7.  To prevent the emergence of future problems or disabilities

From Bailey, D.B., & Wolery, M. (1992). *Teaching infants and preschoolers with disabilities* (2nd ed.). Columbus, OH: Charles E. Merrill; reprinted by permission.

accompany each, misunderstanding of the practice recommendations exists in both disciplines (Bredekamp, 1993; Carta, 1995).

## Myths About Developmentally Appropriate Practice Guidelines

Kostelnik (1992), addressing general early educators, identified nine myths about developmentally appropriate practices, eight of which apply to preschool programs. Bredekamp (1993) discussed the relationship between general and special early childhood education and identified three myths that hold special implications for young children with disabilities. Carta (1995) also discussed myths. These myths, as discussed by these authors, are summarized in this section.

*Myth 1: In Developmentally Appropriate Practice (DAP) Classrooms, Teachers Do Not and Should Not Teach (Bredekamp, 1993; Carta, 1995; Kostelnik, 1992)* The practice guidelines clearly emphasize child choice, child-directed learning, and use of play as the context for learning. These recommendations are based on the assumption that young children learn from interacting with the social and physical environment. Bredekamp (1993) reasons that children learn from interacting with other children and with adults (teachers), and that both parties of any interaction must be active. Thus, in some situations, teachers influence (teach) children through those interactions. Similarly, in some instances, these interactions may occur with groups of children. The guidelines emphasize that large group instruction and teacher-directed instruction should not be used extensively or "most of the time" (Bredekamp, 1987, p. 54). The issue is not whether teachers teach, but whether a range of methods (e.g., teacher responsiveness to child behavior, child-initiated activities, and teacher-initiated activities) is used in a balanced proportion. Use of teacher-directed instruction that precludes child-initiated learning is clearly inappropriate, as is relying solely on child-initiated activities.

*Myth 2: In DAP Classrooms, the Curriculum Solely Emerges from Children's Interests (Bredekamp, 1993; Carta, 1995; Kostelnik, 1992)* The guidelines were written partly because the practices used in many programs were based on how older children are often taught and were not based on children's interests or on the need of young children to be active and engage in play. The guidelines stress following children's lead in activities, providing materials and activities interesting to children, planning activities based on children's interests, responding to and supporting children's engagement with materials, and promoting children's play. This led to the incorrect assumption that the classroom activities, materials, and practices were based only on children's interests and should be devoid of outcomes. The original document (Bredekamp, 1987), however, indicates that children's needs and abilities were to be considered in planning classroom experiences; furthermore, the NAEYC and NAECS/SDE (1991) position statement clearly indicates that the activities in early childhood programs should result in a range of outcomes.

This issue deals with what is meant by the "individually appropriate" component of developmental appropriateness. "A program cannot possibly achieve individual appropriateness without assessing and planning for children's individual needs and interests" (Bredekamp, 1993, p. 263). If a child's needs are considered, then logic dictates that some goals and practices of the curriculum are based on factors other than children's interests. Admittedly, the goals of programs following the developmentally appropriate practices are more broadly stated (e.g., NAEYC & NAECS/SDE, 1991) than is common on the IEPs of young children with disabilities.

***Myth 3: In DAP Classrooms, Academics Should Not Be Addressed (Bredekamp, 1993; Carta, 1995; Kostelnik, 1992)*** As noted, the developmentally appropriate practice guidelines were written in response to the inappropriate emphasis on academics and the practices that accompanied that emphasis. The guidelines and the NAEYC and NAECS/SDE (1991) position statement recognize that children's cognitive development is important but also place emphasis on other areas of development (e.g., social, emotional, communication, physical development). The stress placed in the guidelines on other areas of development and on promoting foundational cognitive skills and processes (e.g., problem solving, exploration) has led some to conclude that classrooms should not include attention to academics. The issue, however, is not whether academics are addressed, but 1) the definition of academic skills for preschoolers, 2) the practices used to address those skills, and 3) the need to emphasize skills from other domains of development as well. Many of the practices that promote children's literacy development are compatible with the guidelines (Teale & Sulzby, 1986; Wolery & Wolery, 1992).

***Myth 4: In DAP Classrooms, the Activities and Schedule Are Not Structured (Kostelnik, 1992)*** The emphasis on child-initiated learning, play, and children's interests may have led some to conclude that classrooms following the developmentally appropriate practice guidelines are unstructured. This depends on how *structure* is defined. If *structure* is defined as children sitting in desks aligned in rows, then developmentally appropriate classrooms are not structured. A more accurate definition of *structure* includes how the classroom is organized, how children gain access to materials, when and how activities and routines occur, and how adults interact with children. Using this definition, the guidelines are a framework for structuring the classroom, and the practice recommendations articulate how that structuring should occur.

***Myth 5: In DAP Classrooms, Teachers Do Not Rely on Other Sources of Knowledge (Bredekamp & Rosegrant, 1992b; Kostelnik, 1992)*** Although the guidelines provide a framework in which decisions are made, adults must draw on other sources of knowledge in implementing them. These other sources include the knowledge bases in child development, curriculum design and implementation, and the content of the disciplines (e.g., literacy, mathematics) being taught (Rosegrant & Bredekamp, 1992). Thus, accomplished early childhood teachers draw on several sources of knowledge, including assessment information on individual children, when designing classrooms, carrying out classroom activities, scheduling activities and routines, and interacting with children.

***Myth 6: In DAP Classrooms, Teachers Must Operate the Classroom in One Specific Way (Carta, 1995; Kostelnik, 1992)*** The guidelines also assist early childhood programs in meeting the NAEYC accreditation system. The accreditation standards and the guidelines, however, are a general framework for making decisions about designing and operating classrooms (Bredekamp & Rosegrant, 1992b). Thus, two programs following the guidelines may implement them differently, with each being consistent with the guidelines, but each being unique in responding to the needs and interests of the children involved. The guidelines are not prescriptions for every situation, but are general rules for intelligent application.

***Myth 7: The DAP Guidelines Are a Fad that Will Wane and Be Replaced by Another Set of Practices (Kostelnik, 1992)*** Educators can justifiably be skeptical about major efforts to reform practice because numerous examples exist in which reform efforts have been prominent, only to lose support and then reappear (Cuban, 1990). The developmentally appropriate practice guidelines are not based exclusively on ecologically valid and methodologically defensible research; rather, they are based on theory, research, logic, and tradition. Two comments are pertinent about this myth. First, the guidelines are evolving. The original document (Bredekamp, 1987) has been expanded and clarified through two more recent statements (Bredekamp & Rosegrant, 1992a; NAEYC & NAECS/SDE, 1991), and, as of early 1996, the guidelines are under revision. Thus, modifications of the guidelines are likely to occur in the future. Second, the guidelines are widely recognized, with more than 300,000 copies disseminated (Bredekamp, 1993), and have had wide influence. Thus, the effects of the guidelines are likely to endure well into the 21st century.

***Myth 8: In DAP Classrooms, Only Children Who Are Developing Typically, Are Caucasian, and Are from Middle-Class Homes Benefit (Bredekamp, 1993; Carta, 1995; Kostelnik, 1992)*** Questions have arisen about the applicability of the developmentally appropriate practice guidelines for children who are not Caucasian, who live in poverty, and who have disabilities (Carta et al., 1991; Delpit, 1988; Jipson, 1991; McGill-Franzen, 1992; Walsh, 1991). The original document (Bredekamp, 1987) acknowledged diversity in culture, ethnicity, language, and ability, but did not clearly articulate practice recommendations that allowed programs to accommodate that diversity appropriately. The leadership of NAEYC (e.g., Bredekamp, 1993) maintains that the individual appropriateness component allows and requires the practices to be adjusted to accommodate individual differences based in culture, ethnicity, language, economic circumstances, and ability. As a result, attempts have been made to clarify the application of the guidelines to diverse groups (e.g., Bowman, 1992; Mallory & New, 1994), including those with disabilities (Bredekamp, 1993; Carta, 1995; Carta et al., 1993).

## Myths About Early Childhood Special Education Practices

Myths also exist about early childhood special education practices and their applications in classrooms. Carta (1995) identified five such myths; these myths and two additional myths are discussed in this section.

***"Myth 1: Most Children with Special Needs Must Be Taught in Very Structured Activities in One-to-One Settings with the Teacher" (Carta, 1995, p. 4)*** To receive services through the infant and toddler program (i.e., Part H of PL 99-457) or to receive special education and related services at the preschool level, each child with disabilities must have an individualized intervention plan (i.e., an IFSP or IEP, respectively). Perhaps emphasis on individualizing intervention led to the assumption that instruction should be implemented individually and rigidly. A cursory reading of the early special education literature, however, indicates that the recommended practice is to embed instruction within naturally occurring activities and routines (Bailey & Wolery, 1992; Barnett & Carey, 1992; Bricker & Cripe, 1992; Cavallaro et al., 1993; Halle, Alpert, & Anderson, 1984; Wolery, 1994a; Wolery & Sainato, in press; Wolery, Werts, & Holcombe, 1994). Furthermore, since 1984, the recommendation has been that "individualized instruction should be provided within the small group setting" (Bailey & Wolery, 1984, p. 103); thus, structured, direct instruction in a one-to-one setting is rarely recommended. For a discussion of the rationale of small group instruction and procedures for implementing it, see Collins, Gast, Ault, and Wolery (1991). The emphasis on small-group instruction, however, does not mean that adults should avoid responsive interactions with individual children as recommended in the developmentally appropriate practice guidelines. Such interactions are useful with young children with disabilities.

*"Myth 2: Activities that Follow Recommended Practices in ECSE [Early Childhood Special Education] Must Be Entirely Teacher-Directed" (Carta, 1995, p. 4, information in brackets added)* Although activities may be designed to fulfill particular purposes (e.g., provide certain experiences, ensure selected goals are achieved), recommendations about the structure of classrooms and activities in early childhood special education are similar to those in developmentally appropriate practices. Bailey and Wolery (1984) made specific recommendations for organizing classrooms for young children with disabilities:

1. "The classroom environment must be arranged and equipped to invite and encourage activity" (p. 103).
2. "The teacher must provide inviting interesting activities" (p. 104).
3. "Children's spontaneous play must be allowed and encouraged" (p. 105).

Other authors have made similar recommendations (e.g., Dunst et al., 1987; Dunst, Lowe, & Bartholomew, 1990; Fewell & Vadasy, 1983; Linder, 1993; Mahoney & Powell, 1986; McEvoy, 1990; McWilliam & Bailey, 1992; Musselwhite, 1986; Sainato & Carta, 1992). The degree to which teacher-directed instruction is employed largely depends on the outcomes that are being promoted (Wolery, 1994b). Furthermore, when teacher-directed instruction is used, teaching opportunities should be embedded within activities (Chiara, Schuster, Bell, & Wolery, 1995; Venn, Wolery, Werts, et al., 1993).

*"Myth 3: In Typical ECSE Practice, Teachers Must Use Artificial Incentives to Get Children to Perform Behaviors" (Carta, 1995, p. 4)* Artificial incentives are used widely in special education, including early childhood special education, but the preference is to avoid such incentives or to use them sparingly (cf. Wolery, 1994c). The recommended practices are to rely on natural consequences (Halle et al., 1984), use activities that solicit and promote engagement (McWilliam & Bailey, 1992), pair artificial reinforcers with natural consequences (Bailey & Wolery, 1992), and thin reinforcement quickly (i.e., use it less often as children master the skills being taught) (Wolery, 1994c).

*"Myth 4: Curricular Content in ECSE Focuses on Academic Subskills or Individual Behaviors that Are Taught Out of Context" (Carta, 1995, p. 4)* The assumption that the early childhood special education curriculum primarily focuses on academic or preacademic skills can be held only if one ignores the literature in the field. Almost every curriculum (e.g., Dunst, 1981; Johnson-Martin, Attermeier, & Hacker, 1990; Johnson-Martin, Jens, & Attermeier, 1986; Neisworth, Willoughby-Herb, Bagnato, Cartwright, & Laub, 1980) addresses multiple developmental domains. Furthermore, most assessment texts and methods of intervention texts advocate addressing multiple developmental domains, and recommendations exist for embedding instruction for multiple goals from multiple domains within the

same activity (Bricker & Cripe, 1992). Thus, the curriculum clearly includes skills beyond academic and preacademic domains.

Considerable discussion has focused on what constitutes the curriculum content for young children with disabilities. In the 1970s, the predominant model was one of teaching developmental milestones originating primarily from developmental measures based on a maturational perspective. This tactic is no longer recommended, however (cf. Dunst, 1981). Alternative perspectives such as cognitive-developmental (such as Piaget's) (Bricker & Bricker, 1974; Dunst, 1981), functional (Neel & Billingsley, 1989), and ecological (Vincent et al., 1980) have emerged. These approaches capture meaningful sequences of development or focus on skills needed to function independently in children's current or future environments. The developmentally appropriate practices were written, in part, to discourage practices designed to prepare children for future environments such as kindergarten and first grade. As a result, concern about preparing children with disabilities for future environments is often expressed by general early educators. Research related to facilitating transitions to such environments indicates that functional classroom skills (e.g., compliance with group rules, playing and working independently of teacher assistance), not academics, are critical (Atwater, Orth-Lopes, et al., 1994).

*"Myth 5: ECSE Recommended Practices Are Completely Behaviorally Based and Do Not Incorporate Developmental Principles" (Carta, 1995, p. 5)* Many early childhood special education practices are based on basic principles of applied behavior analysis. Many are based on several different theoretical perspectives, however, and often on positions emanating from different disciplines (Wolery & Bredekamp, 1994). For example, recommendations on designing classrooms often are based on the insights of constructivists such as Piaget and Vygotsky; recommendations on structuring the social dimensions of classrooms can be traced to social learning theorists such as Bandura; recommendations for promoting social and communicative skills have their roots in various theories of child development and linguistics; and recommendations concerning the broader aspects of intervention are often based on ecological perspectives advocated by Bronfenbrenner. Although the behavioral perspective has been a useful source (Strain et al., 1992), practices are based on other perspectives as well.

*Myth 6: Planning Individualized Early Education Programs for Children with Disabilities Should Be Based Solely on Developmental Assessments (Benner, 1992; McLean et al., in press)* Early childhood special education teams are required to design individualized intervention programs for each child and to base those programs on assessment information. As a result, developmental scales of many different versions are often employed. Although developmental scales provide some useful information in understanding children's current abilities, other strategies of gathering information also should be used. These other strategies include ongoing observations of children in natural activities and routines and interviews with family members and others who know the child well. Each of these measurement strategies (testing, observation, and interviews) is recommended for developing intervention plans.

***Myth 7: More Directive Practices Should Be Used with Children Who Have More Severe Disabilities*** Many of the myths associated with developmentally appropriate practices and with early childhood special education practices arise from misunderstanding the literature or the intent of the recommended practices. In the case of this myth, history is the culprit. It was recommended that the intrusiveness or directiveness of the practices was related to the severity of children's disabilities, with more normalized practices being used with children with mild disabilities and more directive practices being used with children with severe disabilities. As the field has evolved, however, this assumption has been questioned. In practice, even with children with severe disabilities, the classroom environment should be designed based on their interests, preferences, and choices; instruction should be embedded into ongoing activities and routines; and natural consequences should be employed as much as possible (Sailor & Guess, 1983). This shift occurred because of a realization that the instructional practices being used were based more on the nature of the desired outcomes than on the severity of children's disabilities (Wolery, 1994b).

In Figure 1, a continuum of instructional practices in early childhood special education is noted. Also, two types of outcomes are listed: child-initiated behavior and specific child behavior. If engagement and child-selected interactions with the environment are desired, then practices on the left-hand side of the figure are likely to be more successful. If specific child behavior (e.g., using a spoon, answering a specific question, using a particular language form) is desired, however, then the strategies on the right-hand side of the figure are more likely to be successful. Although the same types of procedures are likely to produce similar behavior in children with different levels of disability, application of the procedures may require more systematic use and more careful monitoring with children with severe disabilities.

## Summary of Discipline-Specific Practices

General early childhood education practices are described in numerous sources. An important source is the developmentally appropriate practice guidelines (Bredekamp, 1987), which have been updated and clarified (Bredekamp & Rosegrant, 1992a; NAEYC & NAECS/SDE, 1991). Similarly, special early childhood education practices are described in many sources, but the DEC document (DEC Task Force on Recommended Practices, 1993) is a legitimate starting point. Myths of various types exist about both sets of practices. Given the previous discussion, two questions arise:

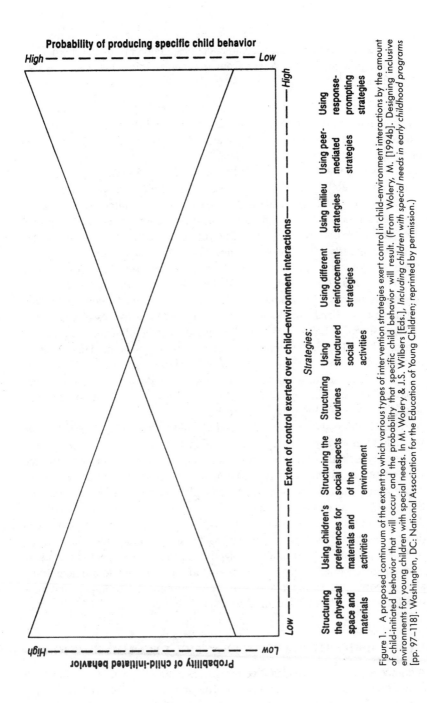

Figure 1. A proposed continuum of the extent to which various types of intervention strategies exert control in child–environment interactions by the amount of child-initiated behavior that will occur and the probability that specific child behavior will result. (From Wolery, M. [1994b]. Designing inclusive environments for young children with special needs. In M. Wolery & J.S. Wilbers [Eds.], *Including children with special needs in early childhood programs* [pp. 97–118]. Washington, DC: National Association for the Education of Young Children; reprinted by permission.)

1. Are the developmentally appropriate practice guidelines and early childhood special education practice recommendations different from one another?
2. If the practices are different from one another, in what ways are they different?

McLean and Odom (1993) analyzed the NAEYC practices and the DEC recommended practices to identify similarities and differences. They concluded that "there did not appear to be any areas in which direct disagreement or conflict exists between the practices recommended by both organizations. Rather, considerable similarity and agreement exist in virtually every area discussed" (p. 289). They did note, however, that different emphases existed in the two sets of practices. Other authors have come to similar conclusions. In short, classrooms following the developmentally appropriate practice guidelines are defensible settings in which young children with disabilities can receive their early education experiences; however, modifications and adjustments of those programs will likely be required to meet the needs of those children (Carta et al., 1991, 1993; Wolery, Strain, & Bailey, 1992). These modifications may focus on increased attention to specified outcomes, including more formalized initial and ongoing assessment activities (Carta, 1995; Wolery, Strain, & Bailey, 1992); shifts toward more family-centered practices (Carta, 1995; McLean & Odom, 1993); more systematic attention to transitions to future placements (Carta, 1995; Wolery, Strain, & Bailey, 1992); and increased attention to teaming and interagency collaboration (Carta, 1995; Wolery, Strain, & Bailey, 1992). These modifications are substantial and should be addressed by intervention teams.

Carta (1995) also suggests that the two fields share common ground from which to promote appropriate early educational services to all children. These include 1) emphasis on individualization, 2) trends toward more authentic and naturalistic assessment activities, 3) emphasis on promoting children's active engagement with the environment, 4) value placed on children's social interactions, and 5) recognition of the need to accommodate children's cultural diversity. Furthermore, Carta (1995) suggests that using some instructional procedures causes the practices of the two fields to be more integrated. These include attending to instructional objectives within ongoing activities, using naturalistic teaching procedures, arranging the environment to promote desirable outcomes, stressing naturalistic or environmental prompts, and purposefully using peers without disabilities.

## BARRIERS TO INTEGRATING PRACTICE RECOMMENDATIONS

A number of authors have identified barriers to integrating young children with disabilities in general early childhood programs. Some of the identified barriers have direct applications to the integration of the practices from the two fields; however, others do not. For example, Smith and Rose (1993) identified potential policy barriers that, although important, may have little relevance to integrating practice recommendations from the two fields.

Odom and McEvoy (1990) identified five barriers to inclusive services: 1) different philosophic and theoretical bases, 2) lack of adequate preparation of both general and special early educators, 3) negative attitudes on the part of the early childhood staff, 4) issues related to monitoring programs that are outside of the public control, and 5) issues related to ensuring that children received the related services they needed. Wolery, Huffman, et al. (1993) asked general early educators to identify barriers to including children with disabilities in general early childhood programs. The most frequently cited barriers were 1) inadequate staff-to-child ratios, 2) lack of adequate personnel preparation and consultation from experts, and 3) architectural and structural barriers. Staff attitudes were not listed as a major barrier by general early educators. Each barrier on these two lists, with the potential exception of issues related to monitoring nonpublic programs, may influence a team's ability to integrate the practice recommendations from general and special early childhood education. Also, Buysse and Wesley (1993) indicated that many early childhood special educators perceive a shift in their roles from providing direct services to children to providing consultative services to general educators; many of them report being dissatisfied with this role shift. On a positive note, however, general early educators indicate that most classroom activities and areas are relatively easy to adapt for children with mild and moderate disabilities (Wolery, Schroeder, et al., 1994).

Thus, although the literature indicates that tremendous potential exists for integrating the practice recommendations from the two fields (Bredekamp, 1993; Carta, 1995), potential problems may exist. Attention must be paid to personnel preparation issues, the philosophical differences on which the practices are based, the new expectations placed on general and special early childhood educators (adding children with disabilities to classrooms that already have inadequate staff-to-child ratios and space, and role shifts requiring new competencies), and providing the related services that children need. Wolery and Bredekamp (1994) suggest that addressing these issues in the context of planning and providing services to individual children with disabilities may be a more effective tactic than addressing these issues for all potential children with disabilities who may be enrolled in a program. For example, rather than attempting to resolve philosophical differences for all practices, the differences can be resolved only for the strategies and practices that are presently needed for the child. Rather than providing staff with training related to serving children with all manner of disabilities, training should be provided based on the disabilities of the particular child who is targeted for enrollment in the program.

## RECOMMENDATIONS FOR
## INTEGRATING PRACTICE RECOMMENDATIONS

A number of sources can be used to guide personnel when integrating young children with disabilities into general early childhood programs (Allen, 1992; Bricker & Cripe, 1992; Peck et al., 1993; Safford, 1989; Striefel, Killoran, & Quintero, 1991; Wolery & Wilbers, 1994). In these sources, suggestions are made for assisting programs in serving children with and without disabilities. These sources advocate for approaching inclusion from a team perspective (Bruder, 1994), involving families in inclusion decisions (Bailey, 1994), and providing training and ongoing assistance to the staff involved (Odom & McEvoy, 1990).

### General Guidelines for Integrating Practice Recommendations

Eight general guidelines can be made for integrating the recommendations from general and special early childhood education. First, the assessment information for the child with disabilities should be organized and analyzed to identify the high-priority goals to be addressed in the classroom (Wolery, 1996a). This, of course, is a team effort that relies heavily on input from family members. Second, classroom areas, materials, activities, and routines should be organized following the principles of developmentally appropriate practices (NAEYC & NAECS/SDE, 1991). Generally, such organization is appropriate for young children with disabilities. Third, the organization and schedule of the classroom should be analyzed to identify times when attention can be devoted to each important goal for the child with disabilities (Bricker & Cripe, 1992). Ideally, each important goal is addressed at multiple times throughout the day, and multiple goals are addressed in each activity or routine of the day. An activity-by-skill matrix is useful for these planning decisions (Bricker & Cripe, 1992). Fourth, independent participation and engagement by the child with disabilities should be promoted in each activity. When this is not possible, supported participation is more desirable than lack of participation (Wolery, 1994a). Fifth, practices and instructional strategies needed to teach the goals in the identified times should be selected. Many options can be used from both the special and general early education literature. These strategies and practices should be selected based on their probable effectiveness and the likelihood of use. Probable effectiveness is based on understanding the existing literature, and likelihood of use is based partly on the degree to which using the practice matches the current style and roles used by program staff. Sixth, all individuals responsible for using any specialized strategies or practices should be taught to use them with a high degree of fidelity (Wolery & Fleming, 1993). Seventh, a system should be developed for monitoring the effects of the interventions that are used (Wolery, 1996b). Eighth, the planned program should be implemented, the effects monitored, and the procedures adjusted as needed based on the monitoring results (Bricker & Cripe, 1992; Wolery & Fleming, 1993).

## Specific Guidelines for Integrating Practice Recommendations

As noted previously, ideally specialized practices are used in ongoing classroom activities and routines. In some cases, simply participating in these activities and routines allows children with disabilities to achieve their goals. In other cases, adjustments (adaptations or modifications) of those activities and routines are required (Losardo & Bricker, 1994). These adjustments constitute the actual integration of practice recommendations from the two fields. Eight guidelines for achieving that integration of practice (cf. Wolery, 1994a; Wolery, Werts, & Holcombe, 1994) are given in this section. Each adjustment is listed, and then examples from the research literature illustrate how the adjustment was accomplished.

*Adjust Activities and Routines by Embedding Instructional Opportunities and Practices in Multiple Activities Throughout the Day*  Some goals can be addressed by making relatively minor adjustments to several activities or routines. For example, Fox and Hanline (1993) taught a young boy with Down syndrome to do a number of behaviors to increase nonverbal communication and functional play. During different activities throughout the day, the child was given opportunities to use the targeted behavior, and a hierarchy of teacher prompts was used. The procedure was a variation of the system of least prompts (Doyle, Wolery, Ault, & Gast, 1988). The child learned to do the behaviors and continued to use them after the training was stopped. Chiara et al. (1995) also embedded an instructional strategy into multiple activities throughout the day. They taught children with and without developmental delays to name pictures by interspersing opportunities to respond to the pictures in several activities each day with at least 15 minutes between each opportunity. They used a constant time-delay procedure (Wolery, Holcombe, et al., 1992) to provide the instruction. Each opportunity was embedded into the ongoing activities in such a way as not to interrupt children's ongoing behavior. All children learned the skills that were taught, and they did so about as rapidly as they learned similar behaviors in structured small group instruction.

*Adjust Activities and Routines by Embedding Instructional Opportunities and Practices in a Single Activity or Routine*  Some goals can be more easily addressed within a single activity. For example, Venn, Wolery, Werts, et al. (1993) used this recommendation to teach three young boys with pervasive developmental disorders to imitate their typically developing peers during daily art activities. Although the children could imitate adults, they did not imitate their peers. The art activity was an ideal time to teach peer imitation because a variety of materials were used, different appropriate uses of the materials were possible, and the teacher was able to watch children and identify times to provide the instruction. A progressive time-delay procedure (Wolery, Ault, & Doyle, 1992) was used. Typically, a child with disabilities and three or four typically developing classmates were in the art area. Five times during the art activity the teacher spoke to the child with disabilities, told him to watch his peer and do what the peer had done, and then prompted the child to do the observed behavior. All three boys learned to imitate their peers without adult assistance.

In another example, Filla, Wolery, and Anthony (1995) taught three children with developmental delays to carry on conversations with their typically developing peers during daily dramatic play activities. Each day a child with disabilities and two typically developing children were allowed to play with a theme box (e.g., boxes of toys that were related to a theme, such as having a picnic, visiting a doctor's office). The teacher used a least prompt procedure (Doyle et al., 1988) to cue conversations between the children. This procedure produced an increase in the frequency of conversations, the number of turns per conversation, and the frequency of initiations to peers.

*Adjust Activities and Routines by Changing what Children Do in Them* Some goals can be addressed by adjusting what children do within existing activities. For example, McEvoy et al. (1988) wanted to increase the frequency of social interactions during free play periods. To achieve this goal, they adjusted what children did within small group activities when children played games and sang songs. The specific adjustment, referred to as affection or friendship activities (McEvoy, Twardosz, & Bishop, 1990), involved increasing the amount of physical and social contact between children during games and songs. This produced an increase in children's social interactions during subsequent free play periods. A similar adaptation known as transition-based teaching (Wolery, Doyle, Gast, Ault, & Simpson, 1993) changes what children do during transitions between classroom activities. To teach a variety of preacademic and language skills, teachers provided a single brief opportunity to do the skill as the transition started. Prompting was provided as needed (often with constant time delay), and the transition was allowed to continue as soon as the child responded. This procedure was quite successful in different classrooms (Werts, Wolery, Holcombe-Ligon, Vassilaros, & Billings, 1992) and with no increases in the duration of the transitions for teachers or children (Wolery, Anthony, & Katzenmeyer, 1995).

*Adjust Activities and Routines by Adapting the Materials and Their Access* Some goals can be achieved by changing the materials used or by changing the rules used to gain access to the materials. For example, Rettig, Kallam, and McCarthy-Salm (1993) wanted to increase the social play of young children with developmental delays. As a result, they compared the effects of "social" toys (e.g., dress-up clothes, dolls, trucks) to "isolate" toys (e.g., crayons, puzzles, beads) (Odom & Strain, 1984). By simply making social toys available, increases occurred in the amount of social play. Likewise, several studies demonstrated that certain shifts in the rules of access can result in more communicative requests (Kaiser, Yoder, & Keetz, 1992). For example, placing certain preferred toys on shelves that are in sight but require children to ask for them can increase the number of requests for materials (Hart & Risley, 1975). These requests can then provide opportunities to use procedures such as incidental teaching, which is a powerful procedure for promoting a wide range of useful language skills (Kaiser et al., 1992).

*Adjust Activities and Routines by Using Shorter but More Frequent Opportunities* Some goals are best taught during functional activities and routines; for example, teaching self-feeding with a spoon should be taught during meals, and teaching children to put on their coats should be taught when children go out to play or leave for the day. Although these routines occur regularly (each day), they may occur infrequently (once or twice per day). In teaching children to feed themselves, Azrin and Armstrong (1973) increased the number of meals children ate but decreased the length of each meal and the amount of food children ate at each meal. This produced rapid acquisition of the self-feeding behaviors.

*Adjust Activities and Routines by Changing the Rules of Access to Particular Areas* Some goals can be addressed most easily in particular areas or activities, but children may avoid them. Similarly, some children switch activities frequently and do not spend sufficient time in each for sustained play and interaction. To address such situations, the rules of access can be switched. For example, if a child leaves one area, then that child is required to go to an area he or she avoids before going to an area that is preferred. Such rule switches can increase the time children spend in the avoided areas and decrease the amount of switching children do between areas (Jacobson, Bushell, & Risley, 1969; Rowbury, Baer, & Baer, 1976).

*Adjust Activities and Routines by Changing the Social Composition or Structure of Activities* Two primary reasons for providing services to children with and without disabilities in the same program are 1) to allow children with disabilities to have competent interactive partners (typically developing peers), and 2) to provide them with competent models to be imitated. DeKlyen and Odom (1989) increased children's social interactions by defining and assigning specific roles during dramatic play activities. This structuring of the roles during play activities produced increases in social interactions between children with and without disabilities. To take advantage of competent peer models and to teach children with disabilities to perform response chains, Werts, Caldwell, and Wolery (in press) structured modeling opportunities. One peer each day was asked to demonstrate the target skill for the child with disabilities. The peer completed each step of the chain and described it while his or her classmate with disabilities watched. This procedure resulted in the children with disabilities learning to do the skills without direct instruction from the adults.

*Adjust Activities and Routines by Teaching Peers to Engage in Facilitative Behavior* An advantage of inclusive programming is that typically developing peers can be taught to help their classmates with disabilities learn desirable skills. Several studies have taught typically developing peers to initiate or respond to the social initiations of their classmates with disabilities, producing increases in social behavior (Odom, Hoyson, Jamieson, & Strain, 1985) or in communicative behavior in free play situations (Goldstein & Ferrell, 1987) and in snack activities (Venn, Wolery, Fleming, et al., 1993). See Goldstein and Kaczmarek (1992) and Strain and Odom (1986) for information on using these procedures.

Thus, a number of adjustments to ongoing classroom activities and routines have been studied to address specific educational goals for young children with disabilities in general early childhood education programs. These adjustments constitute the actual integration of practices from early childhood special and general education fields. The recommendations from general early education are used to design the classroom and to govern interactions adults have with children. The recommendations from special early education are used to address specific goals for children with disabilities within activities and routines being operated in compliance with the developmentally appropriate practice guidelines.

## CONCLUSIONS

The two disciplines have separate histories and practice guidelines, but integration of those practices is possible. Both sets of practices are evolving, and attempts to integrate them will influence that evolution and may produce improved services for all children. The integration of the practices must occur in the context of inclusive classrooms. This chapter illustrates a few suggestions for achieving this integration of practice; however, continued research and training are needed.

## REFERENCES

Allen, K.E. (1992). *The exceptional child: Mainstreaming in early childhood education.* Albany, NY: Delmar.
Anderson, R.C., Heibert, E.H., Scott, J.A., & Wilkinson, I.A.C. (1985). *Becoming a nation of readers: The report of the Commission on Reading.* Washington, DC: U.S. Department of Education.
Atwater, J.B., Carta, J.J., Schwartz, I.S., & McConnell, S.R. (1994). Blending developmentally appropriate practice and early childhood special education: Redefining best practice to meet the needs of all children. In B.L. Mallory & R.S. New (Eds.), *Diversity and developmentally appropriate practices: Challenges for early childhood education* (pp. 185–201). New York: Teachers College Press.

Atwater, J.B., Orth-Lopes, L., Elliott, M., Carta, J.J., & Schwartz, I.S. (1994). Completing the circle: Planning and implementing transitions to other programs. In M. Wolery & J.S. Wilbers (Eds.), *Including children with special needs in early childhood programs: Research and implications for practice* (pp. 167–188). Washington, DC: National Association for the Education of Young Children.

Azrin, N.H., & Armstrong, P.M. (1973). The "mini-meal": A method for teaching eating skills to the profoundly retarded. *Mental Retardation, 11,* 9–13.

Bailey, D.B. (1994). Working with families of children with special needs. In M. Wolery & J.S. Wilbers (Eds.), *Including children with special needs in early childhood programs: Research and implications for practice* (pp. 23–44). Washington, DC: National Association for the Education of Young Children.

Bailey, D.B., & McWilliam, R.A. (1990). Normalizing early intervention. *Topics in Early Childhood Special Education, 10*(2), 33–47.

Bailey, D.B., & Wolery, M. (1984). *Teaching infants and preschoolers with handicaps.* Columbus, OH: Charles E. Merrill.

Bailey, D.B., & Wolery, M. (1992). *Teaching infants and preschoolers with disabilities* (2nd ed.). Columbus, OH: Charles E. Merrill.

Baltes, P.B., Reese, H.W., & Nesselroade, J.R. (1977). *Life-span developmental psychology: Introduction to research methods.* Monterey, CA: Brooks/Cole.

Barnett, D.W., & Carey, K.T. (1992). *Designing interventions for preschool learning and behavior problems.* San Francisco: Jossey-Bass.

Benner, S.M. (1992). *Assessing young children with special needs: An ecological perspective.* White Plains, NY: Longman.

Bennett, W.J. (1986). *What works: Research about teaching and learning.* Washington, DC: U.S. Department of Education.

Bijou, S.W. (1993). *Behavior analysis of child development* (3rd ed.). Reno, NV: Context Press.

Bijou, S.W., & Baer, D.M. (1961). *Child development: A systematic and empirical theory* (Vol. 1). Englewood Cliffs, NJ: Prentice Hall.

Bijou, S.W., & Baer, D.M. (1965). *Child development: Universal stage of infancy* (Vol. 2). Englewood Cliffs, NJ: Prentice Hall.

Bornstein, M.H., & Lamb, M.E. (1992). *Developmental psychology: An advanced textbook* (3rd ed.). Hillsdale, NJ: Lawrence Erlbaum Associates.

Bowman, B.T. (1992). Reaching potentials of minority children through developmentally and culturally appropriate programs. In S. Bredekamp & T. Rosegrant (Eds.), *Reaching potentials: Appropriate curriculum and assessment for young children* (Vol. 1, pp. 128–136). Washington, DC: National Association for the Education of Young Children.

Bredekamp, S. (1987). *Developmentally appropriate practice in early childhood programs serving children from birth through age 8: Expanded edition.* Washington, DC: National Association for the Education of Young Children.

Bredekamp, S. (1991). Redeveloping early childhood education: A response to Kessler. *Early Childhood Research Quarterly, 6,* 199–209.

Bredekamp, S. (1993). The relationship between early childhood education and early childhood special education: Healthy marriage or family feud? *Topics in Early Childhood Special Education, 13,* 258–273.

Bredekamp, S., & Rosegrant, T. (1992a). *Reaching potentials: Appropriate curriculum and assessment for young children* (Vol. 1). Washington, DC: National Association for the Education of Young Children.

Bredekamp, S., & Rosegrant, T. (1992b). Reaching potentials: Introduction. In S. Bredekamp & T. Rosegrant (Eds.), *Reaching potentials: Appropriate curriculum and assessment for young children* (Vol. 1, pp. 2–8). Washington, DC: National Association for the Education of Young Children.

Bricker, D.D. (1986). *Early education of at-risk and handicapped infants, toddlers, and preschool children.* Glenview, IL: Scott, Foresman.

Bricker, D., & Bricker, W.A. (1973). *Infant, toddler, and preschool research and intervention project report: Year III IMRID Behavioral Science Monograph No. 23.* Nashville, TN: Institute on Mental Retardation and Intellectual Development, George Peabody College.

Bricker, D., & Cripe, J.J.W. (1992). *An activity-based approach to early intervention.* Baltimore: Paul H. Brookes Publishing Co.

Bricker, W., & Bricker, D. (1974). An early language training strategy. In R. Scheifelbusch & L. Lloyd (Eds.), *Language perspectives: Acquisition, retardation, and intervention.* Baltimore: University Park Press.

Bronfenbrenner, U. (1977). Toward an experimental ecology of human development. *American Psychologist, 32,* 513–531.

Bruder, M.B. (1994). Working with members of other disciplines. In M. Wolery & J.S. Wilbers (Eds.), *Including children with special needs in early childhood programs: Research and implications for practice* (pp. 45–70). Washington, DC: National Association for the Education of Young Children.

Buysse, V., & Bailey, D.B. (1993). Behavioral and developmental outcomes in young children with disabilities in integrated and segregated settings: A review of comparative studies. *Journal of Special Education, 26,* 434–461.

Buysse, V., & Wesley, P.W. (1993). The identity crisis in early childhood special education: A call for professional role clarification. *Topics in Early Childhood Special Education, 13,* 418–429.

Carta, J.J. (1995). Developmentally appropriate practice: A critical analysis as applied to young children with disabilities. *Focus on Exceptional Children, 27,* 1–16.

Carta, J.J., Atwater, J.B., Schwartz, I.S., & McConnell, S.R. (1993). Developmentally appropriate practices and early childhood special education: A reaction to Johnson and McChesney Johnson. *Topics in Early Childhood Special Education, 13,* 243–254.

Carta, J.J., Schwartz, I.S., Atwater, J.B., & McConnell, S.R. (1991). Developmentally appropriate practice: Appraising its usefulness for young children with disabilities. *Topics in Early Childhood Special Education, 11*(1), 1–20.

Cavallaro, C.C., Haney, M., & Cabello, B. (1993). Developmentally appropriate strategies for promoting full participation in early childhood settings. *Topics in Early Childhood Special Education, 13,* 293–307.

Chiara, L., Schuster, J.W., Bell, J., & Wolery, M. (1995). Small-group massed-trial and individually distributed-trial instruction with preschoolers. *Journal of Early Intervention, 19,* 203–217.

Collins, B.C., Gast, D.L., Ault, M.J., & Wolery, M. (1991). Small group instruction: Guidelines for teachers of students with moderate to severe handicaps. *Education and Training in Mental Retardation, 26,* 18–32.

Cuban, L. (1990). Reforming again, again, and again. *Educational Researcher, 19*(1), 3–13.

DEC Task Force on Recommended Practices. (1993). *DEC recommended practices: Indicators of quality in programs for infants and young children with special needs and their families.* Reston, VA: Council for Exceptional Children.

DeKlyen, M., & Odom, S.L. (1989). Activity structure and social interactions with peers in developmentally integrated play groups. *Journal of Early Intervention, 13,* 342–352.

Delpit, L. (1988). The silenced dialogue: Power and pedagogy in educating other people's children. *Harvard Educational Review, 58*(3), 290–298.

Doyle, P.M., Wolery, M., Ault, M.J., & Gast, D.L. (1988). System of least prompts: A review of procedural parameters. *Journal of The Association for Persons with Severe Handicaps, 13,* 28–40.

Dunst, C.J. (1981). *Infant learning: A cognitive-linguistic intervention strategy.* Hingham, MA: Teaching Resources.

Dunst, C.J. (1985). Rethinking early intervention. *Analysis and Intervention in Developmental Disabilities, 5,* 165–201.

Dunst, C.J., Lesko, J.J., Holbert, K.A., Wilson, L.L., Sharpe, K.L., & Liles, R.F. (1987). A systematic approach to infant intervention. *Topics in Early Childhood Special Education, 7*(2), 19–37.

Dunst, C.J., Lowe, L.W., & Bartholomew, P.C. (1990). Contingent social responsiveness, family ecology, and infant communicative competence. *National Student Speech Language Hearing Association Journal, 17,* 39–49.

Dunst, C.J., Trivette, C.M., & Deal, A. (1994). *Supporting and strengthening families: Volume 1. Methods, strategies and practices.* Cambridge, MA: Brookline Books.

Elkind, D. (1989). *Miseducation: Preschoolers at risk.* New York: Alfred A. Knopf.

Evans, E.D. (1975). *Contemporary influences in early childhood education* (2nd ed.). New York: Holt, Rinehart & Winston.

Fewell, R.R., & Vadasy, P.F. (1983). *Learning through play: A resource manual for teachers and parents.* Allen, TX: DLM Teaching Resources.

Filla, A., Wolery, M., & Anthony, L. (1995). *Promoting children's conversations during play with adult prompts.* Manuscript submitted for publication.

Fox, L., & Hanline, M.F. (1993). A preliminary evaluation of learning within developmentally appropriate early childhood settings. *Topics in Early Childhood Special Education, 13,* 308–327.

Gallagher, J.J., & Ramey, C.T. (Eds.). (1987). *The malleability of children.* Baltimore: Paul H. Brookes Publishing Co.

Gesell, A., Halverson, H.M., Thompson, H., Ilg, F.L., Castner, B.M., Ames, L.B., & Amatruda, C.S. (1940). *The first five years of life: The preschool years.* New York: Harper & Row.

Goldstein, H., & Ferrell, D.R. (1987). Augmenting communicative interaction between handicapped and nonhandicapped preschoolers. *Journal of Speech and Hearing Disorders, 19,* 200–211.

Goldstein, H., & Kaczmarek, L. (1992). Promoting communicative interaction among children in integrated intervention settings. In S.F. Warren & J. Reichle (Eds.), *Causes and effects in communication and language intervention* (pp. 81–111). Baltimore: Paul H. Brookes Publishing Co.

Goodman, J.F. (1992). *When slow is fast enough: Educating the delayed preschool child.* New York: Guilford Press.

Guralnick, M.J. (1978). *Early intervention and the integration of handicapped and nonhandicapped children.* Baltimore: University Park Press.

Guralnick, M.J. (1981). The efficacy of integrating handicapped children in early education settings: Research implications. *Topics in Early Childhood Special Education, 1*(1), 57–71.

Guralnick, M.J. (1990). Major accomplishments and future directions in early childhood mainstreaming. *Topics in Early Childhood Special Education, 10*(2), 1–17.

Guralnick, M.J. (1993). Developmentally appropriate practice in the assessment and intervention of children's peer relations. *Topics in Early Childhood Special Education, 13,* 344–371.

Halle, J.W., Alpert, C.L., & Anderson, S.R. (1984). Natural environment language assessment and intervention with severely impaired preschoolers. *Topics in Early Childhood Special Education, 4*(3), 36–56.

Harel, S., & Anastasiow, N.J. (Eds.). (1985). *The at-risk infant: Psycho/socio/medical aspects.* Baltimore: Paul H. Brookes Publishing Co.

Harris, F.R., Wolf, M.M., & Baer, D.M. (1964). Effects of adult social reinforcement on child behavior. *Young Children, 20,* 8–17.

Hart, B., & Risley, T.R. (1975). In vivo language training: Unanticipated and general effects. *Journal of Applied Behavior Analysis, 8,* 411–420.

Horowitz, F.D. (1987). *Exploring developmental theory: Toward a structural-behavioral model of development.* Hillsdale, NJ: Lawrence Erlbaum Associates.

Hunt, J.M. (1961). *Intelligence and experience.* New York: Ronald Press.

Individuals with Disabilities Education Act of 1990 (IDEA), PL 101-476. (October 30, 1990). Title 20, U.S.C. §§ 1400 et seq.: *U.S. Statutes at Large, 104,* 1103–1151.

Jacobson, J.M., Bushell, D., & Risley, T.R. (1969). Switching requirements in a Head Start classroom. *Journal of Applied Behavior Analysis, 2,* 43–47.

Jipson, J. (1991). Developmentally appropriate practice: Early childhood education as development—Critique of the metaphor. *Early Education and Development, 2*(2), 137–152.

Johnson, J.E., & Johnson, K.M. (1992). Clarifying the developmental perspective in response to Carta, Schwartz, Atwater, and McConnell. *Topics in Early Childhood Special Education, 12,* 439–457.

Johnson, J.E., & Johnson, K.M. (1994). The applicability of developmentally appropriate practice for children with diverse abilities. *Journal of Early Intervention, 18,* 343–346.

Johnson, K.M., & Johnson, J.E. (1993). A rejoinder to Carta, Atwater, Schwartz, and McConnell. *Topics in Early Childhood Special Education, 13,* 255–257.

Johnson-Martin, N., Attermeier, S.M., & Hacker, B. (1990). *The Carolina curriculum for preschoolers with special needs.* Baltimore: Paul H. Brookes Publishing Co.

Johnson-Martin, N., Jens, K.G., & Attermeier, S.M. (1986). *The Carolina curriculum for handicapped infants and infants at risk.* Baltimore: Paul H. Brookes Publishing Co.

Kaiser, A.P., Yoder, P., & Keetz, A. (1992). Evaluating milieu therapy. In S.F. Warren & J. Reichle (Eds.), *Causes and effects in communication and language intervention* (pp. 9–47). Baltimore: Paul H. Brookes Publishing Co.

Kessler, S.A. (1991). Alternative perspectives on early childhood education. *Early Childhood Research Quarterly, 6,* 183–197.

Kostelnik, M.J. (1992). Myths associated with developmentally appropriate programs. *Young Children, 47,* 17–23.

Kozloff, M.A. (1994). *Improving educational outcomes for children with disabilities: Principles for assessment, program planning, and evaluation.* Baltimore: Paul H. Brookes Publishing Co.

Linder, T.W. (1993). *Transdisciplinary play-based intervention: Guidelines for developing a meaningful curriculum for young children.* Baltimore: Paul H. Brookes Publishing Co.

Losardo, A., & Bricker, D. (1994). Activity-based instruction and direct instruction: A comparison study. *American Journal on Mental Retardation, 98,* 744–765.

Lubeck, S. (1991). Reconceptualizing early childhood education: A response. *Early Education and Development, 2,* 168–173.

Mahoney, G., & Powell, A. (1986). *The transactional intervention program teacher's guide.* Rock Hill, SC: Center for Excellence in Early Childhood Education.

Mahoney, G., Robinson, C., & Powell, A. (1992). Focusing on parent-child interaction: The bridge to developmentally appropriate practice. *Topics in Early Childhood Special Education, 12,* 105–120.

Mallory, B.L., & New, R.S. (1994). *Diversity and developmentally appropriate practices: Challenges for early childhood education.* New York: Teachers College Press.

McEvoy, M.A. (1990). The organization of caregiving environments: Critical issues and suggestions for future research. *Education and Treatment of Children, 13,* 269–273.

McEvoy, M.A., Nordquist, V.M., Twardosz, S., Heckman, K.A., Wehby, J.H., & Denny, R.K. (1988). Promoting autistic children's peer interaction in an integrated early childhood setting using affection activities. *Journal of Applied Behavior Analysis, 21,* 193–200.

McEvoy, M.A., Twardosz, S., & Bishop, N. (1990). Affection activities: Procedures for encouraging young children with handicaps to interact with their peers. *Education and Treatment of Children, 13,* 159–167.

McGill-Franzen, A. (1992). Early literacy: What does "developmentally appropriate" mean? *Reading Teacher, 46,* 56–58.

McGonigel, M.J., Woodruff, G., & Roszmann-Millican, M. (1994). The transdisciplinary team: A model for family-centered early intervention. In L.J. Johnson, R.J. Gallagher, & M.J. LaMontagne (Eds.), *Meeting early intervention challenges: Issues from birth to three* (pp. 95–131). Baltimore: Paul H. Brookes Publishing Co.

McLean, M.E., Bailey, D.B., & Wolery, M. (1996). *Assessing infants and preschoolers with special needs* (2nd ed). Columbus, OH: Charles E. Merrill.

McLean, M.E., & Odom, S.L. (1993). Practices for young children with and without disabilities: A comparison of DEC and NAEYC identified practices. *Topics in Early Childhood Special Education, 13,* 274–292.

McWilliam, R.A., & Bailey, D.B. (1992). Promoting engagement and mastery. In D.B. Bailey & M. Wolery (Eds.), *Teaching infants and preschoolers with disabilities* (2nd ed.) (pp. 229–255). Columbus, OH: Charles E. Merrill.

McWilliam, R.A., & Strain, P.S. (1993). Service delivery models. In DEC Task Force on Recommended Practices, *DEC recommended practices: Indicators of quality in programs for infants and young children with special needs and their families* (pp. 40–49). Reston, VA: Council for Exceptional Children.

Musselwhite, C.R. (1986). *Adaptive play for special needs children: Strategies to enhance communication and learning.* Boston: College Hill Press.

National Association for the Education of Young Children and the National Association of Early Childhood Specialists in State Departments of Education. (1991). Guidelines for appropriate curriculum content and assessment in programs serving children ages 3 through 8: A position statement. *Young Children, 46,* 21–38.

Neel, R.S., & Billingsley, F.F. (1989). *Impact: A functional curriculum handbook for students with moderate to severe disabilities.* Baltimore: Paul H. Brookes Publishing Co.

Neisworth, J.T. (1993). Assessment. In DEC Task Force on Recommended Practices, *DEC recommended practices: Indicators of quality in programs for infants and young children with special needs and their families* (pp. 11–18). Reston, VA: Council for Exceptional Children.

Neisworth, J.T., Willoughby-Herb, S.J., Bagnato, S.J., Cartwright, C.A., & Laub, K.W. (1980). *Individualized education for preschool exceptional children.* Rockville, MD: Aspen Publishers Inc.

Norris, J.A. (1991). Providing developmentally appropriate intervention to infants and young children with handicaps. *Topics in Early Childhood Special Education, 11*(1), 21–35.

Novick, R. (1993). Activity-based intervention and developmentally appropriate practice. *Topics in Early Childhood Special Education, 13*, 403–417.

Odom, S.L., Hoyson, M., Jamieson, B., & Strain, P.S. (1985). Increasing handicapped preschoolers' peer social interactions: Cross setting and component analysis. *Journal of Applied Behavior Analysis, 18*, 3–16.

Odom, S.L., McConnell, S.R., & McEvoy, M.A. (Eds.). (1992). *Social competence of young children with disabilities: Issues and strategies for intervention.* Baltimore: Paul H. Brookes Publishing Co.

Odom, S.L., & McEvoy, M.A. (1988). Integration of young children with handicaps and normally developing children. In S.L. Odom & M.B. Karnes (Eds.), *Early intervention for infants and children with handicaps: An empirical base* (pp. 241–268). Baltimore: Paul H. Brookes Publishing Co.

Odom, S.L., & McEvoy, M.A. (1990). Mainstreaming at the preschool level: Potential barriers and tasks for the field. *Topics in Early Childhood Special Education, 10*(2), 48–61.

Odom, S.L., & McLean, M.E. (in press). *Recommended practices in early intervention/early childhood special education.* Austin, TX: PRO-ED.

Odom, S.L., McLean, M.E., Johnson, L.J., & LaMontagne, M.J. (1995). Recommended practices in early childhood special education: Validation and current use. *Journal of Early Intervention, 19*, 1–17.

Odom, S.L., & Strain, P.S. (1984). Classroom-based social skills instruction for severely handicapped preschool children. *Topics in Early Childhood Special Education, 4*, 97–116.

Peck, C.P., & Cooke, T.P. (1983). Benefits of mainstreaming at the early childhood level: How much can we expect? *Analysis and Intervention in Developmental Disabilities, 3*, 1–22.

Peck, C.A., Odom, S.L., & Bricker, D. (Eds.). (1993). *Integrating young children with disabilities into community programs; Ecological perspectives on research and implementation.* Baltimore: Paul H. Brookes Publishing Co.

Piaget, J. (1951). *Play, dreams and imitation in childhood.* New York: Norton.

Piaget, J. (1952). *The origins of intelligence in children.* New York: International University Press.

Piaget, J. (1954). *The construction of reality in the child.* New York: Basic Books.

Rettig, M., Kallam, M., & McCarthy-Salm, K. (1993). The effect of social and isolate toys on social interactions of preschool-aged children. *Education and Training in Mental Retardation, 28*, 252–256.

Rosegrant, T., & Bredekamp. S. (1992). Reaching individual potentials through transformational curriculum. In S. Bredekamp & T. Rosegrant (Eds.), *Reaching potentials: Appropriate curriculum and assessment for young children* (Vol. 1, pp. 66–73). Washington, DC: National Association for the Education of Young Children.

Rosenkoetter, S.E., Hains, A.H., & Fowler, S.A. (1994). *Bridging early services for children with special needs and their families: A practical guide for transition planning.* Baltimore: Paul H. Brookes Publishing Co.

Rowbury, T.G., Baer, A.M., & Baer, D.M. (1976). Interactions between teacher guidance and contingent access to play in developing preacademic skills of deviant preschool children. *Journal of Applied Behavior Analysis, 9*, 85–104.

Safford, P.L. (1989). *Integrated teaching in early childhood: Starting in the mainstream.* White Plains, NY: Longman.

Sailor, W., & Guess, D. (1983). *Severely handicapped students: An instructional design.* Boston: Houghton Mifflin.

Sainato, D.M., & Carta, J.J. (1992). Classroom influences on the development of social competence in young children with disabilities. In S.L. Odom, S.R. McConnell, & M.A. McEvoy (Eds.), *Social competence of young children with disabilities: Issues and strategies for intervention* (pp. 93–109). Baltimore: Paul H. Brookes Publishing Co.

Shepard, L., & Smith, M.L. (1988). Escalating academic demand in the kindergarten: Some nonsolutions. *Elementary School Journal, 89,* 135–146.

Smith, B.J., & Rose, D.F. (1993). *Administrator's policy handbook for preschool mainstreaming.* Cambridge, MA: Brookline Books.

Spodek, B. (1991). Reconceptualizing early childhood education: A commentary. *Early Education and Development, 2,* 161–167.

Spodek, B. (1993). *Handbook of research on the education of young children.* New York: Macmillan.

Stephens, B. (1977). A Piagetian approach to curriculum development. In E. Sontag (Ed.), *Educational programming for the severely and profoundly handicapped* (pp. 237–249). Reston, VA: Division on Mental Retardation of the Council for Exceptional Children.

Strain, P.S. (1983). Generalization of autistic children's social behavior change: Effects of developmentally integrated and segregated settings. *Analysis and Intervention in Developmental Disabilities, 3,* 23–34.

Strain, P.S., McConnell, S.R., Carta, J.J., Fowler, S.A., Neisworth, J.T., & Wolery, M. (1992). Behaviorism in early intervention. *Topics in Early Childhood Special Education, 12*(1), 121–141.

Strain, P.S., & Odom, S.L. (1986). Peer social initiations: Effective intervention for social skills development of exceptional children. *Exceptional Children, 52,* 543–551.

Striefel, S., Killoran, J., & Quintero, M. (1991). *Functional integration for success: Preschool intervention.* Austin, TX: PRO-ED.

Teale, W.H., & Sulzby, E. (1986). *Emergent literacy.* Norwood, NJ: Ablex.

Venn, M.L., Wolery, M., Fleming, L.A., DeCesare, L.D., Morris, A., Sigesmund, M.H. (1993). Effects of teaching preschool peers to use the mand-model procedure during snack activities. *American Journal of Speech-Language Pathology, 2*(1), 38–46.

Venn, M.L., Wolery, M., Werts, M.G., Morris, A., DeCesare, L.D., & Cuffs, M.S. (1993). Embedding instruction in art activities to teach preschoolers with disabilities to imitate their peers. *Early Childhood Research Quarterly, 8,* 277–294.

Vincent, L.J., Salisbury, C., Walter, G., Brown, P., Gruenwald, L.J., & Powers, M. (1980). Program evaluation and curriculum development in early childhood/special education: Criteria of the next environment. In W. Sailor, B. Wilcox, & L. Brown (Eds.), *Methods of instruction for severely handicapped students* (pp. 303–328). Baltimore: Paul H. Brookes Publishing Co.

Vygotsky, L. (1978). *Mind in society: The development of psychological processes.* Cambridge, MA: Harvard University Press.

Walsh, D.J. (1991). Extending the discourse on developmental appropriateness: A developmental perspective. *Early Education and Development, 2,* 110–119.

Werts, M.G., Caldwell, N.K., & Wolery, M. (in press). The effects of fluent peer models on the observational learning of response chains by students with disabilities. *Journal of Applied Behavior Analysis.*

Werts, M.G., Wolery, M., Holcombe-Ligon, A., Vassilaros, M.A., & Billings, S.S. (1992). Efficacy of transition-based teaching with instructive feedback. *Education and Treatment of Children, 15,* 320–334.

214 / WOLERY

Wolery, M. (1994a). Implementing instruction for young children with special needs in early childhood classrooms. In M. Wolery & J.S. Wilbers (Eds.), *Including children with special needs in early childhood programs: Research and implications for practice* (pp. 151–166). Washington, DC: National Association for the Education of Young Children.

Wolery, M. (1994b). Designing inclusive environments for young children with special needs. In M. Wolery & J.S. Wilbers (Eds.), *Including children with special needs in early childhood programs: Research and implications for practice* (pp. 97–118). Washington, DC: National Association for the Education of Young Children.

Wolery, M. (1994c). Instructional strategies for teaching young children with special needs. In M. Wolery & J.S. Wilbers (Eds.), *Including children with special needs in early childhood programs: Research and implications for practice* (pp. 119–150). Washington, DC: National Association for the Education of Young Children.

Wolery, M. (1996a). Using assessment information to plan intervention programs. In M.E. McLean, D.B. Bailey, & M. Wolery (Eds.), *Assessing infants and preschoolers with special needs* (2nd ed.) (pp. 491–518). Columbus, OH: Charles E. Merrill.

Wolery, M. (1996b). Monitoring child progress. In M.E. McLean, D.B. Bailey, & M. Wolery (Eds.), *Assessing infants and preschoolers with special needs* (2nd ed.) (pp. 519–560). Columbus, OH: Charles E. Merrill.

Wolery, M., Anthony, L., & Katzenmeyer, J. (1995). *Transition-based teaching: Effects on the duration of transitions, teachers' behavior, and children's learning.* Manuscript submitted for publication.

Wolery, M., Ault, M.J., & Doyle, P.M. (1992). *Teaching students with moderate and severe disabilities: Use of response prompting strategies.* White Plains, NY: Longman.

Wolery, M., & Bredekamp, S. (1994). Developmentally appropriate practice and young children with special needs: Contextual issues in the discussion. *Journal of Early Intervention, 18,* 331–341.

Wolery, M., Doyle, P.M., Gast, D.L., Ault, M.J., & Simpson, S.L. (1993). Comparison of progressive time delay and transition-based teaching with preschoolers who have developmental delays. *Journal of Early Intervention, 17,* 160–176.

Wolery, M., & Fleming, L.A. (1993). Implementing individualized curriculum in integrated settings. In C.A. Peck, S.L. Odom, & D. Bricker (Eds.), *Integrating young children with disabilities into community programs: Ecological perspectives on research and implementation* (pp. 109–132). Baltimore: Paul H. Brookes Publishing Co.

Wolery, M., Holcombe, A., Brookfield, J., Huffman, K., Schroeder, C., Martin, C.G., Venn, M.L., Werts, M.G., & Fleming, L.A. (1993). The extent and nature of preschool mainstreaming: A survey of general early educators. *Journal of Special Education, 27,* 222–234.

Wolery, M., Holcombe, A., Cybriwsky, C.A., Doyle, P.M., Schuster, J.W., Ault, M.J., & Gast, D.L. (1992). Constant time delay with discrete responses: A review of effectiveness and demographic, procedural, and methodological parameters. *Research in Developmental Disabilities, 13,* 239–266.

Wolery, M., Huffman, K., Brookfield, J., Schroeder, C., Venn, M.L., Holcombe, A., Fleming, L.A., & Martin, C.G. (1993). *Benefits and barriers to preschool mainstreaming: Perceptions of general early childhood educators.* Unpublished manuscript.

Wolery, M., & Sainato, D.M. (in press). General curriculum and intervention strategies. In S.L. Odom & M.E. McLean (Eds.), *Recommended practices in early intervention/early childhood special education.* Austin, TX: PRO-ED.

Wolery, M., Schroeder, C., Martin, C.G., Venn, M.L., Holcombe, A., Brookfield, J., Huffman, K., & Fleming, L.A. (1994). Classroom activities and areas: Regularity of use and perceptions of adaptability by general early educators. *Early Education and Development, 5*, 181–194.

Wolery, M., Strain, P.S., & Bailey, D.B. (1992). Reaching potentials of children with special needs. In S. Bredekamp & T. Rosegrant (Eds.), *Reaching potentials: Appropriate curriculum and assessment for young children* (Vol. 1, pp. 92–111). Washington, DC: National Association for the Education of Young Children.

Wolery, M., Werts, M.G., & Holcombe, A. (1994). Current practices with young children who have disabilities: Issues of placement, assessment, and instruction. *Focus on Exceptional Children, 26*(6), 1–12.

Wolery, M., & Wilbers, J.S. (1994). *Including children with special needs in early childhood programs.* Washington, DC: National Association for the Education of Young Children.

Wolery, M., & Wolery, R.A. (1992). Promoting functional cognitive skills. In D.B. Bailey & M. Wolery (Eds.), *Teaching infants and preschoolers with disabilities* (2nd ed.) (pp. 521–572). Columbus, OH: Charles E. Merrill.

# Chapter 9

# Integrated Early Intervention Practices in Speech-Language Pathology

M. Jeanne Wilcox and Michelle S. Shannon

Historically, services provided by speech-language pathologists (SLPs) have included direct provision of individual treatment with a primary focus on remediation of identified limitations in communication abilities. This diagnostic-prescriptive approach, which is derived from a medical model, has been widely applied in both medical and educational settings (e.g., Miller, 1989). Within educational settings in particular, this service delivery approach has come to be viewed and characterized as the pull-out model, in which children are removed from their classrooms so that the therapist can provide individual speech and/or language treatment. Although the pull-out model is still in use, since the 1980s many SLPs as well as other personnel involved in the provision of intervention services to children with disabilities have questioned the social validity of this model, especially in educational settings. In turn, there has been an increasing emphasis on the importance of and need for provision of speech and language services from a perspective that incorporates integrated practices.

This chapter provides an overview of issues as well as some specific suggestions regarding the design and implementation of integrated speech and language practices in center-based early intervention programs. We remind our readers that this topic is quite broad, and complete coverage of all issues is beyond the scope of this chapter. We have highlighted what we view as the most salient issues and practice needs, and we encourage our readers to view this

217

chapter as a resource, pursuing cited references for those areas in which more detailed information is desired. Our treatment of the topic is organized into two parts. First, we consider parameters of integrated practices and those areas of expertise within the discipline most compatible with an integrated services perspective. We then turn to implementation issues, with a specific focus on, and numerous examples illustrating strategies for achieving, communication and language goals within toddler and preschool classroom settings.

## INTEGRATED PRACTICES:
## COMPONENTS AND APPLICABLE SERVICES

The term *integrated services* has a broad base of meanings and interpretations that vary within as well as across disciplines. This has led to variation in implementation and illustrate that integrated services should be conceptualized not in absolute terms, but rather as a continuum of service delivery options (e.g., American Speech-Language-Hearing Association [ASHA], 1995; Elksnin & Capilouto, 1994; McWilliam, 1995). For many SLPs, integrated services are synonymous with classroom-based intervention, and although the classroom intervention model may be the most common application of integrated services, options range from individual therapy with input from other personnel, to individual therapy with collaborative goal development, to direct or consultative interventions in a natural environment (e.g., home, school, community).

The need for SLPs to rely on integrated practice models in provision of services to young children has arisen from a combination of factors, including 1) the critical importance of social interaction to emerging communication and language skills; 2) a recognition of the importance of providing communication and language opportunities within typical, daily activities; 3) an emphasis on including children with disabilities in typical settings; 4) concerns about generalization of emerging skills; and 5) the need to integrate communication and language goals with other educational goals to achieve academic and social success. Several speech-language clinicians and researchers have described integrated service options and associated implementation issues (e.g., Borsch & Oaks, 1992; Brandel, 1992; Bunce et al., 1995; Cirrin & Penner, 1995; Cooper & Cooper, 1991; Elksnin & Capilouto, 1994; Miller, 1989; Nelson, 1993; Norris & Hoffman, 1990; O'Brien & O'Leary, 1988; Rice, 1995; Silliman & Wilkinson, 1991; Wilcox, Kouri, & Caswell, 1991; Wilcox & Morris, 1995a). Although variations in focus, applicable practices, and implementation exist, there appears to be an emerging consensus regarding three key components of integrated speech-language practices (e.g., ASHA, 1995).

1.  A natural setting must serve as the intervention context. Natural settings vary in accordance with program models and may include homes, schools,

or communities. With regard to young children in center-based settings, the most likely natural setting is a toddler or preschool classroom.

2. Services should be integrated with the natural setting such that intervention strategies can be implemented within the ongoing stream of activities typical for that setting. With respect to early intervention (i.e., toddler or preschool) classrooms, this means that intervention goals and objectives should be linked with curricular content and therapeutic techniques embedded in ongoing activities.

3. The design and delivery of services should involve collaborations with families and other professional and support personnel. These collaborations should include development of goals and objectives as well as direct (i.e., services provided by an SLP) and indirect (i.e., SLP serves as a consultant to another individual who provides the direct service) service delivery procedures.

Most services provided by SLPs to young children are compatible with integrated practices that include classroom-based interventions. This is not to say that individual out-of-class treatment is no longer necessary. Indeed, individual treatment may be necessary to establish or facilitate initial skill acquisition, particularly when treating some speech disorders (e.g., voice, articulation, fluency) and oral-motor problems (e.g., feeding, swallowing). Use of emerging speech and related oral-motor behavior in natural settings (i.e., generalization) is also of critical concern, however, and the integrated practice framework provides the optimum format for addressing this concern.

Areas of practice for SLPs that are prime candidates for classroom-based interventions exclusively include communication (e.g., intentional communication, communication functions, socially appropriate use of language behavior) and language programming (e.g., lexical acquisition, sentence production, morphosyntactic features). Although some clinicians use the pull-out model to facilitate emergence of these communication and language abilities, research (e.g., Rice & Hadley, 1995; Wilcox et al., 1991) indicates that such skills may be facilitated best within classroom contexts. Communication and language skills emerge within the context of interpersonal interaction, and although early intervention classrooms vary along the continuum of high versus low structure, all instruction is interpersonal in nature, thereby affording children with opportunities to acquire and use their communication and language skills. To separate such skills from the ongoing stream of natural interactive opportunities (e.g., pull-out treatment) not only contributes to the chronic problem of generalization of linguistic abilities but also may interfere with learning how to use linguistic abilities in a socially appropriate manner. Generalization and socially appropriate use of linguistic abilities constitute critical concerns that must be addressed in early language interventions (e.g., Fujiki & Brinton, 1994; Kaiser, Yoder, & Keetz, 1992; Rice, 1993; Rice, Sell, & Hadley, 1991;

Windsor, 1995; see also Chapter 6). Provision of language interventions within preschool classrooms provides opportunities for children to acquire linguistic forms and functions necessary for ongoing activities. Furthermore, when such interventions include children with varying abilities (i.e., those developing typically and atypically), many opportunities are also available to learn socially appropriate use of new forms.

Most literature in support of classroom-based speech and language interventions is in the form of program descriptions and SLPs' impressions of effectiveness. Thus, the case for classroom-based interventions, at this time, relies more on beliefs and values than on empirical data. The data, however, are emerging and include 1) case study reports (Christensen & Luckett, 1990; Withey, 1991), 2) pre- and postgroup comparisons (Rice & Hadley, 1995; Wilcox & Morris, 1995b), 3) group comparisons of pull-out versus classroom intervention (Wilcox et al., 1991), and 4) comparisons of different facilitation methods within a classroom (Cole & Dale, 1986; Cole, Dale, & Mills, 1991). The single-case data (case study methods) document improvement for children with various speech and language disorders when treated within classroom settings. Group data reported by Rice and Hadley (1995) as well as Wilcox and Morris (1995b) build a convincing case for the effectiveness of classroom-based interventions for language and phonological disorders.

Rice and Hadley (1995) report language outcome data for 36 children with specific language impairment (SLI) who were enrolled in a language acquisition preschool (LAP) over a 6-year period. The LAP is a demonstration preschool in which one third of the children attending have been identified as having SLI, one third are learning English as a second language, and one third are developing language typically. Language intervention and enrichment activities are incorporated into the curriculum across classroom activities and throughout the class period. General language measures at program entry and exit indicated that all children with SLI demonstrated improvement in communication abilities. Furthermore, comparison with the group of children developing language typically indicated the likelihood that the improvement by the children with SLI exceeded that which would be expected because of maturational factors alone. Wilcox and Morris (1995b) reported phonology outcome data for 32 of these children with SLI. The Goldman-Fristoe Test of Articulation served as the standardized outcome measure for all children and indicated substantial improvements in speech skills.

Cole and Dale (1986) as well as Wilcox et al. (1991) found that children who received language intervention embedded into general classroom activities demonstrated as much progress as children who received direct language instruction within the classroom (Cole & Dale, 1986) and individual language instruction (Wilcox et al., 1991). The Wilcox and colleagues investigation additionally addressed issues regarding generalization. Preschoolers (age range 12–47 months) with language delays were randomly assigned to either an individual pull-out or classroom-based treatment condition. All children produced fewer than 20 true words at the initiation of the investigation. Interactive modeling procedures were used to facilitate acquisition of a core lexicon (10–15 words) in both groups of children. With the exception of setting (i.e., in-class versus out-of-class intervention) variables concerning specific facilitation of language goals (i.e., number of models provided, number of opportunities to use selected words, selection of target words) were controlled; thus, resulting group differences could be attributable to the setting factor. No differences were found in the children's use of target words during treatment. The children who received classroom-based intervention, however, demonstrated a greater degree of productive use of target words in home generalization measures.

Although the empirical, research-oriented basis for integrated therapeutic techniques is emerging, the need for integrated practices is becoming widely recognized. As noted by McWilliam and Bailey (1994), existing research certainly establishes that integrated practices are at least as effective as isolated models. Almost all areas within the scope of SLPs' practice in early intervention are applicable for integrated therapy models to facilitate acquisition of new skills or promote generalization of emerging skills. We shall now turn our attention to strategies for achieving integrated practices in center-based early intervention programs.

## IMPLEMENTATION OF INTEGRATED PRACTICES IN PRESCHOOL CLASSROOMS: GUIDELINES AND EXAMPLES

This section focuses on strategies for achieving goals within the classroom context. Our examples rely on a model in which an SLP is actively involved in the classroom environment. We recognize that classroom-based integrated services include consultant models, and many of our suggestions and facilitation strategies can be taught to teachers or other classroom personnel for those situations in which the SLP serves as a consultant to the classroom teacher.

Most of our examples and discussion include strategies and guidelines for facilitation of language acquisition in young children with language disorders. We think it is important to point out that the classroom is also an appropriate context for the treatment of other communication impairments such as voice, fluency, and speech-sound errors. Indeed, various clinicians (e.g., Andrews & Summers, 1993; Christensen & Luckett, 1990; Cooper, 1991; Cooper & Cooper, 1991; Masterson; 1993; Wilcox & Morris, 1995a, 1995b) have reported high degrees of success in the treatment of such impairments within classroom settings. We choose to focus primarily on language interventions because most young children who are eligible for intervention services have substantial needs in the language domain. Many of the suggestions and examples are also applicable or amenable to treatment of various speech disorders. The classroom is probably the most fertile ground for achieving generalization of emerging speech patterns, because it provides children with opportunities to practice newly learned skills in a natural setting. Although we provide the particulars regarding strategies for facilitating emergence of specific language behavior, it should be remembered that these same strategies can be used to facilitate generalization of many speech behaviors. Because we focus on the classroom context, the examples and suggestions are appropriate for young children attending toddler playgroups and preschool programs covering an age range of approximately 18 months–5 years.

Classroom-based intervention serves as the anchor for most descriptions of integrated speech and language services. We must emphasize, however, that a change in the location of intervention does not constitute, in and of itself, integrated therapy. For example, a clinician can come into a classroom, take a child into a corner, and work on objectives that are isolated from skills that the child needs to be successful in class activities without classroom personnel being aware of the child's goals or strategies for facilitating those goals. In addition to physically locating interventions within a class, successful integrated therapy practices are those that 1) facilitate children's acquisition of communication and language behavior essential to participation in classroom activities, 2) are designed with consideration of varying communication opportunities across the array of typical classroom events or activities, 3) include therapeutic techniques that are integrated into the classroom environment with respect to curriculum content and corresponding activities, and 4) are based on collaborations with families and classroom personnel.

### Essential Skills and Functional Goals

In one of the first descriptions of the roles and responsibilities of an integrated programming team, Campbell (1987) suggested that functional or essential skills should serve as the basis for the organization and delivery of children's services. Chapter 5 reinforces this concept and stresses the critical importance of functional goals to the success of integrated programming efforts. Because a classroom day includes a series of interpersonal activities that vary in focus and intent but still rely on interpersonal communication, it appears simple to integrate communication and language goals into this stream of activities. In reality, this is not so. Typically, communication and language goals are developed with reference to a child's performance on a particular assessment battery. Unfortunately, many standard assessment batteries bear little resemblance to the reality of a child's classroom environment and the communication and language skills needed to succeed in that environment. For example, many SLPs administer some sort of test (either formal or informal) designed to assess receptive and expressive vocabulary. Assume that problems are identified, and consider the following individualized education program (IEP) goal and associated objectives that typically result from vocabulary assessments:

> *Goal:* Elizabeth will increase her receptive and expressive vocabulary.
>
> *Objective 1:* Elizabeth will identify 10 words in each of the following categories with 80% accuracy: Food, clothing, body parts, vehicles, animals.
>
> *Objective 2:* Elizabeth will name 10 words in each of the following categories with 80% accuracy: Food, clothing, body parts, vehicles, animals.

Although the objectives are certainly relevant to the identified goal, they have minimal functional value in the sense that 1) they are not linked to natural opportunities for practice during a typical classroom day, and 2) as they are written, they do not represent skills that are critical for success in typical classroom activities. Central to the development of functional goals and objectives are the concepts of natural opportunities and critical effects. Facilitation of communication and language skills is most easily achieved when targeted behavior corresponds to some aspect of daily activities for which there are natural prompts or cues for performance and for which there are obvious and direct results when behaviors are produced correctly.

Standard communication and language assessment practices typically include 1) administration of some type of formal instrument or developmental checklist, 2) a parent interview, and 3) analysis of a clinician–child or parent–child language sample. Following this protocol will identify areas of concern and need in terms of a child's specific communication and language abilities. Additional information must be gathered on the classroom environment and routines, however, to generate functional goals and objectives. Therapists who regularly work in classrooms already have a good understanding of preschool classrooms, including activities and general skills necessary for participation. Children's abilities to use their skills vary widely, however, and information on their performance in typical classroom activities is essential to the development of functional communication and language goals and objectives. Ideally, this information is gathered through consultation with classroom personnel as well as direct observation of children in their classrooms. Observations should be routine-based and seek to determine a given child's ability to use his or her communication and language skills to participate in that routine as well as opportunities within particular routines for facilitation of specific skills. After considering such parameters as natural cues, critical effects, and routine-based opportunities, the more traditional IEP goal and objective can be rewritten as follows:

> *Goal:* Elizabeth will increase her participation during snack time.
>
> *Objective 1:* Elizabeth will assist in setting up for snack by getting at least three snack items (e.g., food, placemats, cups) as requested by her peers on three consecutive occasions.

*Objective 2:* Elizabeth will make at least three requests for snack items by using labels for desired food and drink items on three consecutive occasions.

*Objective 3:* Elizabeth will respond to at least two peer requests for more food on three consecutive occasions.

*Objective 4:* Elizabeth will request assistance in throwing away her snack items (e.g., napkin, cup) on three consecutive occasions.

Although both the traditional and the more functional goal and objective sequence address improvement of receptive and expressive vocabulary abilities, the functional sequence directly links such improvement with a typical, repeated activity.

Standard assessment procedures should be used to determine specific communication and language needs from a domain or structural perspective (e.g., intentional communication, communication functions, receptive and expressive vocabulary, two-word combinations, grammatical morphemes, kernel sentences). Once these general needs have been determined for a given child, however, daily routines should be examined in collaboration with appropriate personnel and parents to determine appropriate sequences of functional goals and objectives. The classroom experience provides a context for communication and language learning within high-structure activities and low-structure activities. With preplanning, classroom activities in each of these areas can be structured to provide children with multiple opportunities and reasons to communicate.

## Communication Opportunities and Classroom Events

Many events and activities such as arriving and departing class, cleanup, and snack time occur in the classroom quite frequently and take on a routine structure. Based on the study of parent–child interaction, child-language theorists have suggested that routines facilitate language development by providing a repeatable and predictable format within which children can interact and communicate. Within a given routine, the same events typically recur in the same order. Therefore, children learn what to expect within a specific routine, which may allow allocation of more resources to the task of language acquisition (Snow, Perlmann, & Nathan, 1987). Additionally, there are specific times when interactants are expected to take a turn and the words or utterances used for those turns are highly predictable, with a restricted possibility of meanings, thereby allowing children to make an association between a word or phrase and its meaning (Ninio & Bruner, 1978; Ratner & Bruner, 1978). Young children with and without language delays have been found to talk more frequently and use longer utterances within the context of routines (Conti-Ramsden & Friel-Patti, 1987; Snow et al., 1987; Yoder & Davies, 1992; Yoder, Spruytenburg, Edwards, & Davies, 1995).

Many activities within the classroom day can be routinized to increase opportunity and motivation to communicate. Furthermore, once a routine is well established, unexpected modifications (i.e., creation of a novel event) can provide a salient reason for children to communicate. Such modifications may take various forms, including 1) performing a component event of the routine out of logical and typical sequence, 2) using an object necessary to the routine in an unusual manner, 3) forgetting objects needed or turns within a routine, and 4) making objects needed inaccessible (Constable, 1983).

***Highly Structured Activities*** Highly structured activities are usually times when adults in the classroom take the lead and direct the activity such as circle time, story time, or small-group experiences. Such activities should be designed to provide numerous opportunities for children to use communication and language. Reliance on a multitude of directives (e.g., "Put it here") and questions (e.g., "What's this?") may reduce overall communication opportunities as well as the need to provide multiword responses. Communication and language learning are maximized through adults' use of more naturalistic conversational techniques. For example, production of comments such as "You're stirring the Kool-Aid," "You're pouring the water," and so on is more likely to assist children in making a connection between words and actions than questions such as "What are you doing?" During activities, SLPs should encourage creative thinking in children by allowing them to express their ideas. Active participation of children at their individual levels can be accomplished by modifying the activity requirements or using adapted material or devices when necessary. For example, children with limited speech production abilities might use a communication device to initiate requests and/or comment during planned activities.

***Less Structured Activities*** Less structured activities are usually child-directed in that children choose what they will do, how they will do it, and how long they will participate. Examples of less structured activities include free play in interest areas, outdoor play, and snack time. During free play, it is necessary for staff to make activities available that encourage choice making, independent interactions with materials, and social interactions among peers. Children should be encouraged to use their language abilities to make choices and decisions regarding their play. By having children develop a plan before free play, opportunities are provided for children to express themselves verbally and subsequently to act on their own decisions. For children with limited language abilities, a picture symbol communication board representing areas of the room, objects, and peers may be used to make choices, either by pointing or by using single words or phrases. By arranging and equipping the physical environment within an organized framework, children are able to develop independence in choosing, obtaining, and returning materials. Once they are engaged in an activity, the SLP can follow their lead and take advantage of opportunities to facilitate language acquisition through the use of naturalistic teaching strategies such as modeling.

Child-initiated play activities do not always provide multiple opportunities for practicing skills, and it may be necessary for the SLP to structure the environment to allow for practice. For example, if children are putting on clothes in the housekeeping area, the SLP may encourage the idea of going to the store and trying on different clothes. This allows the clinician to increase the need for interaction and communication and, through his or her participation in the activity, model appropriate communication and language skills. Social interaction skills among children can also be encouraged during free play activities through the use of group activities such as art projects or playing house in the dramatic play area. For example, during an art project, the SLP might limit materials to encourage children to take turns, make requests for sharing, and respond to others' requests for obtaining materials. While playing house, an SLP can use prompts and cues to encourage socially appropriate language use with peers. For example, on observing a child cooking food on the pretend stove, the SLP might say, "Mmm that looks good. Who is going to eat it?" or "Ask Mary if she wants some."

## Integrated Therapeutic Techniques

Following determination of activities that will serve as the context for language interventions, the SLP must consider specific therapeutic techniques to use in these activities. In particular, the SLP must determine the necessary levels of cues and prompts to ensure that children linguistically and socially participate to the fullest extent possible. The database on effective language intervention techniques is substantial (see Fey, 1986; Kaiser et al., 1992), and there are numerous strategies that facilitate acquisition of a variety of language skills. Some strategies rely on changes in the physical environment. For children with disabilities, it is important that they are given multiple opportunities to practice a language skill; however, these opportunities should be as natural as possible. Often objects in the physical environment are so accessible to children that they are able to go through the day getting for themselves the things they need or desire. Consequently, few naturally occurring opportunities arise for children to request specific objects or assistance. Manipulation of the physical environment to create communication opportunities can be as simple as hiding regularly used or necessary objects (Constable, 1983) or providing children with choices of objects (Ostrosky & Kaiser, 1991). Hiding objects can facilitate use of question forms and coding negation (i.e., "no truck," "cannot find truck"). Providing choices of two or more options for objects or activities can encourage the use of communication to indicate the child's choice. Additional techniques that exploit or manipulate the physical environment include sabotage strategies (Constable, 1983), such as withholding objects or turns. For example, if the clinician wants children to learn to make requests for food during snack time, providing limited portions creates the need as well as increases opportunities for the children to make requests.

Other intervention strategies focus on ways in which the SLP interacts with a child and the manner in which language targets are brought to a child's attention, that is, made salient. Establishing and maintaining joint attention through following a child's attentional lead is a basic principle in many language intervention programs (e.g., Cole, 1995; Kaiser & Hester, 1994). Early intentional communication is more likely to occur within the context of sharing attention with adults, and several investigations have indicated that a large proportion of children's communications during the prelinguistic, one-word, and early multiword stages are for the purpose of directing another's attention to an object or event on which the child already is focused (Carpenter, Mastergeorge, & Coggins, 1983; Coggins & Carpenter, 1981; Wetherby, Cain, Yonclas, & Walker, 1988). Therefore, one way in which joint attention episodes with adults contributes to ongoing communication and language development is by providing a social context that supports and gives immediate meaning to children's communication attempts.

Joint attention episodes also appear to contribute to language development by providing the context for adult language use to be immediately meaningful to the child. From very early on, adults follow an infant's gaze or pointing gesture and label objects on which the infant already is focused, or they manipulate an object as they label it to attract the infant's attention. It is believed that this facilitates lexical learning by reducing the attentional demands placed on the child. Instead of the child determining the focus of the adult's attention and then applying the adult's label to that focus of attention, if joint attention has already been established, all the child has to do is make an association between the label and the object to which it refers.

Equally as important as the establishment of joint attention is the way in which the SLP provides models of targeted communication and language behavior. A key therapeutic strategy includes semantically contingent models. As children begin to use symbols and string words together, semantically contingent adult responses have been shown to facilitate linguistic development. Such responses continue the topic of conversation by maintaining or adding to the semantic content of what a child says while also highlighting structural aspects of language. Two methods of providing semantically contingent responses include the use of expansions and recasts. Expansions repeat a child's utterance, filling in missing elements (Bunce & Watkins, 1995; Moerk, 1992). For example, a child might say, "Baby crying," and her mother might reply, "The baby is crying." A recast is an utterance that maintains the meaning of the child's utterance but changes one or more semantic, syntactic, or morphological elements. An example of a recast would be producing the utterance, "Big Bird is eating a big cookie," following a child's utterance, "Big Bird sit down." Semantically contingent responses such as expansions and recasts have been shown to facilitate general language growth such as use of semantic relations, verb phrase complexity, and mean length of utterance (Barnes, Gutfreund, Satterly, & Wells, 1983; Fey, Cleave, Long, & Hughes, 1993; Hoff-Ginsberg, 1985; Scherer & Olswang, 1984), as well as specific morphological and syntactic forms (Camarata & Nelson, 1992; Camarata, Nelson, & Camarata, 1994; Newport, Gleitman, & Gleitman, 1977) in children with and without language disabilities.

Overall a variety of strategies are available for use in integrated practices. Table 1 provides brief descriptions of various strategies and examples of use across varying classroom activities. The strategies vary along a continuum of degree of structure from those that make no attempt to elicit specific child productions to those that gently prompt (e.g., "Can you say _____ ?"), to those that specifically request verbal behavior (e.g., "Tell me what you want?"). Although all of these strategies can be effective, there may be various situations in which one is more appropriate. Several investigators have reported aptitude-by-treatment interactions (Cole, Dale, & Mills, 1991; Wilcox et al., 1991, Yoder, Kaiser, & Alpert, 1991) in which a relationship between cognitive abilities and the language intervention technique is apparent. Specifically, all three investigations indicated that children with lower cognitive abilities appear to make greater language gains in the more loosely structured intervention protocols, including those with no specific response requirements. Similarly, children with higher cognitive abilities appeared to demonstrate greater language gains in intervention approaches that were more directive.

### Individualized Group Instruction

Another crucial implementation issue in the design of integrated practices includes the concept of individualized group instruction. A primary concern of many SLPs regarding integrated practices focuses on whether the goals for individual children at different skill levels can be targeted during group activities (Elksnin & Capilouto, 1994). The use of individualized group instruction is necessary to address the varying range of individual communication and language needs and skill levels of children during group activities in the classroom setting. During group activities in inclusive programs, specific modifications based on individual children's abilities are necessary to facilitate maximal participation of all children (including those developing typically). When planning group activities, the clinician must first structure the activity by establishing a regular, predictable routine for the children to follow, such as first singing a greeting song and then allowing a child to choose a song for the group to sing, so that children know what to expect. Next the clinician must link children's individual communication and language goals with the components of the routine. It is also necessary to determine the level of prompts and cues necessary to facilitate participation and learning of individual objectives. For example, some children's goals might be to imitate a sequence of motor

Table 1.  Examples of specific intervention strategies embedded in classroom events

| Facilitating strategies | Event | Goal and example of use |
|---|---|---|
| 1. Sabotage strategies (Constable, 1983) | | |
| Violating routine events: Omit or incorrectly perform a familiar and/or necessary step in an activity or routine. | Outdoor play | Goal: Shaun will use the target sound /g/ at the beginning of words.<br>Implementation: While pushing Shaun on a swing, catch the swing each time it comes back toward you and hold it. As you hold the swing, say, "Go," and then let go of the swing. After several turns, do not say anything and hold the swing while waiting for Shaun to let you know he wants to keep swinging. |
| Withholding objects and turns: Most activities require the use of several materials, and many require turn-taking. During such an activity, withhold an object or turn in an apparent oversight. | Snack | Goal: Tyler and Jeff will initiate communication to request things they want and need.<br>Implementation: During snack time, hand cups out, but "forget" to give cups to Tyler and Jeff. |
| Violating object function or object manipulation: When child is familiar with action schemes for specific objects or object roles that compose routine events, intentionally violate those routines. | Free play | Goal: Brittany will use two-word phrases to indicate what people or objects are doing or what she wants them to do.<br>Implementation: Play with Jack-in-the-Box, which plays the tune to "All Around the Mulberry Bush." After going through the song several times and letting the clown pop up as you sing "Pop goes the weasel," hold your thumb over the lid so that the clown cannot pop up, and sing the song, emphasizing "Pop goes the weasel." |
| Hiding objects: Hide objects necessary or desirable for an activity. | Free play | Goal: Lisa will ask questions beginning with /wh/-question words "what" and "where."<br>Implementation: Remove Lisa's favorite truck from the blocks and vehicles area. When Lisa goes to that center and begins to look for the truck, direct her search so that she eventually locates the toy. Model the question "Where's the truck?" as you search. |

(continued)

Table 1. (continued)

| Facilitating strategies | Event | Goal and example of use |
|---|---|---|
| 2. *Providing choices* (Ostrosky & Kaiser, 1991): Provide child with two or more options for objects or activities. | Opening circle | *Goal:* Michael will point to a picture to request objects and activities. *Implementation:* When Michael is choosing in which free play center he wants to play, hold up two pictures depicting different centers and ask him, "Do you want to play with blocks or cars?" Wait for Michael to indicate his choice. |
| 3. *Interactive modeling* (Camarata, Nelson, & Camarata, 1994; Fey, 1986; Wilcox, 1984; Wilcox, Kouri, & Caswell, 1991): Follow into child's established focus of attention. Do not require imitation of the modeled utterance. | | |
| *Focused stimulation:* Set up situations that verbally and/or nonverbally obligate the use of the target form. Produce many utterances that demonstrate use of the target form in meaningful and functional contexts. May use self-talk, parallel talk, expansions, and recast to emphasize use of the target form. | Outdoor play | *Goal:* Matthew will use a greater number of words to indicate what he wants and needs. *Implementation:* During outside play, Matthew walks over to the swing set and starts to climb up on one of the swings. Adult: "Matthew, want on the swing?" Matthew: Continues to climb onto the swing. Adult: "Climb on the swing." Matthew: Is now sitting on swing. Adult: "Want me to push swing?" Matthew: Nods head. Adult: "Push swing" as she pushes the swing. |
| *Modeling with expansion:* Repeat child utterances, filling in the missing elements. | Small-group activity | *Goal:* David will begin to use the preposition "in" to communicate where objects are located. *Implementation:* At the art table, David says "crayon basket" as he holds a basket of crayons. Respond with "Yes, the crayons are in the basket." |

| | | |
|---|---|---|
| *Modeling with recast:* Produce utterances that maintain semantic context of immediately preceding child utterance, but change semantic, syntactic, or morphological elements. | Snack | *Goal:* Marcy will use the past tense marker "ed" to talk about events that have already happened.<br>*Implementation:* Marcy drops a cracker on the floor and says, "Drop cracker." Answer "Yes, you dropped the cracker on the floor." |
| 4. *Vertical structuring* (plus expansion) (Fey, 1986): Approach child when engaged in an activity and ask a question designed to elicit a multiword response. Complete the following steps: 1) If child produces multiword target, expand the utterance as described under modeling and expansion; 2) If child does not produce targeted production, ask, "Who's this?" or "What's this?" while pointing to an object, picture, etc., to elicit the first noun in the utterance; then await a response; 3) regardless of the child's response, ask, "Who's this?" or "What's this?" while pointing to an object, picture, etc., to elicit the second noun in the utterance, and again await a response; 4) expand child's response by producing an utterance with the semantic–syntactic relationship encoded vertically by child. | Snack | *Goal:* Ellen will use more complex sentences by joining two simple sentences with the word "and."<br>*Implementation:* Ellen is eating a snack. Approach and sit next to her.<br>Adult: "What are you eating for snack?"<br>Ellen: Looks at adult without responding.<br>Adult: Ask "What's this?" while pointing to carrots on Ellen's plate.<br>Ellen: "Carrot."<br>Adult: Ask "What's this?" while pointing to celery on Ellen's plate.<br>Ellen: "Celery."<br>Adult: "That's right, you're eating carrots and celery. Yum." |

*(continued)*

Table 1. (continued)

| Facilitating strategies | Event | Goal and example of use |
|---|---|---|
| 5. *Scaffolding:* Assess the child's abilities in a particular situation, and then provide models and prompts at level slightly higher to facilitate more sophisticated child behavior. | Free play | *Goal:* Kim will use *is* and "*ing*" constructions to describe events that are occurring.<br><br>*Implementation:* Kim is playing with a farm set, pretending to feed various farm animals.<br>Adult: As Kim feeds the pig, "What's the pig doing?"<br>Kim: "Pig eating."<br>Adult: "Pig is eating."<br>Adult: As Kim feeds the cow, "What's the cow doing?"<br>Kim: "Cow eating."<br>Adult: "Cow is eating."<br>Adult: As Kim feeds the duck, "What's the duck doing?"<br>Kim: "Duck eating."<br>Adult: "Duck is eating." |
| 6. *Milieu teaching techniques:*<br>*Mand-model* (Hart & Risley, 1975; Kaiser, Yoder, & Keetz, 1992; Warren, McQuarter, & Rogers-Warren, 1984): Establish mutual focus with child and apply the following steps: 1) Request verbal behavior (e.g., "Tell me what you want."); 2) if child responds appropriately, comply with or acknowledge child's response; 3) if child does not respond, provide an imitative prompt (e.g., "Can you say ball?"); 4) if child responds appropriately, comply with or acknowledge response. If child does not respond, terminate this particular teaching sequence. | Small-group activity | *Goal:* Brett will use words rather than aggressive behavior to communicate with his peers.<br><br>*Implementation:* At the art table, Melanie comes and takes from the table a marker that Brett had been using.<br>Brett: Tries to grab marker back.<br>Adult: "Tell Melanie what you want."<br>Brett: Tries to grab marker again and vocalizes angrily.<br>Adult: "Tell Melanie 'my marker.'"<br>Brett: "My marker."<br>Adult: Intervene to be sure Melanie gives the marker back to Brett. |

*Time delay:* Establish mutual focus with child. Create or wait for a situation in which child needs assistance to continue an ongoing activity. Instead of requesting communicative behavior, be physically available and maintain "expectant" eye contact. If child fails to produce an appropriate communicative behavior, provide a conversationally based imitative prompt.

*Incidental teaching:* Carry out the following steps: 1) Focus attention on child who has initiated an interaction; 2) ask child to expand communicative behavior; 3) prompt or provide a model of an appropriate expansion; 4) acknowledge by imitating and complying with child's communicative behavior.

Structured free play

*Goal:* John will include the sounds /p/ and /b/ at the end of words.
*Implementation:* John is in the housekeeping area setting the table so that the stuffed animals can eat. Sit close to him, holding all of the cups. Look "expectantly" at John while waiting for him to ask for the cups. If he does not ask, prompt a request by saying "need cup." Then give him one at a time, regardless of whether he attempts a response.

Opening circle

*Goal:* Jim will begin to use two-word phrases.
*Implementation:* During opening circle, blow bubbles, then pause for a few moments.
Jim: "More."
Adult: "More. More what, Jim? More bubbles."
Jim: "More."
Adult: "OK, more bubbles," and then blow more bubbles.

233

movements when given partial physical assistance during a music and movement activity. Other children's goals might be to take a turn telling others what to do when provided with a choice modeled by the clinician, such as, "Do you want us to clap hands or turn around?"

During group activities, SLPs must ensure that the necessary modifications are made so that all children are either active or partial participants with very little down time. All children with communication impairments should have a designated form of communication (i.e., speech, sign language, picture board, technological device) to interact with others. For children with sensory impairments such as a visual or hearing impairment, it may be necessary to modify how directions or instructions are given and make adaptations in materials and task requirements. By making these preparations, each child's specific communication and language needs are addressed during the typical classroom activities that occur each day.

To illustrate the design and implementation of individualized group instruction more fully, Table 2 provides examples of language intervention strategies across different classroom activities for the following children:

- **Sam** is a 3-year, 8-month-old child with significant delays in all developmental areas. He enjoys interaction with adults and peers. At this time, he communicates primarily by vocalizing, gesturing, and pointing, but he frequently tries to imitate single words used by others.
- **Andrew** is a 4-year, 6-month-old child who understands language well but demonstrates delayed language production skills. He uses two- to three-word phrases and inconsistently uses early developing grammatical morphemes (e.g., -ing, plural -s, in, on). Andrew follows the classroom routine easily but tends to play alone, initiating few interactions with adults and peers.
- **Maria** is a 4-year, 3-month-old child with a significant phonological disorder characterized by the deletion of final consonants and the substitution of front sounds (e.g., /t/, /d/) for back sounds (e.g., /k/, /g/). Her speech intelligibility is poor; however, this does not deter her from interacting frequently with others.

## Collaboration

A final, critical implementation issue concerns collaboration among other professionals, support personnel, and families. For an integrated therapy model to succeed, there must be at the minimum a collaborative relationship between the speech-language clinician and the general classroom personnel. Ideally, the parents and other personnel involved in the child's education will also be involved. Collaboration allows people with diverse expertise to solve mutually defined problems creatively (Idol, Paolucci-Whitcomb, & Nevin, 1986). This definition of collaboration assumes that all team members are involved in assessment, goal setting, and intervention.

Table 2.  Examples of individualized group instruction for communication and language goals

| | |
|---|---|
| Sam's goal: | Sam will increase his vocabulary to more specifically request things he wants and needs during the class day. |
| Andrew's goal: | Andrew will add "ing" to the end of words to talk about events that are occurring. |
| Maria's goal: | Maria will include consonant sounds at the end of words and target sounds /k/ and /g/ at the beginning and end of words. |

| Classroom events | Targeted behavior and suggested strategies |
|---|---|
| **1. Opening circle** | |
| Sam | When it is time to choose free play centers, Sam will indicate (with the aid of picture cues) in which center he would like to play by saying "blocks," "cars," or "books" on four consecutive days.<br>Suggested strategy: Mand-model |
| Andrew | During discussion of the calendar and weather, Andrew will use phrases such as "The sun shining" and "It raining" to describe the day's weather on four consecutive days.<br>Suggested strategy: Mand-model |
| Maria | Maria will include the /s/ sound at the end of "house" and the /t/ sound at the end of "art" when she chooses a free play center three times a week.<br>Suggested strategies: Focused stimulation, providing choices |
| **2. Free play** | |
| Sam | Sam will use labels to comment on what he is playing with (e.g., "block," "car") two times on four consecutive days.<br>Suggested strategy: Focused stimulation |
| Andrew | Andrew will add "ing" to action words to talk about events that are occurring (e.g., "The baby sleeping," "Phillip coloring," "Building a house") four times on four consecutive days.<br>Suggested strategies: Modeling with expansion, scaffolding |
| Maria | Maria will use the /k/ sound at the beginning of the phrase "clean up" as she tells each of her peers that it is time to "clean up toys" three times on four consecutive days.<br>Suggested strategy: Mand-model |
| **3. Small groups** | |
| Sam | Sam will attempt to produce labels to name objects used in the activity (e.g., "marker," "book") two times on four consecutive days.<br>Suggested strategies: Focused stimulation, sabotage (withholding objects, violating routine steps) |
| Andrew | Andrew will add "ing" to action words when asked questions about what is occurring during small-group activities three times on four consecutive days.<br>Suggested strategies: Focused stimulation, modeling with recast |
| Maria | Maria will use final sounds in words such as "book," "pen," and "spoon," to call an adult's attention to the fact that necessary objects are missing during small-group activities, two times on four consecutive days.<br>Suggested strategies: Sabotage (withholding objects and turns, hiding objects) |

*(continued)*

Table 2. (continued)

| Classroom events | Targeted behavior and suggested strategies |
| --- | --- |
| **4. Outdoor play** | |
| Sam | Sam will say "slide" or "swing" to request a turn on playground equipment on four consecutive days. |
| | Suggested strategies: Focused stimulation, sabotage (withholding objects or turns) |
| Andrew | Andrew will use "ing" on the end of action words to talk about what his peers are doing two times on four consecutive days. |
| | Suggested strategy: Scaffolding |
| Maria | Maria will include the final sound in "slide" and "ball" to request turns during outdoor activities, two times on four consecutive days. |
| | Suggested strategy: Incidental teaching |
| **5. Snack** | |
| Sam | During snack, Sam will ask for another helping by saying "juice" or "cracker" three times during the week. |
| | Suggested strategies: Incidental teaching, time delay |
| Andrew | Andrew will use each of the phrases "eating _____" and "drinking _____" two times in a week. |
| | Suggested strategies: Modeling with expansion, modeling with recast |
| Maria | Maria will use the /k/ sound in words such as "cracker," "carrot," and "cup" to request items during snack time one time on four consecutive days. |
| | Suggested strategy: Time delay |
| **6. Closing circle** | |
| Sam | Sam will tell his peers good-bye, saying "Bye" as he waves his hand, three times on four consecutive days. |
| | Suggested strategies: Modeling with expansion (i.e., expand Sam's verbal behavior of waving to waving and saying "Bye"), mand-model |
| Andrew | Andrew will use the phrase "_____ going home" when asked where classmates are going as they leave the room two times on four consecutive days. |
| | Suggested strategy: Mand-model |
| Maria | Maria will use the /g/ sound at the beginning of "good-bye" three times on four consecutive days. |
| | Suggested strategy: Focused stimulation |

Framing assessment and goal setting within the contexts of children's daily activities and actively and meaningfully involving the parents and team members in these steps familiarizes them with the process of providing integrated services and begins the process of establishing a collaborative relationship. Involving parents and other team members in the assessment and goal-setting process can be accomplished by observing children in typical situations and with the people with whom they regularly interact, as well as by soliciting parents' and teachers' descriptions of children's communication and language abilities.

In a truly collaborative relationship, all members of the team have responsibility for appropriately facilitating acquisition of targeted goals (ASHA, 1991). For this to occur, SLPs must understand the content and objectives of the curriculum and classroom activities, and classroom personnel will most likely need to increase their understanding of the language acquisition process and how social interaction supports communication and language development (Elksnin & Capilouto, 1994; Montgomery, 1992; Russell & Kaderavek, 1993). Parents and other professionals may be unaware of the things that they are already doing or can do within typical interactions with children that facilitate language and communication growth (e.g., following the child's focus of attention, providing consistent labels). SLPs can illustrate use of these strategies by 1) providing opportunities for parents and teachers to observe them facilitating language within an activity, 2) directly training parents and teachers in language facilitation techniques, and 3) planning team-teaching activities. Active participation in these processes allows all team members to recognize the benefits of providing speech and language services within the naturalistic context of the classroom (Borsch & Oaks, 1992; Montgomery, 1992).

Collaboration requires a commitment to building a cooperative relationship with all team members. This involves establishing rapport with parents and other intervention professionals, possibly by discovering and discussing mutual interests (Borsch & Oaks, 1992). Flexibility is also required. Individuals need to be prepared to change or expand the boundaries of what they perceive as their professional role to truly share responsibility for a child's achievement of agreed-upon goals (ASHA, 1991; Brandel, 1992). Additionally, maintaining a collaborative relationship requires an investment of time. Regularly scheduled meetings for the purpose of monitoring and adapting individual children's programs ensures that, to some degree, team members come together to plan and implement services.

## CONCLUSIONS

We have identified three key components of integrated speech and language services, consisting of 1) use of natural environments as intervention contexts; 2) development of goals, objectives, and therapeutic activities that are embedded in the ongoing stream of activities; and 3) collaborations with families and other personnel. With regard to center-based early intervention, we have suggested that the classroom is a natural and appropriate context for the facilitation of communication and language skills. Most areas within the scope of SLPs' practice are compatible with the integrated therapy model, and classroom-based interventions in particular. Although individual pull-out treatments are appropriate in some instances, particularly for treatment of certain speech disorders, the classroom is the optimal environment to facilitate generalization of emerging abilities. With respect to language abilities, the classroom serves as an ideal environment for facilitation of initial skills. That is, early language intervention goals may best be achieved within a classroom-based intervention model. Data from two reports provide convincing support for this conclusion (Rice & Hadley, 1995; Wilcox et al., 1991). This research is in an emergent phase and more is certainly needed, but when the findings are coupled with reported case studies, group outcome data, and the general clinical impressions that classroom environments are optimal for facilitating acquisition and socially appropriate use of linguistic abilities, the advantage is even more apparent.

Integrating language intervention services into the classroom requires more than just conducting therapy within the physical confines of the class-room. Functional integration of services requires embedding language facilitation techniques into the regular activities and events that take place during the class day so that children may participate to the fullest extent possible. Additionally, clinicians must be prepared to share the responsibility for planning, implementing, and monitoring communication and language intervention programming. This requires building meaningful relationships to teach parents, therapists from other disciplines, and classroom personnel how to enhance communication and language development.

## REFERENCES

American Speech-Language-Hearing Association. (1991). A model for collaborative service delivery for students with language-learning disorders in the public schools. *ASHA, 33*(Suppl.5), 44–50.

American Speech-Language-Hearing Association. (1995). *Inclusive practices for children and youth with communication disorders: Draft technical report.* Unpublished report.

Andrews, M., & Summers, A. (1993). A voice stimulation program for preschoolers: Theory and practice. *Language, Speech, and Hearing Services in Schools, 24,* 140–145.

Barnes, S., Gutfreund, M., Satterly, D., & Wells, G. (1983). Characteristics of adult speech which predict children's language development. *Journal of Child Language, 10,* 65–84.

Borsch, J., & Oaks, R. (1992). Effective collaboration at Central Elementary School. *Language, Speech, and Hearing Services in Schools, 23,* 367–368.

Brandel, D. (1992). Collaboration: Full steam ahead with no prior experience. *Language, Speech, and Hearing Services in Schools, 23,* 369–370.

Bunce, B., & Watkins, R. (1995). Language intervention in a preschool classroom: Implementing a language-focused curriculum. In M. Rice & K. Wilcox (Eds.), *Building a language-focused curriculum for the preschool classroom: Volume 1. A foundation for lifelong communication* (pp. 39–71). Baltimore: Paul H. Brookes Publishing Co.

Bunce, B., Watkins, R., Eyer, J., Torres, R., Ray, S., & Ellsworth, J. (1995). The language-focused curriculum in other settings. In M. Rice & K. Wilcox (Eds.), *Building a language-focused curriculum for the preschool classroom: Volume 1. A foundation for lifelong communication* (pp. 199–220). Baltimore: Paul H. Brookes Publishing Co.

Camarata, S., & Nelson, K. (1992). Treatment efficiency as a function of target selection in the remediation of child language disorders. *Clinical Linguistics and Phonetics, 6,* 167–178.

Camarata, S., Nelson, K., & Camarata, M. (1994). Comparison of conversational-recasting and imitative procedures for training grammatical structures in children with specific language impairment. *Journal of Speech and Hearing Research, 37,* 1414–1423.

Campbell, P. (1987). The integrated programming team: An approach for coordinating professionals of various disciplines in programs for students with severe and multiple handicaps. *Journal of The Association for Persons with Severe Handicaps, 12,* 107–116.

Carpenter, R., Mastergeorge, A., & Coggins, T. (1983). The acquisition of communicative intentions in infants eight to fifteen months of age. *Language and Speech, 26,* 101–116.

Christensen, S., & Luckett, C. (1990). Getting into the classroom and making it work. *Language, Speech, and Hearing Services in Schools, 21,* 110–113.

Cirrin, F., & Penner, S. (1995). Classroom-based and consultative service delivery models for language intervention. In M. Fey, J. Windsor, & S. Warren (Eds.), *Language intervention: Preschool through the elementary years* (pp. 333–362). Baltimore: Paul H. Brookes Publishing Co.

Coggins, T., & Carpenter, R. (1981). The communicative intention inventory: A system for observing and coding children's early intentional communication. *Applied Psycholinguistics, 2,* 235–252.

Cole, K. (1995). Curriculum models and language facilitation in the preschool years. In M. Fey, J. Windsor, & S. Warren (Eds.), *Language intervention: Preschool through the elementary years* (pp. 39–60). Baltimore: Paul H. Brookes Publishing Co.

Cole, K., & Dale, P. (1986). Direct language instruction and interactive language instruction with language-delayed preschool children: A comparison study. *Journal of Speech and Hearing Research, 29,* 206–217.

Cole, K., Dale, P., & Mills, P. (1991). Individual differences in language delayed children's responses to direct and interactive preschool instruction. *Topics in Early Childhood Special Education, 11,* 99–124.

Constable, C. (1983). Creating communicative context. In H. Winitz (Ed.), *Treating language disorders: For clinicians by clinicians* (pp. 97–120). Baltimore: University Park Press.

Conti-Ramsden, G., & Friel-Patti, P. (1987). Situational variability in mother-child conversations. In K. Nelson & A. van Kleeck (Eds.), *Children's language: Volume 6* (pp. 43–63). Hillsdale, NJ: Lawrence Erlbaum Associates.

Cooper, C. (1991). Using collaborative/consultative service delivery models for fluency intervention and carry over. *Language, Speech, and Hearing Services in Schools, 22,* 152–153.

Cooper, E., & Cooper, C. (1991). A fluency disorders prevention program for preschoolers and children in the primary grades. *American Journal of Speech-Language Pathology, 1,* 28–31.

Elksnin, L.K., & Capilouto, G.J. (1994). Speech-language pathologists' perceptions of integrated service delivery in school settings. *Language, Speech, and Hearing Services in Schools, 25,* 258–267.

Fey, M. (1986). *Language intervention with young children.* San Diego, CA: College-Hill Press.

Fey, M., Cleave, P., Long, S., & Hughes, D. (1993). Two approaches to the facilitation of grammar in children with language impairment: An experimental evaluation. *Journal of Speech and Hearing Research, 36,* 141–157.

Fujiki, M., & Brinton, B. (1994). Social competence and language impairment in children. In R. Watkins & M. Rice (Eds.), *Specific language impairments in children* (pp. 123–143). Baltimore: Paul H. Brookes Publishing Co.

Goldman, R.M., & Fristoe, M. (1969). *Goldman-Fristoe Test of Articulation.* Circle Pines, MN: American Guidance Service.

Hart, B., & Risley, T. (1975). Incidental teaching of language in the preschool. *Journal of Applied Behavior Analysis, 8,* 411–420.

Hoff-Ginsberg, E. (1985). Some contributions of mothers' speech to their children's syntactic growth. *Journal of Child Language, 24,* 367–385.

Idol, L., Paolucci-Whitcomb, P., & Nevin, A. (1986). *Collaborative consultation.* Austin, TX: PRO-ED.

Kaiser, A., & Hester, P. (1994). Generalized effects of enhanced milieu teaching. *Journal of Speech and Hearing Research, 37,* 1320–1340.

Kaiser, A., Yoder, P., & Keetz, A. (1992). Evaluating milieu teaching. In S. Warren & J. Reichle (Eds.), *Causes and effects in communication and language intervention* (pp. 9–48). Baltimore: Paul H. Brookes Publishing Co.

Masterson, J. (1993). Classroom-based phonological intervention. *American Journal of Speech-Language Pathology, 1,* 5–9.

McWilliam, R.A. (1995). Integration of therapy and consultative special education: A continuum in early intervention. *Infants and Young Children, 7,* 29–38.

McWilliam, R.A., & Bailey, D.B., Jr. (1994). Predictors of service delivery models in center-based early intervention. *Exceptional Children, 61,* 56–71.

Miller, L. (1989). Classroom-based language intervention. *Language, Speech, and Hearing Services in Schools, 20,* 153–170.

Moerk, E. (1992). *A first language taught and learned.* Baltimore: Paul H. Brookes Publishing Co.

Montgomery, J. (1992). Perspectives from the field: Language, speech, and hearing services in schools. *Language, Speech, and Hearing Services in Schools, 23,* 363–364.

Nelson, N. (1993). *Language disorders in context: Infancy through adolescence.* New York: Macmillan.

Newport, E., Gleitman, H., & Gleitman, L. (1977). Mother, I'd rather do it myself: Some effects and noneffects of maternal speech style. In C. Snow & C. Ferguson (Eds.), *Talking to children: Language input and acquisition.* Cambridge, England: Cambridge University Press.

Ninio, A., & Bruner, J. (1978). The achievement and antecedents of labelling. *Journal of Child Language, 5,* 1–15.

Norris, J., & Hoffman, P. (1990). Language intervention within naturalistic environments. *Language, Speech, and Hearing Services in Schools, 21,* 72–84.

O'Brien, M., & O'Leary, T. (1988). Evolving to the classroom model: Speech-language services for the mentally retarded. *Seminars in Speech and Language, 20,* 153–169.

Ostrosky, M., & Kaiser, A. (1991). Preschool classroom environments that promote communication. *Teaching Exceptional Children, 23,* 6–10.

Ratner, N., & Bruner, J. (1978). Games, social exchange and the acquisition of language. *Journal of Child Language, 5,* 391–401.

Rice, M. (1993). "Don't talk to him: He's weird": A social consequences account of language and social interaction. In A. Kaiser & D. Gray (Eds.), *Enhancing children's communication: Research foundations for intervention* (pp. 139–158). Baltimore: Paul H. Brookes Publishing Co.

Rice, M. (1995). The rationale and operating principles for a language-focused curriculum for preschool children. In M. Rice & K. Wilcox (Eds.), *Building a language-focused curriculum for the preschool classroom: Volume 1. A foundation for lifelong communication* (pp. 27–38). Baltimore: Paul H. Brookes Publishing Co.

Rice, M., & Hadley, P. (1995). Language outcomes of the language-focused curriculum. In M. Rice & K. Wilcox (Eds.), *Building a language-focused curriculum for the preschool classroom: Volume 1. A foundation for lifelong communication* (pp. 155–169). Baltimore: Paul H. Brookes Publishing Co.

Rice, M., Sell, M., & Hadley, P. (1991). Social interactions of speech- and language-impaired children. *Journal of Speech and Hearing Research, 34,* 1299–1307.

Russell, S., & Kaderavek, J. (1993). Alternative models for collaboration. *Language, Speech, and Hearing Services in Schools, 24,* 76–78.

Scherer, N., & Olswang, L. (1984). Role of mothers' expansions in stimulating children's language production. *Journal of Speech and Hearing Research, 27,* 387–396.

Silliman, E., & Wilkinson, L. (1991). *Communication for learning: Classroom observation and collaboration.* Rockville, MD: Aspen Publishers, Inc.

Snow, C., Perlmann, R., & Nathan, D. (1987). Why routines are different: Toward a multiple-factors model of the relation between input and language acquisition. In K.E. Nelson & A. van Kleeck (Eds.), *Children's language* (Vol. 6, pp. 65–97). Hillsdale, NJ: Lawrence Erlbaum Associates.

Warren, S., McQuarter, R., & Rogers-Warren, A. (1984). The effects of mands and models on the speech of unresponsive language-delayed preschool children. *Journal of Speech and Hearing Disorders, 49,* 43–52.

Wetherby, A., Cain, D., Yonclas, D., & Walker, V. (1988). Analysis of intentional communication of normal children from the prelinguistic to the multi-word stage. *Journal of Speech and Hearing Research, 31,* 240–252.

Wilcox, K., & Morris, S. (1995a). Speech intervention in a language-focused curriculum. In M. Rice & K. Wilcox (Eds.), *Building a language-focused curriculum for the preschool classroom: Volume 1. A foundation for lifelong communication* (pp. 73–92). Baltimore: Paul H. Brookes Publishing Co.

Wilcox, K., & Morris, S. (1995b). Speech outcomes of the language-focused curriculum. In M. Rice & K. Wilcox (Eds.), *Building a language-focused curriculum for the preschool classroom: Volume 1. A foundation for lifelong communication* (pp. 171–180). Baltimore: Paul H. Brookes Publishing Co.

Wilcox, M. (1984). Developmental language disorders: Preschoolers. In A. Holland (Ed.), *Language disorders in children* (pp. 101–128). San Diego, CA: College-Hill Press.

Wilcox, M., Kouri, T., & Caswell, S. (1991). Early language intervention: A comparison of classroom and individual treatment. *American Journal of Speech-Language Pathology, 1,* 49–62.

Windsor, J. (1995). Language impairment and social competence. In M. Fey, J. Windsor, & S. Warren (Eds.), *Language intervention: Preschool through the elementary years* (pp. 213–240). Baltimore: Paul H. Brookes Publishing Co.

Withey, C. (1991). Creating an environment to facilitate communication growth within a language unit. *Child Language Teaching and Therapy, 7,* 115–126.

Yoder, P., & Davies, B. (1992). Do children with developmental delays use more frequent and diverse language in verbal routines? *American Journal of Mental Retardation, 97,* 197–208.

Yoder, P., Kaiser, A., & Alpert, C. (1991). An exploratory study of the interaction between language teaching methods and child characteristics. *Journal of Speech and Hearing Research, 34,* 155–167.

Yoder, P., Spruytenburg, H., Edwards, A., & Davies, B. (1995). Effect of verbal routine contexts and expansions on gains in the mean length of utterance in children with developmental delays. *Language, Speech, and Hearing Services in Schools, 26,* 21–32.

# Chapter 10

# Physical Therapy

## Beverly Rainforth and Pamela Roberts

### HISTORICAL AND CULTURAL BACKGROUND

Physical therapy practice in early intervention has been shaped by complex interactions between the development of the profession of physical therapy, evolution of various philosophical and societal views of disability and treatment, and passage of federal legislation that includes physical therapy among the services available to young children with disabilities and their families. In some ways, the development of physical therapy practice in early intervention and schools parallels changes in the general field. Physical therapy as a profession has a longer history of a more prescriptive relationship with medicine than with education. This culture of professional values, roles, and relationships has shaped and continues to shape professional education, practice guidelines, and the delivery of services to young children and their families.

### Origins of Physical Therapy

The profession of physical therapy originated in the United States during World War I when the Surgeon General established Reconstruction Aid Programs to rehabilitate soldiers injured in the war. Both physical and occupational therapy grew out of these Reconstruction Aid Programs. In the 1920s and 1930s, physical therapists turned to civilian needs, and, by World War II, the profession was well established. During these early years, physical therapists worked under the direction of physicians and provided primarily short-term rehabilitation for adults recovering from illness or injury.

Preparation of this chapter was supported, in part, by Grant No. HO86V40007 from the U.S. Department of Education to Allegheny-Singer Research Institute and State University of New York at Binghamton. The statements herein do not necessarily represent policies of the U.S. Department of Education, and no official endorsement should be inferred.

As early as the 1950s, the physical therapist's role in providing services to children was beginning to be defined outside of the curative, short-term rehabilitation model. Dr. Julius Richmond, former Surgeon General, described his vision for therapists as a part of interdisciplinary teams collaborating to treat the "whole child" with an emphasis on prevention (Richmond, 1950). Physical therapists became important additions to the team of individuals working to save lives and to minimize long-term disability for children and adults with polio in the 1950s. It was during this time that physical therapists became experts in specific muscle testing and muscle reeducation.

In the 1960s, pediatric physical therapy began a transition from the primarily orthopedic orientation for rehabilitation of children with polio to the "neurotherapeutic" orientation that became the model for serving children with a wide range of long-term disabilities (Stuberg & Harbourne, 1994). At the same time, a number of other areas of physical therapy practice evolved, expanding the scope of practice to include multiple areas and specializations. Throughout this period, physical therapy reflected a medical, problem-oriented philosophy that identified problems, goals, and interventions with the belief that surgery, physical treatments, and exercise would have a curative effect.

## Development of the Profession

Three major evolutions have marked the development of physical therapy as a profession: evolution from a prescriptive to a direct access base of practice; evolution from hospital-based practice settings to multiple settings, including private practice; and evolution of professional education and specialization with an increased research base generated by physical therapists. Each of these evolutions was guided and directed by the American Physical Therapy Association (APTA), the national organization that sets the guidelines and code of ethics for the practice of physical therapy and the evaluative criteria for the accreditation of programs that educate professionals in the field.

***Direct Access*** When the profession began, physical therapists worked under the direct supervision of physicians. All physical therapists needed a prescription from a physician to evaluate new patients and then could provide only those services specifically prescribed by a physician. This historical relationship between physical therapists and physicians within the traditional medical model dictated both the settings in which therapists worked and the autonomy of their day-to-day decision making. From 1935 through 1977, the APTA code of ethics and guide for professional conduct used language that supported a referral relationship with physicians, meaning that physicians would refer patients for physical therapy without developing explicit prescriptions (Myers, 1995).

Physical therapy practice is governed by state law, however, and, until the 1970s, most state practice acts did not allow physical therapists to practice without a physician's prescription. The profession began to develop its own identity as this prescriptive relationship gave way to the referral relationship and later to "direct access" (services without physician's referral). In 1957, Nebraska became the first state with a practice act to allow direct access, and California followed in 1968. In the 1970s, the models for evaluation and practice without referral evolved quickly after the World Confederation for Physical Therapy changed its codes of ethics (Myers, 1995). The number of states permitting direct access grew from 2 in 1968 to 30 in 1993, with most of these states changing their practice acts between 1985 and 1990. Fourteen additional states now allow physical therapists to evaluate a potential client before obtaining physician referral. Table 1 shows the referral requirement for physical therapy services in each state.

Because of these changes, physical therapy now can be a point of entry for consumers, including young children and their families, to receive services and referral to other members of a service team as appropriate. Direct access can reduce the time before services are available and improve access to support services such as early intervention, where the traditional medical model may not be the most efficient, accessible, or effective way to serve children and their families.

***Diversity in Practice Settings*** During the profession's early years, physical therapists practiced primarily in hospitals and occasionally in physicians' offices (Myers, 1995). As the profession developed, major shifts also occurred in the settings where physical therapists practice. From

Table 1. Referral requirement for physical therapy services in each state

| *States permitting direct access* | | | |
|---|---|---|---|
| Alaska | Iowa | Nebraska | South Dakota |
| Arizona | Kentucky[a] | Nevada | Texas[a] |
| California[a] | Maine[a] | New Hampshire[a] | Utah |
| Colorado | Maryland[a] | New Mexico[a] | Vermont |
| Florida[a] | Massachusetts | North Carolina[a] | Washington[a] |
| Idaho[a] | Minnesota[a] | North Dakota | West Virginia |
| Illinois[a] | Montana | Rhode Island[a] | Wisconsin[a] |

| *States permitting evaluation without referral but requiring physician referral for treatment* | | | |
|---|---|---|---|
| Connecticut | Kansas | New Jersey | Tennessee |
| District of Columbia | Lousiana | New York | Wyoming |
| Georgia | Michigan | Oklahoma | |
| Hawaii | Mississippi | Pennsylvania | |

| *States and territories requiring physician referral for evaluation and treatment* | | | |
|---|---|---|---|
| Alabama | Indiana | Oregon | Virgin Islands |
| Arkansas | Missouri | Puerto Rico | Virginia |
| Delaware | Ohio | South Carolina | |

[a]With certain restrictions.
Adapted from American Physical Therapy Association (1994).

1978 to 1993, the percentage of physical therapists practicing in hospitals decreased by 46% with corresponding increases in nontraditional settings such as home care, rehabilitation outpatient settings, and private practices (Myers, 1995).

Despite the dramatic increase in physical therapist practice outside of hospitals, only a small portion of physical therapists practice explicitly in pediatric areas of educationally related early intervention services, early childhood programs, and school programs. The APTA estimates that 7%–10% of practicing physical therapists work in pediatrics (Stuberg & McEwen, 1993). A 1990 survey conducted by the APTA Section on Pediatrics found that 46% of the 1,725 responding pediatric physical therapists practiced in school settings (Sweeney, Heriza, & Markowitz, 1994). Within the broad practice of physical therapy, however, only 3.5% of the therapists who responded to an APTA survey in 1993 indicated that schools were their primary practice site (Myers, 1995). Therefore, although a significant portion of pediatric physical therapists practice in school settings, these therapists still comprise a relatively small, specialized portion of the total profession.

***Professional Education and Specialization***   Important indicators of the development of a profession are the interrelated processes of self-determination in the scope of practice, self-accountability in documenting the efficacy of practice, and control of the accreditation process. Although the American Physiotherapy Association accredited physical therapy education programs from 1928 to 1936, the American Medical Association held this authority from 1936 to 1977. In 1977, APTA resumed shared responsibility, and in 1983, APTA became the sole accrediting agency for physical therapist and physical therapist assistant educational programs. Accreditation standards must ensure that physical therapists entering the profession have a basic level of competence to practice in the ever-expanding range of settings with increasing demands for autonomous critical decision making. Educational curricula burst with the growing knowledge base of the field across all settings and special interest areas. With increasing competition for time and emphasis, entry-level curricula must reflect the competencies necessary for the high percentage of physical therapists and physical therapist assistants who predictably will practice in settings outside of pediatrics.

Fortunately, greater autonomy has also corresponded with pursuit of advanced study and specialization within the field of physical therapy. Although entry-level programs must prepare generalists to provide physical therapy for clients with varied needs in diverse settings, many therapists acquire advanced degrees in areas of specialization and/or develop expertise through intense continuing education.

To recognize members' special interests and to encourage professional growth, APTA formed a Pediatric Section in 1974 and began a specialist certification program in 1978. In 1985, APTA certified the first pediatric specialist, to formally recognize physical therapists with advanced clinical knowledge, experience, and skills in pediatrics. By 1995, 79 physical therapists were certified as pediatric specialists, and more than 4,000 therapists belonged to the Pediatric Section (American Physical Therapy Association, personal communication, May 25, 1995). In addition, many physical therapists participate in continuing education related to pediatrics and read specialized journals such as *Pediatric Physical Therapy* and *Physical and Occupational Therapy in Pediatrics.*

The Maternal and Child Health (MCH) Bureau of the U.S. Department of Health and Human Services was a strong influence on the development of pediatric physical therapy as a specialty area. MCH provided leadership through funding for advanced training in pediatric physical therapy. The University Affiliated Programs, originally funded under MCH initiatives, provided an umbrella to promote coordinated research, professional education, and services for persons with developmental disabilities, further encouraging physical therapist specialization (Campbell, 1994).

Increased professionalization and specialization have certainly had positive effects on the field of physical therapy and the quality of services that therapists can provide. Specialization has offered physical therapists access to the knowledge base and opportunities to expand the research base for a steadily increasing focus on service-related issues for young children and their families. Although a common thread in all MCH programs has been an emphasis on interdisciplinary practice and research (Campbell, 1994), the trends toward professionalization and specialization have inadvertently worked against this emphasis: specialization both emanates from and promotes greater autonomy, which builds barriers to the collaborative interactions that are especially important in providing integrated services to young children and their families. Although the tensions between autonomy and collaboration remain, struggling with complexities of this kind is a natural part of a professional evolution.

The profession of physical therapy has evolved along several dimensions since the 1940s. As physical therapists develop greater professional identity, the older models and relationships are often viewed negatively as "physician-dominated." Another view is that physicians, who had provided direct services in all aspects of rehabilitation before World War I, engaged in role release to physical therapists. Today physical therapists struggle with many of the same dilemmas as physicians once did: whether to keep trying to provide all services through direct, hands-on treatment; to whom to release roles; how much training and supervision to provide; and when authority for decision making must be held, delegated, or simply shared with others recognized as having equal status. As pediatric physical therapists have considered these issues, some guidance has also come from outside the profession.

## OUTSIDE INFLUENCES ON PEDIATRIC PHYSICAL THERAPY

Current practice of pediatric physical therapy has been influenced by at least two separate developments: philosophical views of disability and intervention, and state and federal mandates.

### Philosophical Views of Disability and Intervention

The traditional medical model in which many physical therapists were prepared was a paternalistic model. Professionals were viewed as "experts" who advised patients and their families regarding the correct course of action, and compliance was expected. Patients often were defined in terms of their diagnosis or disability, as reflected in references to patients in terms such as "the CP child" or even "the CP."

These attitudes are changing; physical therapists recognize that a patient is a consumer of physical therapy services and the most important member of the team. The consumer is viewed as a person, not a diagnosis; when a diagnosis or disability is relevant to a discussion, the person is referred to as "a child with cerebral palsy." In early intervention programs, physical therapists now recognize that consumers of their services include both the child with a disability and family members. Physical therapists also recognize that, as consumers, families have the right to be active members of the decision-making team, and physical therapists have the responsibility both to encourage that participation and to respect the outcomes.

Operationalizing this philosophy of consumerism requires physical therapists to adopt other new views and strategies. For example, the basic philosophy of assessment and intervention is moving from a developmental neuromotor emphasis to a model of "disablement." Harris and Portela (1994) described one such model:

> Based on the World Health Organization classification system of function, a model of disablement developed by Nagi in the 1960's and recent work by Guccione, Haley's model of childhood disablement includes three measurement constructs that are important to functional assessment: 1) capability of the child to perform discrete functional skills; 2) the child's performance of functional activities; and 3) the child's ability to perform social, family and personal roles. (p. 136)

This major shift in how therapists approach assessment of both baseline performance and changes over time supports the model of integrated therapy services because therapists now consider movement within the context of function, rather than focus on movement (or disordered movement) as an isolated entity. In the same trend, physical therapists previously focused more on the diagnosis and corresponding "impairment" than on how a disability influences a person's lifestyle. By recognizing that many things besides a medical diagnosis affect the quality of life for children and their families, physical therapists are becoming empowered to measure those things that are important to quality of life for each individual child and family.

With reorganization of health services into preferred provider networks and with increasing pressure to show efficient and effective care for every dollar spent, "outcome accountability" has become the focus of health care in the 1990s. For physical therapists working in early intervention, this "efficiency model" has the potential either to depersonalize services or to enhance the consumer orientation. As informed participants, families can help define desired outcomes, such as decreased costs in the future, greater independence for their child with a disability, or opportunities for their child to have greater choices.

Every shift in philosophy takes time to become the representative philosophy of the profession. More physical therapists are being exposed to these new paradigms, but many still function with influences of the older medical diagnostic-curative model. Integrating the new philosophies into practice will require not just exposure to these beliefs but corresponding changes in how physical therapists plan and provide services. Some changes in practice that support integrated services in early intervention are outlined in the next paragraph.

First, teams need a shared vision of a desirable future for their consumers, that is, for each individual child with disabilities and his or her family. A family may indicate that a desirable future for their child would be to attend kindergarten at the neighborhood school, to have playmates in the neighborhood, and to participate in a variety of leisure activities with family and friends in the local community. The physical therapist, as part of the early intervention team, can then help the family identify abilities and supports necessary to make the vision a reality. Physical therapy services are provided to address the needs, goals, and priorities the family identifies, which might range from refining movements that enhance the child's feelings of success during play to determining therapeutic positioning that enables the child to use an augmented communication system. Adequacy of services is evaluated in terms of family satisfaction with both processes and outcomes. Although many physical therapists find this change in roles challenging at first, empowering consumers enables both consumers and therapists to experience new levels of satisfaction.

## State and Federal Mandates

In 1965, physical therapy was identified as a reimbursable service under Medicare and Medicaid legislation, increasing access for people who were elderly or poor (Social Security Amendments of 1965, PL 89-97). Physical therapy services were also covered by private insurance. As a result, children with developmental disabilities could receive physical therapy in a hospital setting or as an outpatient. Many services available to children crossed agencies and spanned both federal and state initiatives. At the state level, clinics for children with disabilities were often organized as "Services for Crippled Children" with different terminology, depending on the state in which the family received services.

Although children had greater access to services across these multiple agencies, interagency coordination was often weak and the medical orientation of Medicaid, state clinics, and health insurance had undesirable effects. Rather than reinforcing the shift toward functional outcomes and quality-of-life issues, eligibility for these services reinforced the medical diagnostic model where the "label" or diagnosis rather than the functional needs of the child and family determined the service program. These systems built their reimbursement frameworks around physician diagnosis and prescription as the base for intervention provided by the other professionals on the team. As early members of these teams, physical therapists were closely tied to the physician prescriptive process that the system reinforced following a medical model of services.

Nonprofit organizations, such as the United Cerebral Palsy Associations and Easter Seal Foundation, also expanded their programs for children during this time. Although not part of the mandated service system, these agencies followed the accepted medical model. An unfortunate result was that clinical services often dominated educational programs and therapy seemed to compete with, rather than support, the education of children with multiple needs.

**Physical Therapy as a Related Educational Service** In 1975, the Education for All Handicapped Children Act, PL 94-142, explicitly named physical therapy as a related service and part of the educational team mandated to plan and implement free, appropriate public education programs in least restrictive environments for all school-age children. Although this brought thousands of physical therapists into the schools, therapists typically removed children from classes to provide direct treatment, much as they had in hospitals and rehabilitation centers. This medical model was further strengthened in the schools by a growing practice of billing third-party payers for physical therapy, with regulations often allowing reimbursement for direct but not consultative services.

In response, the Pediatric Section of APTA published *Physical Therapy Practice in Educational Environments: Policies and Guidelines,* which promoted alternative service models (Martin, 1990). These guidelines clarify that, in special education, physical therapy is a "related educational service," intended to assist a child to derive greater benefit from the educational program than if physical therapy were not provided. In an educational program, therefore, physical therapists need to work closely with other members of the educational team to plan and implement a coordinated program. Physical therapy is viewed as a support to education rather than a medical service.

**Physical Therapy as a Related Service for Preschool Children** In 1986, the Education for All Handicapped Children Act was amended (PL 99-457) to establish services for infants, toddlers, and preschool children, and physical therapists expanded their services into a variety of early childhood settings, including child care centers and preschool programs. Because physical therapy is a related service for preschoolers, the same principles and guidelines apply as for school-age children. Coordination and integration of services with those of other disciplines are essential, and provision of services during routine preschool and child care activities is highly desirable. Routine activities provide physical therapists with countless opportunities to conduct assessment, develop interventions, and embed either direct or indirect services, such as during transitions between activities (mobility), positioning to participate in the activities (e.g., postural control, use of positioning equipment), and participating in play and self-care (Rainforth, York, & Macdonald, 1992). These routines also provide meaningful contexts for physical therapists to collaborate with other team members for comprehensive assessment, program planning, and instruction (Linder, 1990, 1993). When physical therapists find that sensorimotor needs cannot be addressed within existing routines, collaboration with early childhood educators usually results in creation of needed opportunities, often to the benefit of all children.

When physical therapy is a related educational service, there are two levels of service that might be written into a student's individualized education program (IEP) to meet his or her unique needs (Martin, 1990).

Indirect services involve the physical therapist and other members of the educational team exchanging information to improve the amount or quality of the student's participation. Indirect services may involve general consultation or specific child/procedure consultation. General consultation is aimed at information sharing and problem solving, such as determining a furniture arrangement that enables a child to move his or her wheelchair to all areas of the early childhood classroom more independently. Specific child/procedure consultation is aimed at providing more consistent intervention; thus, a teacher and teacher assistant might learn to apply a student's splints, teach him or her to bend to get toys from a shelf, and teach him or her to climb the ladder to the slide. The physical therapist would work directly with the student to assess his or her abilities and needs and to determine effective intervention strategies but would use treatment time to help classroom staff improve their skills. Special education teams place high priority on indirect services because students can work on sensorimotor skills many times each day, not just when the physical therapist is present.

Direct services are the hands-on treatment provided by the physical therapist. These are not necessarily provided in a separate room, however, and may be provided during free play activities, story time and dramatic play, center activities, snack, or a variety of other early childhood activities. The early childhood teacher and physical therapist can maximize opportunities to work on sensorimotor needs identified as priorities by making time to plan together. Whether physical therapy is provided through indirect or direct services, the relevance of physical therapy to the educational program is improved when assessment and treatment occur in the student's routine early childhood education activities (Martin, 1990).

***Physical Therapy Services for Infants and Toddlers*** Whereas the Education of the Handicapped Act Amendments of 1986 (PL 99-457) identified physical therapy as a related educational service for preschoolers, it authorized new roles with infants and toddlers. First, when the infant's or toddler's primary disability is sensorimotor, physical therapy might be the primary service rather than a support to education. When physical therapy is "the profession most immediately relevant to the infant's or toddler's or family's needs," a therapist might serve as service coordinator "responsible for the implementation of the plan and coordination with other agencies and persons" (20 U.S.C. § 1477(d)(6)). And when infants and toddlers have multiple needs, physical therapy is one of many services that must be coordinated and integrated, just as with older children. In any of these roles, physical therapists may provide some direct treatment to infants and toddlers, but their first priority is to work with families, caregivers, and other team members.

Two considerations distinguish physical therapy services for infants and toddlers from services for preschoolers and older children. First, the developmentally appropriate practice for infants and toddlers, even without disabilities, is to limit the number of adults who handle them each day (Bredekamp, 1991). This is even more important for infants and toddlers with disabilities, whose sensorimotor organization may leave them with poor coping mechanisms (Zeitlin & Williamson, 1994). Thus, physical therapy services are focused on family members and other care providers to prepare them as the "primary interventionists" for their infant or toddler.

The second consideration for infants and toddlers, even without disabilities, is that daily living routines are their curriculum (Bredekamp, 1991). Like preschool activities, daily living routines offer numerous opportunities for physical therapy assessment and intervention (Rainforth & Salisbury, 1988). For example, a physical therapist may note that during diapering, a toddler has spasticity in his or her trunk and legs and is unable to cooperate by lifting his or her legs, rolling, and sitting. After discussing the situation with the toddler's parent and child care provider, the physical therapist works with them to try other positions for diapering (e.g., sidelying), to normalize tone, and to teach the toddler how to move his or her legs and trunk to help with diapering. Because diapering occurs many times each day, the embedded interventions will occur frequently, increasing the likely benefit for the child. Daily routines are important contexts for identifying and responding to family and caregiver needs, teaching primary interventionists, and integrating physical therapy with services of other disciplines. For families and other caregivers, this approach allows infants and toddlers to participate more successfully in daily living activities and reduces the need to add "treatment sessions" to already busy schedules. Although these roles and strategies may be new for many physical therapists, they have been advocated as best practices with infants and toddlers since the early 1970s (see, e.g., Patterson et al., 1976).

The APTA Task Force on Early Intervention (1991) has developed a document entitled *Competencies for Physical Therapists in Early Intervention.* These competencies address traditional areas such as screening, assessment, development of treatment objectives, and treatment, as applied to children from birth to 5 years. There are also competencies for knowledge of family systems theory and family-focused services, law, research, and administration related to physical therapy in early intervention. One area applies specifically to physical therapists as team members and includes the following competencies:

> 8.6 Demonstrate skill in formal and informal teaching of students, families, paraprofessionals, and professionals concerning physical therapy in early intervention.
> 8.8 Demonstrate the ability to monitor the implementation of physical therapy recommendations by other team members.
> 8.12 Demonstrate the ability to relinquish a domain specific role during the transdisciplinary process.

These competencies reaffirm the importance of physical therapists working with teams in nontraditional ways that support integrated early intervention services.

In 1990, the Individuals with Disabilities Education Act (IDEA) (PL 101-476) reauthorized PL 99-457, reasserting the importance of physical therapy as a service in early intervention and educational programs. In fact, Gandy (1993) noted that "pediatric physical therapy is the only specialty area of [physical therapy] practice governed by federal legislation" (p. 129). Physical therapists have been increasingly responsive to special education mandates, critically examining their service models to maximize treatment effectiveness and efficient use of resources.

## PHYSICAL THERAPY PRACTICE AND INTEGRATED SERVICES

Most aspects of pediatric physical therapy are conducive to integrated services. Often, however, providing integrated services requires that therapists consider creative alternatives to traditional practices and role definitions.

### Relationship to Other Disciplines

Physical therapists have skills and responsibilities that complement and overlap with many other disciplines. The growing shortage of physical therapists in almost all service settings and geographic areas makes it essential that all physical therapy services be maximized. Table 2 shows several areas of need and some disciplines that may contribute to addressing those needs. When referring to this table, it is important to realize that disciplines often contribute different perspectives on one area of need. For example, an important daily living activity for a young child with disabilities is mealtime. A physical therapist may focus on sitting posture and head control; an occupational therapist may focus on use of utensils; a speech therapist may focus on oral-motor skills for eating and communication skills to indicate preferences; and an early childhood educator may focus on social aspects of mealtime or steps in the mealtime routine. Family members have important contributions to the team also because they provide important information about eating habits and feedback about the utility of various methods during typical mealtimes.

To use team members most effectively, it is important to determine the child's and family's specific needs, and then determine who can best address those needs, recognizing that skills vary among professionals within the same discipline. Physical therapists' skills vary tremendously depending on initial preparation, work experiences, and continuing education. One physical therapist may not have the skills to address any of the previously mentioned needs at mealtime; another may have skills in positioning, oral-motor aspects of eating, and using utensils. Because occupational therapists and physical therapists have many overlapping skills, early intervention programs may adopt a "developmental therapist" model in which one therapist serves as primary therapist for a team and the other therapist serves as consultant. This approach maximizes use of available staff and reduces the number of team members who must coordinate on a daily basis. Once again, it is the team, rather than the physical therapist or any other professional, that determines who assumes responsibility for which aspects of each child's program.

### Physical Therapist Roles and Role Release

Regardless of an individual's specific skills, all physical therapists have responsibilities for certain roles, such as assessment, treatment planning, ongoing evaluation of treatment effectiveness, and revision of the treatment plan in

Table 2. Needs addressed by physical therapy and other disciplines

| Area of need | Other disciplines |
| --- | --- |
| Gross motor development | |
| Birth–18 months | Occupational therapy<br>Nursing<br>Education |
| 18 months–6 years | Occupational therapy<br>Education |
| Daily living activities | Occupational therapy<br>Education<br>Speech therapy (eating)<br>Rehabilitation counseling |
| Adaptations | Occupational therapy<br>Rehabilitation engineering<br>Orthotics and prosthetics |

response to evaluation. In early intervention settings, physical therapists also have important roles in prescribing equipment, consultation, and training. Each of these activities, whether a direct or indirect service to a child, is performed directly by the physical therapist. It is in these activities that therapists draw on their years of education and experience, their intuition, and clinical judgments to make decisions. In the process, therapists share their thoughts with other team members, and children undoubtedly benefit from this shared knowledge. In general, however, these roles are not formally released to other members of the team. For example, during a team assessment, a physical therapist could point out that a child cannot be credited with "stands at rail" because he or she cannot stand in the absence of strong extensor tone. Although this information is useful to others, and may be generalizable, it is hardly sufficient preparation for others to conduct the next annual review without the physical therapist or to assess other children.

Although much has been written about "role release" (see also Chapter 2), this strategy usually applies only to use of intervention strategies. In most instances, physical therapists can teach parents and other team members to use specific intervention strategies safely and effectively with specific children and in specific situations. Sometimes a therapist may have difficulty specifying which strategies to teach others, such as when a child is learning new skills quite rapidly and thus the corresponding intervention is changing rapidly. Even in these cases, the physical therapist can usually identify a core set of handling skills to teach others for application in daily routines. Physical therapists often use so-called specialized techniques (e.g., myofascial release) in functional contexts and teach these techniques to others, to reduce the day-to-day influence of disability and to provide the child with more opportunities to learn motor control. Ultimately, however, these are team decisions, not decisions made unilaterally by a physical therapist. For example, if the physical therapist believes that an effective strategy is too complex to teach others, the therapist still has a responsibility to the child and other team members to determine ways the child can experience similar success in the therapist's absence. Similarly, if a therapist feels that equipment such as therapy balls or net swings belongs only in a therapy room, teams must discuss how the same benefits can be achieved in integrated settings using other strategies or materials. In some instances, a team may conclude that the equipment was never really needed; in others, a team may arrange for more equipment in a classroom, to be enjoyed by all children.

Physical therapists may also have concerns about safety related to role release, particularly when children are medically fragile. For example, a physical therapist may feel that it is too dangerous for others to exercise a child with severe osteoporosis. However, without teaching others to move the child safely, the child is in danger of injury during routine care such as dressing and positioning. In most instances, the potential benefits to a child outweigh the dangers, especially when the therapist uses generally accepted treatment procedures, develops a written plan, and provides systematic instruction to the person who will implement the plan. In situations where a physical therapist may see a dilemma in sharing specialized knowledge and skills with other members of the early intervention team, the physical therapist has responsibility for bringing this dilemma to the team. Only in this way can dilemmas be resolved through informed judgment by the team members who *share* responsibility for the child's program.

## Legal and Ethical Codes

Questions are sometimes raised about the legality and ethics of physical therapists, as licensed professionals, engaging in role release. Physical therapists are licensed by the states in which they practice, and although state practice acts vary somewhat, most specify that only a licensed physical therapist can claim to provide physical therapy services. Therefore, an early childhood special education program could not claim that its teacher, trained and supervised by a physical therapist, was fulfilling the IEP requirement for 2 hours per week of physical therapy, even if the teacher provided outstanding sensorimotor intervention. Only a physical therapist can fulfill that requirement; however, that time might be spent consulting with and training various team members. Some practice acts specify techniques that a physical therapist cannot perform (e.g., acupuncture), but a review of practice acts provided by 43 states and 2 territories reveals that none specify techniques that can be performed only by a physical therapist (Rainforth, 1996).

The APTA (1991) has set a code of ethics for physical therapists, found in Table 3, and a guide for professional conduct, which briefly expands on each of the principles in the code. Although binding only APTA members, the standards set through the association have more broadly influenced standards of practice and legal regulations. Review of the code and guide reveals considerable support and guidance for physical therapists working in teams.

Overall, the principles require therapists to "be responsive and mutually supportive of colleagues and associates" (APTA, 1991, 1.1.c.p). Principle 5, guidelines for fees, advises therapists to "attempt to ensure that providers, agencies, or other employers adopt physical therapy fee schedules that are reasonable and that encourage access to necessary services" (APTA, 1991, 5.1.c.). By making recommendations for physical therapy consultation and management of services, when appropriate, rather than always direct, individual services, physical therapists can influence important decisions that affect both access to and the cost of services. Under Principle 7, the guidelines allow for and encourage a consumer advocacy and protection role. This role is especially important when teams consider families as contributing and valued members of teams. Physical therapists also have a responsibility to inform and educate families of children with disabilities about the scope and limitations of the physical therapist's role.

Table 3. Physical therapy code of ethics

| | |
|---|---|
| *Principle 1:* | Physical therapists respect the rights and dignity of all individuals. |
| *Principle 2:* | Physical therapists comply with the laws and regulations governing the practice of physical therapy. |
| *Principle 3:* | Physical therapists accept responsibility for the exercise of sound judgment. |
| *Principle 4:* | Physical therapists maintain and promote high standards for physical therapy practice, education, and research. |
| *Principle 5:* | Physical therapists seek remuneration for their services that is deserved and reasonable. |
| *Principle 6:* | Physical therapists provide accurate information to the consumer about the profession and about those services they provide. |
| *Principle 7:* | Physical therapists accept the responsibility to protect the public and the profession from unethical, incompetent, or illegal acts. |
| *Principle 8:* | Physical therapists participate in efforts to address the health needs of the public. |

From American Physical Therapy Association. (1991). *Code of ethics and guide for professional conduct.* Alexandria, VA: Author; reprinted by permission.

Thus, the teamwork and role release required to provide integrated early intervention services are allowed, even encouraged, by legal and ethical standards. Physical therapists still face numerous challenges in achieving this goal, however.

## BARRIERS TO INTEGRATED PRACTICES

In a study of early childhood special educators, speech-language pathologists, occupational therapists, and physical therapists working with young children with disabilities, physical therapists had the lowest preference for integrated models of service, regardless of family preference or child characteristics (McWilliam & Bailey, 1994). Another study of physical therapists working with school-age children revealed significant discrepancies between actual and ideal practice of a team approach in student evaluation, service delivery, team dynamics, and administrative support (Effgen & Klepper, 1994). In this study, 46% reported they always or usually worked with students in a separate therapy room (outside the classroom), but only 25% thought this was ideal. Only 39% reported always or usually having regular team meetings, although 91% thought it would be ideal; and only 10% reported their school district provided training in interdisciplinary teamwork, while 86% considered that ideal. These findings are discouraging and contrary to practices advocated by professional literature and by the Pediatric Section of APTA. Undoubtedly, some of these attitudes reflect the historical and cultural background of the discipline. Other factors seem to contribute to this continued preference for isolated physical therapy services. Some of these barriers are now discussed, along with progress made in the 1990s.

## Professional Preparation for Teamwork

The majority of today's physical therapists were prepared to work in multidisciplinary teams in medical settings (see, e.g., Rainforth, 1985). The medical terminology routinely used by physical therapists has further served to categorize physical therapists as medical professionals and sometimes to alienate them from families and other team members. Even when therapists report that they are well prepared to function in a team, those beliefs are not always supported by behavior in actual work settings.

The interactions of therapists who appear to model integrated services often include establishing shared visions, setting goals that are consumer and family centered and congruent with those of other professionals, sharing roles with teammates, and overlapping roles and responsibilities with teammates (Giangreco, 1995). The definition of a *master clinician* is broadening to include not just those therapists who generate and choose alternative and successful strategies specific to individuals and their situations, but also those therapists who seek out and use interdisciplinary and transdisciplinary strategies to provide coordinated, congruent, effective, and efficient services.

## Generalist Versus Specialist Preparation

Entry-level physical therapy education programs face the challenge of preparing students to 1) serve a range of populations, from pediatric to geriatric; 2) address a range of needs, including orthopedic, neurologic, and cardiopulmonary; and 3) work in a range of settings, including acute care hospitals, extended care facilities, specialized clinics, community health, and private practice. Accreditation standards for entry-level programs are extensive, requiring a strong foundation in basic and applied sciences and physical therapy methods using a variety of modalities. New developments in all areas of physical therapy continually compete for space in the curriculum. Pediatric physical therapy is a relatively small and specialized area, and practice in educational settings is a smaller subspecialty, one of very few in a nonmedical setting. Furthermore, there is a shortage of pediatric physical therapy faculty, limiting advocacy for and ability to teach this specialized content (Stuberg & McEwen, 1993). Therefore, it is unlikely that pediatrics will assume a more prominent position or receive a greater allocation of resources relative to other areas of physical therapy in the entry-level curriculum in the near future.

Given the status of pediatrics, it is encouraging to find that 93% of entry-level programs require coursework in pediatrics (Cherry & Knutson, 1993). Most of these programs reported including at least 11–20 contact hours in each of three areas: child development, pediatric disorders, and management of pediatric conditions, with some programs offering more than 60 hours in management of pediatric conditions. Programs typically had only 2–4 hours of laboratory experience in pediatrics, but 85% of programs offered a clinical affiliation in pediatrics. Unfortunately, affiliations in pediatrics are limited (Gandy, 1993), and a program with a strong pediatric component may also promote experience in settings where children with disabilities are isolated from children without disabilities (Turner, 1993).

Because few entry-level programs have pediatric affiliations, and because many physical therapists without specialized training or experience in pediatrics fill vacancies in early intervention, the APTA Task Force on Early Intervention (1991) advised that "new graduate or physical therapy generalists must work under the preceptorship of a therapist experienced in pediatrics until basic pediatric competencies are achieved" (p. 77). Staff development in integrated early intervention programs may play an important role in fulfilling both the immediate need for pediatric physical therapists and the need to prepare future faculty for entry-level physical therapy education programs.

Although the ability of entry-level programs to increase the content to explicitly focus more time on pediatric issues may be discouraging, there is optimism that the general trends of education will support many of the skills necessary for integrated related services. Pediatrics is not the only arena where the need for more collaborative decisions is growing and where the roles of the patient and family have increasing contributions to the vision and focus for intervention for that individual. Role release is being promoted in geriatric facilities and inpatient rehabilitation units as they work to effectively and efficiently provide integrated services. Strategies such as activity-based planning and shared goals with goal matrixes are being adopted in these settings to coordinate multiple interventions. Educational planning documents from APTA show increasing attention to basic education on issues that have been in the limelight in pediatrics since the 1970s. Increasing emphases on communication, cultural sensitivity, delegation of physical therapy–related services, collaboration with diverse individuals, alternative scheduling, and natural context functional outcomes for physical therapists in all practice settings will support the preparation of physical therapists who can cross the medical model gap and provide educationally relevant services to young children and their families (APTA Education Division, 1995).

## Shortage of Physical Therapists

There is a national shortage of physical therapists, not just in pediatrics or educational settings, but with all consumer populations and in all service settings. Although many think these shortages will not be remedied soon, some believe that the environment of health care reform through managed care and reorganization toward patient-centered teams, rather than discipline-specific departments, is slowing the rise in need. It is unlikely that merely raising salaries or using other recruitment and retention strategies will increase the number of therapists in pediatrics in the near future. Therefore, programs must focus on using available expertise more efficiently. This chapter has described several strategies to increase efficiency without sacrificing quality of services. One approach is for physical therapists to coordinate and integrate their methods with those from other disciplines, with other team members accepting responsibility for daily implementation of intervention plans. Another approach is to identify areas of overlap between physical therapy and other disciplines so other team members might fulfill roles traditionally assigned to physical therapists. Teams cannot afford to have rigid territorial boundaries drawn around the practice of physical therapy or other disciplines; rather, flexibility needs to characterize decisions about who provides services and how. Finally, when physical therapy is a low priority relative to other needs, families and their teams would benefit from focusing on the higher priorities rather than diluting the impact of all services (Giangreco, 1995). In addition, programs could devise ways to support clinical education opportunities for therapists in early intervention, early childhood education, and school system practice settings. The presence of more practicum opportunities for therapists, although requiring a commitment to the clinical educational role, may in the long run increase the number of therapists comfortable with a position providing integrated related services.

### Role of Physical Therapist Assistants

Beginning in the 1970s, the APTA authorized training of physical therapist assistants (PTAs). The specific legal recognition of the physical therapist assistant differs from state to state, with some states requiring licensure of the PTA and other states simply defining the role through statutory language in physical therapist licensure. PTAs are trained primarily at the associate degree level and work under the supervision of a physical therapist in the delivery of physical therapy services. Their duties include assisting the physical therapist in implementing treatment programs according to the plan of care, training patients in exercises and activities of daily living, conducting treatments, using special equipment, administering modalities and other treatment procedures, and reporting to the physical therapist on the patient's responses (Commission on Accreditation in Physical Therapy Education, 1992). The PTA's role varies with the setting but includes team interactions as delegated and coordinated through the physical therapist.

Because of the shortage of physical therapists, many educational programs have looked to PTAs to fulfill some physical therapist responsibilities. PTAs work under supervision of physical therapists, who conduct initial and follow-up evaluations and design and modify interventions. The overall focus in PTA education is to prepare PTAs who, as educated clinicians, can implement a plan of care designed by a physical therapist, regardless of area of specialization (Zaslow & Benedetto, 1994). The Draft Position Statement on the Utilization of Physical Therapist Assistants in the Provision of Pediatric Physical Therapy asserts that "physical therapist assistants can be appropriately utilized in pediatric practice settings with the exception of the medically unstable, such as neonates in the NICU" (APTA Section on Pediatrics, 1995, p. 14). In a center-based early intervention program, a PTA might implement interventions recommended by the physical therapist, for example, by facilitating motor participation of a toddler with severe cerebral palsy during a weekly play group, or by helping plan and implement the gross motor program at a preschool that includes several children with sensorimotor needs.

Curricula for PTA programs include areas directly related to the pediatric population. Normal and abnormal motor development, developmental milestones, basic neurophysiology, transfer training, gait training, and activities of daily living are identified by faculty as evidence of preparation to practice under the direction of a physical therapist in pediatric settings, including early intervention and schools. Some of the same core areas of curriculum lacking for physical therapists are lacking for PTAs: family systems, collaborative teaming, cultural systems, and specific information on mandated educational services identified under IDEA.

The use of the paraprofessional in all areas of practice is increasingly considered a strategy both to remedy the shortage of providers and to offer less expensive yet more effective services. Services for young children and their families are likely to be part of this trend. The challenge will be to integrate the use of the assistant into service models that support the educationally appropriate, collaborative, functional, and contextually relevant services. As in any situation where PTAs are used, the responsibility for the effectiveness of the service will in large part be determined by the skill with which the physical therapist delegates, monitors, and supervises the contributions of the assistant.

## Traditional Referral and Reimbursement Models

Payment for services in the traditional medical model often tied reimbursement, and therefore service access, to physician referral for services. In some states, physical therapists are still required, by law, to have a physician referral before providing services. In states that do not yet have "direct access," this reimbursement relationship often complicates and increases costs of physical therapy services. Additionally, although not required by state practice acts, reimbursement rules and regulations for Medicare, Medicaid, and traditional third-party insurance programs often require a physician referral to qualify for payments. Even stricter rules and regulations exist in managed care settings where specified "gatekeepers" dictate the number, type, and frequency of reimbursable services. In some service settings, physical therapists are the only members of the team with this professional constraint. For some settings and agencies, reimbursement for physical therapy services is contingent on the physical therapist providing direct hands-on treatment, which limits the scope of available services and supports. These constraints have created frustration among consumers, physical therapists, other professionals on their teams, and employers. Fortunately, changes are under way in these systems.

The number of states seeking and gaining direct access for physical therapy services by consumers increases each year. In states with direct access, the physical therapist's increased autonomy has not decreased interactions with other health professionals. Instead, interdisciplinary collaboration has increased to include relevant referral both to physical therapists from physicians and others, and from physical therapists to other health, education, and social service providers.

Patient education, home evaluations, and adaptive equipment consultations are now listed as reimbursable interventions, despite an insurance system that is still oriented primarily toward fees for medical services. Although the number of consumers and of therapists working in managed care, health maintenance organizations, and prospective payment systems is increasing, a full transition away from the medical model, crisis intervention, and fee-for-service system has yet to occur. Change is slow. The APTA is working to increase the scope of reimbursable services. Concurrently, studies are helping identify the patterns of physical therapy service with outcomes correlated with decreased health care costs. Minimizing the frequency and duration of services while still reaching the consumer's, family's, and society's goals for independence and maximum functional abilities is a goal of the profession.

With the advent of educational payment for physical therapy as a related service under PL 94-142, physical therapists' reliance on medically oriented insurance reimbursement diminished. Unfortunately, a rising trend of school systems' billing public and private medical insurance providers confuses the educational versus medical benefits of physical therapy and hinders broader interdisciplinary and transdisciplinary approaches in these nontraditional settings. Professional organizations and consumer advocacy groups at the federal and state levels have begun to identify strategies to address this problem. The state of Iowa, for example, has changed Medicaid rules and guidelines so that the IEP is the sole documentation required for services in the school setting. Other states are considering similar changes. A continuing issue is whether such changes will be written to include the indirect and consultative services that are so important in educational settings.

## Accountability

Accountability is both a barrier and a solution for many of the issues raised in this chapter. Pediatric physical therapists must document provision of services for third-party payers, for IEPs and individualized family service plans, and for families and other team members. However, there has been confusion between documentation that a service has been provided and that the service is effective. This confusion has encouraged physical therapists in early intervention services to maintain traditional service models because of the ease of documenting provision of episodic therapy service (e.g., 30 minutes, three times per week).

Although it is still necessary to document that children receive the recommended type and amount of service, much greater emphasis is now placed on the outcomes of services. Early intervention teams are becoming more skilled at identifying functional outcomes that incorporate perspectives of physical therapists, developing intervention plans that embed methods used by physical therapists, and conducting ongoing assessment of both quantitative and qualitative aspects of child performance. In the process, physical therapists are learning to augment their intuition (which has guided decision making for many years) with careful analysis of children's sensory and movement abilities and needs and to organize their treatments into systematic instruction (Campbell & Stewart, 1986; Watts, 1985). These changes have been made possible through a team approach and have resulted in better support for integrated early intervention services.

Physical therapists and the teams to which they belong are accountable for helping children achieve one set of shared goals and must critically examine past practices with regard to their effectiveness in promoting child outcomes.

## CONCLUSIONS

The profession of physical therapy originated as a medical service and still retains many vestiges of this medical model. Since the 1970s, and with leadership from APTA, many physical therapists have specialized in pediatrics and adopted new roles as educational team members in a variety of school and early intervention settings. Although entry-level physical therapy curricula help prepare therapists for these and other consumer-oriented roles, advanced programs and continuing education offer pediatric therapists growing opportunities for specialization.

Although physical therapy still faces barriers to the practice of integrated early intervention services, the profession is examining past practices and developing new strategies that address current needs. Increasing comfort with role release and recognition that the practice of physical therapy for young children with disabilities overlaps with many other disciplines have allowed physical therapists to assume a variety of primary and support roles in early intervention teams. As a result, physical therapists now participate in teams that are more individualized, child and family centered, and highly effective, all while using resources more efficiently.

## REFERENCES

American Physical Therapy Association. (1991). *Code of ethics and guide for professional conduct.* Alexandria, VA: Author.

American Physical Therapy Association. (1994). *State licensure reference guide.* Alexandria, VA: Author.

APTA Education Division. (1995, February). *Coalitions for consensus: A normative model of professional education (draft document).* Alexandria, VA: American Physical Therapy Association.

APTA Section on Pediatrics.(1995, March). Draft position statement on the utilization of physical therapist assistants in the provision of pediatric physical therapy. *Section on Pediatrics Newsletter, 5*(1), 14–16.

APTA Task Force on Early Intervention. (1991). Competencies for physical therapists in early intervention. *Pediatric Physical Therapy, 3*(2), 77–80.

Bredekamp, S. (1991). *Developmentally appropriate practice in early childhood programs serving children from birth through age 8.* Washington, DC: National Association for the Education of Young Children.

Campbell, P.H., & Stewart, B. (1986). Measuring changes in movement skills with infants and young children with handicaps. *Journal of The Association for Persons with Severe Handicaps, 11*(3), 153–161.

Campbell, S.K. (1994). Perspective: The maternal and child health connection. *Pediatric Physical Therapy, 6*(3), 154–156.

Cherry, D.B., & Knutson, L.M. (1993). Curriculum structure and content in pediatric physical therapy: Results of a survey of entry-level physical therapy programs. *Pediatric Physical Therapy, 5*(3), 109–116.

Commission on Accreditation in Physical Therapy Education. (1992). *Revision of the evaluative criteria for accreditation of education programs for the preparation of physical therapist assistants (second draft).* Alexandria, VA: Author.

Education for All Handicapped Children Act of 1975, PL 94-142. (August 23, 1977). Title 20, U.S.C. §§ 1400 et seq.: *U.S. Statutes at Large, 89,* 773–796.

Education of the Handicapped Act Amendments of 1986, PL 99-457. (October 8, 1986). Title 20, U.S.C. §§ 1400 et seq.: *U.S. Statutes at Large, 100,* 1145–1177.

Effgen, S.K., & Klepper, S.E. (1994). Survey of physical therapy practice in educational settings. *Pediatric Physical Therapy, 6*(1), 15–21.

Gandy, J.S. (1993). Survey of academic programs: Exploring issues related to pediatric clinical education. *Pediatric Physical Therapy, 5*(3), 128–133.

Giangreco, M. (1995). Related services decision-making: A foundational component of effective education for students with disabilities. *Physical and Occupational Therapy in Pediatrics, 15*(2), 47–67.

Harris, S.R., & Portela, A.L.M. (1994). Research in pediatric physical therapy: Past, present and future. *Pediatric Physical Therapy, 6*(3), 133–138.

Individuals with Disabilities Education Act of 1990, PL 101-476. (October 30, 1990). Title 20, U.S.C. §§ 1400 et seq.: *U.S. Statutes at Large, 104,* 1103–1151.

Linder, T. (1990). *Transdisciplinary play-based assessment: A functional approach to working with young children.* Baltimore: Paul H. Brookes Publishing Co.

Linder, T. (1993). *Transdisciplinary play-based intervention: Guidelines for developing a meaningful curriculum for young children.* Baltimore: Paul H. Brookes Publishing Co.

Martin, K. (Ed.). (1990). *Physical therapy practice in educational environments: Policies and guidelines.* Alexandria, VA: Pediatric Section, American Physical Therapy Association.

McWilliam, R.A., & Bailey, D.B. (1994). Predictors of service delivery models in center based early intervention. *Exceptional Children, 61*(1), 56–71.

Myers, R.S. (1995). Historical perspective, assumptions, and ethical considerations for physical therapy practice. *Saunders manual of physical therapy practice.* Philadelphia: W.B. Saunders.

Patterson, E.G., D'Wolf, N., Hutchison, D.J., Lowry, M., Schilling, M., & Siepp, J. (1976). *Staff development handbook: A resource for the transdisciplinary process.* New York: United Cerebral Palsy Associations of America, Inc.

Rainforth, B. (1985). *Collaborative efforts in the preparation of physical therapists and teachers of students with severe handicaps.* Unpublished doctoral dissertation, University of Illinois, Urbana-Champaign.

Rainforth, B. (1996). *Analysis of physical therapy practice acts: Implications for therapists in educational settings.* Manuscript in preparation.

Rainforth, B., & Salisbury, C.L. (1988). Functional home programs: A model for therapists. *Topics in Early Childhood Special Education, 7*(4), 33–45.

Rainforth, B., York, J., & Macdonald, C. (1992). *Collaborative teams for students with severe disabilities: Integrating therapy and educational services.* Baltimore: Paul H. Brookes Publishing Co.

Richmond, J.B. (1950). The role of the physical therapist in the total care of the child. *Physical Therapy Review, 30*(9), 371–374.

Social Security Amendments of 1965, PL 89-97. (July 30, 1965). Title I, U.S.C. §§ 401–425: *U.S. Statutes at Large, 79,* 329–339.

Stuberg, W., & Harbourne, R. (1994). Theoretical practice in pediatric physical therapy: Past, present, and future considerations. *Pediatric Physical Therapy, 6*(3), 119–125.

Stuberg, W., & McEwen, I. (1993). Faculty and clinical education models of entry-level preparation in pediatric physical therapy. *Pediatric Physical Therapy, 5*(3), 123–127.

Sweeney, J.K., Heriza, C.B., & Markowitz, R. (1994). The changing profile of pediatric physical therapy: A 10 year analysis of clinical practice. *Pediatric Physical Therapy, 6*(3), 113–118.

Turner, D. (1993). A model for entry-level pediatric physical therapy education. *Pediatric Physical Therapy, 5*(3), 117–122.

Watts, N.T. (1985). Decision analysis: A tool for improving physical therapy practice and education. In S.L. Wolf (Ed.), *Clinical decision making in physical therapy* (pp. 7–23). Philadelphia: F.A. Davis Co.

Zaslow, L., & Benedetto, M. (1994). Is the PTA an untapped resource in pediatric physical therapy? *PT Magazine of Physical Therapy, 2*(3), 52–54.

Zeitlin, S., & Williamson, G.G. (1994). *Coping in young children: Early intervention practices to enhance adaptive behavior and resilience.* Baltimore: Paul H. Brookes Publishing Co.

# Chapter 11

# Occupational Therapy

## Winnie Dunn

Occupational therapy began during World War I as an effort to rehabilitate disabled soldiers and civilian patients (Willard & Spackman, 1978); the workers were originally called reconstructive aides. These individuals recognized that those injured during the war needed something more than a patch for their wounds; they needed to have something useful to do. The reconstructive aides provided a means for these individuals to recapture purpose in their lives. This simple concept forms the basis for the profession: Individuals need to engage in purposeful activities. Purposeful activities give meaning to an individual's existence and create a framework for organizing life.

Occupational therapy principles and services expanded beyond those with physical impairments to include those with mental illness shortly after World War I. Services continued to expand within these two primary areas through World War II. In the postwar period, services for individuals with developmental disabilities and pediatric disorders were developed; this emphasis continues today.

Many federal legislative mandates address the need for occupational therapy within their rules and regulations (e.g., PLs 94-142, 99-457). As laws are passed and implemented, the scope of occupational therapy expands and is clarified in relation to the needs of many individuals.

## IMPACT OF LEGISLATION ON
## SERVICES FOR CHILDREN AND FAMILIES

Most programs available to children and families today have evolved from the advocacy, legislative, and litigation efforts that occurred in the 1970s (Meyen, 1982). The actions of the 1970s, however, were made possible by efforts that began around the turn of the 20th century (Hanft, 1991; Meyen, 1982).

### Early Legislative Influences

During the 1800s, persons with disabilities were treated benevolently, with communities providing facilities to care for them (Finch, 1985). In the early

1900s, communities viewed persons with disabilities as defective, which led to the promulgation of large institutions to house them (Hanft, 1991).

In 1912, the federal government established the Children's Bureau, whose purpose was to investigate problems of childhood such as infant mortality, child labor, aid requirements for mothers of young children, and juvenile delinquency (Hanft, 1991). By the 1930s, many mothers were dying in childbirth, and 1% of all children born had disabilities. Congress passed the Social Security Act in 1935 (PL 74-271). Title V of this act provided funds for programs for both mothers and children (i.e., the beginning of maternal and child health programs and Crippled Children's Services). By the 1960s, the Social Security Act also contained Title XIX, the Medicaid provisions, which provided support for medical needs (Hanft, 1991).

A number of factors influenced public policies during the middle of the 20th century (Menzler, 1986). With veterans returning from war, new treatments needed to be developed and implemented. Additionally, as these individuals were being rehabilitated, the public began to view disabilities differently. The civil rights movement also contributed to a changing perception about individuals with disabilities as those deserving rights to learn, work, and live in the community. In addition to the civil rights movement, advocacy groups increased attention given to individual's rights. Perhaps most importantly, the economy expanded greatly during the 1960s, providing the opportunity for many public programs to be funded.

All of these early legislative actions provided the environment in which Americans were reconceiving their beliefs about individuals with disabilities and the contributions they could make to society. These were important milestones that enabled mid-1990s initiatives such as interdisciplinary services, family-centered care, and full inclusion to be possible.

## Public School Mandates

During the 1960s and early 1970s, Congress addressed the need for children with disabilities to have an education. The civil rights and rehabilitation movements had provided the opportunity to change beliefs that otherwise would have prohibited any consideration of early intervention or educational services for children with disabilities.

With the passage of PL 94-142, the Education for All Handicapped Children Act of 1975, Congress established that all children, regardless of disability, are entitled to a free, appropriate public education. This act addressed all children of school age and mandated not only educational services but also related services, including occupational therapy.

This mandate placed occupational therapy services into an entirely new arena for practice. Occupational therapists previously had served children within medical environments such as children's hospitals and residential care facilities. Within the medical model, professionals act as experts, identifying the problem through special procedures and designing and implementing a treatment plan based on professional judgments. Professionals providing services within the medical model typically expect the individual to comply with the treatment designed by the professional. Professionals make decisions based on their expertise, frequently with little consideration for variables such as motivation, resources, or environmental supports. The professional typically decides what is best for the individual and family, and there are common protocols for particular diagnoses and problems.

The passage of PL 94-142 led to many reforms in the service provision approaches and strategies classically used by occupational therapists. The educational environment has a different philosophy and beliefs about how children are served, and so has pushed occupational therapists to reconceptualize their services within the educational model. In this model, the providers consider what services will support students in their educational endeavors. Services are best provided within the context of actual learning experiences rather than as a clinical treatment performed outside of the school routine. The section on service provision in this chapter further describes best practices within the educational model.

## Early Intervention Legislation

During the first 10 years of enactment of PL 94-142, it became clear that it was not in children's best interests to wait to serve them until they were of school age. Additionally, more infants and toddlers were surviving because of advanced technology but needed services throughout their early development (Mather & Weinstein, 1988). Thus, in 1986, Congress enacted the Education of the Handicapped Act Amendments (PL 99-457) to extend those specified services to children ages 3–5 years. PL 99-457 also established incentives for states to provide early intervention programs for children birth–3 years and their families. This law established the importance of addressing the needs of children and families from their perspective, rather than from the professionals' perspective.

Occupational therapy is a primary service available to children and families in the early intervention systems; in the preschool and school-age populations, occupational therapy is considered a related service (i.e., provided only as needed to facilitate educational outcomes). Hanft and Humphrey (1989) reported that in a survey of 555 pediatric occupational therapists, 57% worked exclusively with infants and toddlers.

## SOCIOCULTURAL INITIATIVES SINCE THE MID-1980s

Since 1985, many initiatives have begun that are the result of shifts in sociocultural beliefs and values. Responding to the emerging beliefs that persons with disabilities are vital members of the community, Congress has enacted additional legislation, including the Technology-Related Assistance for Individuals with Disabilities Act of 1988 (PL 100-407), which provides mechanisms to create community support for persons to gain access to assistive technology, and the Americans with Disabilities Act of 1990 (ADA) (PL 101-336), which mandates work, living, and community adaptations to provide all persons with access to community resources. These laws clearly acknowledge that we need to make our environments more available to all persons. This is a great benefit to families who have a member with a disability, and all children will be able to grow up believing that they are capable of contributing to society and accepting others.

In the education environment, these sociocultural shifts have manifested themselves in the full inclusion movement. These initiatives state that all children are to be educated together; children will not typically be served in separate classrooms or schools. Many authors have offered curricular models and instructional strategies for making integration and inclusion successful (e.g., Sailor et al., 1989; Stainback & Stainback, 1990). Study findings demonstrate that students with disabilities can learn in heterogeneous groups (Idol, 1987; Palinscar, 1986). These education directions create a new environment for providers, families, and children.

## SERVICE PROVISION ISSUES

With all the changes in sociocultural beliefs and the new environments in which occupational therapists are being asked to participate, it is critical that professionals consider what service provision strategies create the best fit for these demands. The old ways of doing things are no longer acceptable.

### Principles

Occupational therapists consider activities of daily living (ADL), work and productive activities, and play and leisure to be the three key areas of performance (see Table 1). Three core principles guide the occupational therapy service provision process in early intervention. First, the occupational therapist identifies the outcomes that caregivers and providers have selected for the child and assesses and plans within the framework of those functional outcomes. Second, the occupational therapist searches for opportunities to address functional performance needs when the child and care provider are typically engaging in those tasks, rather than during a contrived practice period. Third, interdisciplinary collaboration produces the most pertinent methods for successfully addressing functional outcomes. Each of these general principles is now discussed.

***Interventions Address Desired Outcomes*** When individuals are unable to perform tasks in any of the areas listed in Table 1, the occupational therapist considers why the problem exists by analyzing task performance. The

Table 1. Performance areas addressed in occupational therapy

| Activities of daily living | Work and productive activities | Play or leisure activities |
|---|---|---|
| 1. Grooming<br>2. Oral hygiene<br>3. Bathing/showering<br>4. Toilet hygiene<br>5. Personal device care<br>6. Dressing<br>7. Feeding and eating<br>8. Medication routine<br>9. Health maintenance<br>10. Socialization<br>11. Functional communication<br>12. Functional mobility<br>13. Community mobility<br>14. Emergency response<br>15. Sexual expression | 1. Home management<br>  a. Clothing care<br>  b. Cleaning<br>  c. Meal preparation/ cleanup<br>  d. Shopping<br>  e. Money management<br>  f. Household maintenance<br>  g. Safety procedures<br>2. Care of others<br>3. Educational activities<br>4. Vocational activities<br>  a. Vocational exploration<br>  b. Job acquisition<br>  c. Work or job performance<br>  d. Retirement planning<br>  e. Volunteer participation | 1. Play or leisure exploration<br>2. Play or leisure performance |

Adapted from American Occupational Therapy Association (1994).

occupational therapist particularly addresses the sensorimotor, cognitive, and psychosocial aspects of performance. Table 2 presents essential performance components of tasks (American Occupational Therapy Association, 1994). The occupational therapist uses formal and informal assessment, skilled observation, interview, records review, and history taking to obtain pertinent information. No matter how detailed the assessment strategies become, the occupational therapist always keeps a focus on the desired performance outcome (Table 1), which may be identified through the individual referral sources, other team members, or family members. It is irrelevant, for example, to address a low motor test score if there are no indications that selected ADL, work, or play and leisure activities are affected. Occupational therapists address specific performance component deficits (see Table 2) that may be present *only* if they interfere with the individual's ability to perform necessary or desired life tasks.

***Desired Outcomes Occur in Relevant Contexts*** The contexts in which individuals perform their daily life tasks can facilitate or create barriers to performance (Dunn, Brown, & McGuigan, 1994; Schaaf & Mulrooney, 1989). Occupational therapists believe strongly that these contexts play a key role in the individual's ability to carry out desired or necessary tasks. For example, if the household is too noisy, the baby may not be able to get to sleep.

If the drawer is too crowded, the toddler may not be able to find the spoon; if the drawer is equipped with compartments and objects are sorted in them, however, the child may be more successful.

Objects, persons, and places all serve as parts of the environment. The occupational therapist considers the properties of all these parts and how they might be contributing to or interfering with the child's performance. Pierce (1991) conducted a study of infant acquisition of object rules and concluded that occupational therapists need to consider the pervasive influence of the environment on skill and rule acquisition. Pierce suggests that sometimes therapists may trade efficiency (i.e., setting up a clinically controlled situation) for potentially more powerful effects in natural environments. Timing of interventions within the naturally occurring schedule of the day is also a critical feature of contextually based interventions (e.g., teaching feeding skills during mealtime) (Dunn, Brown, & McGuigan, 1994).

The occupational therapist uses contextual information to decide whether the environment needs to be adapted to become more user-friendly for the child or whether the child can improve sensorimotor, cognitive, or psychosocial skills to manage the environment more successfully (Dunn, 1990). Many times both strategies are useful.

Occupational therapists support the use of natural environments because natural environments carry with them inherent properties that support functional behavior. For example, the bathroom contains sinks, which remind us to wash our hands; the classroom has peers who respond spontaneously to our actions. When a child can be supported to acquire skills in natural environments, the environment will provide cues for the behavior throughout the day.

***Collaboration Produces Pertinent Methods for Functional Outcomes*** Occupational therapists view children's needs in relation to the functional implications for their lives (Dunn, 1991b). This perspective lends itself well to the collaborative process of problem solving. Other professionals and family members have unique perspectives on a particular situation that are complementary to the occupational therapy perspective. Occupational therapists recognize the value of others' viewpoints as important for creating an optimal intervention plan that fits into the children's and families' lifestyles and life environments. Collaboration with other professionals enables the team to create interventions that incorporate all facets of the individual's needs into the recommended life routines (Dunn, 1992; Idol, Paolucci-Whitcomb, & Nevin, 1987).

## Models

Occupational therapists use three primary service provision models in practice settings: direct service, monitoring, and consultation (Chandler, Dunn, & Rourk, 1989; Dunn, 1988b; Dunn & Campbell, 1991). This wide range of service provision models enables the occupational therapist to design a

Table 2. Performance components addressed in occupational therapy

| Sensorimotor component | Cognitive integration and cognitive component | Psychosocial skills and psychological components |
|---|---|---|
| 1. Sensory<br>  a. Sensory awareness<br>  b. Sensory processing<br>    1) Tactile<br>    2) Proprioceptive<br>    3) Vestibular<br>    4) Visual<br>    5) Auditory<br>    6) Gustatory<br>    7) Olfactory<br>  c. Perceptual skills<br>    1) Stereognosis<br>    2) Kinesthesia<br>    3) Pain response<br>    4) Body scheme<br>    5) Right–left discrimination<br>    6) Form constancy<br>    7) Position in space<br>    8) Visual closure<br>    9) Figure ground<br>    10) Depth perception<br>    11) Spatial relations<br>    12) Topographical orientation | 1. Level of arousal<br>2. Orientation<br>3. Recognition<br>4. Attention span<br>5. Initiation of activity<br>6. Termination of activity<br>7. Memory<br>8. Sequencing<br>9. Categorization<br>10. Concept formation<br>11. Spatial operations<br>12. Problem solving<br>13. Learning<br>14. Generalization | 1. Psychological<br>  a. Values<br>  b. Interests<br>  c. Self-concept<br>2. Social<br>  a. Role performance<br>  b. Social conduct<br>  c. Interpersonal skills<br>  d. Self-expression<br>3. Self-management<br>  a. Coping<br>  b. Time management<br>  c. Self-control |

(continued)

Table 2. (continued)

| Sensorimotor component | Cognitive integration and cognitive component | Psychosocial skills and psychological components |
|---|---|---|
| 2. Neuromuscular<br>  a. Reflex<br>  b. Range of motion<br>  c. Muscle tone<br>  d. Strength<br>  e. Endurance<br>  f. Postural control<br>  g. Postural alignment<br>  h. Soft tissue integrity<br>3. Motor<br>  a. Gross coordination<br>  b. Crossing the midline<br>  c. Laterality<br>  d. Bilateral integration<br>  e. Motor control<br>  f. Praxis<br>  g. Fine coordination/dexterity<br>  h. Visual-motor integration<br>  i. Oral-motor control | | |

Adapted from American Occupational Therapy Association (1994).

comprehensive program for a child, taking into account environmental, task, and other support factors.

***Direct*** Occupational therapists provide direct service when they carry out individualized intervention plans with one child or a small group of children. The occupational therapist has immediate and ongoing contact with the child or children and carries out specialized intervention techniques that can be implemented safely only by occupational therapists. Hanft and Humphrey (1989) found that occupational therapists working in early intervention report that they perform direct services as a primary role. Direct service provides the therapist with opportunities to explore refinements for interventions and gives children access to specialized interventions. Occupational therapists employ direct service to introduce new behaviors into the child's repertoire, establish more adaptive behavioral schemes, alter maladaptive behavioral patterns, or build tolerance for sustaining performance in activities.

With the many changes in legislative mandates and sociocultural beliefs about persons with disabilities, there have been shifts in the prevailing opinions about the appropriate setting for direct service activities (e.g., Dunn & Campbell, 1991). Historically, occupational therapists have provided direct service outside the child's life environments (i.e., in a separate room with specialized equipment). Although there may be times when separation is useful to the therapeutic process, recommended practices suggest that separating children from their typical environments should occur only when other options are not manageable. For example, if the child is very distracted by other events, objects, or persons in the life environment, separation may enable the child to focus on the therapeutic task. These instances, however, are infrequent in early intervention programs, which emphasize the same developmental priorities within the daily routine that the child needs to address from an occupational therapy perspective (Dunn, 1991c).

As more children have been integrated into natural settings for school, daily living, and leisure activities, it has become clear that many direct service techniques and strategies can be applied within these natural settings. There are many advantages to this method. First, the child being served is in a comfortable and familiar setting, which can be more conducive to participation. Second, the environment itself is a rich source of stimuli that can be incorporated into therapeutic activities. Third, the environment can provide naturally occurring cues or opportunities to perform desired tasks that otherwise have to be artificially created in isolated clinical settings. Fourth, the natural environment is a rich source of motivation and reinforcement for task performance, which can also support functional behavior.

It is also critical to consider the impact of establishing a skill in an isolated, controlled environment compared to establishing a skill within the naturally occurring context. It is more likely that the skills developed in the natural context will be resilient to interruptions and supported by cues in the environment. When a child acquires a skill in isolation, the child may not recognize how that skill fits into the daily routine and therefore does not apply that skill when it is needed.

The sociocultural shifts in the society in general also affect early intervention programs. Families expect their children to be involved with other same-age peers in their early intervention programs and recognize the importance of these interactions as part of improving functional performance in daily life (Hanft, 1989). Providers and families are identifying the positive outcomes that are possible when specialized expertise is applied within the daily routine, including positive effects on the overall curriculum for all children.

*Monitoring* Occupational therapists monitor or supervise services when they create intervention plans and oversee other persons who implement the plan in the child's environment. Monitoring can improve the therapeutic benefit of activities that are a routine part of the child's day or week, because it is unlikely that the occupational therapist will be available every time the task is performed. By designing specific intervention strategies, the occupational therapist can have a positive impact on those life routines; the child is not neglected because the occupational therapist cannot be there. Eating, dressing, socialization, play, and personal hygiene programs are frequent targets of monitored intervention.

After the occupational therapist designs the intervention strategies, the therapist meets with the person who will be carrying out the intervention on a regular basis (e.g., teacher, aide, parent). The purpose of this meeting is to teach the techniques to the person, observe the person performing the techniques, and address any behavioral indications that tell the person that the techniques are failing or should be discontinued. The occupational therapist has the obligation to ensure that the intervention is carried out safely and therapeutically; when these assurances cannot be made, the monitored program is stopped and an alternative plan is created (Dunn, 1988b; Dunn & Campbell, 1991). When the occupational therapist is certain that the program will be implemented safely and that the person knows when to discontinue a technique and call for assistance, the monitored program is initiated. The occupational therapist keeps in regular contact with the implementor (at least bimonthly) to update the intervention and address any questions.

Monitoring provides an excellent way to extend the expertise of the occupational therapist into the child's daily routines. Family members, teachers, aides, and other service providers can participate in monitored programs. The advantage for the child receiving service is that the therapeutic techniques are embedded into the naturally occurring routines, affording more opportunities for practice, increasing the possibility for generalization of skills, and providing the child with the opportunity to participate in the task. The advantage for the service or care providers is that they can use therapeutic techniques to carry out the routines that they were already using with the child. This frequently makes the routines easier to complete and more successful. Occupational therapists have particular expertise in analyzing the components of daily life tasks and are excellent resources for service providers. Monitoring provides a vehicle for this interaction.

*Consultation* Professionals in many disciplines have discovered the value of providing consultation as a service provision option (Idol et al., 1987; West & Idol, 1987). Consultation differs from monitoring in that the consultant provides expertise to enable others to meet their specified goals. The specific problems may have been identified and defined by family members, other professionals, or other providers (e.g., baby sitter); the consultant works within the framework of this problem identification process to gather additional information and to formulate possible recommendations.

The literature suggests that a collaborative style of consultation is most preferred (Idol et al., 1987; Pryzwansky & White, 1983). Idol and colleagues (1987) provide the benchmark definition for collaborative consultation:

> Collaborative consultation is an interactive process that enables people with diverse expertise to generate creative solutions to mutually defined problems. The outcome is enhanced, altered, and produces solutions that are different from those that the individual team members would produce independently. (p. 1)

This definition identifies that interventions created within a collaborative consultation process represent a consolidation of expertise from several perspectives. Interventions no longer resemble the disciplines, but rather look like children performing functional tasks (Dunn, 1992). Occupational therapists bring unique skills to the collaborative process, particularly in the functional application of skills to the performance of necessary or desired life tasks.

The occupational therapist who serves as a consultant meets with the consultee to clarify the problem to be addressed. In this role, the occupational therapist must use active listening and careful interviewing skills to delineate the problem. Sometimes the occupational therapist has conducted assessments and brings this information to the discussion. When the individuals are satisfied that they have defined the problem as clearly as possible, they begin to explore alternatives to resolve the problem. For occupational therapists, intervention options include teaching service providers a skill that they can continue to use independently; adapting the tasks, materials, or environment to make the activity more user-friendly; adjusting the demands of the task; or designing strategies to remediate the problem (Dunn & Campbell, 1991). The occupational therapist maintains regular contact with the consultee to provide adequate support for the success of the interventions.

Consultation can extend the impact of the knowledge base of occupational therapy into natural life environments. Occupational therapy facilitates the functional performance of life tasks. Therapists have to construct artificial life task opportunities in isolated direct service situations (Dunn & Campbell,

1991). When a consultative model is used to facilitate naturally occurring opportunities, the environment can cue and reinforce functional performance. Consultation also affords other team members with opportunities to broaden their skills as well. The occupational therapist's ability to analyze tasks and create functional modifications is well suited to the consultative model of service provision.

## Approaches

As with service provision models, there are several service provision approaches available to the occupational therapist. Dunn, Brown, and McGuigan (1994) have outlined five intervention approaches enabling the occupational therapist to intervene at a variety of levels to achieve the best outcome for the child. Each of the intervention approaches addresses different factors that can affect performance.

***Establish or Restore*** The establish or restore approach (sometimes called the remedial approach) is the most familiar to service providers and has been frequently emphasized in preservice education. In this approach, the professional identifies the child's strengths and needs and creates strategies to alleviate the problems. Although many strategies exist to establish or restore skills, most require validation through systematic research. For example, Fewell (1988) found that preschool children who had received intensive gross motor interventions during 1 year achieved significant gains in gross motor scores on the Peabody Developmental Motor Scales, but did not maintain these gains in a subsequent school year.

These approaches have grown from the traditional medical model of intervention, which seeks to resolve a problem altogether. This is certainly a desirable outcome when it is possible; however, many of the performance problems that children in early intervention programs face are attributable to conditions that persist throughout the developmental period and perhaps throughout life. Sometimes it may not be in children's and families' best interest to focus only on remedial approaches; this focus may prohibit the child from having important peer or developmental opportunities. For example, if providers limited themselves to remediating only a child's oral communication problem, they might miss opportunities to encourage other forms of functional communication, such as gesturing, eye contact, and facial expressions that enable the child to participate with peers and providers.

***Adapt*** As in remedial approaches, the therapist, using an adaptive or compensatory approach, also identifies the child's strengths and needs. Instead of trying to fix the problem, however, an occupational therapist employs an adaptive strategy to work around the problem to enable performance. Prevailing practices frequently emphasize establishing new skills (i.e., remediating limitations), but the remedial approach can place too much emphasis on the child as the source of the problem. Adaptive approaches provide an opportunity to acknowledge that more accessible environments and tasks can be designed for children. Kemmis and Dunn (1996) found that adaptation and remedial strategies were equally successful for weekly plans created by teacher–therapist dyads.

For example, if a young child has poor stability in a chair during snack, a compensatory intervention would be to locate a chair with sides to make it easier for the child to stay in the chair throughout the snack period. This intervention does not improve the child's postural control, which involves a remedial approach. In an adaptive approach, the provider focuses on the desired task performance and identifies ways to ensure that the child is able to participate, regardless of a particular problem. Finding a more supportive chair acknowledges the child's postural control difficulty and makes an environmental adaptation to support the child to participate in snack time with peers.

Whenever providers or families change tasks, materials, or environments to accommodate a particular child's needs, they have employed an adaptive approach. It is in children's best interest to employ adaptive approaches. It is not necessary to resolve all problems by remediating them. Sometimes finding a way around the problem can provide the child with opportunities to participate, creating interest and motivation for performance. Occupational therapists are particularly skilled at designing adaptations, because they have knowledge of both the child's abilities and characteristics of tasks and the environment.

*Alter* This approach involves systematically identifying the skills and needs of the child and the characteristics of the environment to discern the best possible match for the child. When providers see that a child becomes very disruptive in a particular situation, they have the option to help the child handle the situation (i.e., a remedial approach), they can change the environment in some way to reduce the possibility of an outburst (i.e., an adaptive approach), or they can identify an alternative environment that is a better match for the child's temperament. The alter approach acknowledges both the child's current capabilities and the environmental variables, but does not set out to change either one; the therapist intervenes by finding an alternate environment that is a better match for the child. For example, if the child is unable to maintain control in a particular classroom because of the morning routine, the team may choose to move the child to a new classroom that has a more compatible morning routine. This strategy does not require the child to develop new skills and does not force either teacher to change his or her morning routines, but rather seeks to make the best fit with available resources.

Sometimes in early intervention programs, providers focus so heavily on helping the children to improve their skills that opportunities to capitalize on the available resources (both the child's and the environment's) are missed. Young children are in a continuous state of learning; it is not always necessary to make them manage every situation. The alter approach has the therapeutic benefit of providing a more facilitatory environment that affords the child the opportunity to behave in an adaptive manner.

*Prevent* Professionals also recognize that there are risk factors that may interfere with future development; in these situations, providers use the prevent approach. Anticipating the possible future outcome from the child's current condition, the therapist intervenes to minimize the effects of the foreseen outcome (Dunn, Campbell, Oetter, & Berger, 1989). Professionals frequently select this approach for children with Down syndrome because as they grow and develop, children with this disability have a high chance of having low muscle tone, which can interfere with sensorimotor development. Therapists use a prevention approach to create numerous activities that enhance muscle tone and postural stability to prevent interference of low muscle tone in later movement milestones. A team may also select a prevention approach for a preschooler who is more active than other children and avoids manipulative toys. If this trend continues in this child's play, eye–hand coordination skills might be affected. By providing an environment that is structured to encourage the child to interact with objects more frequently, visual-motor problems may be averted.

*Create* A create approach is used to promote the optimal evolution of a child's skills and abilities. Unlike the other approaches, which focus on a child's difficulties, this approach does not presume that the child has any particular delay or disability. Community-based programs established for all young children are applying a creation approach, including child care programs, tumbling and dance programs, and library reading programs. A creation approach is used frequently in early intervention programs when families collaborate with professionals to provide an optimal developmental environment for their children.

It is sometimes difficult for service providers such as occupational therapists to consider their roles in creation approaches to intervention. The profession has emphasized addressing children's problems and needs. This view can limit opportunities to create successful environments for all children, as well as provide a broader range of opportunities for children with disabilities. A creation approach reminds us that young children with disabilities are still young children who want to play and discover themselves and their world. By creating environments that promote optimal development, we offer children with disabilities the chance to explore their own interests and abilities in naturally occurring ways.

## Use of Models and Approaches

The service provision models and approaches can be used in any combination to address individualized needs. It is inaccurate to characterize the direct service model as an automatically restorative or remedial approach to intervention, or to always use an adaptive approach with monitoring or consultation. Each service provision model can be used with each service provision approach successfully. This creates many more options for service providers as they address the complex needs of young children. Table 3 provides examples of various combinations of service provision approaches and models being used to address various problems.

## Providing Early Intervention Services in Community Settings

Occupational therapy services are provided in every type of early intervention program in the community, including the family home, child care centers, special education programs, and integrated early intervention and preschool programs. The service provision models and approaches previously described can all be applied to every setting. The ultimate objective of occupational therapy within every setting is for the child to accomplish necessary and desired life tasks.

More early intervention programs are developing as the Individuals with Disabilities Education Amendments of 1991 (PL 102-119) are implemented. Occupational therapists most frequently address regulation of the infant's state, functional caregiving strategies, development of motor and cognitive skills, socialization, and play.

The family is the central focus of early intervention services, even in center-based programs, because young children receive much of their support for development from family members. Team members interact to intertwine various frames of reference to the benefit of the family and child. Although some direct service is warranted with this age group, it is much more useful for the therapist to employ monitoring and consultation to help both the early intervention providers and the family better care for and facilitate the child's development. Prevention and promotion (i.e., "create") are common approaches for all team members; however, young children can also profit from adaptive approaches, which enable children to have access to tasks more easily. Case-Smith (1991) suggests that occupational therapists are well suited to be case managers in family-centered care because of their functional view of child and family needs and broad range of intervention options.

## Assessment in Early Intervention Programs

When occupational therapists serve early intervention programs, they must consider relevant methods for assessment. The first consideration is the referral: What do the family and early intervention providers need and want the child to do? All data are collected within this framework. There are very few formal assessments that are appropriate for infants and toddlers (Cook, 1991), but formal assessments typically provide measures only of status (e.g., developmental level, component skills). In early intervention programs, occupational therapists need to identify not only the child's status but also the factors

Table 3. Examples of combinations of service provision approaches and models

|  | Service provision approaches | | | | |
| Service provision models | Establish/restore (remediate) | Adapt (compensate) | Alter | Prevent | Create (promote) |
| --- | --- | --- | --- | --- | --- |
| Direct | Facilitate neck extensor muscles so child can look at friends when playing | Fabricate a splint to enable the child to hold the cup at snack time | Select a community preschool based on the level of noise the child can manage | Facilitate weight bearing during infancy to prevent possible delays in walking | Provide a play program for the community for all children to attend |
| Monitoring | Supervise the teacher's aide to facilitate tone for reaching during a game | Supervise a feeding program that minimizes the time for eating and enables socialization | Work with parents to identify which community locations will be best for their family outings | Create a "positions alternatives" chart for the aides to prevent skin breakdowns | Oversee the development of a morning preschool routine that optimizes early development possibilities |
| Consultation | Teach classroom staff how to incorporate enhanced sensory input into play routines during free time | Show teachers how to change the pieces of a game so all children can handle the pieces | Provide the team with information from skilled observations that enables them to select the best play partner for a child | Teach a parent a range-of-motion sequence to prevent deformities | Assist the child care provider to develop a comprehensive curriculum |

282

that facilitate or create barriers to performance during functional tasks (Case-Smith, 1993). Observing the child during early intervention routines, interviewing teachers and family members, conducting ecological assessments, and recording the child's responses to task and environmental adaptations are all appropriate methods for completing a comprehensive assessment.

### RECOMMENDED PRACTICES IN INTEGRATING EARLY INTERVENTION SERVICES

#### Relationship to Other Disciplines

Occupational therapy focuses on the functional abilities of individuals as they attempt to perform desired and necessary life tasks. This emphasis complements the focus of other disciplines, highlighting the importance of the interdisciplinary team. Table 4 summarizes the overlap between occupational therapy and other disciplines and provides strategies that can be used to coordinate services. This is meant not to represent a comprehensive analysis, but only to provide a sample of key areas of interest as these professions collaborate on teams. Humphrey and Link (1990) convened an expert panel to identify priorities and recommendations for preparation to work in early intervention. This panel identified interdisciplinary skills, including communication, and valuing others' perspectives as high-priority skills. Lawlor and Henderson (1989) interviewed 118 pediatric therapists, two thirds of whom reported providing services as part of a team.

#### Key Issues for Participating on Teams

All members of the team face several challenges as they serve children as a collaborative unit rather than as single disciplines (see Chapter 2). Team members must hold the value that the picture is not complete with only one point of view. This is sometimes difficult for professionals to embrace because most learned their disciplines in isolation from other disciplines. Policy changes are necessary to alter this course and enable professionals to be trained together, thus instilling the value of multiple points of view.

Mather and Weinstein (1988) discuss the evolving partnership between therapists and educators in early intervention programs. They point out that in the beginning, teachers have found the medical model approach of programming to be foreign to them, particularly in linking many component-level tasks and performance in the early intervention curriculum. They give the example of relating shoulder control to fine motor skills in the classroom. Mather and Weinstein also acknowledge, though, that therapists were unfamiliar with curriculum design, making it difficult for therapists to relate their concerns for specific children to this overall plan. They then give some successful adaptations that the disciplines have made to make partnerships successful. As

Table 4. Relationship between occupational therapy and other disciplines and strategies for coordinating services

| Discipline | Overlap with occupational therapy | Strategies for coordination of services |
|---|---|---|
| Physical therapy | Understanding the human body and its function and capacities; understanding the developmental process across the life span | PT can provide preparatory work to increase tolerance/capacity for activity; OT can apply the capacities to the desired functional task |
| Social work | Recognition of the importance of individuals living and working in the community; understanding the importance of family supports | SW can provide specific links to the community for the family and can facilitate movement through the systems to obtain desired resources and placements when needed; OT can prepare the child and family to function within desired settings |
| Special education | Understanding the cognitive aspects of performance; understanding task analysis | SPED can provide the cognitive tasks that are appropriate for the child; OT considers the sensorimotor, cognitive, and psychosocial aspects of the particular cognitive tasks; they collaborate to create a single intervention |
| Psychology | Understanding the psychosocial aspects of performance | PSY can provide in-depth background regarding the psychosocial aspects and their context within the family; OT supports these endeavors through skilled observation about how these difficulties interfere with functional skill performance |
| Speech-langage pathology | Knowledge of the oral-motor structures; knowledge of the swallow patterns; knowledge of the nonverbal aspects of communication | SLP can provide swallowing interventions; OT can address food acquisition and oral-motor control; SLP can provide expertise regarding the selection of the proper augmentative communication device; OT addresses functional aspects of communication (e.g., access to augmentative communication device) |

From Dunn, W. (1992). Occupational therapy evaluation. In F.R. Brown, E.H. Aylward, & B.K. Keogh (Eds.), *Diagnosis and management of learning disabilities: An interdisciplinary/lifestyle approach* (2nd ed.). San Diego, CA: Singular Publishing Group; reprinted by permission.

therapists began to understand the curriculum, they began to offer suggestions for the curriculum that were improvements for all the children. Teachers became more aware of the individual differences that may affect play activities. New schemata for assessing children emerged, with a combined emphasis on individual skills and functional performance. These successes led to common ground for problem solving and documentation.

Everyone is a winner when the team creates the best solution for a child and family, a solution that fits the family's lifestyle and the child's learning or play preferences, and when it addresses key functional needs and desires. Everyone loses when one discipline dominates unnecessarily, causing the solution to largely reflect that discipline rather than the family's and the child's lifestyle.

Team members must value the child's and family's needs more than the visibility of their own disciplines. Sometimes one discipline may need to withdraw a recommendation because it is not in the overall best interest of the child and family. For example, the occupational therapist may identify serious oral-motor problems that interfere with talking and eating. Oral-motor intervention for talking would not be appropriate, however, if the team determined that an augmentative communication device was a better option. The occupational therapist might refocus attention to the reaching and pointing skills needed to gain access to the communication device.

It is critical for all team members to be equal collaborators in program planning. Group leadership can be flexible, depending on the case being addressed. It becomes important to team members to have other team members present (and not just their reports); more flexible scheduling ensures that critical points of view are represented (Rainforth, York, & Macdonald, 1992). Many of these issues are related to a lack of knowledge about collaboration and how to operationalize it within teams. Idol and colleagues (1987) provide a benchmark discussion of the principles of collaborative consultation and methods for developing these skills.

Professional training focuses our attention on the children receiving services; when they acquire a new skill, we see it happen; when they see us, they show pleasure. Teamwork requires a new focus on other adult professionals who do not give this same direct, concrete feedback. Team members must learn how to recognize and give each other reinforcement for work well done. Many authors have suggested the use of the Integrated Programming Team Model to describe the functional operation of service provision, which extends the operation of the interdisciplinary team (Campbell, 1987a, 1987b; Dunn, 1991a, 1991b; Giangreco, 1986a, 1986b). Integrated models offer the professional team members guidance on reorganizing skills and expertise to be constructive in natural settings.

## Concepts of Integrating Services

The concept of integrating therapeutic interventions into educational environments and daily tasks is not a new one to the related-services disciplines (Dunn,

Moore, Brown, & Westman, 1994). For example, the philosophical constructs of occupational therapy are based on the concept of purposeful activity or those tasks that have meaning for the individual, believing that this characteristic provides intrinsic motivation to persist in reaching goals (Breines, 1984; Clark, 1979; Fidler & Fidler, 1978; Hinojosa, Sabari, Rosenfeld, & Shapiro, 1983; Kircher, 1984; Steinbeck, 1986; West, 1984). Kircher (1984) and Steinbeck (1984) both found that persons without disabilities persisted significantly longer on an identical task of exertion when the task had an identifiable purpose rather than when perceived merely as an exercise. Gliner (1985) proposed that professionals create normal life events within which to learn motor skills, suggesting that actor and environment are inseparable.

Giangreco, Edelman, and Dennis (1991) report on professional practices that facilitate or interfere with integrated services. Practices such as writing individual discipline goals and recommendations before meetings, writing separate reports, and selecting placement based on available services are practices that interfere with integrated programming. Giangreco and colleagues (1991) suggest more group goal and recommendation development, with an emphasis on goals and recommendations that are not associated with a particular discipline, but rather focus on children's needs and strengths.

Several related-services authors have reported positive outcomes for children when professionals implement newer models of service provision. Dunn (1990) compared the use of direct intervention and consultation in preschool programs for children with developmental delays. Findings reveal that both service provision models yield the same percentage of individualized education program (IEP) goals being met (approximately 70%). When teachers collaborated in a consultation model, however, they reported that the occupational therapist contributed to 24% more of the efforts to meet the goals on the IEP. Peck, Killen, and Baumgart (1989) demonstrated that consultation can facilitate teachers' developing effective interventions on simple language goals for children with disabilities. Additionally, teachers generalized the techniques to new situations that were not part of the initial project. Giangreco (1986b) compared isolated therapy services with integrated occupational and physical therapy services (i.e., teachers and therapists collaborate to design the intervention) for a student with multiple disabilities. The student performed significantly better during the integrated intervention phase, supporting the effectiveness of integrating teacher and therapist expertise. Jones (1983) combined several therapy techniques with behavioral techniques to investigate eating problems in children with mental retardation. Combined therapeutic approaches were most effective at supporting the children to eat solid foods.

The related-services literature indicates that integrating the ideas from several disciplines can be an effective means of serving children and youth with disabilities. These few examples need to be elaborated to create a consolidated framework for systematic decision making. The successful related-services strategies also need to be integrated with regular and special education approaches to create more effective learning environments for all children.

Dunn (1991b) has described a model for comprehensive integration delineating the various types of integration desired for children with disabilities (see Figure 1) to ensure that children are included in relevant settings and have the appropriate interdisciplinary supports necessary to make the learning experience successful for the children (with and without disabilities) and their teachers. This model provides guidance about the particular contributions professionals can make to integration and inclusion.

*Peer integration* occurs when typical children and children with special needs are placed together for activities (i.e., included in early intervention programs). *Functional integration* occurs when therapeutic and instructional strategies are applied within a child's life environments (e.g., home, school, extracurricular activities) to make these environments more user-friendly for the child. For example, an occupational therapist may construct a plate adaptation (i.e., a guard on the side to keep food inside the plate) to enable the child to participate in snack activities. *Practice integration* occurs when various professionals and families collaborate to design a combined approach that addresses a child's unique needs within a particular context. An occupational therapist may, for example, work on upper extremity reach and grasp, not as an end in

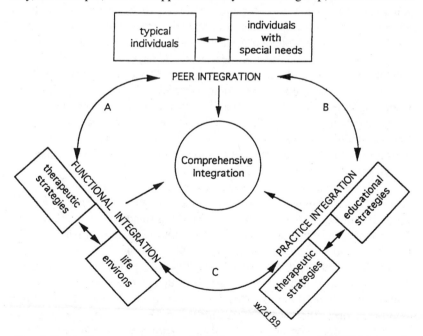

Figure 1. Model of the components of comprehensive integration. (From Dunn, W. [1991b]. Integrated related services. In L.H. Meyer, C.A. Peck, & L. Brown [Eds.], *Critical issues in the lives of people with severe disabilities* (p. 354). Baltimore: Paul H. Brookes Publishing Co.; reprinted by permission.)

itself, but as a means for a child to use a switch, point to a communication board, eat independently, or manipulate objects.

When all three types of integration are present in early intervention service systems for children, *comprehensive integration* (i.e., full inclusion) results. Comprehensive integration requires not only that the child be included in the regular early intervention environment but also that the interdisciplinary team members work collaboratively to make learning more functional and applicable to that setting and the child's needs. When professionals are knowledgeable about the application of their particular discipline's expertise, they can incorporate appropriate techniques into practice integration routines or functional integration adaptations. When children develop additional skills from functional and practice integration activities, they can participate more fully in typical environments. A key difference between segregated and integrated opportunities for children is the knowledge and skills of professionals in facilitating comprehensive integration (Dunn, 1991b).

## Theoretical Constructs in Daily Routines

One of the biggest challenges that occupational therapists face in early intervention programs is the need to make their expertise relevant in this setting. One factor in applying the more familiar frames of reference to the needs of young children in early intervention programs is that the specific interventions were designed for a direct service model of service provision. Another factor is that frequently the occupational therapist working in a community-based early intervention program provides services within an interdisciplinary team and is the only occupational therapist in the program. This means that other team members are usually unfamiliar with the theories and frames of reference that guide problem solving for the occupational therapist. In this situation, occupational therapists organize information to ensure that it is clear (i.e., jargon-free) and understandable to the other team members. Many good recommendations have not been implemented, because the provider did not understand the meaning or relevance of the task for the child.

There is much to learn about recommended practices in early intervention services. Several studies on early intervention practices have raised questions about the efficacy of these services. When using standardized developmental motor tests as the outcome measures of early intervention treatments, findings have been equivocal (e.g., Palmer et al., 1988; Parette & Hourcade, 1984a, 1984b; Piper et al., 1986). Ottenbacher (1989) analyzed the power of statistical tests from 49 early intervention articles. He found that these studies had a high probability of Type II errors in the conclusions (i.e., not enough children in studies to detect differences), suggesting that professionals may be at risk for making inaccurate decisions about what is in children's best interest. Gorga (1989) summarized the current literature on the efficacy of early intervention treatment practices and concluded that greater care needs to be taken in the decisions about appropriate outcomes for early intervention services. Gorga advocated interdisciplinary study of effectiveness, which include measurements of changes through the treatment, functional abilities, and quality of life as appropriate target outcomes.

*Applying Sensory Integration in Early Intervention* The theory of sensory integration creates a mechanism by which to understand and explore the relationship between children's behavior and neural processing (Fisher, Murray, & Bundy, 1991). The neuroscience literature provides much of the evidence that documents the operation of the nervous system in support of the neuroscience constructs of sensory integrative theory (Dunn, 1988b). Many of the studies in the literature report reliability and validity work done as part of the development and refinement of the tests used by therapists to diagnose sensory integrative deficits. A number of studies have been conducted to test the application of these neuroscience constructs to intervention regimes with children. Ottenbacher (1982a) conducted an analysis of the studies examining the effectiveness of sensory integration. Although he found 49 potential studies, only 8 met the experimental criteria he had set. In analyzing these 8 studies, he found that those participating in sensory integration therapy performed significantly better overall than the control groups, suggesting that sensory integration has some potential effect. In a series of articles debating the issue of using sensory integration with children with mental retardation, authors point out the evidence suggesting the useful and questionable features of practices (Arendt, MacLean, & Baumeister, 1988; Burns, 1988; Cermak, 1988; Clark & Primeau, 1988; Dunn, 1988a; Kimball, 1988; Ottenbacher, 1988). As with the more general early intervention literature, there is a need for additional work to advance knowledge about the impact of sensory integration on children's performance.

The theory of sensory integration contains many critical concepts that can provide guidance about how to interpret children's behavior. These theoretical concepts have remained elusive to many interdisciplinary colleagues because of difficulties in making the concepts accessible to them. When concepts remain unclear, the rich knowledge and insights that are possible from this frame of reference are lost, and the child may receive less than optimal programming.

In an attempt to remedy this situation, Dunn (1991c) designed some materials to make the sensory processing parts of this frame of reference accessible to other team members and to provide an interdisciplinary basis for assessment and intervention planning. First, a team member needs to understand basic principles that underlie sensory processing. Table 5 contains the names of the sensory systems in the first column and a list of descriptor words with definitions and a simple example of each in the second and third columns. The descriptor words are divided into two groups: the arousal or alerting descriptors and the discrimination or mapping descriptors. The types of stimuli

Table 5. Arousal/alerting and discrimination/mapping descriptors of the sensory system

| Sensory system | Arousal/alerting descriptors[a] | Discrimination/mapping descriptors[b] |
|---|---|---|
| For all systems | Unpredictable: the task is unfamiliar; the child cannot anticipate the sensory experiences that will occur in the task. | Predictable: sensory pattern in the task is routine for the child, such as diaper changing—the child knows what is occurring and what will come next. |
| Somatosensory | Light touch: gentle tapping on the skin; tickling (e.g., loose clothing making contact with skin).<br><br>Pain: brisk pinching; contact with sharp objects; skin pressed in small surface (e.g., when skin is caught in between chair arm and seat).<br><br>Temperature: hot or cold stimuli (e.g., iced drinks, hot foods, cold hands, cold metal chairs).<br><br>Variable: changing characteristics during the task (e.g., putting clothing on requires a combination of tactile experiences).<br><br>Short duration stimuli: tapping, touching briefly (e.g., splashing water).<br><br>Small body surface contact: small body surfaces, as when using only fingertips to touch something. | Touch pressure: firm contact on the skin (e.g., hugging, patting, grasping). Occurs both when touching objects or persons, or when they touch you.<br><br>Long duration stimuli: holding, grasping (e.g., carrying a child in your arms).<br><br>Large body surface contact: large body surface contacts include holding, hugging; also includes holding a cup with the entire palmar surface of hand. |
| Vestibular | Head position change: the child's head orientation is altered (e.g., pulling the child up from lying on the back to sitting).<br><br>Speed change: movements change velocity (e.g., the teacher stops to talk to another teacher when pushing the child to the bathroom in his wheelchair).<br><br>Direction change: movements change planes, such as bending down to pick something up from the floor while carrying the child down the hall.<br><br>Rotary head movement: head moving in an arc (e.g., spinning in a circle, turning head side-to-side). | Linear head movement: head moving in a straight line (e.g., bouncing up and down, going down the hall in a wheelchair).<br><br>Repetitive head movement: movements that repeat in a simple sequence (e.g., rocking in a rocker). |

| | | |
|---|---|---|
| Proprioception | Quick stretch: movements that pull on the muscles (e.g., briskly tapping on a muscle belly). | Sustained tension: steady, constant action on the muscles, pressing or holding on the muscle (e.g., using heavy objects during play).<br>Shifting muscle tension: activities that demand constant changes in the muscles (e.g., walking, lifting, and moving objects). |
| Visual | High intensity: visual stimulus is bright (e.g., looking out the window on a bright day).<br>High contrast: a lot of difference between the visual stimulus and its surrounding environment (e.g., cranberry juice in a white cup).<br>Variable: changing characteristics during the task (e.g., a TV program is a variable visual stimulus). | Low intensity: visual stimulus is subdued (e.g., finding objects in the dark closet).<br>High similarity: small differences between visual stimulus and its surrounding environment (e.g., oatmeal in a beige bowl).<br>Competitive: the background is interesting or busy (e.g., the junk drawer, a bulletin board). |
| Auditory | Variable: changing characteristics during the task (e.g., a person's voice with intonation).<br>High intensity: the auditory stimulus is loud (e.g., siren, high-volume radio). | Rhythmic: sounds repeat in a simple sequence/beat (e.g., humming; singing nursery songs).<br>Constant: the stimulus is always present (e.g., a fan noise).<br>Competitive: the environment has a variety of recurring sounds (e.g., the classroom, a party).<br>Noncompetitive: the environment is quiet (e.g., the bedroom when all is ready for bedtime).<br>Low intensity: the auditory stimulus is subdued (e.g., whispering). |
| Olfactory/gustatory | Strong intensity: the taste/smell has distinct qualities (e.g., spinach). | Mild intensity: the taste/smell has nondistinct or familiar qualities (e.g., Cream of Wheat). |

From Dunn, W. (1991c). The sensorimotor systems: A framework for assessment and intervention. In F.P. Orelove & D. Sobsey, *Educating children with multiple disabilities: A transdisciplinary approach* (2nd ed.) (pp. 37–39). Baltimore: Paul H. Brookes Publishing Co.; reprinted by permission.

[a]"Arousal/alerting stimuli tend to generate "noticing" behaviors. The individual's attention is at least momentarily drawn toward the stimulus (commonly disrupting ongoing behavior). These stimuli enable the nervous system to orient to or notice a stimulus that may require a protective response. In some situations, an arousing stimulus can become part of a functional behavior pattern (e.g., when the arousing somatosensory input from putting on the shirt becomes predictable, a discrimination/mapping characteristic).

[b]Discrimination/mapping stimuli are those that enable the individual to gather information that can be used to support and generate functional behaviors. The information yields spatial and temporal qualities of body and environment (the content of the maps) that can be used to create purposeful movement. These stimuli are more organizing for the nervous system.

represented in the arousal/alerting column tend to be those that get the child to notice what is going on; many times this noticing, or attentional behavior, is only momentary and can be disruptive to ongoing performance. Arousal or alerting responses are important because they enable children to orient to potentially important stimuli in their environments.

The types of stimuli represented in the discrimination/mapping column tend to be those that enable the child to gather information. These stimuli tend to contribute information to the construction of maps of self and environment in the nervous system that can be used to plan and execute functional behaviors. Discrimination and mapping information tends to be more organizing for the nervous system.

Armed with this information, team members can begin to discuss the sensory features of a child's performance. Figure 2 provides a worksheet for considering the sensory components of task performance. The first two columns contain the same sensory descriptor words that are defined in Table 5. The team identifies a target task for the child and marks any of the sensory descriptors that occur during the typical performance of the task (in the columns headed "What does the task routine hold?"). The three columns (A, B, C) are used only when a task is more complex and has to be considered in parts (e.g., preparing a meal); for young children, this usually is not necessary. The next column provides space for considering the actual context in which the target child performs the task; different environments contain different sensory features that may make a difference in the child's ability to perform the task. Finally, the team reviews the pattern of sensory qualities in the task and discusses possible adaptations that can be made to increase the possibility of the child performing the task.

Figure 3 contains a completed sensory component worksheet about a child who needs to wash her face. This task contains many sensory experiences, all of which can be either helpful or disruptive to the child's performance. The team identified a large number of ways to restructure the task of face washing (see last column of Figure 3). If the team were to change many of these features at once, however, then the team would not know what was helpful for the child. Therefore, the team would need to select which interventions it believed were most likely to improve the child's performance and introduce them one-at-a-time into the face-washing routine. By systematically creating one adaptation at a time, the team learns more about the child's responsiveness and can use this information to plan additional interventions for other activities.

When piloting these strategies with teams in the Midwest, I discovered that team members (e.g., teachers, aides, related service providers) began to think that the arousal or alerting stimuli were bad ones and the discrimination or mapping stimuli were good ones for intervention. Based on solid neurological principles (e.g., Kandell, Schwartz, & Jessell, 1992), all of the sensory descriptors are useful to the nervous system and the child if selected and used properly. This discovery led to the development of Table 6, which is organized

| Routine/task Sensory characteristics | What does the task routine hold? A | B | C | What does the particular environment hold? | What adaptations are likely to improve functional outcome? |
|---|---|---|---|---|---|
| **Somatosensory** Light touch (tap, tickle) | | | | | |
| Pain | | | | | |
| Temperature (hot, cold) | | | | | |
| Touch pressure (hug, pat, grasp) | | | | | |
| Variable | | | | | |
| Duration of stimulus (short, long) | | | | | |
| Body surface contact (small, large) | | | | | |
| Predictable | | | | | |
| Unpredictable | | | | | |
| **Vestibular** Head position change | | | | | |
| Speed change | | | | | |
| Direction change | | | | | |
| Rotary head movement | | | | | |
| Linear head movement | | | | | |
| Repetitive head movement—rhythmic | | | | | |
| Predictable | | | | | |
| Unpredictable | | | | | |

Figure 2. Sensory components of task performance (worksheet). (From Dunn, W. [1991c]. The sensorimotor systems: A framework for assessment and intervention. In F.P. Orelove & D. Sobsey, *Educating children with multiple disabilities: A transdisciplinary approach* (2nd ed.) (p. 67). Baltimore: Paul H. Brookes Publishing Co.; reprinted by permission.)

*(continued)*

Figure 2. (continued)

| Routine/task Sensory characteristics | | What does the task routine hold? A  B  C | What does the particular environment hold? | What adaptations are likely to improve functional outcome? |
|---|---|---|---|---|
| Proprioceptive | Quick stretch | | | |
| | Sustained tension | | | |
| | Shifting muscle tension | | | |
| | Predictable | | | |
| | Unpredictable | | | |
| Visual | High intensity | | | |
| | Low intensity | | | |
| | High contrast | | | |
| | High similarity (low contrast) | | | |
| | Competitive | | | |
| | Variable | | | |
| | Predictable | | | |
| | Unpredictable | | | |

| | | | | | | |
|---|---|---|---|---|---|---|
| Auditory | Rhythmic | | | | | |
| | Variable | | | | | |
| | Constant | | | | | |
| | Competitive | | | | | |
| | Noncompetitive | | | | | |
| | Loud | | | | | |
| | Soft | | | | | |
| | Predictable | | | | | |
| | Unpredictable | | | | | |
| Olfactory/ gustatory | Mild | | | | | |
| | Strong | | | | | |
| | Predictable | | | | | |
| | Unpredictable | | | | | |

Task Components:
A = _____
B = _____
C = _____

| Routine/task Washing face | | What does the task routine hold? | | | What does the particular environment hold? (classroom sink) | What adaptations are likely to improve functional outcome? |
| Sensory characteristics | | A | B | C | | |
|---|---|---|---|---|---|---|
| | Light touch (tap, tickle) | X | | | | Turn water off to decrease splashing. |
| Somatosensory | Pain | | | | | |
| | Temperature (hot, cold) | X | | | | Try alternative water temperatures. |
| | Touch pressure (hug, pat, grasp) | X | | | | Pat face instead of rubbing cloth on face. |
| | Variable | X | | | | Pat large face area. |
| | Duration of stimulus (short, long) | L | | | | |
| | Body surface contact (small, large) | L | | | | Try washing one part only; begin with chin area. |
| | Predictable | X | | | | |
| | Unpredictable | | | | | (NOTE: Make sure routine is consistent day-to-day.) |

Figure 3.   Sensory components of task performance (sample). (From Dunn, W. [1991c]. The sensorimotor systems: A framework for assessment and intervention. In F.P. Orelove & D. Sobsey, *Educating children with multiple disabilities: A transdisciplinary approach* [2nd ed.] [p. 68]. Baltimore: Paul H. Brookes Publishing Co.; reprinted by permission.)

| | | | | | | |
|---|---|---|---|---|---|---|
| Vestibular | Head position change | X | | | | Alter water source so you do not have to bend head down (e.g., in a pan or tub). |
| | Speed change | | | | | |
| | Direction change | X | | | | Keep head up so you do not have down–up pattern. |
| | Rotary head movement | | | | | |
| | Linear head movement | X | | | | Keep head up; if need arousal, place items on counter to encourage more head turning. |
| | Repetitive head movement—rhythmic | | | | | |
| | Predictable | | | | | |
| | Unpredictable | | | | | |
| Proprioceptive | Quick stretch stimulus | | | | | |
| | Sustained tension stimulus | X | | | | Move objects to decrease head control requirements. |
| | Shifting muscle tension | X | | | | |

*(continued)*

297

Figure 3. (continued)

| Routine/task Sensory characteristics | What does the task routine hold? A | B | C | What does the particular environment hold? (classroom sink) | What adaptations are likely to improve functional outcome? |
|---|---|---|---|---|---|
| Visual | | | | | |
| High intensity | | | | | |
| Low intensity | | | | | |
| High contrast | | | | | |
| High similarity (low contrast) | X | | | X Other objects | Use dark washcloths and light soap; use dark containers on light counter; remove extra items from counter. |
| Competitive | X | | | X On sink | |
| Variable | | | | X Counter changes day-to-day | |
| Predictable | X | | | | If arousal is needed, vary placement of items. |
| Unpredictable | | | | | |

| | | | | |
|---|---|---|---|---|
| Auditory | Rhythmic | X | | Prepare wet cloth; do not have running tap water. |
| | Variable | X | | Use tub of water instead of running water. |
| | Constant | | | |
| | Competitive | | X Other students | Move child to the bathroom alone. |
| | Noncompetitive | X | | |
| | Loud | | X Teacher's voice | Provide physical prompts and decrease talking. |
| | Soft | | | |
| | Predictable | X | | |
| | Unpredictable | | X Unplanned | |
| Olfactory/ gustatory | Mild | X | | If arousal is needed, use strong-smelling soap. |
| | Strong | | | |
| | Predictable | X | | |
| | Unpredictable | | | |

Task Components:    A = _____
                    B = _____
                    C = _____

like Table 5 but contains different content. Table 6 provides the team members with a simple explanation of the reason why they might select a particular sensory feature to have a therapeutic benefit. In addition to an explanation, the table contains an example derived from children's activities. For example, light touch is useful to increase alertness in a child, particularly if the child is lethargic; it generally would not be a good idea to use light touch stimuli with a child who is already overly excited.

Another strategy to get team members thinking about sensory factors is to help them conceptualize potential problems within daily life tasks. Table 7 provides examples of observable behaviors that indicate difficulty with sensory processing during daily life tasks. The information from a table such as this one can be used to create referral or observational assessment forms, generate discussion in team meetings, and explain a child's difficulties to family members.

These materials are only examples of the ways that occupational therapists can present their theoretical knowledge to make it available and understandable to their team members. Other team members are more likely to follow through with a suggestion to turn the water off while a child is washing her face if they understand that the sound of the water may disrupt the child's attention and concentration on the task. When occupational therapists can embed their specialized knowledge into daily routines, children have many more opportunities to develop and generalize their skills with proper supports.

*Applying Neurodevelopmental Treatment in Early Intervention* Neurodevelopmental treatment (NDT) is another common frame of reference that occupational therapists employ in their problem solving. NDT was originally conceived as a direct service intervention for infants and young children with cerebral palsy (Bobath & Bobath, 1984); others have suggested that it can be applied to the needs of children with Down syndrome (Harris, 1981), children with mental retardation (Ellis, 1967), and children with learning and behavior problems (Dunn & DeGangi, 1992).

There has been much controversy about the efficacy of NDT. Ottenbacher and colleagues (1986) conducted a meta-analysis of NDT studies; six of them had an early intervention population. They found that there was a small treatment effect, suggesting that most of those who received NDT or some combined intervention including NDT perform better after intervention. Two single-subject design studies on NDT with young children also showed positive effects of NDT on immediate measures of muscle, postural, and motor activity (Harris & Riffle, 1986; Laskas, Mullen, Nelson, & Wilson-Broyles, 1985). These studies did not indicate any possible long-term effects on functional performance.

Other studies have provided more equivocal results. Harris (1988) and Stern and Gorga (1988) reviewed the collective evidence on NDT and raised critical questions about how studies are designed, how interventions are applied, what outcome measures are selected, and what impact NDT may or may not have on long-term functional outcomes. More work is needed to identify

Table 6. Reasons for incorporating various sensory qualities into integrated intervention programs

| Sensory system | Arousal/alerting descriptors | Discrimination/mapping descriptors |
|---|---|---|
| For all systems | *Unpredictable:* to develop an increasing level of attention to keep the child interested in the task/activity (e.g., change the position of the objects on the child's lap tray during the task). | *Predictable:* to establish the child's ability to anticipate a programming sequence or a salient cue; to decrease possibility to be distracted from a functional task sequence (e.g., use the same routine for diaper changing every time). |
| Somatosensory | *Light touch:* to increase alertness in a child who is lethargic (e.g., pull cloth from child's face during peek-a-boo). *Pain:* to raise from unconsciousness; to determineability to respond to noxious stimuli when unconscious (e.g., flick palm of hand or sole of foot briskly). *Temperature:* to establish awareness of stimuli; to maintain attentiveness to task (e.g., use hot foods for spoon eating and cold drink for sucking through a straw). *Variable:* to maintain attention to or interest in the task (e.g., place new texture on cup surface each day so child notices the cup). *Short duration:* to increase arousal for task performance (e.g., tap child on chest before giving directions). *Small body surface contact:* to generate and focus attention on a particular body part (e.g., tap around lips with fingertips before task of eating). | *Touch pressure:* to establish and maintain awareness of body parts and body position; to calm a child who has been overstimulated (e.g., provide a firm bear hug). *Long duration:* to enable a child to become familiar, comfortable with the stimulus; to incorporate stimulus into functional skill (e.g., grasping the container to pick it up and pour out contents). *Large body surface contact:* to establish and maintain awareness of body parts and body position; to calm a child who has been overstimulated (e.g., wrap child tightly in a blanket). |
| Vestibular | *Head position change:* to increase arousal for an activity (e.g., position child prone over a wedge). | *Linear head movement:* to support establishment of body awareness in space (e.g., carry child around the room in fixed position to explore its features). |

*(continued)*

Table 6. (continued)

| Sensory system | Arousal/alerting descriptors | Discrimination/mapping descriptors |
|---|---|---|
| Vestibular | *Speed change:* to maintain adequate alertness for functional task (e.g., vary pace while carrying the child to a new task). <br> *Direction change:* to elevate the level of alertness for functional task (e.g., swing child back and forth in arms prior to positioning him at the table for a task). <br> *Rotary head movement:* to increase arousal prior to functional task (e.g., pick child up from prone (on stomach) facing away to upright facing toward you to position for a new task). | *Repetitive head movement:* to provide predictable and organizing information; to calm a child who has been overstimulated (e.g., rock the child). |
| Proprioception | *Quick stretch:* to generate additional muscle tension to support functional tasks (e.g., tap muscle belly of hypotonic muscle while providing physical guidance to grasp). | *Sustained tension:* to enable the muscle to relax, elongate, so body part can be in more optimal position for function (e.g., press firmly across muscle belly while guiding a reaching pattern; add weight to objects being manipulated). <br> *Shifting muscle tension:* to establish functional movement patterns that contain stability and mobility (e.g., prop and reach for a toy; reach, fill, and lift spoon to mouth). |
| Visual | *High intensity:* to increase opportunity to notice object; to generate arousal for task (e.g., cover blocks with foil for manipulation task). <br> *High contrast:* to enhance possibility of locating the object and maintaining attention to it (e.g., place raisins on a piece of typing paper for prehension activity). <br> *Variable:* to maintain attention to or interest in the task (e.g., play rolling catch with a clear ball that has moveable pieces inside). | *Low intensity:* to allow the visual stimulus to blend with other salient features; to generate searching behaviors because characteristics are less obvious (e.g., find own cubbyhole in back of the room). <br> *High similarity:* to establish more discerning abilities; to develop skills for naturally occurring tasks (e.g., scoop applesauce from beige plate). <br> *Competitive:* to facilitate searching; to increase tolerance for natural life circumstances (e.g, obtain correct tools from equipment bin). |

(continued)

Table 6. (continued)

| Sensory system | Arousal/alerting descriptors | Discrimination/mapping descriptors |
|---|---|---|
| Auditory | *Variable:* to maintain attention to or interest in the task (e.g., play radio station after activating a switch).<br>*High intensity:* to stimulate noticing the person or object; to create proper alerting for task performance (e.g., ring a bell to encourage the child to locate the stimulus). | *Rhythmic:* to provide predictable and organizing information for environmental orientation (e.g., sing a nursery rhyme while physically guiding motions).<br>*Constant:* to provide a foundational stimulus for environmental orientations; especially important when other sensory systems (e.g., vision, vestibular) do not provide orientation (e.g., child recognizes own classroom by fan noise and calms down).<br>*Competitive:* to facilitate differentiation of salient stimuli; to increase tolerance for natural life circumstances (e.g., after child learns to look when her name is called, conduct activity within busy classroom).<br>*Noncompetitive:* to facilitate focused attention for acquiring a new and difficult skill; to calm a child who has been overstimulated (e.g., move child to quiet room to establish vocalizations).<br>*Low intensity:* to allow the auditory stimulus to blend with other salient features; to generate searching behaviors because stimulus is less obvious (e.g., give child a direction in a normal volume). |
| Olfactory/ gustatory | *Strong intensity:* to stimulate arousal for task (e.g., child smells spaghetti sauce at lunch). | *Mild intensity:* to facilitate exploratory behaviors; to stimulate naturally occurring activities (e.g., smell of lunch food is less distinct, so child is encouraged to notice texture, color). |

From Dunn, W. (1991c). The sensorimotor systems: A framework for assessment and intervention. In F.P. Orelove & D. Sobsey, *Educating children with multiple disabilities: A transdisciplinary approach* (2nd ed.) (pp. 70–73). Baltimore: Paul H. Brookes Publishing Co.; reprinted by permission.

Table 7. Examples of observable behaviors that indicate difficulty with sensory processing during daily life tasks

| Sensory system | Personal hygiene | Dressing | Eating | Homemaking | School/work | Play |
|---|---|---|---|---|---|---|
| Somatosensory | Withdraws from splashing water<br>Pushes washcloth/towel away<br>Cries when hair is washed and dried<br>Makes face when toothpaste gets on lips, tongue<br>Tenses when bottom is wiped after toileting | Tolerates a narrow range of clothing items<br>Prefers tight clothing<br>More irritable with loose-textured clothing<br>Cries during dressing<br>Pulls at hats, head gear, accessories | Only tolerates food at one temperature<br>Gags with textured food or utensils in mouth<br>Winces when face is wiped<br>Hand extends and avoids objects and surfaces (finger food, utensils) | Avoids participation in tasks that are wet, dirty<br>Seeks to remove batter that falls on arms | Cries when tape or glue gets on skin<br>Overreacts to pats, hugs; avoids these actions<br>Only tolerates one type of paper, only wooden objects<br>Hands extend when attempting to type | Selects a narrow range of toys, textures similar<br>Can't hold on to toys/objects<br>Rubs toys on face, arms<br>Mouths objects |
| Proprioception | Can't lift objects that are heavier, such as a new bar of soap<br>Can't change head position to use sink and mirror in same task | Can't support heavier items (e.g., belt with buckle, shoes)<br>Fatigues prior to task completion<br>Misses when placing arm or leg in clothing | Uses external support to eat (e.g., propping)<br>Tires before completing meal<br>Can't provide force to cut meat<br>Tires before completing foods that need to be chewed | Drops equipment (e.g., broom)<br>Uses external support such as leaning on counter to stir batter<br>Difficulty pouring a glass of milk | Drops books<br>Becomes uncomfortable in a particular position<br>Hooks limbs on furniture to obtain support<br>Moves arm, hand in repetitive patterns (self-stimulatory) | Unable to sustain movements during play<br>Tires before game is complete<br>Drops heavy parts of a toy/game |

| | | | | | | |
|---|---|---|---|---|---|---|
| Vestibular | Becomes disoriented when bending over the sink<br>Falls when trying to participate in washing lower extremities | Gets overly excited/distracted after bending down to assist in putting on socks<br>Cries when moved around a lot during dressing | Holds head stiffly in one position during mealtime<br>Gets distracted from meal after several head position changes | Avoids leaning to obtain cooking utensil<br>Becomes overly excited after moving around the room to dust | Avoids turning head to look at persons, to find source of a sound<br>After being transported in a wheelchair, more difficult to get on task<br>Moves head in repetitive pattern (self-stimulatory) | Avoids play that includes movement<br>Becomes overly excited or anxious when moving during play<br>Rocks excessively<br>Craves movement |
| Visual | Can't find utensils on the sink<br>Difficulty spotting desired item in drawer<br>Misses when applying paste to toothbrush | Can't find buttons on patterned or solid clothing<br>Overlooks desired shirt in closet or drawer<br>Misses armhole when donning shirt | Misses utensils on the table<br>Has trouble getting foods onto spoon when they are a similar color to the plate | Can't locate correct canned item in the pantry<br>Has difficulty finding cooking utensils in the drawer | Can't keep place on a page<br>Can't locate desired item on communication board<br>Attends excessively to bright or flashing objects | Trouble with matching, sorting activities<br>Trouble locating desired toy on cluttered shelf |

*(continued)*

Table 7. (continued)

| Sensory system | Personal hygiene | Dressing | Eating | Homemaking | School/work | Play |
|---|---|---|---|---|---|---|
| Auditory | Cries when hair dryer is turned on<br>Becomes upset by running water<br>Jerks when toilet flushes | Distracted by clothing that makes noise (e.g., crisp cloth, accessories) | Distracted by noise of utensils against each other (e.g., spoon in bowl, knife on plate)<br>Can't keep eating when someone talks | Distracted by vacuum cleaner sound<br>Distracted by TV or radio during tasks | Distracted by squeaky wheelchair<br>Intolerant of noise others make in the room<br>Overreacts to door closing<br>Notices toilet flushing down the hall | Play is disrupted by sounds<br>Makes sounds constantly |
| Olfactory/ gustatory | Gags at taste of toothpaste<br>Jerks away at smell of soap | Overreacts to clothing when it has been washed in a new detergent | Tolerates a narrow range of foods<br>Becomes upset when certain hot foods are cooking | Becomes upset when house is being cleaned (odors of cleaners) | Overreacts to new person (new smells)<br>Intolerant of scratch-n-sniff stickers<br>Smells everything | Tastes or smells all objects before playing |

From Dunn, W. (1991c). The sensorimotor systems: A framework for assessment and intervention. In F.P. Orelove & D. Sobsey, *Educating children with multiple disabilities: A transdisciplinary approach* (2nd ed.) (pp. 62–66). Baltimore: Paul H. Brookes Publishing Co.; reprinted by permission.

the best ways to test the principles of NDT and to make a stronger effort to relate the outcomes of this intervention to functional performance.

Therapists have applied NDT primarily within a direct service model, but there are many concepts within NDT that can be applied within the daily routines of the early intervention program (Dunn, 1991c; Dunn & DeGangi, 1992). Dunn and DeGangi (1992) suggest that there are several key factors from NDT principles that can be applied in early intervention programs. First, knowledge about proper positioning can be beneficial for all children in an early intervention program. Proper positioning provides children with access to cues from the environment and provides adults with strategies for moving children who are not ambulatory.

Second, occupational therapists can provide the team with information about the effects of muscle tone on performance using an NDT perspective (Dunn & DeGangi, 1992). Rather than discuss the technical aspects of low and high muscle tone, it is more useful to point out the effects of tone on the child's abilities. When the care staff understand the reasons for particular recommendations, they are more likely to carry out the recommendations consistently. For example, when a child has increased extensor tone, the body arches back and the child is difficult to position in sitting for subsequent tasks, such as toileting. Simple handling and carrying techniques can minimize the power of extensor tone and enable the care staff to keep the child in a more flexed position when being carried, thereby making toileting easier to accomplish.

Children with high muscle tone (e.g., spasticity) may also adaptively use that tone to support themselves while reaching for a cookie that is out of reach. In this case, the motivation to complete this task interacts with the usually negative effects of the high muscle tone, enabling the child to perform successfully. During a typical direct service therapeutic interaction in which the therapist was working on reaching, the child may not have demonstrated the reaching ability.

Third, the NDT perspective offers the therapist knowledge about how to teach others specific therapeutic techniques. For example, the therapist can teach early intervention staff how to provide physical guidance and facilitation to movements within functional tasks (Campbell, 1987a). If the other team members know how to provide appropriate input and support during desired tasks, the child has many more opportunities to experience and practice functional movements. Embedding the facilitation techniques into daily routines is also more motivating for the child; exercising is not nearly as much fun as tasks we enjoy for any of us.

Finally, Dunn and DeGangi (1992) suggest that therapists can teach others about recognizing, interpreting, and responding to young children's cues, using both an NDT and sensory integration perspective. By teaching early intervention team members and families what to notice about the child, and how to interpret the behaviors the child exhibits, the therapist is giving more options for creating a successful outcome for the child. For example, if a child cries when the teachers hold him or her, the teachers may immediately think of hunger, thirst, or soiled diapers as the cause of the discomfort. If the teachers act on these hypotheses, and the child continues to cry, they may be out of ideas for intervening with the child. From an NDT and sensory integration perspective, the child may be responding to the places where he or she is being touched, the firmness of the touch, or the movements associated with being held. The therapist can then offer alternative hypotheses for the crying and therefore create additional suggestions for intervention. The therapist and teacher then collaborate to test each idea and determine which is correct, enabling the early intervention team to learn more refined information about the child over time.

*Applying Interdisciplinary Frames of Reference to Functional Skills* The most important aspect of having specialized knowledge is being able to apply it to relevant problems. Table 8 provides an example of applying four common early intervention frames of reference to the same problem: drinking from a cup. No one perspective is adequate to consider all

Table 8.  Parameters considered for a child who needs to learn to drink from a cup independently

| Frame of reference/ perspective | Factors to consider |
| --- | --- |
| Neurodevelopmental | What is the status of muscle tone (e.g., hypertonus, hypotonus)? Does muscle tone interfere with movement (e.g., tightness restricts movement, low tone prohibits child from moving)? What is the base of support (e.g., legs, pelvis, back supporting body weight when sitting)? How is the trunk aligned for the task? How can I support functional movement (e.g., use facilitation or inhibition)? |
| Sensory integrative | Does the child notice the stimulus (e.g., voice command, cup of liquid)? How does the child respond to positioning (e.g., light touch, touch pressure)? What are characteristics of cup surface (e.g., on hand, on lips)? Will the grasping pattern further enable adaptive responses, or will it interfere with movement (e.g., the tension for gripping may enhance extension muscle tone, then the child cannot get the cup to his mouth)? |
| Behavioral | Is the child interested in drinking from cup? Does the child like the liquid being used? Is the child thirsty? How does the child know it's time to drink (e.g., what cues are used—verbal prompt, physical prompt)? |
| Cognitive | Does the child understand what he or she is supposed to do? Does the child have the perceptual skills to accomplish the task (e.g., can he find the cup on the table with other eating utensils)? Can the child generalize skills from one cup to another? From one setting to another? |

From Dunn, W. (1991c). The sensorimotor systems: A framework for assessment and intervention. In F.P. Orelove & D. Sobsey, *Educating children with multiple disabilities: A transdisciplinary approach* (2nd ed.) (p. 59). Baltimore: Paul H. Brookes Publishing Co.; reprinted by permission.

relevant factors. Teams can identify more variables with multiple perspectives and have a better chance of identifying possible interventions. This is the goal of all team interactions.

## CONCLUSIONS

Occupational therapy is a key profession on the interdisciplinary early intervention team. Occupational therapy addresses the needs and desires of children and families to participate in activities that are meaningful in their lives. Therapists address this goal of participation by considering 1) the child's sensorimotor, cognitive, and psychosocial skills and deficits; 2) the features of the tasks the child and family wish to perform; and 3) the characteristics of the environment in which the task occurs. Occupational therapists are particularly skilled at creating adaptations that make tasks and environments more user-friendly.

Because occupational therapists employ a contextual view of the child's performance, they have many skills that complement those of other disciplines. Occupational therapists value the collaboration of other colleagues and families because multiple points of view create a more complete picture of performance and expand intervention possibilities.

## REFERENCES

American Occupational Therapy Association. (1994). *Uniform terminology for occupational therapy: Application to practice*. Rockville, MD: Author.

Americans with Disabilities Act of 1990, PL 101-336. (July 26, 1990). Title 42, U.S.C. §§ 12101 et seq.: *U.S. Statutes at Large, 104*, 327–378.

Arendt, R.E., MacLean, W.E., Jr., & Baumeister, A.A. (1988). Critique of sensory integration therapy and its application in mental retardation. *Journal of Mental Retardation, 92*, 401–411.

Bobath, K., & Bobath, B. (1984). The neurodevelopmental treatment. In D. Scrutton (Ed.), *Management of the motor disorders of children with cerebral palsy* (pp. 6–18). Philadelphia: J.B. Lippincott.

Breines, E. (1984). An attempt to define purposeful activity. *American Journal of Occupational Therapy, 38*, 543–544.

Burns, Y.R. (1988). Sensory integration or the role of sensation in movement. *Journal of Mental Retardation, 92*, 412.

Campbell, P.H. (1987a). Integrated programming for students with multiple handicaps. In L. Goetz, D. Guess, & K. Stremel-Campbell (Eds.), *Innovative program design for individuals with dual sensory impairments* (pp. 159–188). Baltimore: Paul H. Brookes Publishing Co.

Campbell, P.H. (1987b). The integrated programming team: An approach for coordinating professionals of various disciplines in programs for students with severe and multiple handicaps. *Journal of The Association for Persons with Severe Handicaps, 12*(2), 107–116.

Case-Smith, J. (1991). Occupational and physical therapists as case managers in early intervention. *Physical and Occupational Therapy in Pediatrics, 11*(1), 53–70.

Case-Smith, J. (Ed.). (1993). *Pediatric occupational therapy and early intervention.* Stoneham, MA: Butterworth-Heinemann.

Cermak, S.A. (1988). Sensible integration. *Journal of Mental Retardation, 92,* 413–414.

Chandler, B., Dunn, W., & Rourk, J. (1989). *Guidelines for occupational therapy services in school systems* (2nd ed.). Rockville, MD: American Occupational Therapy Association.

Clark, F., & Primeau, L.A. (1988). Obfuscation of sensory integration: A matter of professional predation. *Journal of Mental Retardation, 92,* 415–419.

Clark, P.N. (1979). Human development through occupation: Theoretical frameworks in contemporary occupational therapy practice, Part 1. *American Journal of Occupational Therapy, 33,* 505–514.

Cook, D. (1991). The assessment process. In W. Dunn (Ed.), *Pediatric occupational therapy* (pp. 35–72). Thorofare, NJ: Slack.

Dunn, W. (1988a). Basic and applied neuroscience research provides a base for sensory integration theory. *Journal of Mental Retardation, 92,* 420–422.

Dunn, W. (1988b). Models of occupational therapy service provision in the school system. *American Journal of Occupational Therapy, 42*(11), 718–723.

Dunn, W. (1990). A comparison of service provision models in school-based occupational therapy services. *Occupational Therapy Journal of Research.*

Dunn, W. (1991a). Dimensions of performance. In C. Christiansen & C. Baum (Eds.), *Occupational therapy: Overcoming human performance deficits* (pp. 230–257). Thorofare, NJ: Slack.

Dunn, W. (1991b). Integrated related services. In L.H. Meyer, C.A. Peck, & L. Brown (Eds.), *Critical issues in the lives of people with severe disabilities* (pp. 353–377). Baltimore: Paul H. Brookes Publishing Co.

Dunn, W. (1991c). The sensorimotor systems: A framework for assessment and intervention. In F.P. Orelove & D. Sobsey, *Educating children with multiple disabilities: A transdisciplinary approach* (2nd ed.) (pp. 33–78). Baltimore: Paul H. Brookes Publishing Co.

Dunn, W. (1992). Consultation: How, when, and why. In C.B. Royeen (Ed.), *AOTA self study series on schools: Lesson 5.* Rockville, MD: American Occupational Therapy Association.

Dunn, W., Brown, T., & McGuigan, A. (1994). The ecology of human performance: A framework for considering the effect of context. *American Journal of Occupational Therapy, 48*(7), 595–607.

Dunn, W., & Campbell, P. (1991). Designing pediatric service provision. In W. Dunn (Ed.), *Pediatric Occupational Therapy* (pp. 139–159). Thorofare, NJ: Slack.

Dunn, W., Campbell, P., Oetter, P., & Berger, E. (1989). *Guidelines for occupational therapy services in early intervention and preschool services.* Rockville, MD: American Occupational Therapy Association.

Dunn, W., & DeGangi, G. (1992). Sensory integration and neurodevelopmental treatment for educational programming. In C.B. Royeen (Ed.), *AOTA self study series on schools.* Rockville, MD: American Occupational Therapy Association.

Dunn, W., Moore, W., Brown, T., & Westman, K. (1994). *Development of a consolidated model for providing inclusive education and related services for children and youth with disabilities.* Unfunded OSEP Grant.

Education for All Handicapped Children Act of 1975, PL 94-142. (August 23, 1977). Title 20, U.S.C. §§ 1400 et seq.: *U.S. Statutes at Large, 89,* 773–796.

Education of the Handicapped Act Amendments of 1986, PL 99-457. (October 8, 1986). Title 20, U.S.C. §§ 1400 et seq.: *U.S. Statutes at Large, 100*, 1145-1177.

Ellis, E. (1967). *Physical management of developmental disorders (Clinics in Developmental Medicine No. 26).* London: Spastics International Medical Publications/ Heinemann.

Fewell, R. (1988). Follow-up findings of a program for motor skill achievement. *Topics in Early Childhood Special Education, 7*(4), 70.

Fidler, G.S., & Fidler, J.W. (1978). Doing and becoming: Purposeful action and self actualization. *American Journal of Occupational Therapy, 32,* 305-310.

Finch, E. (1985). Deinstitutionalization: Mental health and mental retardation services. *Psychosocial Rehabilitation Journal, VIII*(3), 36-47.

Giangreco, M.F. (1986a). Delivery of therapeutic services in special education programs for learners with severe handicaps. *Physical and Occupational Therapy in Pediatrics, 6*(2), 5-15.

Giangreco, M.F. (1986b). Effects of integrated therapy: A pilot study. *Journal of The Association for Persons with Severe Handicaps, 11*(3), 205-208.

Giangreco, M., Edelman, S., & Dennis, R. (1991). Common professional practices that interfere with the integrated delivery of related services. *Remedial and Special Education, 12*(2), 16-24.

Gliner, J.A. (1985). Purposeful activity in motor learning theory: An event approach to motor skill acquisition. *American Journal of Occupational Therapy, 39,* 28-34.

Gorga, D. (1989). Occupational therapy treatments practices with infants in early intervention. *American Journal of Occupational Therapy, 43*(11), 731-736.

Hanft, B. (1989). Early intervention: Issues in specialization. *American Journal of Occupational Therapy, 43*(7), 431-434.

Hanft, B. (1991). Impact of federal policy on pediatric health and education programs. In W. Dunn (Ed.), *Pediatric occupational therapy* (pp. 273-284). Thorofare, NJ: Slack.

Hanft, B., & Humphrey, R. (1989). Training occupational therapists in early intervention. *Infants and Young Children, 1*(4), 54-65.

Harris, S.R. (1981). Effects of neurodevelopmental therapy on improving motor performance in Down's syndrome infants. *Developmental Medicine and Child Neurology, 23,* 477-483.

Harris, S. (1988). Early intervention: Does developmental therapy make a difference? *Topics in Early Childhood Special Education, 7*(4), 20-32.

Harris, S.R., & Riffle, K. (1986). Effects of ankle-foot orthoses on standing balance in a child with cerebral palsy. *Physical Therapy, 66,* 663-667.

Hinojosa, J., Sabari, J., Rosenfeld, M.S., & Shapiro, M.S. (1983). Purposeful activities. *American Journal of Occupational Therapy, 37,* 805-806.

Humphrey, R., & Link, S. (1990). Preparation of occupational therapists to work in early intervention programs. *American Journal of Occupational Therapy, 44*(9), 828-833.

Idol, L. (1987). Group story mapping: A comprehension strategy for both skilled and unskilled readers. *Journal of Learning Disabilities, 20,* 196-205.

Idol, L., Paolucci-Whitcomb, P., & Nevin, A. (1987). *Collaborative consultation.* Austin, TX: PRO-ED.

Individuals with Disabilities Education Amendments of 1991, PL 102-119. (October 7, 1991). Title 20, U.S.C. §§ 1400 et seq.: *U.S. Statutes at Large, 105,* 587-608.

Jones, T.W. (1983). Remediation of behavior-related eating problems: A preliminary investigation. *Journal of The Association for the Severely Handicapped, 8*(4), 62-71.

Kandell, E., Schwartz, J., & Jessell, T. (Eds.). (1992). *Principles of neural science.* New York: Elsevier/North Holland.

Kemmis, B., & Dunn, W. (1996). *A study of remedial and compensatory intervention in school contexts.* Manuscript submitted for publication.

Kimball, J.C. (1988). The emphasis is on integration, not sensory. *Journal of Mental Retardation, 92,* 423–424.

Kircher, M.A. (1984). Motivation as a factor of perceived exertion in purposeful versus nonpurposeful activity. *American Journal of Occupational Therapy, 38,* 165–170.

Laskas, C.A., Mullen, S.L., Nelson, D.L., & Wilson-Broyles, M. (1985). Enhancement of two motor functions of the lower extremity in a child with spastic quadriplegia. *Physical Therapy, 65,* 11–16.

Lawlor, M., & Henderson, A. (1989). A descriptive study of the clinical practice patterns of occupational therapists working with infants and young children. *American Journal of Occupational Therapy, 43*(11), 755–764.

Mather, J., & Weinstein, E. (1988). Teachers and therapists: Evolution of a partnership in early intervention. In J. Neisworth, S. Garwood, & R. Fewell (Eds.), *Topics in Early Childhood Special Education* (pp. 1–9). Austin, TX: PRO-ED.

Menzler, C. (1986). *The advocacy for change training manual.* Washington, DC: National Association of Developmental Disability Councils.

Meyen, E.L. (1982). *Exceptional children in today's schools: An alternative resource book* (pp. 35, 587). Denver, CO: Love Publishing Co.

Ottenbacher, K. (1982a). Sensory integration therapy: Affect or effect. *American Journal of Occupational Therapy, 36*(9), 571–578.

Ottenbacher, K. (1982b). Occupational therapy and special education: Some concerns related to Public Law 94-142. *American Journal of Occupational Therapy, 36*(2), 81–84.

Ottenbacher, K.J. (1988). Sensory integration—myth, method, and imperative. *Journal of Mental Retardation, 92,* 425–426.

Ottenbacher, K. (1989). Statistical conclusion validity of early intervention research with handicapped children. *Exceptional Children, 55*(6), 534–540.

Ottenbacher, K., Biocca, Z., DeCremer, G., Bevelinger, M., Jedlovec, K.B., & Johnson, M.B. (1986). Quantitative analysis of the effectiveness of pediatric therapy: Emphasis on the neurodevelopmental treatment approach. *Physical Therapy, 66,* 1095–1101.

Palinscar, A. (1986). The role of dialogue in providing scaffolded instruction. *Educational Psychologist, 21*(1&2), 73–98.

Palmer, F.B., Shapiro, B.K., Wachtel, R.C., Allen, M.C., Hiller, J.E., Harryman, S.E., Mosher, B.S., Meinert, C.L., & Capute, A.J. (1988). The effects of physical therapy on cerebral palsy. *New England Journal of Medicine, 318,* 803–808.

Parette, H.P., Jr., & Hourcade, J.J. (1984a). A review of therapeutic intervention research on gross and fine motor progress in young children with cerebral palsy. *American Journal of Occupational Therapy, 38,* 462–468.

Parette, H.P., Jr., & Hourcade, J.J. (1984b). How effective are physiotherapeutic programmes with young mentally retarded children who have cerebral palsy? *Journal of Mental Deficiency Research, 28,* 167–175.

Peck, C.A., Killen, C.C., & Baumgart, D. (1989). Increasing implementation of special education instruction in mainstream preschools: Direct and generalized nondirective consultation. *Journal of Applied Behavioral Analysis, 22,* 197–210.

Pierce, D. (1991). Early object rule acquisition. *American Journal of Occupational Therapy, 45*(5), 438–449.

Piper, M.C., Kunos, V.I., Willis, D.M., Mazer, G.L., Ransay, M., & Silver, K.M. (1986). Early physical therapy effects on the high-risk infant: A randomized controlled trial. *Pediatrics, 78,* 216–224.

Pryzwansky, W.B., & White, G.W. (1983). The influence of consultee characteristics on preferences for consultation approaches. *Professional Psychology Research and Practices, 14*(4), 457–461.

Rainforth, B., York, J., & Macdonald, C. (1992). *Collaborative teams for students with severe disabilities: Integrating therapy and educational services.* Baltimore: Paul H. Brookes Publishing Co.

Sailor, W., Anderson, J.L., Halvorsen, A.T., Doering, K., Filler, J., & Goetz, L. (1989). *The comprehensive local school: Regular education for all students with disabilities.* Baltimore: Paul H. Brookes Publishing Co.

Schaaf, R., & Mulrooney, L. (1989). Occupational therapy in early intervention: A family centered approach. *American Journal of Occupational Therapy, 43*(11), 745–754.

Social Security Act of 1935, PL 74-271. (August 14, 1935). Title 42, U.S.C. §§ 301 et seq.: *U.S. Statutes at Large, 15,* 687–1774.

Social Security Act Amendments of 1965, PL 89-97. (July 30, 1965). Title I, U.S.C. §§ 401–425: *U.S. Statutes at Large, 79,* 329–339.

Stainback, W., & Stainback, S. (Eds.). (1990). *Support networks for inclusive schools: Interdependent integrated education.* Baltimore: Paul H. Brookes Publishing Co.

Steinbeck, T.M. (1986). Purposeful activity and performance. *American Journal of Occupational Therapy, 40,* 529–534.

Stern, F.M., & Gorga, D. (1988). Neurodevelopmental treatment (NDT): Therapeutic intervention and its efficacy. *Infants and Young Children, 1,* 22–32.

Technology-Related Assistance for Individuals with Disabilities Act of 1988, PL 100-407. (August 19, 1988). Title 29, U.S.C. §§ 2201 et seq.: *U.S. Statutes at Large, 102,* 1044–1065.

West, J.F., & Idol, L. (1987). School consultation (Part I): An interdisciplinary perspective on theory, models, and research. *Journal of Learning Disabilities, 20,* 388–408.

West, W.L. (1984). A reaffirmed philosophy and practice of occupational therapy for the 1980s. *American Journal of Occupational Therapy, 38,* 15–23.

Willard, H., & Spackman, C. (1978). *Occupational therapy* (5th ed.). Philadelphia: J.B. Lippincott.

# Chapter 12

# Collaborative Consultation Across Seven Disciplines

*Challenges and Solutions*

## P.J. McWilliam

The preceding chapters address issues and strategies related to integrated therapy for four professional disciplines: early childhood special education, speech-language pathology, physical therapy, and occupational therapy. Many eligible infants and preschoolers receive services from these disciplines, and professionals representing these disciplines are frequently active members of early intervention assessment and intervention teams. It is not surprising that these four disciplines are often thought of as constituting the core of early intervention services.

Other disciplines, however, are involved in early intervention, and their role was not forgotten in the legislation governing services to infants and toddlers. Part H of PL 102-119, the Individuals with Disabilities Education Act Amendments of 1991, lists 11 disciplines that should be actively involved in early intervention efforts in every state to provide comprehensive services to children and their families. Professionals within these 11 disciplines include 1) early childhood special educators, 2) speech-language pathologists, 3) physical therapists, 4) occupational therapists, 5) psychologists, 6) nurses, 7) social workers, 8) physicians, 9) nutritionists, 10) audiologists, and 11) vision specialists.

Few children require the involvement of professionals from all 11 disciplines, but many children and families are involved to some degree with one or more professionals outside the four disciplines discussed in the previous chapters. The degree of involvement of the other seven disciplines varies considerably from one child and family to another. For some, involvement may consist of only a single assessment or a brief consultation. For others, a

315

professional from one of these disciplines may be the primary service provider and perhaps even the service coordinator (e.g., Dietz & Ferrell, 1993; Roush & McWilliam, 1990). Furthermore, the intensity of services required by any given child and family may change over time. The level of involvement of any discipline is determined on a case-by-case basis, taking into consideration such factors as the diagnosis of the child, the priorities of the family, the availability of alternative resources, the skills of other disciplines working with the child and family, and the environments in which the child lives and plays.

The nature of the work performed by professionals across the seven disciplines covered in this chapter is quite diverse. For example, on the surface, there is little in common between an audiologist diagnosing a young child's hearing impairment and prescribing amplification devices and a social worker obtaining food stamps, safe housing, and Supplemental Security Income (SSI) payments for a teenage mother of two in the inner city. What comparison is there between a psychologist who has been asked to consult with a classroom program about a child who is hitting or biting other children and a nutritionist who is asked to assist in the development of a diet for a child with Prader-Willi syndrome? Even within the same discipline, the work scope of these professionals is quite broad, and considerable knowledge and skill are required to fulfill the many functions each professional may be called on to perform. There are, however, a number of challenges that these seven disciplines have in common in integrating their work to provide services to young children and their families. This chapter discusses the challenges faced by these disciplines and describes some practical strategies for providing more integrated services.

## CHALLENGES TO SUCCESSFUL INTEGRATION

Although the professional literature is replete with pleas for interdisciplinary coordination, teaming, and interagency collaboration in early intervention (e.g., Bruder & Bologna, 1993; Klein & Campbell, 1990; Matkin, 1985; McGonigel & Garland, 1988; McGonigel, Woodruff, & Roszmann-Millican, 1994; Woodruff & McGonigel, 1988), the reality in many communities is a fragmented or patchwork service delivery system for infants, preschoolers, and their families (Baroni, Tutbill, Feenan, & Schroeder, 1994; Bruder & Bologna, 1993; McGarr, Dwyer, & Holland, 1995). It is rare enough for a program to have a speech-language pathologist, occupational therapist, or physical therapist on staff. These services are often provided on a part-time, contractual basis by private therapists or are provided by another community agency. It is almost unheard of for a program to have a nurse, audiologist, physician, or vision specialist on staff, even on a contractual basis. Occasionally, a program has a psychologist or social worker on staff, but even this is not standard practice (Odom & McEvoy, 1990; Wolery et al., 1994).

Professionals from these seven disciplines mostly will be employed by and work within an agency external to classroom-based programs. They may work in clinic settings, hospitals, private practice, or other publicly funded human services agencies. Regardless of the type of agency in which they work, the result is often the same: When called in as consultants, these professionals are frequently virtual strangers to the classroom teacher, other team members, and the child and family. There is often little, if any, time available for relationship building or teaming, especially when the professional is called in on an emergency basis or for a one-time-only consultation. The consulting professional is at a further disadvantage because he or she is usually unaware of the philosophy, policies, procedures, or even the scope and nature of services offered by the program with which he or she is consulting.

In some cases, two community agencies may serve many of the same children and families. When this happens, collaboration at the administrative level may solve some problems (Woodruff & Sterzin, 1988). Rarely, however, does it solve all of the problems, and this situation may be more the exception than the rule (Melaville & Blank, 1991). There are too many instances in which agencies serve very few of the same children and families and in which professionals within these seven disciplines are consulting with home-based or classroom-based programs for the first time.

Cross-agency work can be further complicated when agency policies and procedures place restrictions on how consulting professionals are allowed to provide their services. For example, an audiologist working in a hospital-based clinic may be aware of the efforts needed to ensure integrated services for a child with a hearing impairment in a community child care center, but may be unable to carry through with what is needed. The medical model adhered to by the clinic and the hospital's sources of funding may dictate the amount of time the audiologist can devote to any one client, where services take place, the type of services that are provided, and what constitutes billable hours (Fox, Wicks, McManus, & Newacheck, 1992).

Where the work of consulting professionals is conducted may be one of the greatest challenges to integrated services and may be partially determined by the discipline itself. For example, the work of an audiologist is typically conducted in a hospital clinic or private office because that is where the necessary equipment is located. Similarly, the overall nature of social work frequently places social workers in family's homes and community settings. Within each discipline, however, variations in the type of services provided result in different locations. For example, a psychologist conducting a standardized assessment typically does so in a private office or a clinic setting, whereas a psychologist consulting for a child exhibiting behavior problems is more likely to do so in the family's home or in the classroom environment.

To what extent can the work of professionals in these disparate locations be integrated into the classroom environment? Can the psychologist conducting an assessment in an evaluation clinic, the audiologist working in a hospital clinic, or the social worker visiting the family's home contribute significantly to the child's progress and day-to-day functioning within the classroom environment? Or must these professionals also conduct at least part of their work in the classroom setting to be truly effective?

Even when services are conducted within the classroom, these professionals are usually limited by the duration and intensity of services that they can offer any one child or program. For some, coordination within the classroom may consist of one or two visits, such as the psychologist who is contracted to assist with a child exhibiting behavior problems. For others, such as a vision specialist serving as an itinerant teacher for a child with severe visual impairment, visits to the classroom may be as often as once or twice a week for as long as the child remains enrolled in the classroom program. For still others, such as a nurse teaching self-catheterization skills to an older preschooler with spina bifida, a high level of services may be provided for a relatively short amount of time.

Whatever the duration or intensity of services, few, if any, of these professionals are in the classroom all day and every day. Even those who can be in the classroom all day do so only for a limited time. How can we ensure that the time spent by consulting professionals in the classroom is put to best use? Does the time spent in the classroom have a positive influence on the child's progress and day-to-day functioning when the consulting professional is not there, or after consultation services have ended?

Another issue that consulting professionals face is defining what their role is in working with parents (File & Kontos, 1992). This is often unclear and can be quite confusing, especially for those professionals who believe strongly in a family-centered approach to services. When services are requested and paid for by a classroom-based program, who is the primary service recipient—the individual child, the classroom teacher, or the family? When parents and classroom staff are in agreement on what the child needs and how services are to be provided, the question may be unnecessary. But what happens when there is disagreement between the teacher and the parents? And how can the professional know what the parents think is important for their children and themselves if the professionals do not have contact with the parents?

In some situations, the primary contact of the consulting professional may be with the parents, even when the services are requested by the classroom program. This is typically the case when a child is evaluated by an external agency or receives therapy in a clinic-based setting and the parent brings the child to these settings for services. It is also the case for social workers who conduct home visits. In such situations, what responsibility, if any, does the professional have for communicating and coordinating activities with the classroom program?

In summary, the challenges to integrating the services provided by professionals within these seven disciplines are many. These professionals are typically not regular members of early intervention teams. The services they provide may or may not even be in the same location as the classroom program. The time they have available for providing services is usually limited, and their roles related to working with families and facilitating home–school coordination may be unclear.

Failure to address these challenges and develop strategies for improving the integration of services may threaten the quality and effectiveness of services for many children and families enrolled in early intervention programs. It is unrealistic to think that the challenges and limitations previously described can be resolved quickly. The structures of services in most states and local communities have long-standing traditions. Furthermore, the cost of making the necessary changes is likely to be prohibitive on the tight budgets of most human services programs. To make improvements, however, some changes in how services are provided may be necessary.

First, strategies are needed to ensure that the services provided by consulting professionals address the functional needs of children and families—that the areas of child development and behavior addressed by their services are important to families and are immediately relevant to the child's ability to function effectively in his or her daily routines at home and in the classroom. Second, strategies are needed to ensure that the interventions that consulting professionals develop are practical, that they are easily implemented by parents and teachers within the context of daily routines. Third, strategies are needed to ensure that the effectiveness of interventions is maintained over time, and that parents and teachers are sufficiently knowledgeable and skilled to handle any difficulties that may arise after consultation services have ended. The remainder of this chapter further delineates the need for strategies in these three areas and provides alternative methods within each area for achieving more integrated service delivery.

## SOLUTIONS FOR CONSULTING PROFESSIONALS

### Identifying Functional Goals

The reasons why children are referred to any of the disciplines discussed in this chapter are enormously diverse. Children may be referred for assessment or diagnosis if, for example, they are suspected of having a hearing impairment, are exhibiting developmental delays, or show symptoms that indicate a possible medical or psychiatric condition that may warrant treatment. Children may also be referred for discipline-specific interventions, such as controlling aggressive or destructive behavior, or mobility training and braille awareness for a child who is blind.

Whatever the reason for referral, it is likely that the consulting professional knows little about the characteristics of the settings in which the child lives and plays or how the child functions within his or her daily routines. Further-more, the consultant is not likely to have a full understanding of parents' or teachers' concerns or their perceptions and expectations of the child. Obtaining this type of information is the first order of business if the consulting profes-sional is to develop interventions that are practical and meaningful. But how is such information obtained, especially when referral information is vague and contacts with children and caregivers are brief?

Two basic strategies may be used to identify functional goals: 1) observing the child within the context of daily routines, and 2) interviewing the child's parents and teachers. These two strategies are discussed separately below; it should be noted, however, that a combination of observing and interviewing usually produces the best results.

**Observing**    Observing the child within the context of his or her daily living environments provides the consulting professional with four important pieces of information. First, the consultant sees what skills the child needs to function successfully within the physical structure and routines of home or school. Second, the consultant observes how the child uses the skills he or she has and any adaptations the child makes to participate in daily routines. Third, the consultant can see how parents, teachers, and other children respond to the child. Fourth, the consultant is afforded a glimpse of the resources available in the environment and any constraints imposed on parents or teachers (e.g., time, space, materials, child–staff ratios) that may affect their ability to imple-ment interventions with the child.

The more time a consultant can spend watching a child within his or her daily routines, the more the consultant will learn. However, the amount of time consultants can spend observing is probably limited. If so, consultants can ask parents or teachers what they think is most important to observe and when the best times are to visit the home or classroom to observe these particular aspects of the child's behavior.

There are some situations that do not permit the consulting professional to visit and observe children in their daily living environments. For example, a psychologist who works in a diagnostic and evaluation clinic, an audiologist who conducts hearing tests in a hospital or private office, or a nutritionist or nurse working in a public health facility may not have the time to make visits. In such cases, teachers, parents, or other therapists can videotape the child and show the tapes to the consultant as a reasonable substitute for direct observa-tion. Videotaping may, in fact, be advantageous in that it provides more opportunities for parents or teachers to record those situations and aspects of child behavior that they think are important for the consultant to see.

**Interviewing**    Sometimes neither direct observation nor videotaping is possible. In other situations, observation may be feasible in the classroom, but not in the child's home, or vice versa. In either case, interviewing parents and teachers can provide some of the information that would otherwise be obtained through observation. It should be remembered, however, that information obtained through interviewing may be biased by the perspective of the parent or teacher being interviewed. Although their perspectives are important, if the consultant were to directly observe the same situation, the consultant's interpretation probably would be slightly different as a result of his or her professional training, knowledge, and experience. In other words, valuable information may be lost if the consultant is not afforded a clear picture of the child within the context of daily routines.

The purpose of interviewing parents and teachers is twofold: 1) to obtain background information relevant to the reason for the child's referral, and 2) to understand what the parents' and teachers' priorities are for the child. Background information such as birth histories, diagnoses, developmental progress, and intervention strategies can be obtained from medical reports and other professional records. Whenever possible, such written documents should be requested and reviewed before the consultant assesses the child or prescribes interventions.

Consultants should keep in mind, however, that past records may be invalid, such as when a child's behavior during past testing was not amenable to obtaining an accurate assessment or if subsequent testing did not substantiate a previous diagnosis and if this updated information is not in the reports the consultant receives. Rather than accepting past records at face value or assuming that all the relevant information is in them, consultants can talk with caregivers about the child's background and the reports the consultants have received. They can ask parents or teachers what reports are most important and whether the information in them is accurate and complete. They can inquire about additional records and whether there is anything else that should be known about the child that may not be in the child's records. In addition to becoming better informed, consultants who ask these questions are communicating that they want to provide quality services, that they value the information parents and teachers have to offer, and that they respect their opinions about the child's needs. Even more important than obtaining background information is that talking with caregivers allows consultants to find out what parents or teachers want from their services, that is, what consultants can offer that will be useful in caring for the child on a day-to-day basis and in planning for the child's future.

Consultants often work in agencies that serve a large number of clients; thus, referrals and appointments may be handled by a receptionist or someone other than the professional who will be providing services. Although efficient in terms of how professional time is used, handling referrals in this manner can result in delivery of services that do not address the concerns of parents and teachers. For instance, suppose a child is referred to a developmental evaluation clinic for a psychological evaluation. The clinic's receptionist schedules an appointment, and, when the child arrives, the psychologist is prepared for and conducts a routine assessment of cognitive functioning and adaptive skills. This information may be exactly what the parents or teachers had hoped to receive. Then again, the child's level of cognitive functioning may be of relatively little concern to them. For example, they may be more concerned that the child does not sleep well at night or is difficult to manage in the classroom or that repeated efforts to toilet-train the child have been ineffective. Even if the child comes to the clinic for a routine psychological evaluation, the psychologist may be able to provide some insight into or assistance with these concerns. To provide such assistance, however, the psychologist must first know that these concerns exist, and that can happen only if the psychologist communicates with parents and teachers.

The same holds true for any professional who conducts assessments or evaluations. For example, much time is usually involved in conducting audiological assessments and ensuring that amplification devices are properly adjusted to meet the child's needs. But how much time is spent talking with teachers and parents about the child's day-to-day functioning at home and at school? Maybe the teacher is concerned that the child does not join in the play of other children in the classroom. Maybe the car rides to school and back home are miserable for the parent and the child because it is difficult to communicate in this situation. These and other concerns that parents or teachers may have probably can be addressed by the audiologist if he or she is aware that these concerns exist.

What methods can consultants use to uncover caregivers' concerns and priorities? There are three basic strategies: 1) reviewing existing documents, 2) having parents and teachers complete surveys or questionnaires, and 3) talking directly to parents and teachers. Reviewing existing documents such as individualized family service plans (IFSPs) or individualized education programs (IEPs) may provide some insight on what is being worked on with the child at home and in the classroom. If the process used in developing and updating these documents is conducted in an ideal manner, these documents may be helpful. Unfortunately, this is not always the case, and the document itself rarely reveals what process was used in its development. The document may be outdated or incomplete; thus, it may not portray a complete picture of what is important to parents or teachers.

Having parents or teachers complete a brief questionnaire is a strategy for obtaining more updated and detailed information than an IFSP or IEP may provide. Questionnaires can be mailed or given to caregivers before the first contact with the consultant, or they can be completed during the initial meeting. Separate, and perhaps even different, questionnaires may be given to parents and classroom teachers to obtain information about the child in both the home and school settings. The format and content of questionnaires will vary depending on the particular discipline for which they are used and on the various services that can be offered. Questionnaires may consist of a list of child behaviors (e.g., toileting, getting along with peers, compliance, attention, feeding), rating scales on which parents or teachers are asked to indicate how concerned they are about each behavior as it relates to the particular child. Questionnaires may also be less structured, perhaps asking only a few open-ended questions about the child's strengths and needs and caregivers' concerns for the future. Alternatively, parents and teachers may only be asked to list on a sheet of paper what their primary concerns are and what they hope to gain as a result of the assessment or consultation.

Questionnaires may appear to be the easiest and most efficient method of obtaining information about caregivers' priorities. This is not the preferred method of parents, however. Most parents prefer informal conversations with professionals over the use of questionnaires for sharing information about themselves and their children (Bailey & Blasco, 1990). Furthermore, question-naires may restrict parents' and teachers' responses to only those items that are on the survey, and any additional concerns they have may go unmentioned. Paper-and-pencil methods also do not allow the give and take of information that is achieved through direct conversations. Conversations with parents and teachers allow the professional to ask follow-up questions, thus gaining more complete understanding of their concerns. Although talking with parents and teachers takes more time than the other two methods, the payoff may be worth the time if it results in providing more meaningful services.

Conversations with caregivers need not always involve scheduled appoint-ments for a face-to-face interview. Sometimes all that is needed is a brief phone call. For example, if a professional is scheduled to conduct a routine evaluation of a child, he or she could call the child's parents and teachers ahead of time to remind them of the upcoming appointment. At the same time, they could be asked if there is anything they are particularly concerned about or are working on with the child at home or at school that the consultant should look at or discuss with them when the child comes in for testing.

For example, suppose a nutritionist has been asked to provide an analysis of a child's diet. A phone call can make a big difference in the usefulness of the information the nutritionist gives to the child's caregivers. When requesting a 5-day dietary intake, the nutritionist can call the parents to explain the forms they have been given and encourage them to jot down any concerns they may have about the child's eating or diet. At the same time, the nutritionist can ask if there is any particular concern that he or she can help with or should keep in mind when analyzing the child's dietary intake. Perhaps the parents are concerned that the child may not be getting the amount of calcium needed, but the child does not like milk or other dairy products. Maybe they are concerned about giving meat to the child, for fear that the child's inefficient chewing caused by cerebral palsy may result in choking. Whatever the concerns or issues might be, after asking such questions, the nutritionist would be better prepared to conduct a dietary analysis that addresses caregivers' concerns and to make useful recommendations. In this particular situation, the nutritionist's report may provide suggestions for food substitutes or supplements or even include recipes that specifically address the child's intolerance for dairy products or meat.

Informal conversations can also take place while working with the child. Parents or teachers can be invited to sit in the testing room during a psychological assessment, or they can be offered the opportunity to sit in the booth during an audiological evaluation. They can then be asked questions throughout the assessment and be encouraged to talk about what the child can and cannot do at home or school and what they would most like to see the child accomplish next. Armed with this knowledge, the information and suggestions provided by the consultant are more likely to be useful and used.

Informal conversations or interviews with parents and teachers can also take place in conjunction with direct observations of the child at home or in the classroom. While watching, the consultant can ask questions about what the child is doing, whether it is typical for him or her, and what, if anything, parents or teachers would like the child to be able to do differently within each routine observed. This is the first step toward intervention planning—finding out what is important to those who provide the child's daily care. If intervention plans do not address parents' and teachers' priorities, it is unlikely that they will follow through with the plans that are developed. In other words, the work of the consultant may be doomed before it ever begins.

This does not mean, however, that consultants should automatically work on the first priority that parents or teachers identify for the child. Before any final decisions are made, caregivers deserve the benefit of the consultant's expertise. After all, if parents and teachers knew exactly what was important and what they should do, the consultant's services would never have been requested in the first place. Take, for example, the situation of an itinerant teacher of the visually impaired who consults with a preschool classroom for a young boy who is blind. In talking with the classroom teacher, the consultant discovers that one of the teacher's biggest concerns is the child's table manners. The child always puts his fingers in his food and bends his head to his plate, sniffing everything before he eats it. The teacher prides herself on teaching the children good table manners and finds his behavior unacceptable.

An explanation from the consultant with regard to why the young boy is engaging in such behavior may be all that is needed to increase the teacher's tolerance for the child's eating habits; thus, the teacher would no longer view this aspect of the child's development as the priority it originally was. Perhaps, too, the consultant notices when observing the child that he tends to stick with one toy or activity for prolonged periods rather than switching more frequently from one activity to another as the sighted children in the class tend to do. Alternatively, maybe the consultant notices that the other children have not befriended the boy. Usually, the other children avoid him, but sometimes they are outwardly negative in response to his social overtures. If the teacher has not voiced concern about these issues, the consultant should mention them, explaining that transitions between activities and social interactions are two of the most frequent difficulties for children who are blind (Erwin, 1993, 1994). With this knowledge, the teacher may be more observant of these aspects of the child's behavior and agree that intervention may be needed in these areas.

Teachers also may be limited in their knowledge about the development and needs of young children with hearing impairments (Roush & Matkin, 1994), the dietary requirements and behavioral characteristics of children with Prader-Willi syndrome (Raab, 1986), or the complex and multifaceted needs of children with human immunodeficiency virus (HIV) and their families (Lesar & Maldonado, 1994). For instance, teachers who have limited knowledge about HIV may focus their concerns on protecting the other children in the classroom rather than on protecting the child with HIV, who is probably at greater risk. Medical consultants, nurses, nutritionists, psychologists, and social workers have a great deal of information to offer teachers about the effects of HIV on children and families (Lesar & Maldonado, 1994).

By sharing their knowledge, experience, and perspectives, consultants put parents and teachers in a better position to identify appropriate goals for intervention. They may not always accept or agree with consultants' ideas and opinions, but at least they have more information with which to guide their decisions. When they do not agree, little can be gained by consultants' pushing their opinions any further. In fact, when there is a disagreement between what caregivers and consultants see as priorities for a child, the wisest course of action is usually to go along with the priorities of parents and teachers. By respecting and responding to their priorities first, they may become more receptive to suggestions offered by the consultant. It should also be remembered that information sharing is a two-way street. Although consultants may have more information about and experience with a specific disability or intervention techniques, parents and teachers have more information about the individual child and how he or she functions within the context of daily routines.

## Designing Interventions

When designing and implementing interventions, consultants may be tempted to tell parents or teachers what they should do, show them how to do it, or do it themselves. This is not surprising, considering the target of intervention for the child is usually something the consultant has been specifically trained to address. Furthermore, it is not always easy for consultants to abandon the role of expert in favor of less directive methods of consultation (Pugach & Johnson, 1989). Under what circumstances should consultants do it themselves when designing and implementing interventions? When should they take a more indirect approach, sharing the responsibility with parents, teachers, and other therapists?

If consultants could pull children out of the home or classroom, fix them, and then return them to their natural environments without the need for additional interventions, the expert model would seem to be the most efficient use of everyone's time. Unfortunately, such situations are rare. There are few areas of child behavior or development that are amenable to a "fix 'em up and put 'em back" approach to consultation. Even in the prescription of hearing aids, which may seem to be a relatively straightforward and uncomplicated intervention, the likelihood of success is severely reduced unless parents and teachers are involved and committed to their proper use (Roush & Gravel, 1994).

Children's learning and skill performance are highly dependent on the environments in which they live and play, including the physical characteristics of those environments, the types and scheduling of activities, and the responsiveness of adults and other children within these settings. Even when a consultant provides frequent or intense services, the majority of a child's time is still spent at home and school without the benefit of the consultant's presence. After the consultant's work is finished, maintenance of the child's successes will depend on the efforts of parents and teachers. Thus, parents and teachers should be included in planning children's interventions from the very beginning, and interventions should be conducted within natural contexts whenever possible.

Collaborative models of consultation are often recommended for working with classroom teachers (Erin, 1988; File & Kontos, 1992; Idol, Paolucci-Whitcomb, & Nevin, 1986; Phillips & McCullough, 1990; Pugach & Johnson, 1988), and research has shown that teachers prefer collaborative consultation over more directive approaches (Babcock & Pryzwansky, 1983; Pryzwansky & White, 1980). A basic assumption of collaborative consultation is equality in the relationships between consultants and consultees. Although the consultant is responsible for facilitating the input of caregivers, the purpose of such facilitation is to ensure that both parties have an opportunity to contribute their ideas and expertise in developing interventions for children. Thus, information sharing and joint problem solving constitute the core of the collaborative approach.

Based on their review of research on consultation, File and Kontos (1992) concluded that, in addition to professional expertise, consultants must have highly developed skills in interpersonal relationships and communication to be truly effective. In fact, consultants' interpersonal and communication skills have been shown to be good predictors of teachers' satisfaction with consultation (Schowengerdt, Fine, & Poggio, 1976; Weissenberger, Fine, & Poggio, 1982). These skills include communicating clearly, demonstrating sincere caring and empathy, and showing respect for the consultee (West & Cannon, 1988). The ability to elicit information from the consultee (Bergan & Tombari; 1976) and the availability of the consultant to engage in joint problem solving throughout the implementation of interventions (West & Cannon, 1988) also contribute to the success and perceived usefulness of consultation.

There are three major reasons for soliciting parents' and teachers' input and working with them in designing interventions: 1) to obtain information about any previous attempts that have been made to produce desired changes in child behavior, 2) to gain a better understanding of the resources available for implementing interventions and any potential barriers to success, and 3) to increase the likelihood that parents and teachers will be motivated and committed to implementing interventions and following through with procedures to maintain or continue treatment gains.

The first step is to find out what parents or teachers are currently doing to achieve their goals for the child, and what they have tried in the past. The consultant may ask the following types of questions to obtain this information:

- Is this something that you have worked on already? If so, please describe what you have done.
- How successful have your past attempts been?
- How satisfied were you with the results of your past attempts?
- If your past attempts were less than successful, why do you think they did not work?
- Based on your past attempts, what do you think it would take to produce the desired results (e.g., time, money, materials, knowledge, skills)?

In posing these questions, the consultant not only discovers what has been tried but also gains information about parents' and teachers' expectations for the child and what resources are available in the home or classroom. Equally important, the consultant conveys respect for the knowledge and ideas that parents and teachers have to offer, thus setting the stage for joint problem solving.

The next step is to determine what changes in intervention strategies are needed to accomplish child goals. Regardless of where the consultant's work with the child actually takes place, parents and teachers should be involved in making these decisions, and, whenever possible, their ideas should be incorporated into intervention plans. The benefits of soliciting teachers' input in the development of intervention plans were demonstrated in a study conducted by Peck and colleagues (Peck, Killen, & Baumgart, 1989). In this study, a consultant asked general teachers in community-based child care centers to develop interventions that addressed the IEP goals of children enrolled in their classrooms. The consultant served only as a facilitator; all interventions were completely teacher-generated. Using a multiple baseline design, Peck and colleagues (1989) showed that teachers routinely implemented the strategies that they developed for addressing the children's IEP goals, and the children made progress toward these goals. In addition, two out of three teachers began using these intervention strategies in settings that had not been targeted originally for intervention.

There are times, however, when parents and teachers are unsure of what to do and rely on the consultant for suggestions. How can a collaborative approach be used in these situations? First, when a consultant suggests specific treatment strategies, he or she should provide a full explanation of the procedures and the reasons for using them. This should be done using language that is easily understood by parents and teachers. Second, parents and teachers should be given some degree of input or choice in the decisions. One way to do this is to present several options for addressing child goals. Parents or teachers can choose from these alternatives or, at the very least, be included in evaluating the pros and cons of each option before any final decisions about intervention are reached. Another way to involve parents and teachers is to ask them to assist in fleshing out the details of intervention plans. This may include identifying specific routines where interventions will first be implemented, identifying resources to carry out plans, or selecting specific toys or other materials that are suitable for the child and therefore likely to enhance the effectiveness of the intervention procedures.

When parents and teachers are active participants in the selection and development of intervention procedures, they develop a sense of ownership of the plan and will be more likely to commit to and support its success. If parents and teachers have at least a basic understanding of the principles on which selected interventions are based, they may be more likely to follow through with interventions in the absence of the consultant, make minor adjustments when interventions are not working, or apply their new knowledge when working on other skills with the same child or with other children who have similar needs.

## Implementing Interventions

When consultants have sufficient latitude in their jobs to offer choices regarding where interventions are implemented, parents and teachers can be included in making this decision. In some situations, however, agency policies may dictate where services can take place, and consultants must work within these constraints. The following discussion is divided into three parts in accordance with where the consultant's work may take place: 1) in-class, 2) out-of-class, and 3) a combination of in-class and out-of-class intervention. Each section includes a discussion of when this approach may be preferred over others and how consultants can effectively collaborate with classroom teachers. Although the terms *in-class* and *out-of-class* are used here, similar issues and solutions exist when considering the differences between interventions that are implemented in families' homes and those that are provided in settings outside the home environment (e.g., clinics, private offices).

***In-Class Interventions***    Whenever possible, in-class interventions should be considered. They have the distinct advantage of teaching child behaviors within the settings where they are ultimately expected to occur—the child's daily routines at school or at home. This intervention eliminates difficulties in generalizing gains made in therapy to other settings. To conduct in-class interventions, however, consultants need to travel to classroom sites and have sufficient time available for working with children and teachers. Any resources or specialized equipment needed to implement interventions must also be either available in the classroom or easily transported there. In-class intervention may not be the best choice if the classroom setting is too distracting for learning to occur, or if the intervention may result in too much disruption of classroom routines for other children. Even so, in-class interventions should not be ruled out too hastily. As stated earlier, the classroom or home is where the child will eventually be expected to perform skills that are learned in therapy.

In-class interventions are particularly advantageous when targeted child behaviors are those that will be expected to occur throughout a number of daily routines. Teaching sign language to a child, teaching mobility and self-help skills to a child who is blind or has a visual impairment, and teaching compliance to a child with behavior difficulties are all examples of the types of child behaviors that should probably be taught within the classroom or home setting. In-class interventions are also advantageous when working on child behaviors that are likely to be elicited and maintained by specific setting events in the classroom or by the behavior of adults or other children within these environments. For example, it is extremely difficult to work on a child's behavior problems during mealtimes or naptime outside of these natural contexts.

When conducting in-class interventions, consultants have two basic approaches from which to choose: 1) working directly with the child themselves or 2) having teachers implement the interventions. There are two advantages to working directly with the child. First, the consultant has the skills and knowledge necessary for implementing the procedures and making adaptations in accordance with the child's responsiveness to the intervention. Therefore, the consultant may be more successful than a teacher who would have to learn these skills at the same time he or she was implementing the intervention. Second, the consultant who implements interventions in the classroom serves as a model for teachers, showing rather than just telling them how to conduct interventions with the child. If the child is responsive to the consultant and the intervention appears to be effective, the teacher may be motivated to take on responsibility for and become involved in implementing the procedures.

There are also disadvantages to consultants' working directly with the child in the classroom. It can be very time-consuming, and not every consultant can devote the amount of time needed to produce the desired results. Another potential disadvantage is that teachers may not feel invested in the intervention if they are not implementing it themselves. They may even view the consultant's working with the child as relief from their own responsibility for the child and as an opportunity to accomplish other things. When this happens, the consultant is unlikely to function as an effective model for the teacher, because the teacher will probably not be watching.

The ultimate outcome of in-class intervention is the transfer of responsibility for implementation from the consultant to the classroom teacher. This should be discussed in the joint planning of the intervention, and specific agreements can be made to ensure that the teacher is involved throughout implementation and acquires the skills needed to eventually assume full responsibility.

The traditional approach to in-class intervention is for the teacher to implement the interventions with the child and for the consultant to serve as a guide and resource for the teacher. With this approach, the teacher assumes responsibility from the beginning; but without proper support from the consultant, this approach may be relatively ineffective. Even if a collaborative approach has been employed in developing the procedures for intervention and the teacher is highly motivated, complications can arise in the initial transition from planning interventions to their actual implementation. Unforeseen difficulties, such as the failure of equipment, or an unresponsive child may cause a teacher to lose enthusiasm and confidence in procedures, and he or she may stop implementing them or do so only halfheartedly.

Teachers usually need the greatest amount of support from consultants when they first begin to implement new interventions. Frequent visits to the classroom and telephone conversations with the teacher can make a difference. The consultant needs to be available to help the teacher troubleshoot and problem-solve and to encourage the teacher's efforts. In fact, the availability of the consultant throughout implementation to adapt procedures, model interventions, and provide general support to teachers has been identified as a crucial competency for consultants (West & Cannon, 1988).

With sufficient training and support from consultants, teachers can implement interventions traditionally considered beyond their abilities and capable of being implemented only by qualified personnel from other disciplines. For example, Robertson, Alper, Schloss, and Wisniewski (1992) demonstrated that preschool teachers can effectively implement a procedure for teaching self-catheterization skills to a child with mylomeningocele (spina bifida) in a classroom setting. The simulation training and sequential prompt hierarchy procedures used by the teachers in this study previously had been conducted only by qualified medical personnel in clinic and hospital settings. As pointed out by Robertson and colleagues (1992), many schools do not have full-time nurses, and to provide inclusive placements for children with health impairments or who are medically fragile, teachers may need to assume responsibility for some procedures that would normally be conducted by medical personnel.

Flexibility on the part of consultants is important if teacher-implemented procedures are to be successful. For example, in the case of teaching self-catheterization skills to a child, teachers who are unfamiliar or uncomfortable with the procedure may need a lot of support and guidance from a trained nurse during the initial stages of implementation. As the teachers become more skilled and confident in handling the procedure on their own, less of the nurse consultant's time is required. Flexibility also may be required of consultants within other disciplines when helping teachers or parents develop and implement interventions. For example, the need for community-based, flexible consultation services for children with behavioral and emotional problems is described in a case study presented by an innovative program in Maryland (Hunt, Mayette, Feinberg, & Baglin, 1994). The case describes a behavioral consultant's work with a 12-month-old with multiple disabilities that include a sleep disorder. The child's sleep disorder was extremely stressful for the mother, to the point where the professionals working with the family felt there was a potential for child abuse. In combination with other strategies (e.g., feeding schedules), the mother elected to use a Cry-It-Out approach to get the child to sleep. The mother needed a lot of support and reassurance to follow through with the procedure. Support from the consultant included being on call for the mother 24 hours a day, 7 days a week.

For the first 3 weeks of implementing the procedure, the mother called frequently, sometimes several times per day, and talked to the consultant for anywhere from a few minutes to an hour at a time. Some of these calls occurred at night when the child was crying and the mother "needed advice or encouragement to stick with the program" (Hunt et al., 1994, p. 65). The mother's need for support lessened over time as the child showed improvement, but calls to the consultant resumed on several occasions when the child had relapses. The authors point out that consultation services were effective with this family because " . . . support services were available 'as needed' rather than on the traditional school or clinic schedule" (p. 66). In this case study, a parent was the primary recipient of consultation services, but teachers implementing behavioral programs could also benefit from flexible consultation time.

***Out-of-Class Interventions*** There are times when consultants' work with children takes place outside of the classroom. In some situations, it may not be by choice, such as when agency policies do not allow in-class intervention. In other situations, it may be more appropriate for interventions to take place elsewhere, such as when needed equipment is not available in the classroom, when interventions would be overly disruptive to classroom routines and other children, or when the target child would be too distracted in the classroom for learning to occur. Regardless of the reason, when a child is removed from his or her natural environment and interventions are implemented without teachers being present, there is always a risk that teachers will be less invested in the interventions. As a result, later transfer of child gains from the therapy environment to the classroom may be jeopardized. This may be true even when teachers have been involved in decisions regarding the interventions that take place outside of the classroom.

How can consultants who provide services outside of the classroom minimize this risk? One way is to maintain frequent, ongoing communication with teachers throughout the implementation phase (McWilliam, 1995). This can be accomplished through phone calls, brief written notes, FAX messages, e-mail, or brief classroom visits. In some cases, it may be feasible for the teacher to observe a therapy session. If this is not possible, the consultant can videotape at least a portion of a therapy session and send the tape to the classroom teacher. Having the teacher observe the therapy session is of little help, however, if it is not accompanied by a discussion of what the consultant is doing in the session and why. Whatever the means of ongoing communication, its purposes are to keep classroom staff aware of what the consultant is working on with the child and what progress is being made and to solicit the input of teachers in decision making.

Perhaps the greatest risk to coordination with classroom programming occurs when the consultant's primary contact is with a child's parents. Either the parents may take the child to the consultant's office or the consultant may provide home-based services. Both of these methods are common for nutritionists, psychologists, social workers, public health nurses, and audiologists. Although these consultants may know that classroom teachers or other professionals are involved with the child and family, they may have no direct contact with them. If teachers are not informed about what a consultant is working on with a child and family outside of the classroom, then they may be unaware of stresses the family may be experiencing, they may not know how they can be supportive, and their work with the child may not support, and may even conflict with, that of the consultant. For this reason, there are an increasing number of pleas (e.g., Hunt et al., 1994; Lesar & Maldonado, 1994; McGonigel, 1994; Robertson et al., 1992; Woodruff, Driscoll, & Sterzin, 1992) for coordination between these disciplines and educational programs for infants and preschoolers with disabilities. These calls for increased coordination include recommendations that all disciplines involved with a child and family contribute to the development of a comprehensive intervention plan (IEP or IFSP).

Hunt et al.'s (1994) case study of the 12-month-old with a sleeping disorder provides a good example of how a consultant working in the home environment can coordinate his or her work with that of educators and other therapists. In this situation, the behavioral consultant had frequent communication with the early intervention program, including all of the therapists who worked with the child. In addition to working directly with the parent and child, the consultant provided the other therapists with ideas about how they could support the mother. Later, when the consultant became aware of the magnitude of stress that the mother was experiencing, the consultant met formally with the early intervention team, and the IFSP was revised to reflect a primary focus on establishing a sleep schedule for the child. All other in-home therapies were suspended until this goal was accomplished.

*Combined Approaches* Combining in-class and out-of-class interventions also can be used to collaborate with teachers and to ensure that skills learned in therapy are transferred to the classroom. The two approaches may be used simultaneously or in sequence. For example, suppose a vision specialist is consulting with a preschool about a child who needs mobility training. The vision specialist and the teacher might agree that the child would benefit from intensive one-on-one instruction outside of the classroom because the child is highly distractible and the classroom is overstimulating. Using a sequential approach, the consultant would work on mobility skills outside of the classroom until a certain level of mastery was achieved and then work with the child in the classroom to ensure generalization of mobility skills to classroom routines. The consultant might accomplish the same goals by employing a simultaneous approach; that is, the consultant could work with the child outside the classroom while providing the classroom teacher with suggestions for meeting the child's independent mobility needs within specific routines of the day (e.g., getting to the bathroom, finding a seat at morning circle).

As McWilliam (1995) points out, the location of services (in-class versus out-of-class) is only one dimension along which therapy models may vary. In Chapter 4, McWilliam identifies five additional dimensions:

1.  The degree to which other children are involved
2.  Whether the therapist uses a directive or responsive approach to interactions with the child
3.  The extent to which therapists work on functional skills
4.  Whether the therapist employs a hands-on approach or a consultative approach
5.  Whether therapy is provided within the context of classroom routines or without regard to classroom routines

McWilliam (1995) suggests that "each dimension of service delivery can range from segregated to integrated and that the dimensions constitute different domains of therapist behavior" (p. 32). Using various combinations of therapist behaviors along each of McWilliam's six dimensions of service delivery, one sees that a relatively large number of approaches to consultation are possible. McWilliam's model may serve as an excellent tool for identifying the various options that may be used in providing consultation and in deciding on the best choice, or combination of choices, for any given child and situation.

The following is an example in which various therapy models were used to provide integrated services. In this case, a therapist was asked to consult with a preschool about a child who had a severe expressive speech disorder. After discussing the various options available for increasing expressive language, the child's teacher and parents agreed that they wanted to try teaching the child sign language. At first, the consultant worked on sign language within the context of the child's regular classroom routines, using signs with the child during play with peers (e.g., block building, pretend play, using Play-Doh). The consultant hoped not only to teach the child signs that were functional within daily routines but also to serve as a model for the teacher. In addition, the consultant served as a resource for the teacher, showing her signs for words that she thought would be useful during the school day.

The consultant soon realized, however, that this approach was not effective. First, the classroom was extremely active and the child was easily distracted, so it was difficult to get the child to attend to the use of signs within routines. Second, the busy classroom was not conducive to conversations with the teacher. When the therapist was playing with a group of children, the teacher tended to leave that activity and attend to situations in other areas of the classroom. Third, neither the teacher nor the parents seemed comfortable learning and using signs. They appeared to need more support and encouragement than could be offered when the therapist was working with the child during classroom routines. This was particularly problematic for the parents because their work schedules did not allow them to be in the classroom during the day.

The therapist met with the parents and teacher to discuss these issues, and they came to an agreement on a new approach to consultation. Once per week the parents came to the classroom at the end of the school day, after the other children had gone home. The parents brought their older child, whom they had picked up from after-school care on their way to the classroom. For approximately 1 hour, the parents, teacher, and therapist played in the classroom with the two children. The classroom site was selected because it was a convenient place for the parents and teacher to meet and because the toys and activities available in the classroom were familiar to the child. Thus, the child would be engaging with materials that would also be available during regular classroom routines.

During this hour after school, the therapist joined the child in whatever play activity he chose (e.g., Play-Doh, puzzles, blocks). The parents, teacher, and sibling also were included in the activity. Following the child's lead, the therapist signed to the child during play and emphasized salient words related to the activity. For example, while playing "restaurant," the therapist repeatedly used signs such as THANK YOU, PLEASE, MORE, GOOD, EAT, and DRINK.

Using this new approach, the child soon began to imitate the therapist's signing. The teacher, parents, and even the child's older sibling also began using the signs they had watched the therapist use, and they asked what the signs were for other words. Over time the parents and teacher became more comfortable using signs and took a more active role in signing with the child during these after-school play sessions. As they did, the therapist reduced her direct interactions with the child and became more of a prompter from the sidelines, supplying needed signs as the parents and teacher played with the child and sibling. In addition to the after-school sessions, the therapist supplied the parents and teachers with books on signing and had them keep a list of words they commonly used in the classroom and at home so that they could learn the signs for these words, too.

Why was this approach effective? First, therapy was conducted within the child's natural environment, even if it was not during regular school routines. Second, by including the parents and teacher in the sessions, the therapist served as an effective model and showed them how they could teach the child during the course of everyday play. Third, the therapist was available to the parents and teachers to provide information and encouragement during their first awkward attempts to use sign language. Fourth, by including the parents and the teacher, interventions were occurring both at home and at school.

Perhaps the most important reason for this therapist's success was that she recognized when her first approach was not working and was willing and able to change her methods of consultation. Each situation a consultant encounters is unique. The characteristics of the child, the family, the teacher, and the home and school environments all play a role in determining the type of consultation strategies that will be most effective. Although it is tempting to develop a single strategy or "recipe" for providing consultation that can be used for every situation, the uniqueness of each situation calls for an individualized approach. In addition, the consultation strategies used in providing services to any one child may need to be combined or changed over time to achieve and maintain desired changes in child behavior.

## Follow-Up

An important but often neglected aspect of consultation is follow-up. When consultation services end and parents or teachers need to continue interventions or to implement maintenance procedures, there is a risk that progress may be disrupted. Even if the child has made significant progress and parents or teachers are highly motivated to continue their efforts, any number of things can go wrong. Intervention procedures may lose their effectiveness, the child may develop other problems, or parents and teachers may be distracted by more pressing priorities and lose motivation or fall back into old habits.

One strategy for ensuring continued progress is to discuss such possibilities at the close of consultation activities. Based on their experiences, consultants can talk to parents and teachers about things that may go wrong, what they can do to prevent them from happening, and how to deal with them effectively if they do occur. For example, at the close of services, the consultant can provide a written document that outlines procedures for continued progress and maintenance. This gives the parents or teachers something to refer to if problems arise and they need a reminder of what to do. Such a document can also include a list of things to look for that may be indicative of either a procedure that is no longer working or the development of additional problems that may require intervention. Parents or teachers can use this list of warning signals to identify when it may be appropriate to resume contact with the consultant or enlist other means of assistance.

Although such measures may be helpful, their effectiveness can be short-lived. Closing discussions have a tendency to be forgotten, and a written document may make its way into the back of a file, therefore failing to serve as an effective reminder to parents and teachers. The most effective way for consultants to ensure continued progress is to conduct periodic follow-up contacts. One method is for the consultant to send a letter to parents or teachers, asking how things are going and inviting them to call if they have any concerns, questions, or additional issues they would like to discuss. At the very least, a letter can remind parents and teachers about the importance of implementing procedures and may serve as a booster shot if motivation has begun to wane. Such a letter can also remind parents and teachers that the consultant is available to provide assistance if needed. A phone call or visit to the home or classroom adds a personal touch and may be perceived as a more sincere offer to provide assistance than a formal letter. In addition, phone calls and visits let consultants know the status of child progress, rather than assuming that things are going well unless the parent or teacher responds to their letter and tells them otherwise. Thus, as time permits, consultants should consider these options for conducting follow-up.

## CONCLUSIONS

Professionals within the seven disciplines addressed in this chapter face numerous challenges in coordinating their efforts with those of other early intervention professionals. Although the involvement of these professionals in the lives of many infants and preschoolers with disabilities and their families is critical, they usually are not regular members of early intervention teams. These professionals often work within agencies that are not supportive of activities aimed at coordinating their services with those of other early intervention professionals. Heavy caseloads and stringent regulations that govern where, when, and how long services can be provided often work against such efforts. Although there is increasing awareness of the need to improve coordination with other disciplines and programs, significant changes in administrative policies and the structure of community services are unlikely to occur in the near future.

Faced with these challenges, consulting professionals within these disciplines may want to abandon efforts to coordinate their services and use what little time they have available to provide direct, hands-on services to children and their families. Looked at another way, perhaps the best use of such limited time is to ensure that those who can devote more time to intervention (e.g., parents and teachers) are provided with the knowledge, skills, and confidence they need to be effective in their daily work. A number of strategies for working with parents and classroom teachers are described in this chapter, all of which are based on a collaborative model of consultation. A checklist for collaborative consultation, provided in Figure 1, summarizes the various strategies suggested in this chapter for identifying goals, designing interventions, and implementing intervention plans.

### Identifying goals for intervention
- [ ] Consultant is aware of the environmental demands placed on the child at home and at school (e.g., adult expectations, daily routines, schedules, reactions of other children).
- [ ] Consultant is aware of how the child performs within the context of daily routines and adapts to environmental demands.
- [ ] Consultant is aware of parent and teacher priorities for the child (i.e., areas of concern, desires for change).
- [ ] Consultant shares his or her knowledge and perspective to make parents and teachers informed decision makers in identifying child goals.
- [ ] Consultant conveys respect for parents' and teachers' ideas, opinions, perspectives, and priorities.

### Designing interventions
- [ ] Consultant is aware of past efforts to accomplish child goals (e.g., strategies used, amount of progress, satisfaction with methods and results, barriers encountered).
- [ ] Consultant solicits ideas and opinions from parents and teachers about strategies for achieving child goals.
- [ ] Parents and teachers actively participate in development of intervention strategies (e.g., generating ideas, identifying potential resources, making decisions).
- [ ] Parents' and teachers' ideas are incorporated into intervention plans.
- [ ] Plans include strategies for ensuring generalization and maintenance of treatment gains to home and school environment.
- [ ] Interventions designed for implementation by parents and teachers fit easily into daily routines.
- [ ] Plans include the identification of resources needed by parents and teachers to carry out interventions at home and school (e.g., time, money, materials, support).

### Implementating intervention plans
- [ ] Consultant provides parents and teachers with full explanation of procedures, using language that is easily understood.
- [ ] Consultant informs all interested parties (e.g., teachers, parents, other therapists) about intervention procedures.
- [ ] Consultant ensures that interventions are documented and communicated through inclusion on child's IFSP/IEP.
- [ ] Consultant maintains ongoing communication with all interested parties about progress and any changes in intervention strategies.
- [ ] Progress is frequently monitored in all settings where interventions take place or where change is desired, and strategies are revised when necessary.
- [ ] Consultant has frequent contact with parents and teachers during initial stages of intervention in home and school settings.
- [ ] Consultant is available on an as-needed basis to provide support and encouragement to parents and teachers and to assist in troubleshooting when problems arise.
- [ ] Consultant conducts follow-up activities to monitor continued progress and to offer additional support as needed.

Figure 1. Checklist for collaborative consultation.

## REFERENCES

Babcock, N.L., & Pryzwansky, W.B. (1983). Models of consultation: Preferences of educational professionals at five stages of service. *Journal of School Psychology, 21,* 359–366.

Bailey, D.B., & Blasco, P.M. (1990). Parents' perspectives on a written survey of family needs. *Journal of Early Intervention, 14*(3), 196–203.

Baroni, M.A., Tutbill, P., Feenan, L., & Schroeder, M. (1994). Technology-dependent infants and young children: A retrospective case analysis of service coordination across state lines. *Infants and Young Children, 7*(1), 69–78.

Bergan, J.R., & Tombari, M.L. (1976). Consultant skill and efficiency and the implementation and outcomes of consultation. *Journal of School Psychology, 41,* 3–14.

Bruder, M.B., & Bologna, T. (1993). Collaboration and service coordination for effective early intervention. In W. Brown, S.K. Thurman, & L.F. Pearl (Eds.), *Family-centered early intervention with infants and toddlers: Innovative cross-disciplinary approaches* (pp. 103–128). Baltimore: Paul H. Brookes Publishing Co.

Dietz, S.J., & Ferrell, K.A. (1993). Early services for young children with visual impairment: From diagnosis to comprehensive services. *Infants and Young Children, 6*(1), 68–76.

Erin, J.N. (1988). The teacher-consultant: The teacher of visually handicapped students and collaborative consultation. *Education of the Visually Handicapped, 20*(2), 57–63.

Erwin, E.J. (1993). Social participation of young children with visual impairments in integrated and specialized settings. *Journal of Visual Impairment and Blindness, 5,* 138–142.

Erwin, E.J. (1994). Social competence in young children with visual impairments. *Infants and Young Children, 6*(3), 26–33.

File, N., & Kontos, S. (1992). Indirect service delivery through consultation: Review and implications for early intervention. *Journal of Early Intervention, 16*(3), 221–233.

Fox, H.B., Wicks, L.B., McManus, M.A., & Newacheck, P.W. (1992). Private and public health insurance for early intervention specialists. *Journal of Early Intervention, 16*(2), 109–122.

Hunt, F.M., Mayette, C., Feinberg, E., & Baglin, C.A. (1994) Integration of behavioral consultation in an intervention setting. *Infants and Young Children, 7*(2), 62–66.

Idol, L., Paolucci-Whitcomb, P., & Nevin, A. (1986). *Collaborative consultation.* Austin, TX: PRO-ED.

Individuals with Disabilities Education Act Amendments of 1991, PL 102-119. (October 7, 1991). Title 20, U.S.C. §§ 1400 et seq.: *U.S. Statutes at Large, 105,* 587–608.

Klein, N.K., & Campbell, P. (1990). Preparing personnel to serve at-risk and disabled infants, toddlers, and preschoolers. In S.J. Meisels & J.P. Shonkoff (Eds.), *Handbook of early childhood intervention* (pp. 679–699). New York: Cambridge University Press.

Lesar, S., & Maldonado, Y.A. (1994). Infants and young children with HIV infection: Service delivery considerations for family support. *Infants and Young Children, 6*(4), 70–81.

Matkin, N. (1985). Effective communication: Interactive interdisciplinary teamwork. In E. Cherow (Ed.), *Hearing impaired children and youth with developmental disabilities.* Washington, DC: Gallaudet College Press.

McGarr, B., Dwyer, J., & Holland, M. (1995). Delivering nutrition services in early intervention in rural areas. *Infants and Young Children, 7*(3), 52–62.

McGonigel, M.J. (1994). The individualized family service plan: Philosophy and conceptual framework. In J. Roush & N.D. Matkin (Eds.), *Infants and toddlers with hearing loss: Family-centered assessment and intervention* (pp. 99–112). Timonium, MD: York Press.

McGonigel, M.J., & Garland, C.W. (1988). The individualized family service plan and the early intervention team: Team and family issues and recommended practices. *Infants and Young Children, 1*(1), 10–21.

McGonigel, M.J., Woodruff, G., & Roszmann-Millican, M. (1994). The transdisciplinary team: A model for family-centered early intervention. In L.J. Johnson, R.J. Gallagher, M.J. LaMontagne, J.B. Jordan, J.J. Gallagher, P.L. Hutinger, & M.B. Karnes (Eds.), *Meeting early intervention challenges: Issues from birth to three* (2nd ed.) (pp. 95–132). Baltimore: Paul H. Brookes Publishing Co.

McWilliam, R.A. (1995). Integration of therapy and consultative special education: A continuum in early intervention. *Infants and Young Children, 7*(4), 29–38.

Melaville, A.I., & Blank, M.J. (1991). *What it takes: Structuring interagency partnerships to connect children and families with comprehensive services.* Washington, DC: Education and Human Services Consortium.

Odom, S.L., & McEvoy, M.A. (1990). Mainstreaming at the preschool level: Potential barriers and tasks for the field. *Topics in Early Childhood Special Education, 10*(2), 48–61.

Peck, C.A., Killen, C.C., & Baumgart, D. (1989). Increasing implementation of special education instruction in mainstream preschools: Direct and generalized effects of nondirective consultation. *Journal of Applied Behavior Analysis, 22*(2), 197–210.

Phillips, V., & McCullough, L. (1990). Consultation-based programming: Instituting the collaborative ethic in schools. *Exceptional Children, 56*, 291–304.

Pryzwansky, W.B., & White, G.W. (1983). Resistance to school-based consultation: A behavioral analysis of the problem. *Psychology in the Schools, 20*, 311–320.

Pugach, M.C., & Johnson, L.J. (1988). Rethinking the realtionship between consultation and collaborative problem-solving. *Focus on Exceptional Children, 21*(4), 108.

Pugach, M.C., & Johnson, L.J. (1989). The challenge of implementing collaboration between general and special education. *Exceptional Children, 56*, 232–235.

Raab, E.J. (1986). *Understanding Prader-Willi syndrome: A literature review for educators and families.* Edina, MN: Prader-Willi Syndrome Association.

Robertson, J., Alper, S., Schloss, P.J., & Wisniewski, L. (1992). Teaching self-catheterization skills to a child with myelomeningocele in a preschool setting. *Journal of Early Intervention, 16*(1), 20–30.

Roush, J., & Gravel, J. (1994). Acoustic amplification and sensory aids for infants and toddlers. In J. Roush & N.D. Matkin (Eds.), *Infants and toddlers with hearing loss: Family-centered assessment and intervention* (pp. 65–79). Timonium, MD: York Press.

Roush, J., & Matkin, N.D. (1994). *Infants and toddlers with hearing loss: Family-centered assessment and intervention.* Timonium, MD: York Press.

Roush, J., & McWilliam, R.A. (1990). A new challenge for pediatric audiology: Public Law 99-457. *Journal of the American Academy of Audiology, 1*, 196–208.

Schowengerdt, R.V., Fine, M.J., & Poggio, J.P. (1976). An examination of some bases of teacher satisfaction with school psychological services. *Psychology in the Schools, 13*, 269–275.

Weissenberger, J.W., Fine, M.J., & Poggio, J.P. (1982). The relationship of selected consultant/teacher characteristics to consultation outcomes. *Journal of School Psychology, 20*, 263–270.

West, J.F., & Cannon, G.S. (1988). Essential collaborative consultation competencies for regular and special education. *Journal of Learning Disabilities, 21,* 56–63.

Wolery, M., Venn, M.L., Holcombe, A., Brookfield, J., Martin, C.G., Huffman, K., Schroeder, C., & Fleming, L.A. (1994). Employment of related service personnel in preschool programs: A survey of general early educators. *Exceptional Children, 61*(1), 25–39.

Woodruff, G., Driscoll, P., & Sterzin, E.D. (1992). Providing comprehensive and coordinated services to children with HIV infection and their families. In A. Crocker & T.A. Cohen (Eds.), *HIV infection and developmental disabilities* (pp. 105–112). Baltimore: Paul H. Brookes Publishing Co.

Woodruff, G., & McGonigel, M.J. (1988). Early intervention team approaches: The transdisciplinary model. In J.B. Jordan, J.J. Gallagher, P.L. Hutinger, & M.B. Karnes (Eds.), *Early childhood special education: Birth to three* (pp. 163–181). Reston, VA: Council for Exceptional Children.

Woodruff, G., & Sterzin, E.D. (1988). The transagency approach: A model for serving children with HIV infection and their families. *Children Today, 17*(3), 9–14.

# III

# Future Directions

# Chapter 13

# Implications for the Future of Integrating Specialized Services

## R.A. McWilliam

Integrated therapy has been a long time coming and has a long way to go. This chapter discusses what is needed to advance the use of integrated therapy in early intervention. The development of this approach to providing specialized services has implications for practice and requires substantive but manageable change. It also has implications for personnel preparation and policy. Also discussed are the types of research still needed in this area.

### PRACTICE IMPLICATIONS

For practitioners in early intervention, the advent of integrated therapy has an impact on their work with other professionals and with parents, on planning interventions, and on allocation of time. One of the unfortunate consequences of early intervention originating in two theoretical paradigms, the medical model and the educational model, is that occupational, physical, and speech-language therapists, vision specialists, and nurses operate in one framework, and early childhood special educators, general early childhood educators, and social workers operate in another. (Members of other disciplines, such as psychologists, can be found working in either the medical or educational model.) Medical-model interventionists are specialists, and much of their acculturation in training programs is based on developing their identity as such. They concentrate on so much discipline-specific content that they cannot foresee adding infant or family content in other than the most cursory of ways. In many training programs, students are taught about their discipline across the life span. Generalists (e.g., early childhood special educators) must learn about many areas but are restricted in the age range; that is, they specialize in early childhood content. Changes in the field have meant that early interventionists have also had to become well-trained in working with families, meaning that their expertise is even more diffuse.

Because of the way specialists are trained and because it makes sense to have division of labor, primary responsibility for the specialty areas (i.e., special education, physical therapy, occupational therapy, speech-language pathology) rests with specialists from each discipline. "Responsibility" in this case refers to assessment and intervention planning that requires expert knowledge and skill. According to principles of transdisciplinary service delivery, implementation of the interventions does not have to be the responsibility of specialists (McCormick & Goldman, 1979). If the team, not the individual therapist, feels that the recommended activities to improve the child's learning, fine motor skills, perceptual skills, gross motor skills, or communication can be performed by nonspecialists, the extent to which the specialist needs to conduct direct therapy is attenuated.

This postulate may not go over well with traditionalists in the specialty areas, but it does not diminish either the extent to which specialists need to have solid expertise in their field or the extent to which they are needed in early intervention. If families and classroom teachers are primarily responsible for implementing therapy, which families have long done, specialists are going to be needed to guide them. One of the reasons why change to an integrated therapy approach has been slow may be distrust that regular caregivers such as teachers and parents are implementing therapeutic activities properly or often enough. Overcoming this distrust will occur only when both regular caregivers (especially classroom teachers) and specialists work together to embed therapy in regular caregiving routines. Teachers need conditions that make this possible, such as a reasonable number of children and adequate support in terms of therapist consultation and classroom assistance (e.g., from classroom aides). Therapists need skills in passing on their expertise to nonspecialists and the mindset that others can implement the majority of interventions in their specialty area.

## Recognizing Limitations of Direct Therapy

Direct therapy occurs when therapists use hands-on work with a child to help the child acquire particular skills; in physical therapy, such work may also be designed to maintain range of motion to prevent contractures. In early intervention, the question is, What is the value of once- or twice-a-week therapy sessions? In two studies, we found that parents attributed much value to their therapy sessions (McWilliam & Tocci, 1995; McWilliam, Young, & Harville, 1995). When we asked them, however, "What is it about those sessions that's so valuable?" they said it was the information they themselves gained. Some families were not involved in their children's therapy sessions; they took the child to a clinic, left the child with the therapist, and returned at the end of the session. These families also gave some credit to therapy until they were asked, "Does your child learn skills during the session that he (or she) then uses at home?" The families were not sure about this, and, in fact, this line of questioning had to stop because it appeared to make families uncomfortable.

We can draw some important conclusions from these findings. First, the value of so-called direct therapy may not be in the hands-on work with the child, unless it is used to demonstrate activities to do with the child. One wonders whether therapists realize this; further research is needed to explore therapy sessions in which caregivers are present. Second, the intensity of therapy (i.e., how often sessions are provided) should be based on the amount of support caregivers need to implement the activities on their own. Caregivers who need a lot of reassurance or instruction in very small steps presumably need more support—that is, more therapy sessions—than do caregivers who confidently and comprehensively implement what therapists recommend. This leads to a question of how often intensity decisions are based on family or teacher needs. The third conclusion is that pull-out therapy in the absence of a caregiver to benefit from modeling may not be effective. Research is needed to test this hypothesis. Studies of children in classroom-based programs do not support such a discouraging picture for pull-out therapy; children make almost as much progress with out-of-class models as they do with in-class models (see Chapter 4). This leads to the fourth conclusion: It is hard to separate the effects of pull-out therapy from the effects of general classroom programming. This is discussed further in the section on the whole environment. The fifth conclusion is that the effects of segregated therapy—and, indeed, integrated therapy—may best be appreciated over the long term. Although it is extremely unlikely that children can generalize from therapy sessions to nontherapy sessions in the short term (McWilliam & Scarborough, 1994), there is the possibility that therapists' interventions (in combination with nontherapists' interventions) over a number of years contribute to child progress.

Direct therapy should therefore be viewed in its proper perspective. The conclusions do not diminish the value of therapists or of therapy, but they do suggest that the value of the interventions is mediated by how much regular caregivers gain from therapy sessions.

## Talking to Families

What are parents hearing to make them think, at least initially, that direct therapy is necessary and responsible for their children's progress? They have told us that both doctors and therapists themselves say that their children need therapy (McWilliam, Young, & Harville, 1995). Early interventionists from many disciplines, accustomed to traditional methods of service delivery, reinforce this notion and describe therapy as a specialist's working directly with the child. If therapy is represented as something to be provided in a direct, segregated manner, however, then families expect that model. When integrated therapy is later discussed, it may sound like a watered-down version of the original thing. Professionals not only need to be more careful when describing therapy, they also need to describe integrated therapy as a viable alternative. Ideally, all six models described in Chapter 4 would be explained when therapy is first discussed.

## Working with Other Adults

Working effectivly in early intervention now requires skill and a willingness to collaborate with other adults, not just with children. Although it may be argued that this is nothing new to specialists, changes in the field mean that the consultancy part of the job has changed, too. No longer can specialists adopt an expert model of consultation in which they do their own assessment, make independent recommendations about the need for their particular brand of intervention (i.e., therapy), and assume that other adults in the child's life will do what the specialists say. Collaboration means that a multidisciplinary view of the child is required, the need for therapy is decided *after* outcomes or goals are decided, and specialists and generalists together negotiate who needs to do what to achieve those outcomes or goals (Giangreco, Cloninger, & Iverson, 1993).

## Recommending Therapy During the Planning Process

Why is it important to recommend therapy not at the time of referral and assessment, but instead during the individualized family service plan (IFSP)/ individualized education program (IEP) process? To use specialists' time effectively, it should be allocated when needed to attain outcomes or goals on which the family has decided. If therapy is decided upon in advance of outcomes or goals, a number of principles are transgressed.

First, it is likely that outcomes or goals will be chosen to fit the therapy, rather than the other way around. For example, if occupational therapy is recommended, even if the family does not have concerns about fine motor or visual perception but was told that occupational therapy would be a good idea, the occupational therapist will recommend goals. After all, the IFSP/IEP must contain reasons for the service.

Second, expensive services to achieve the outcomes or goals may needlessly be put in place. A child's family may want him or her to work on coming to stand, but if they and the child care staff can work on this outcome or goal, why have physical therapy? If the child has been diagnosed with cerebral palsy, the question can become a passionate issue. Some therapists would be afraid that the parents and other caregivers would not work with the child correctly. With the pessimism about the effectiveness of neurodevelopmental therapy in favor of a dynamic systems model (for a review, see Thelen, 1995), however, more therapists acknowledge that children with cerebral palsy learn skills through diverse pathways. If the need area can be addressed adequately by regular caregivers, allocation of much expensive therapy time is a waste.

Third, the team that carries out intervention should decide on allocation of therapy time; the decision should not be made by people who do not have to live with the consequences. Referrals, by definition, come from outside the team, and, in some communities, assessments for eligibility are conducted by people other than those in the intervention program. When someone tests a child and tells the parents that the child has delays in language and therefore needs speech therapy, the parents go to the early intervention program with that expectation. Even if the professionals on the team feel that the language delays can be addressed without speech-language services, the family may feel that the program is not offering sufficient service. After all, the experts who tested the child said speech therapy is indicated. It is a simple rule: Services follow goals, not vice versa.

The dual purposes of the IFSP or IEP contribute to the confusion about the relationship between goals and services. The document is both a curriculum (list of goals) and a contract for services to be provided (although it is not necessarily a contract in the legal sense). Naturally, bureaucrats are concerned about the latter function because they are held responsible for breaches on the part of service providers. It is therefore common for the focus of IFSP/IEP meetings to be primarily on the services to be provided. It takes conscientiousness by professionals to focus first on outcomes or goals and second on what therapies, given existing family and professional resources, are needed to achieve the outcomes or goals.

## Planning Functional Interventions

The more functional the interventions, the more likely a range of people can address them. In a study of 100 randomly selected IFSPs, functionality was defined as 1) goals the child or family needs for success in their current environments, 2) strategies appropriate for the child's and family's natural contexts, and 3) behaviors the child or family member(s) will perform (McWilliam, Harbin et al., 1995). Both outcomes or goals and strategies can range in functionality. Table 1 shows nonfunctional and functional goals and reasons why they are nonfunctional. In this table, the functional column does not provide the functional equivalent of what is listed in the nonfunctional column, because a characteristic of nonfunctional goals and strategies is often that they are fundamentally inappropriate.

Nonfunctional goals and strategies by definition may be difficult for teachers or families to conduct. Sometimes they are nonfunctional because they cannot be understood; jargon precludes comprehension. Some strategies are nonfunctional because the teacher cannot fathom how to address the goal. This is especially likely in interventions based on highly particularized theories such as sensory integration, where, for example, children may be given

Table 1. Nonfunctional and functional goals

| Nonfunctional | Problem | Functional |
| --- | --- | --- |
| For child to remain on target, she will achieve all of the following: copy a circle; imitate a cross; snips on line using scissors. | For a child under 3 years of age, this goal is not *necessary.* | To increase self-help skills, the child will alert the caregiver when he needs to "go potty." |
| Child will string 10–15 large beads independently. | Stringing beads is not critical to development. | Child (age 2 years, 9 months) will sleep through the night 90% of the time. |
| Child will increase attention span to complete tasks presented and to fully engage in therapy. | Focuses on tasks performed in therapy sessions. | Child will participate in songs and finger plays during circle time for 1) 3 minutes, then 2) 5 minutes. |
| Child's cognitive and language development will be enhanced through story activities, finger play, puppet games, tapes, musical games | Does not state what child will do. | Child will use a pincer grasp to place food and his medication in his mouth, daily. |

chewies (lengths of rubber tubing) to address their attention deficit disorders; the theory is that the attentional problems are caused by sensory integration disorders, which are helped by chewing on the chewy (Scheerer, 1992). When outcomes and strategies are meaningful, directly address the problem, and can be implemented in the child's regular environments, then integrated therapy is enhanced.

## Considering the Whole Environment

During focus groups on integrated services (McWilliam, Young, & Harville, 1995), we posed the following scenario: There are two children who are the same age and same gender and have the same disability. Both have spastic quadriplegia, affecting them identically. They both also receive weekly home visits from a general early interventionist. One child however, lives with two upper socioeconomic status parents, with the mother staying home to be with her child. This mother has a college education and has read everything she could find on raising babies and on cerebral palsy. She faithfully implements any activities her home visitor suggests, and she feels she is doing a good job incorporating therapy into everyday routines. The other child lives with his young mother and four siblings, all under the age of 8. This mother, who left school when she was 14 to have her first child, stays home with the younger children, but she is always tired and worried. She does not understand a lot of the things doctors and early interventionists have told her. Even though she realizes she should be doing things to help her child with cerebral palsy, she cannot remember them all and finds it very hard to fit the activities in with all the other things she has to do during the day.

Should both children receive the same amount of physical therapy? Everyone in the focus groups agreed that the second child should receive more frequent physical therapy because he was not getting therapeutic activities at home, whereas the first child was. One person, however, felt that such a decision was discriminatory against the first child, which reveals either a traditional diagnosis orientation to therapy allocation or a sensitivity to families. Traditionally, diagnosis is a strong determinant of both the need for therapy and the allocation of therapy time (e.g., all children with cerebral palsy should receive weekly physical therapy). This scenario suggests that such a basis for allocating services is wasteful.

If the first mother, however, wanted weekly physical therapy in addition to her weekly early intervention home visits, this would create the greatest challenge to integrated therapy: the potential clash between responsiveness to families' desires and cost-effective allocation of therapy resources. This issue reinforces the importance of fully informing families of the benefits and limitations of different models of service delivery. If the first mother realized that the primary benefit of a physical therapist's visits was to check on child progress and to recommend activities, she would quite possibly be satisfied with monthly or less frequent sessions. This would be especially true if she felt that the generalist who visited her home had ready access to consultation with the physical therapist. If, however, the mother had been led to believe that the physical therapist's hands-on work with the child substantially helped the child, it would not be surprising if she wanted such intense services.

## Using Different Models of Service Delivery

Potential service delivery models (as described in Chapter 4) are consultation, individual-during-routines, group activity, one-on-one in classroom, small-group pull-out, and individual pull-out. Our data show that therapists tend to use the same service delivery model for most children during most of their sessions (McWilliam, Scarborough, & Chaudhary, 1995). Furthermore, therapists from different disciplines within a particular program tended to use the same service delivery model. Although it is possible that one or more of the models (e.g., individual-during-routines or consultation) may meet child and classroom needs most of the time, it is more probable that children and classrooms can benefit from using a number of models at one time or another. Rather like the cascade of services advocated in special education, where children should be able to move easily from one type of service to another, therapy should be that flexible.

Ideally, therapists begin with the assumption that individual-during-routines or consultation will work, moving to less integrated models only if those do not work. Changes in the child, in classroom personnel, or in children enrolled can prompt a more segregated approach. The child is served in a more integrated manner again as soon as the opportunity arises.

## Scheduling and Cost Implications

Therapists and teachers are hostages to their schedules in classroom programs; the case of an occupational therapist scheduled to work with a given child every Tuesday and Thursday from 10:00 to 10:30 A.M. is an example. If she wants to use an individualized-during-classroom model, ideally the children are engaged in activities including small objects so that she can work on fine motor skills. (This example assumes that fine motor skills are the target of the therapist's intervention.) Ensuring that children are so engaged puts pressure on the classroom teachers to schedule appropriate activities at that time and make sure that the group keeps to the schedule. If the group runs behind schedule and the occupational therapist comes during story time, she is of less use to the child and teachers than if they are on schedule. If the therapist runs late, the same type of problem can arise. If she comes in 15 minutes late, teachers might have to prolong the activity or cut short the amount of time for which the occupational therapist can be maximally useful. Thus, strict individualized schedules promote segregated service delivery.

For families, the inviolable schedule is a double-edged sword. It works against them when their children and the classrooms they are in can benefit from more of a therapist's input. The only recourse families typically have is to ask for a formal review of the IFSP/IEP. A strict schedule however, can reassure families that their children are receiving whatever they think is the critical mass (i.e., the appropriate amount).

Strict schedules are a boon for accountability. Administrators can look at therapists' schedules to see how therapy time is allocated, and therapists can use their schedules when they report the amount of therapy provided to each child.

Flexible schedules have two characteristics. First, time is allotted to children on a monthly basis, so that, on any given day, therapists can use their time as best fits the conditions of that day. Those conditions include how children are feeling, who is in attendance, classroom activities, and teachers' preferences for when the therapist should come into the classroom. Therapists need to take careful note of the amount of time they spend with individual children to ensure that all children receive what is promised on the IFSP/IEP. The second characteristic of the flexible schedule is that therapists can work with more than one child at a time.

Integrated therapy also is beneficial for costs. When a speech-language pathologist goes into a classroom that has three children needing his services, he may join a small group that includes two of those children. As he plays with the children, perhaps using responsive teaching or some other naturalistic intervention technique, he is providing speech-language services to both children. The individualized strict schedule would have implied that he should be working only with the child scheduled for therapy at that time. The challenge for therapists working with more than one child at a time is accountability. If the speech-language pathologist spent 30 minutes working with both children, then both children received 30 minutes of the speech-language pathologist's time; the distinction is subtle but important. In terms of accountability for how time is spent, regardless of cost, it can be argued that a total of 60 minutes of service was received. But that does not mean that, if the therapist were on contract or reimbursed by Medicaid, he should be paid for 60 minutes of work when he worked only 30 actual minutes. Common practice is to divide the time for reimbursement purposes; each child is assumed to have received 15 minutes of service.

Assuming that the therapist is contracted to provide a total of 30 minutes for each child per week, because he has spent a total of only 30 minutes in this session, he still owes them 15 minutes each. So, on the next day, he spends 30 minutes with both children; again, for reimbursement purposes, this is documented as 15 minutes per child. The paying agency has paid for 1 hour of therapist time, as dictated by the contract and the children's IFSPs/IEPs; but in fact each child has received twice as much of the therapist's time. This example shows how integrated therapy still requires as much therapy time as traditional models but is more beneficial in terms of costs.

## CHANGE

Moving from a traditional pull-out approach to specialized services requires various degrees of change for many practitioners and administrators. Changes are likely to be needed in making recommendations, service delivery models, contracts, and evaluations. Implications for overcoming resistance are also discussed in this section.

### Separate Assessment from Therapy Recommendations and Join Intervention Planning to Therapy Recommendations

The importance of saving therapy recommendations for the IFSP/IEP process has been discussed previously under practice implications. This section elaborates on that point in terms of a suggested change for professionals.

Child assessments are done either by the same people who will provide services or by others. Others may consist of special evaluation teams or, in the case of children who have just entered a new program, professionals from the previous program. Regardless of who does the assessment, recommendations often include that the child receive therapy and sometimes even the amount of therapy per week.

What happens when professionals who will not be providing services make recommendations for therapy? The family logically links therapy with the treatment for the problem. During intervention planning, they expect therapy to be provided. The professionals on the intervention team are under pressure to provide specialized therapy, even if they feel that the nonspecialized intervention (e.g., classroom programming or home visits) can address the family's concerns and priorities. The problem is only partly who is recommending therapy. More generally, the problem lies in when the suggestion of therapy is made.

Therapy should be a means to the end, not the end itself. If a child is found to be delayed in cognitive development, evaluators can recommend areas of cognition on which the child might work. How to achieve those goals (ends) should be reserved for the intervention-planning process. Ideally, assessment and intervention planning occur more or less simultaneously (see McWilliam, 1992), in which case therapy might be mentioned as a service (means) to address the outcomes or goals. In reality, formal assessments are often conducted before intervention planning, so it is premature to recommend therapy because the outcomes or goals are not decided at that point. Outcomes or goals that appear on the IFSP/IEP should be decided by the intervention team, which includes the family.

Thus, the two main reasons for separating therapy recommendations from assessment and marrying them to intervention planning are 1) therapy is a means, not an end, and 2) it introduces to or reinforces for parents the faulty assumption that therapy is the only treatment for the problem. Clearly, in some settings, therapy may be the best way to address the family's concerns and priorities, but this should be decided only in the context of the whole intervention environment. That environment includes family and program resources.

## Use the Continuum of Six Models

As described in Chapter 7, the continuum of six service delivery models can be used to help move therapists toward a more integrated approach. Administrators and professional peers (and even parents) can encourage the therapist who always uses pull-out therapy to consider, as the first step, working with a small group in the therapy room. From there, the therapist can go into the classroom and work with a child off to the side (i.e., one-on-one in classroom). Once the therapist is comfortable with that model, he or she can consider running small-group activities in the classroom with the target child. Therapists who are not used to integrating their work with that of teachers will find it easier to begin using group therapy by bringing in their own small-group activities. As that method becomes more familiar, they may be persuaded to coordinate activities with the teacher and even to take on coteaching responsibilities while in the classroom. Some therapists are never comfortable with group instruction, particularly with large groups; the challenge of meeting the target children's needs while managing other children is too great. Group activity is one model that may not work in the progress up the continuum; those therapists may move directly from one-on-one in classroom to individual-during-routines. The essential differences between these two models are that in the latter 1) the child's activity is set by the classroom teacher or schedule, not by the therapist; 2) therapy may take place in the middle of things, not off to the side; and 3) the teacher is involved to some extent, not isolated from what the therapist does. Finally, when therapists and teachers have been truly working together for a while (teachers also have to make some changes), the therapist can step back and focus on helping the teacher meet the child's individualized needs for which the therapist previously took primary responsibility. The core of the next change, from individual-during-routines to consultation, is that the teacher rather than the child becomes the client.

Progressing up the continuum in this manner is predicated on the assumptions that children's needs can be met adequately with increasingly integrated models and that families approve of these shifts. Our data on service use reveal that therapists currently do not decide on models based on the children's needs or on family preferences (McWilliam & Tocci, 1995). Ideally, however, the intervention team (including parents) is equally as interested in children's needs being met in increasingly integrated settings as they are in expanding the therapist's repertoire of available models. Again, the importance of talking frankly to families about the limitations of segregated models and about the benefits of integrated models is underscored.

## Include Integrated Therapy in Contracts

Therapy services are often provided by individuals or agencies under contract to the early intervention program. Administrators and nontherapist early interventionists have reported that one of the barriers to integrated services is their lack of control over models used by contract therapists (McWilliam, Young, & Harville, 1995). Although many excellent pediatric therapists work in early intervention as private providers, the nature of contract work seems to produce an expert model of consultation (as defined in File & Kontos, 1992). Perhaps this is explained by the itinerant schedule that some private providers must keep or by the outsider status of such therapists. Thus, the program staff often do not feel that they can dictate how the often highly paid specialist should practice.

A segregated approach by one or more members of the team, however, violates the spirit of interagency collaboration inherent in the Education of the Handicapped Act Amendments of 1986, PL 99-457, and the collaboration desired for preschoolers with disabilities. An underused remedy to this situation is in the wording of the contract. Administrators can specify in the contract that integrated models will be used unless contraindicated for a specific reason (e.g., family preference, fitting equipment, testing, experimenting with a new procedure). The current default model is usually individual pull-out; *default* means that many contract therapists do not systematically consider the range of possible models. If a default model is to be employed, the contract should specify that the model should be individual-during-routines. This model is integrated but avoids the concern of a lack of hands-on therapy that is inherent in the consultation model. The contract should further specify that, as indicated by child, family, and classroom needs, the other five models may be used as appropriate for specific situations.

### Incorporate Integrated Therapy into Evaluations

Evaluations are often considered to be synonymous with child assessment. This section, however, refers to the broader meaning, which includes appraisal of student and staff performance as well as of interventions. A simple way to incorporate integrated therapy into performance evaluations is to have therapists or teachers document which of the six models of service delivery along the continuum (McWilliam, 1995) was used at each therapy session. This documentation allows the supervisor (e.g., program director) to determine the extent to which different models are used and the extent to which therapy is integrated with classroom routines. The information is most useful when the supervisor uses it to ask, for example, why all the children in a particular class receive the same service delivery model. The staff member may or may not have good reasons, but at least the stage is set for talking about individualized therapy decisions.

Evaluations of interventions should include an assessment of the extent to which interventions are working. This is related to the issue of treating therapy as a means, not as an end. For example, when a child is receiving occupational therapy to address self-feeding, presumably the team evaluates the child's progress on that skill. If the child is not making as much progress as hoped for, the teacher and others should determine how well classroom interventions are implemented. This extends the evaluation to include assessment of the intervention. If it appears that classroom interventions are not working, four follow-up questions can be asked:

1. *How functional is the intervention?* An outcome or goal or a recommended strategy that is not really necessary for the child to be successfully engaged in classroom activities is unlikely to be properly addressed in the classroom.
2. *What classroom changes are needed to support the intervention?* Classroom activities may be either too unstructured or too structured to allow for the successful implementation of a therapist's recommendations. Other potential classroom barriers include inadequate materials, problems with child peers, and scheduling problems (e.g., following highly active routines with very quiet routines). The supervisor and team should determine

whether reasonable classroom changes can be made to allow the therapy-related interventions to be better integrated.

3. *What is the quality of consultation?* Interventions may not occur in classrooms, owing to problems in collaboration between the teacher and specialists. For example, recommendations may not be specific enough (McWilliam & Spencer, 1993), or they may be overprescriptive. Many other consultation obstacles are also possible. Resolving the problem of inadequate intervention implementation in the classroom requires an assessment of the quality of consultation.

4. *Is the teacher simply not "following through"?* This question should follow the three above. Research shows that teachers do not consistently carry out therapy-related interventions (McWilliam & Scarborough, 1994; McWilliam & Spencer, 1993). It should not be automatically assumed, however, that teacher performance is at fault until the possibilities of nonfunctional recommendations, unhelpful classroom factors, and poor consultation have been explored. In general, if a teacher is not carrying out individualized interventions because of laziness or a belief that he or she should not have to work on these interventions, administrative action (e.g., moving the child to another classroom or removing the teacher) should be undertaken. The same standard should, of course, apply to the intractable therapist, once other valid reasons have been ruled out.

## Overcome Resistance

Change would not be as difficult as it is if it were not for individuals' resistance. If it were simply a question of teaching a new set of skills, ensuring that the instruction is clear and that the learners have the basic ability to understand what is required would be all that was needed. A shift to an integrated therapy approach, however, requires more than teaching skills; resistance from therapists, teachers, and parents needs to be addressed.

*From Therapists* Perhaps the major source of therapists' resistance is a perception that an integrated approach means a decrease in their status as specialists. Nontherapist early interventionists have reported that they believe they are perceived to have a lower status than therapists (McWilliam, Young, & Harville, 1995). The behaviors of segregated therapy suggest that the therapist has highly particularized techniques that need to be accomplished in a quiet, private place and that only the expert can really manage. In contrast, therapists may see being in classrooms, working with teachers, and handling nontherapy-related duties (e.g., managing disruptive behavior) as demeaning. It is important to convey to therapists that their expertise is absolutely vital to successful early intervention. Segregated approaches may be needed for certain types of testing and for trying out equipment or new interventions.

But expertise should not be equated with segregated behavior. Where therapists' expertise is needed is in their using their specialized knowledge and skills 1) to join with other team members in identifying functional interventions, 2) to recommend strategies that fit into the child's ecology, 3) to work with the child in contexts where the child needs the skills, and 4) to work with teachers to ensure that intervention is not confined to therapy sessions. The more skilled and knowledgeable the therapist, the better he or she is at fulfilling these functions. It can be said that the real experts in early intervention specialized therapies are those who use an integrated approach. This needs to be conveyed to therapists who resist changing from a segregated approach.

***From Teachers*** Resistance from teachers is presumably motivated by something different from therapists'. Two possible sources are the fear that an integrated approach will result in more work and the feeling that someone who does not have to do the work is telling them what to do. It may be true that meeting the individual needs of some children adds to teachers' burdens; administrators need to take that into consideration when they constitute classes. But integrating therapy does not automatically mean more work for the classroom teacher. Good collaboration entails combining both the teachers' and the specialists' strengths. Teachers who show how their developmentally appropriate practices help children with disabilities have an easier time with this collaboration than those who do not see this strength. By the same token, specialists who see teachers' inherent strengths foster good collaboration. The more the team can conceive of integrated therapy as a matter of making slight adjustments to existing practices, the less teachers will feel that another duty has been forced on them.

A potential source of resistance is the feeling of one professional that something is being forced on him or her by another professional. This feeling argues for a collaborative rather than an expert approach to consultation by therapists (File & Kontos, 1992). Integrated therapy should be undertaken with the assumption that both teachers and specialists want the child to do well in the classroom and that both want to ensure that the family's concerns and priorities are addressed. Therapists are well advised to adopt a philosophy with teachers similar to early interventionists' family-centered philosophy with families— that is, being responsive to their concerns, establishing a friendly relationship, being sensitive to their underlying issues, and adopting a holistic approach (i.e., seeing the strengths and needs of the whole classroom environment).

Overcoming teachers' resistance, therefore, requires 1) not adding to their responsibilities, but helping them succeed with their existing responsibilities; and 2) making them partners in planning classroom intervention, not lower-status therapy aides.

***From Parents*** Why would parents resist integrated therapy if it is such a good idea? Focus group findings suggest four predominant reasons: 1) professionals and other parents have made one-on-one direct therapy sound like the most beneficial or the only model; 2) parents want as much of every treatment as they can get for their children, especially in the early years;

3) segregated therapy sounds like an undiluted dose of a good thing; and 4) they have seen success with segregated therapy (McWilliam, Young, & Harville, 1995). Each reason is completely understandable and, in some cases, reflects an astutely well-informed evaluation of services for their children. In many cases, however, families may be deluded by faulty assumptions. Professionals wanting to overcome parents' resistance need to tread carefully, respecting the reality of parents' perspectives while gently introducing the possibility that alternatives exist.

A two-pronged approach to dealing with families' adopting assumptions about therapy from others is to 1) change the professional community's ways of describing therapy to families and 2) point out to families that therapy can be provided in a number of ways, of which the segregated approach is only one.

Addressing the more-is-better philosophy also can be handled in two ways. First, professionals can tell parents that because segregated therapy appears to be working, it is worth expanding the locations where the child benefits from the therapist, perhaps alternating sessions between the therapy room and the classroom. This is also a way of addressing the fourth source of resistance, families' seeing the success of segregated therapy. A second method to address the more-is-better philosophy is to estimate the amount of time that therapy can be conducted in the classroom, compared to the amount of time that a therapist has to work with the child in a pull-out setting. Such a comparison should be handled ethically, with a minimum of disingenuousness, because 1) even when therapists use a segregated approach, classroom teachers often address skills that therapists address; and 2) classroom teachers do not necessarily carry out interventions when the therapist is not in the room. To be honest with families, professionals should point out that only *effective* integrated services would result in more time being spent on the individualized interventions.

Addressing the perception that only undiluted therapy is good requires professionals to apply their expertise in child development and disabilities. Unlike adults and older children, who can take weekly lessons to learn a skill, young children, especially those with developmental delays, cannot be expected to retain a lot of information from or benefit from repeated practice in one concentrated session. Numerous studies have shown that dispersed-trial learning is more effective than massed-trial learning (e.g., Chiara, Schuster, Bell, & Wolery, in press; Helmstetter & Guess, 1986; Wolery, Doyle, Gast, Ault, & Simpson, 1993). Therefore, in classroom programs, the ongoing pull-out therapy should occur only if the teacher is in the session to learn as much as possible for later classroom implementation. Because teachers cannot reasonably be expected to leave their classrooms for each child's therapy sessions, however, it makes more sense for the therapist to work with the child and teacher in the classroom. If we must have a pharmacological analogy, integrated therapy should be presented, not as a watered-down version of pull-out therapy, but like a time-release capsule.

Finally, professionals need to be prepared to deal with families' experiences with segregated therapy as a successful approach. As previously mentioned, integrated therapy can be presented as an expansion of segregated therapy. The family may feel that "if it ain't broke, don't fix it" or that they should not "mess with a good thing." It is hard for professionals to point out, or for therapists to admit, that therapy is usually conducted in such a nonexperimental way (i.e., data are not systematically collected, using single-subject evaluation designs) that what it is about therapy that seems to work or whether an alternative model of service delivery may work even better is not really known. If parents are fully informed about the pros and cons of different models, they are more likely to see the advantage of at least trying an integrated approach, on the off chance that it will result in even more child progress.

The importance of handling parents' resistance with great sensitivity must be reiterated. It is not the job of professionals to convince parents that they are wrong; instead, they must help the families become informed consumers (cf. McWilliam, Lang, et al., 1995).

## PERSONNEL PREPARATION IMPLICATIONS

This chapter begins with implications for practice, followed by ways to manage change, because an integrated approach can start immediately. For this paradigm shift to become institutionalized, however, training programs need to change. This section discusses nine implications for personnel preparation.

### Infusing Content Across Disciplines

Now that early intervention services are found in all 50 U.S. states and in U.S. territories, this discipline or subdiscipline is well accepted in many American universities. Preparation for working with young children with disabilities and their families is often a subdiscipline within occupational therapy, physical therapy, special education, and speech-language pathology. Especially in the medical allied health professions (e.g., occupational therapy, physical therapy, speech-language therapy), early intervention content can constitute a very small part because the training programs take a life-span approach. This results in students' learning early intervention content within their own discipline rather than in courses listed across departments. It would be beneficial for the future of integrated therapy either to infuse content from other disciplines within departmental training or to have cross-disciplinary courses.

### Specializing in Pediatrics

Desperate to overcome the shortage of specialists, early intervention programs have had to use occupational therapists, physical therapists, and speech-language pathologists who do not have pediatric training or experience (McWilliam, Young, & Harville, 1995). Although a life-span approach may be considered adequate within the therapies, many states have moved quickly to establish a separate certificate for early childhood special education, and education associations have jointly formulated standards for working with infants, toddlers, preschoolers, and their families (Division for Early Childhood, National Association for the Education of Young Children, & Association of Teacher Educators, 1995). The culture of collaboration, a developmental approach, and the importance of ecological relevance in early intervention demands pediatric expertise for practitioners of all disciplines. Although it is difficult to add content to already full curricula, professional associations (e.g., the American Occupational Therapy Association, the American Physical Therapy Association, the American Speech-Hearing-Language Association) and university training programs should make provisions for therapists to acquire specializations in pediatrics. These might be accomplished through postgraduate internships or in-service courses. The more therapists understand what early intervention is all about, the more hope there is for successful integrated therapy.

## Using Early Childhood Settings for Clinical Experience

For students who have an interest in working in early intervention, a practicum or internship in an early childhood setting would give them experience that might increase their sensitivity to what is needed in early intervention. Perhaps all students should spend some time in such settings in the hope that more future practitioners might choose pediatrics. When students' clinical experience in their training programs is limited to clinic-based services, it is unlikely that they will develop the requisite attitudes and skills to implement integrated services.

## Training Teachers in Embedded Instruction or Therapy

Teachers need to be trained to fulfill their role in integrated therapy. In particular, they need to be prepared to adapt classroom activities to incorporate individualized interventions (e.g., suggestions from therapists) and to adapt interventions to fit into classroom routines. Special education teachers, who are expected to know about both classroom management and disability-related intervention, can be trained to assume the role of mediator between therapists and general early childhood teachers. A mediator may help meet some of the challenges of integrated therapy, but this resource is not always available. If collaboration between specialists and teachers is successful, however, a mediator would not be needed. Therefore, general early childhood teachers also should be trained in embedding individualized instruction and therapy within general classroom routines. As efforts to bridge the gap between general and special education proceed, personnel trainers need to remember the importance of bridging the gap between general education and specialized therapies.

## Training in IFSP/IEP Process and Product

The critical role of intervention planning has been emphasized throughout this book. This is the point at which functional interventions are decided, and it presents an opportunity for deciding 1) if therapy is needed to address those needs and 2) how therapy will be provided. For integrated therapy to be successful, professionals need training in family-centered, routines-based intervention planning (see McWilliam, 1992) and in developing family-centered, functional IFSPs/IEPs (McWilliam, Harbin, et al., 1995).

## Building the Early Intervention Culture

The culture of early intervention was mentioned previously in the section on specializing in pediatrics. The early intervention culture, which goes beyond pediatric specialization, can be defined as beliefs and practices in working with young children with disabilities that emphasize the importance of inter-disciplinary and interagency collaboration as well as a family-centered approach. It is described as a culture because it involves more than just skills or practices; collaborative and family-centered attitudes are essential. Furthermore, a culture suggests that people identify with it and feel a sense of belonging. Such a culture already exists in the Division for Early Childhood of the Council for Exceptional Children, in interagency collaboration councils, and in early intervention programs. If faculty in personnel preparation programs can acculturate future professionals to these values, it will at least complement (if not counteract) the medical-model training they receive. This acculturation will be beneficial in drawing together professionals from different disciplines, which will help in the integration of services.

## Training in Consultation Skills

One therapist in our focus groups on specialized therapies plaintively remarked that she was not trained to work with adults and now saw what a gap this was in her professional preparation (McWilliam, Young, & Harville, 1995). When working with young children with disabilities, therapists and teachers need to collaborate with other professionals and with families. Training only in working directly with children may be of little use if those techniques cannot be taught to the child's regular caregivers.

It is not only specialists, including consulting early childhood special educators, who need to be trained in consultation skills, however. Classroom teachers need to be informed consumers of and partners in this consultation. Informed consumers have learned different models of service delivery, what constitutes functional interventions, and different models of consultation. Partners in consultation have learned how and when to ask for help, to make suggestions, and to negotiate. Thus, consultation skill training should be a part of personnel development, including in-service training, for therapists, early childhood special educators, and early childhood general educators.

## Training for Use of a Continuum of Service Delivery Models

Unless specialists know the options available for using different service delivery models, they are likely to use the model in which they were trained, the model used by most other specialists in a given program, or the model that gives them most control over the therapy or instruction session. The first step then, is to alert them to the options. In Chapter 7 and earlier in this section, six models are described: individual pull-out, small-group pull-out, one-on-one in classroom, group activity, individual-during-routines, and consultation. This has been described as a continuum, in the order presented, from most segregated to most integrated (McWilliam, 1995). Training in the appropriate use of the continuum focuses on 1) assessing different environmental features of the therapy session (e.g., presence of other children, functionality of therapy goals, classroom characteristics), 2) starting with individual-during-routines, and 3) moving up or down the continuum as the need arises.

## Training Doctors About Early Intervention Services

Early interventionists have already undertaken efforts to train doctors about when to refer children and families for early intervention services. What is still needed is to teach doctors what early intervention involves and does not involve. It involves (or should involve) a holistic approach including all disciplines; it does not involve (or should not involve) segmented therapy services.

## POLICY IMPLICATIONS: HOW SHOULD MONEY BE ALLOCATED?

The ultimate issue in policy is how governmental resources should be allocated. Resource allocation also gives policy makers an opportunity to establish regulations. The regulations must be followed in order for a state or a program to receive public funds. The areas in which policy can affect delivery of therapy services are, first, funding of training programs and therapy positions and, second, reimbursement regulations for Medicaid.

## More Training and Hiring Slots

The more therapists available, the lower the costs for therapy and therapists. To have more therapists, university programs need to produce more graduates, which is complicated but resolvable with adequate policy support. Universities need funds to support faculty, and the ratio of faculty members to students is prescribed by the professional associations (e.g., American Physical Therapy Association, American Occupational Therapy Association, American Speech-Hearing-Language Association) for the training programs to be accredited.

The associations keep the ratios low to maintain adequate quality of instruction. Because of the limited number of faculty that a university can afford, given the relatively small number of students in these graduate programs, only a small number of training slots are available. It is thus a circular problem. If the ratios were not so small, more students could be admitted, which would increase the number of faculty that could be funded for that department. If states could fund more faculty positions, more students could be admitted. A two-pronged approach therefore seems necessary. Associations should grant waivers to training programs to expand faculty-to-student ratios, and states should fund therapy training programs. Given the critical shortage of therapists in early intervention, requests for these policy changes can be made on humanitarian grounds. They can also be made on fiscal grounds. Until there is an adequate threshold of therapists, the costs to taxpayers will be extremely high for publicly supported therapy.

Do the professional associations keep faculty-to-student ratios low, and therefore graduate numbers low, only to maintain the quality of instruction? Although this is undoubtedly a major motivation, it should also be considered that the effect of this accreditation requirement is to increase the market value of the associations' members. If associations do not see training more therapists as being in their best interest, two arguments may be persuasive. First, special dispensations can be given for pediatric specialty training programs only. This would not affect the overall number of physical therapists, occupational therapists, or speech-language pathologists. Second, a backlash might eventually occur, with states rebelling against the high costs of therapy and authorizing more services to be provided by therapy assistants, bachelor's-level professionals, or generalists such as special educators who have received in-service training. The best solution would be for states and universities to work collaboratively with the professional associations to solve the shortage problem.

Another route for chaneling funds is to increase allocations for Part H of the Individuals with Disabilities Education Act Amendments (PL 102–119) and preschool programs, specifically so that they can hire more therapists. This solution has a number of pitfalls, however. First, legislators might take funds from other cost-effective services (e.g., nontherapist early interventionists) to pay for more therapists. Second, allocation of more funds would strengthen the market value of therapists, who could simply increase their rates without seeing substantially more children. Nevertheless, in some communities where therapists are simply not available to families, an infusion of money could allow agencies to attract therapists.

Integrated services are not a way to save money on therapy in the short run. High-quality services require therapists to work collaboratively with teachers and families, so there must be enough time available for therapists to spend time in classrooms, in team meetings, in IFSP/IEP meetings, and in consultation. Research in service delivery models has not been conducted long enough to know whether improved collaboration and more functional services will result in less need for therapy in the long run.

## Medicaid Reimbursement for and State Endorsement of Six Models

Funding only direct hands-on therapy is too restrictive. Practitioners report that they do not spend as much time talking to teachers, observing in classrooms, or attending planning meetings as they would like, because they cannot receive Medicaid reimbursement for such activities (McWilliam, Young, & Harville, 1995). State policies on recognized methods of treatment also favor one-on-one treatment. One solution is to sanction the six models in the continuum of service delivery (McWilliam, 1995).

## RESEARCH IMPLICATIONS

Research into models for the delivery of therapeutic and instructional services is not extensive, probably because it is hard to do. Chapter 4 describes a program of research into integrated versus isolated treatment, and other chapters cite studies related to adjunct topics such as generalization, consultation, and team-based change. Three approaches to research that enhance knowledge of effective treatment models are random assignment, longitudinal research, and aptitude-by-treatment interaction.

### Random Assignment

Random assignment of children to different models of therapy or specialized instruction provides the necessary controls for studying the relative effects of those models. The benefits of this type of group design are that threats to internal validity, such as therapist differences and treatment integrity (i.e., the extent to which a particular model is used), can more easily be accounted for. The challenges, however, are that random assignment prevents practitioners and families from making clinical judgments about treatment models and that models are not able to change for individual children during the study. Perhaps the best known random assignment study involving one of the therapies is that of Palmer and colleagues (1988), which has been criticized by physical therapists on the ground that the therapy the physical therapy group received was inappropriate, that the study did not last long enough for the effects of physical therapy to become apparent, and that the outcome measures were inappropriate. Nevertheless, considering that practitioners have shown an interest in using more integrated models (McWilliam & Bailey, 1994), it seems advisable to secure the support of therapists to investigate the most effective methods of treatment, such as through random assignment group designs.

## Longitudinal Research

Although different models of service delivery have not been found to differ substantially in short-term effects on children's acquisition and generalization of skills addressed, it is possible that prolonged exposure to contrasting models might have differential effects. Traditional longitudinal designs, in which different groups receive different treatments constant over time, pose the same challenges as those described earlier for random assignment: Practitioners and families are not likely to endorse a single model, especially for the long term. One statistical model that researchers should explore is growth curve analysis, as described in Burchinal, Bailey, and Snyder (1994). These authors point out that hierarchical linear models, unlike other repeated-measures designs, maintain the importance of individuals' growth curves, allow for better growth curve estimates, and do not rest on the assumption of independence of individuals' repeated observations. One practical advantage for the researcher is that "case-wise deletion is not performed with incomplete or inconsistently timed data" (p. 417). If the design (i.e., assignment to treatments) can be accomplished, therefore, statistical models exist for appropriate interpretation of the repeated measures (e.g., developmental quotients, goal attainment).

## Aptitude-by-Treatment Interaction

As in most discussions of intervention effectiveness with children with special needs, one reasonable statement is, *it depends on the child.* When practitioners were asked about the extent to which they used integrated services, child characteristics (e.g., age, disability level) accounted for about 40% of the variance when no other variables were considered (McWilliam & Bailey, 1994). After considering the practitioner's discipline, family preferences, the practitioner's age and experience, and the practitioner's caseload characteristics, however, child characteristics accounted for only about 10% of the variance in practitioners' reported typical and ideal practices. It only partly depended on the child. Research on aptitude-treatment interactions (ATI) in education has yielded significant results, most often showing that higher-structure instruction works better for children with lower ability levels and motivation and that lower-structure instruction works better for children with higher ability and motivation (for a review, see Snow, 1989). This same general ATI effect has been found in early language intervention (Yoder, Kaiser, & Alpert, 1991; Yoder, Warren, & Hull, 1995). Snow suggests that ATI findings argue for intervention within what Vygotsky (1978) called the zone of proximal development and within what Elshout (1985) called the zone of tolerable problematicity. Bailey (in press) has translated concepts of ATI into curricular implications in early intervention, including models of specialized service delivery. He argues that the researcher needs to consider at least five factors when evaluating curricula: 1) definitions of the curricula,

2) the match of curricula to child needs, 3) verification of treatment implementation, 4) documentation of outcomes, and 5) documentation of family and professional preferences.

Random assignment, longitudinal designs, and aptitude-by-treatment interaction research are three methodological directions needed in research on service delivery models. The time is ripe for moving, in practice, beyond models of convenience to models that work for individual children and families. In research, the time is ripe for moving toward analysis of the quality of therapy and special education.

## CONCLUSIONS

Integrated therapy requires a shift in conceptualizations about practice, personnel preparation, and policy. Some changes have started, with increasing attention in the literature about the benefits of collaboration and transdisciplinary service delivery. Actually, these ideas are not new, but the acceptance of alternatives to traditional pull-out services continues to be slow. The current mire of resistance will be traversed only when practitioners, training faculty, and policy makers all make some movement toward more integrated approaches. As reported in Chapter 4 and again in the present chapter, practitioners appear to be hampered by their training and by policies that encourage segregated service delivery. Trainers are hampered by professional associations and policies that indicate a preference for one-on-one direct therapy. Finally, policy makers are hampered by conflicting information from the field and by increasing costs with diminishing resources. The need for research to continue explaining the differential effects of service delivery models has never been greater.

---

### Case Study *Shamika*

Ultimately, what is discussed in this book needs to be evaluated in terms of the effects on Shamika, the people in her life, and all other children like her. Shamika is 4 years old and has quadriplegic spasticity, mental retardation, low levels of engagement, and wonderfully strong assertiveness. Her mother dotes on her, as can be seen by Shamika's beautiful clothes and intricate hair adornments. Shamika attends an integrated preschool, where three quarters of the children are typically developing. The teacher, Marion, has a master's degree in early childhood education and has been working with young children

*(continued)*

*(continued)*

for 25 years. Another teacher works in the classroom, along with a part-time assistant. Three therapists work with Shamika: Catherine, the physical therapist; Olga, the occupational therapist; and Dave, the speech-language pathologist. In addition to the therapists, an early childhood special education teacher, Barbara, provided consultation and served as service coordinator. All these people want the best for Shamika and her mother, but, 2 years ago, their versions of the best differed.

Shamika's mother wanted her to go to school at a happy place that did not resemble a hospital. She thought Shamika should get as much professional help as possible because she did not know all the special things that could be done for a child with so many problems. She therefore enrolled Shamika in this particular program because the teacher, Marion, was supposed to be good with kids, and, just as importantly, the full array of specialists was available to work with her daughter.

Marion welcomed Shamika to the classroom because she believed that children were more alike than they were different. She considered it her responsibility to include Shamika in all activities, one way or another. She thought that, if the child could just be exposed to the same experiences as the other children, and be exposed to those children themselves, she would blossom.

Catherine looked forward to the challenge of working with Shamika. She had previously worked with other children with cerebral palsy and was confident about using her eclectic program of a little bit of neurodevelopmental therapy, a little bit of Bobath, and a little bit of motor planning. Her only anxiety was the lack of a therapy room at the preschool. She would have to set up a therapy space with mats and equipment in the foyer.

Olga's first step was to ask Marion what skills Shamika was expected to perform in the classroom. Marion told her what other children Shamika's age were expected to do, but admitted that she did not know if Shamika would be able to do them. Olga therefore decided that her role would be to go into the classroom and work with Shamika on some specific skills, such as taking food from a spoon and hitting a switch connected to a battery-operated toy.

*(continued)*

*(continued)*

Dave had never worked with a child with such severe levels of spasticity or retardation. He was unsure about Shamika's potential to communicate. Her mother wanted her to communicate "any way we can get her to." The teacher felt that, after exposure to chattering peers, Shamika would come out of her shell. The occupational therapist said that controlling the switch-operated toy was the first step toward using an augmentative communication device. Dave was unsure what he could do, so, during therapy sessions, he took Shamika to any isolated part of the preschool he could find and tried providing her with auditory stimulation (i.e., tapes through a headset), tried physically assisting her to babble (i.e., grasping the chin and lips to form "buh-buh-buh-buh"), and tried gentle mandibular massage to stimulate any vocalizations.

Barbara considered her main job to be ensuring that Shamika got all the therapies listed on her IFSP. Once she was assured that Catherine, Olga, and Dave were each able to work directly with Shamika for the listed amount of time, Barbara turned her attention to the classroom. Marion had a lively classroom, with many activities going on in different parts of the room. There were materials of all kinds everywhere. Children talked to each other almost all day long. The three staff members rotated from child to child and from zone to zone, using children's engagement as opportunities to teach them. But Shamika was just there, not involved. She was moved quite often so she could be around other kids. But she was oblivious to the activities and the children. She sat in an adult's lap during circle time, but she could not do the finger plays or activities or sing the songs, let alone do the hokey-pokey.

This picture of Shamika's start at the preschool shows a commitment by everyone to do the best for her, based on their individual interests, expertise, and background. Barbara's observation, however, revealed that Shamika spent much of the day nonengaged. When she spoke to the therapists individually, they all said that when they worked with her she responded well and that they felt she was making slow but steady progress. Marion was concerned about Shamika's lack of involvement, but felt that what Shamika was seeing and hearing would, when she was developmentally ready, click in.

*(continued)*

*(continued)*

Barbara talked about the situation with Shamika's mother. She had to strike a balance between giving an honest picture of what was going on in the classroom and not criticizing any of her colleagues. Barbara and the mother decided to get together with all the team so that everyone knew everyone else's point of view. Once the logistical nightmare of arranging such a meeting was overcome, the team decided it should work more closely together, with two ultimate outcomes for Shamika: She would learn specific skills that her mother considered priorities, and she would be meaningfully engaged during increasing percentages of the day.

Jumping forward to the present, 2 years after Shamika was first enrolled in the program, shows a couple of extremely fortunate situations that helped ensure improvement in services. First, Shamika was not forced to change classrooms just because she turned 3 and just because she now had an IEP instead of an IFSP. Second, the team miraculously was composed of the same professionals she had at the beginning. With 2 years of experimentation, constant talking (collaboration), and a common goal, Shamika's services looked very different. Now Catherine went into the classroom where she had helped Marion design a corner space where any child could lie around (e.g., for story time) or where an adult could play with Shamika while doing range-of-motion exercises. More important, for most therapy sessions, Catherine came into the classroom. She tended to take Shamika to the new quiet area, but Marion joined her as often as possible. When Catherine was not in the classroom, Marion found a few times each day to do most of the same exercises.

Olga still came into the classroom, but, instead of doing her own thing, she took note of where Shamika was and what was generally going on with the other children, and worked to help Shamika participate at some level in the same or similar activities. She assisted in Shamika's becoming a popular member of the class when she created a number of switch toys for her (e.g., a train that went around on a track); the other children really liked these toys, but the rule was that they had to play with Shamika.

Dave had found a purpose. He worked out a series of lesson plans with Marion and the other therapists, and he came into the classroom

*(continued)*

*(continued)*

and organized language- and print-rich activities. Shamika was always one of the children, and the other therapists helped Dave find methods for getting her involved. But his larger purpose was to join forces with Marion so that she could facilitate more communication among children, especially those with language delays, and so that he could become more comfortable working with groups of children.

Barbara spent a lot of time ensuring communication among all the players. She organized meetings, interviewed the players on the run, and wrote down everything. She made sure everyone knew what everyone else was concerned about, what they were doing, and what they thought was most important. She also spent more time in and out of the classroom with Marion; she found that by observing Shamika and what went on in the classroom and processing with Marion, she could help Marion turn her experienced, naturally responsive interactions with all children into focused, contingent interactions with Shamika. Barbara became a resource and a support for Marion, and Marion in turn became Barbara's reality check; Marion spoke up whenever a specialist came up with bizarre or unworkable suggestions.

Services were now integrated.

## REFERENCES

Bailey, D.B., Jr. (in press). Evaluating the effectiveness of curriculum alternatives for high risk infants and preschoolers. In M. Guralnick (Ed.), *The effectiveness of early intervention: Second generation research.* Baltimore: Paul H. Brookes Publishing Co.

Burchinal, M.R., Bailey, D.B., Jr., & Snyder, P. (1994). Using growth curve analysis to evaluate child change in longitudinal investigations. *Journal of Early Intervention, 18,* 403–423.

Chiara, L., Schuster, J.W., Bell, J.K., & Wolery, M. (in press). Small-group massed-trial and individually distributed trial instruction with preschoolers. *Journal of Early Intervention.*

Division for Early Childhood, National Association for the Education of Young Children, & Association of Teacher Educators. (1995). Personnel standards for early education and early intervention: Guidelines for licensure in early childhood special education. *Communicator, 21*(2), insert.

Education of the Handicapped Act Amendments of 1986, PL 99–457. (October 8, 1986). Title 20, U.S.C. 1400 et seq.: *U.S. Statutes at Large, 100,* 1145–1177.

Elshout, J.J. (1985). *Problem solving and education.* Paper presented at the First Conference of the European Association for Research on Learning and Instruction, Leuven, Belgium.

File, N., & Kontos, S. (1992). Indirect service delivery through consultation: Review and implications for early intervention. *Journal of Early Intervention, 16,* 221–233.

Giangreco, M.F., Cloninger, C.J., & Iverson, V.S. (1993). *Choosing options and accommodations for children: A guide to planning inclusive education.* Baltimore: Paul H. Brookes Publishing Co.

Helmstetter, E., & Guess, D. (1986). Application of the individualized curriculum sequencing model to learners with severe sensory impairments. In L. Goetz, D. Guess, & K. Stremel-Campbell (Eds.), *Innovative program designs for individuals with dual sensory impairments.* Baltimore: Paul H. Brookes Publishing Co.

Individuals with Disabilities Education Amendments of 1991, PL 102–119. (October 7, 1991). Title 20, U.S.C. 1400 et seq.: *U.S. Statutes at Large, 105,* 587–608.

McCormick, L., & Goldman, R. (1979). The transdisciplinary model: Implications for service delivery and personnel preparation for the severely and profoundly handicapped. *AAESPH Review, 4,* 152–161.

McWilliam, R.A. (1992). *Family-centered intervention planning: A routines-based approach.* Tucson, AZ: Communication Skill Builders.

McWilliam, R.A. (1995). Integration of therapy and consultative special education: A continuum in early intervention. *Infants and Young Children, 7*(4), 29–38.

McWilliam, R.A., & Bailey, D.B. (1994). Predictors of service delivery models in center-based early intervention. *Exceptional Children, 61,* 56–71.

McWilliam, R.A., Harbin, G.L., Porter, P., Vandiviere, P., Mittal, M., & Munn, D. (1995). *An evaluation of family-centered coordinated Part H services in North Carolina: Part 1—family-centered service provision.* Frank Porter Graham Child Development Center, University of North Carolina, Chapel Hill.

McWilliam, R.A., Lang, L., Vandiviere, P., Angell, R., Collins, L., & Underdown, G. (1995). Satisfaction and struggles: Family perceptions of early intervention services. *Journal of Early Intervention, 19,* 43–60.

McWilliam, R.A., & Scarborough, A. (1994, September). *Does therapy carry over to the classroom? How to make early intervention more effective.* Paper presented at the North Carolina Association for the Education of Young Children/Division for Early Childhood Annual Study Conference, Greensboro, NC.

McWilliam, R.A., Scarborough, A., & Chaudhary, A. (1995). [Patterns of service delivery models and ratings of individualized progress] Unpublished raw data. Frank Porter Graham Child Development Center, University of North Carolina, Chapel Hill.

McWilliam, R.A., & Spencer, A.G. (1993). *Integrated versus pull-out speech-language services in early intervention: A mixed-method study.* Manuscript submitted for publication.

McWilliam, R.A., & Tocci, L. (1995). [Case studies of families' service use: Interview transcripts] Unpublished raw data. Early Childhood Research Institute: Service Utilization, Frank Porter Graham Child Development Center, University of North Carolina, Chapel Hill.

McWilliam, R.A., Young, H.J., & Harville, K. (1995). *Specialized therapy: Perceptions of stakeholders.* Manuscript in preparation.

Palmer, F.B., Shapiro, B.K., Wachtel, R.C., Allen, M.A., Hiller, J.E., Harryman, S.E., Mosher, B.S., Meinert, C.L., & Capute, A.J. (1988). The effects of physical therapy on cerebral palsy: A controlled trial in infants with spastic diplegia. *New England Journal of Medicine, 318,* 803–808.

Scheerer, C.R. (1992). Perspectives on an oral motor activity: The use of rubber tubing as a "chewy." *American Journal of Occupational Therapy, 46,* 344–352.

Snow, R.E. (1989). Aptitude-treatment interaction as a framework for research on individual differences in learning. In P.L. Ackerman, R.J. Sternberg, & R. Glaser

(Eds.), *Learning and individual differences: Advances in theory and research.* San Francisco: W.H. Freeman.

Thelen, E. (1995). Motor development: A new synthesis. *American Psychologist, 50,* 79–95.

Vygotsky, L.S. (1978). *Mind in society.* Cambridge, MA: Harvard University Press.

Wolery, M., Doyle, P.M., Gast, D.L., Ault, M.J., & Simpson, S. (1993). Comparison of progressive time delay and transition-based teaching with preschoolers who have developmental delays. *Journal of Early Intervention, 17,* 160–176.

World Health Organization. (1980). *International classification of impairments, disabilities, and handicaps.* Geneva, Switzerland: Author.

Yoder, P.J., Kaiser, A.P., & Alpert, C.A. (1991). An exploratory study of the interaction between language teaching methods and child characteristics. *Journal of Speech and Hearing Research, 34,* 155–167.

Yoder, P.J., Warren, S.F., & Hull, L. (1995). Predicting children's response to prelinguistic communication intervention. *Journal of Early Intervention, 19,* 74–84.

# Index

*Page numbers followed "t" or "f" indicate tables or figures, respectively.*

transdiciplinary, 87
use of, 281–282, 282*t*
*see also* Collaborative consultation;
    Medical model; Service delivery,
    models; Team
Modeling
    interactive, 221, 230*t*
    with recast, 227–228, 231*t*
    by therapists to teachers, 176
Monitoring, 61, 191, 202–203, 276–277,
    282*t*
    by families, 181–182
Motor planning, 12
Motor skills, 126–127, 129–132, 274*t*
Multidisciplinary approach, 152
Multidisciplinary team, 34–35
Muscle testing and reeducation, 244
Muscle tone, 307


NAECS/SDE, *see* National Association
    of Early Childhood Specialists, in
    State Department of Education
NAEYC, *see* National Association for
    Education of Young Children
National Association for Education of
    Young Children (NAEYC), 185,
    187
*see also* Developmentally appropriate
    practice (DAP)
National Association of Early Childhood
    Specialists, in State Department
    of Education (NAECS/SDE),
    189, 189*t*–190*t*
Natural consequences, 196
NDT, *see* Neurodevelopmental treatment
Neurobehavioral motor intervention,
    129–132, 136
Neurodevelopmental approach, 129–130
Neurodevelopmental treatment (NDT),
    303–308, 308*t*
Neuroscience, 289
Normalization, 21, 153
North Carolina Interagency
    Coordinating Council, Children
    and Families Committee of, 98
Notebook approach, 62
Nurses, 254*t*, 315–316, 318, 325
Nutritionists, 315, 323–325

Objectives
    authentically individualized, 113, 113*f*
    functional, 109–110
    highest-priority, 170
    IEP, 108–109
Observation, 116, 320
Occupational therapy, 19, 254, 254*t*
    decision making and, 58
    generalization from, 94–96, 95*t*
    historical background of, 267–268
    integrated services and, 75
    monitoring and, 276–277
    performance areas addressed in, 271*t*,
        273–274*t*
    principles in, 270–272, 271*t*
    relationship to other disciplines, 283,
        284*t*
    research related to, 72
    in schools, 268–269
Olfactory system, 291*t*, 295*f*, 302*t*, 306*t*
Outcomes, *see* Goals


Paraprofessional, 261
Parents
    consultant contact with, 332–333
    decision-making authority and, 57–58
    evaluation by, 164
    expectations of, 172–173
    participation and therapy allocation,
        156
    parent–child interactions, 224
    professional contact with, 318,
        322–324
    resistance from, 356–358
    therapy sessions and, 344–346
    *see also* Families
Peabody Developmental Motor Scales,
    278
Pediatrics, 154, 246–247, 358–359
Peers, 205–206, 287, 287*t*
Person-centered planning, 61
Personnel preparation, 358–361
Pervasive developmental disorders,
    203–204
Phonology, 138
Physical therapy, 315–316
    allocation of, 349
    competencies in, 253
    decision-making authority and, 58
    development of, 244–247